The Network Society:
From Knowledge to Policy

Edited by
Manuel Castells
Wallis Annenberg Chair Professor of
Communication Technology and Society
University of Southern California,
Los Angeles
and Research Professor,
Open University of Catalonia, Barcelona

Gustavo Cardoso
Professor of Information and Communication Sciences,
Department of Information Sciences and Technology,
ISCTE, Lisbon, Portugal

This book was published with the support of the
Presidência da República Portuguesa and of the
Fundação Luso Americana para o Desenvolvimento.

Castells, Manuel and Cardoso, Gustavo, eds., *The Network Society: From Knowledge to Policy*. Washington, DC: Johns Hopkins Center for Transatlantic Relations, 2006

Center for Transatlantic Relations
The Paul H. Nitze School of Advanced International Studies
The Johns Hopkins University
1717 Massachusetts Ave., NW Suite 525
Washington, DC 20036, USA
Tel: (202) 663-5880
Fax: (202) 663-5879
Email: transatlantic@jhu.edu
http://transatlantic.sais-jhu.edu

ISBN 0-9766434-5-6

Table of Contents

Part III: Organizational Reform and Technological Modernization in the Public Sector

Part IV: Media, Communication, Wireless and Policies in the Network Society

Figures

Tables

Notes on Contributors

Jorge Sampaio was born in Lisbon on September 18th 1939. In 1961 he graduated in Law—Lisbon University. Whilst at university he was involved in various academic activities that marked the start of a persistent political action against the dictatorship. In 1995, Jorge Sampaio stood for the presidential elections. He enjoyed the support of personalities, both independent and from other political areas, who played significant roles in the political, cultural and economic life of the country. On January 14th 1996 he was elected on the first ballot. He was sworn in as President of the Republic on March 9th. He ran for a second term of office and was re-elected on the first ballot on January 14th 2001, for another five-year term. In 1991 he published a collection of his political essays entitled A Festa de um Sonho." In 1995 a new work of his was published under the title *Um Olhar sobre Portugal*, setting out his views on domestic problems in response to concerns expressed by Portuguese opinion-makers in various areas of society. In 2000 he published a book called *Quero Dizer-vos*, in which his present views on the challenges faced by the Portuguese society are laid out. His presidential speeches have been published in a series intitled *Portugueses*.

Manuel Castells is the Wallis Annenberg Chair Professor of Communication Technology and Society at the Annenberg School of Communication, University of Southern California, Los Angeles. He is also Research Professor of Information Society at the Open University of Catalonia (UOC) in Barcelona, professor Emeritus of Sociology and of Planning, at the University of California at Berkeley and Distinguished Visiting Professor of Technology and Society at the Massachusetts Institute of Technology.

Gustavo Cardoso is an associated researcher at CIES/ISCTE and Professor of Technology and Society at ISCTE in Lisbon. He also collaborates with the Department of Communications and Performance Studies of the University of Milan and with the Portuguese Catholic University. His international cooperation in European research networks brought him to work with IN3 (Internet Interdisciplinary Institute) in Barcelona, COST A20 "The Impact of the Internet in Mass Media" and COST A24 "The Evolving Social Construction of Threats." Since 1996 he is adviser on Information Society and telecommunications policies for the Portuguese Presidency.

Dale W. Jorgenson is the Samuel W. Morris University Professor at Harvard University. He received a BA in economics from Reed College in Portland, Oregon, in 1955 and a PhD in economics from Harvard in 1959. After teaching at the University of California, Berkeley, he joined the Harvard faculty in 1969 and was appointed the Frederic Eaton Abbe Professor of Economics in 1980. He has directed the Program on Technology and Economic Policy at the Kennedy School of Government since 1984 and served as Chairman of the Department of Economics from 1994 to 1997.

Khuong M. Vu is visiting Assistant Professor of Finance at the School of Management at Suffolk University. He is a PhD candidate at Harvard University, Kennedy School of Government Dissertation: "Information and Communication Technology and Global Economic Growth: Contribution, Impact, and Policy Implications." His BA was obtained at Hanoi National University, Vietnam. His professional activities include being Senior Advisor, Development Alternative Inc./On the Frontier Advised the Vietnam Competitiveness Initiative Project, funded by USAID to enhance Vietnam's international competitiveness and global integration, Senior Consultant, World Bank, Summer 2003, for survey of key participants in the Sister City and Development Partnership between Seattle, WA and Haiphong, Vietnam; Former Project Leader, MPDF/IFC, Vietnam; Former Strategy Analyst, Prime Minister's Advisory Council, Vietnam; Former Chief Economic Adviser and Deputy Chief of City Government Office, Vietnam.

Luc Soete is joint Director of the United Nations University Institute for New Technologies (UNU-INTECH) and the Maastricht Economic Research Institute on Innovation and Technology (MERIT). He is Professor of International Economics (on leave) at the Faculty of Economics and Business Administration, University of Maastricht. Since January 2004, he is also member of the Dutch Adviesraad voor Wetenschap en Technologie (AWT).

Jane Fountain is Associate Professor of Public Policy at the John F. Kennedy School of Government at Harvard University. She is also founder and Director of the National Center for Digital Government, and Co-Chair of the Information, Technology and Governance Faculty Group. Her research is focused at the intersection of institutions, global information and communication technologies, and governance. Fountain is the author of *Building the Virtual State: Information Technology* *and Institutional Change* (Brookings Institution Press, 2001), which was awarded an Outstanding Academic Title 2002 by *Choice*, and *Women in the Information Age* (Cambridge University Press, forthcoming).

James Katz is professor of communication at Rutgers, The State University of New Jersey. Currently he is investigating how personal communication technologies, such as mobile phones and the Internet, affect social relationships and how cultural values influence usage patterns of these technologies. Prof. Katz has had a distinguished career researching the relationship among the domains of science and technology, knowledge and information, and social processes and public policy. His award-winning books include *Perpetual Contact: Mobile Communication, Private Talk and Public Performance* (co-edited with Mark Aakhus), *Connections: Social and Cultural Studies of the Telephone in American Life*, and *Social Consequences of Internet Use: Access, Involvement, Expression* (co-authored with Ronald E. Rice).

Ronald E. Rice is the Arthur N. Rupe Professor in the Social Effects of Mass Communication at the University of California, Santa Barbara, USA. He is the author of widely cited books and articles in communication and information sciences. Dr. Rice received his Ph.D. from Stanford University. Before coming to UCSB, he was the chair of the Department of Communication at Rutgers University.

Sophia K. Acord is pursuing her doctorate in the sociology of art at the University of Exeter in Britain. Her current work focuses on cultural aspects of the distribution of power. She has previously co-authored articles with Profs. Katz and Rice in the area of social consequences of communication technology.

Betty Collis is head of the research team "Technology for Strategy, Learning and Change" in the Faculty of Behavioural Sciences at the University of Twente in The Netherlands. As leader of a five-year collaborative research project with the Learning and Leadership Development organization of Shell International Exploration and Production (Shell EP-LLD), she is also head of the research team for Shell EP-LLD. In both roles she studies changes in organizations related to their use (or non-use) of technologies.

Geoff Mulgan is the director of the Institute of Community Studies in east London, which had been the main vehicle through which Lord Michael Young created over 60 organizations including the Open

University and the Consumers Association. He has also become a visiting professor at LSE and UCL, and a senior fellow at the Australia New Zealand School of Government. Between 1997 and 2004 he had a number of roles in government: he established and directed the government's Strategy Unit and served as head of policy in the Prime Minister's office. Before that he was founder and director of Demos, described by the Economist as the UK's most influential think-tank; chief adviser to Gordon Brown MP; a consultant and lecturer in telecommunications; and an investment executive. He began his career in local government in London.

Marcelo Branco is an advisor to the Presidency of the Brazilian Republic for the Information Society. He is also the coordinator of the "Projeto Software Livre Brasil" (www.softwarelivre.org). In his academic work he has collaborated with the University of Cadiz (Spain), he is honorary professor at the Instituto Superior Tecnológico CEVATEC in Lima (Perú) and a member of the scientific council of the International Master in Free Software of the Universitat Oberta de Catalunya (UOC, Open University of Catalonia, Spain).

Jonathan Taplin is Adjunct Professor at USC Annenberg School of Communication. His Areas of specialization are in International Communication Management and the field of digital media entertainment. Taplin began his entertainment career in 1969 as Tour Manager for Bob Dylan and The Band. In 1973 he produced Martin Scorsese's first feature film, Mean Streets which was selected for the Cannes Film Festival. In 1984 Taplin acted as the investment advisor to the Bass Brothers in their successful attempt to save Walt Disney Studios from a corporate raid. This experience brought him to Merrill Lynch, where he served as vice president of media mergers and acquisitions. Taplin was a founder of Intertainer and has served as its Chairman and CEO since June 1996. Intertainer was the pioneer video-on-demand company for both cable and broadband Internet markets.

Imma Tubella is Professor of Communication Theory and Vice-rector for Research at the Open University of Catalonia (UOC), Barcelona. Her research interests concern the relationship between media and identity. She is a member of the Board of the Catalan Broadcasting Corporation. Among other publications, she is a co-author of *La Societat Xarxa a Catalunya* (2003).

Francois Bar is Associate Professor of Communication in the Annenberg School for Communication at the University of Southern California. He is a steering committee member of the Annenberg Research Network on International Communication. Prior to USC, he held faculty positions at Stanford University and at the University of California at San Diego. Since 1983, he has been a member of the Berkeley Roundtable on the International Economy (BRIE), at UC Berkeley, where he previously served as program director for research on telecommunications policy and information networking. He has held visiting faculty appointments at the University of Toronto, the University of Paris-XIII, Théséus, and Eurécom.

Hernan Galperin is an Assistant Professor at the Annenberg School for Communication, University of Southern California. He holds a B.A. in Social Sciences from the University of Buenos Aires, Argentina, and a Ph.D. from Stanford University. Dr. Galperin's research and teaching focus on the international governance and impact of new communication and information technologies. His research has been published in article collections and scholarly journals such as the Federal Communications Law Journal, Telecommunications Policy, the Journal of Communication, and Media, Culture, & Society. His new book, *New TV, Old Politics* (Cambridge University Press, 2004) examines the political economy of digital TV in the U.S. and Europe. He is currently working on a project that examines the impact of new wireless networking technologies such as Wi-Fi in developing nations.

Jeff Cole joined the USC Annenberg School for Communication as Director of the newly formed Center for the Digital Future and as a Research Professor. Prior to joining USC, Cole was a longtime member of the UCLA faculty and served as Director of the UCLA Center for Communication Policy, based in the Anderson Graduate School of Management. At UCLA and now at USC Annenberg, Cole founded and directs the World Internet Project, a long-term longitudinal look at the effects of computer and Internet technology on all aspects of society, which is conducted in over 20 countries. At the announcement of the project in June 1999, Vice President Al Gore praised Cole as a "true visionary providing the public with information on how to understand the impact of media."

William Mitchell is Academic Head of the Program in Media Arts and Sciences, Professor of Architecture and Media Arts and Sciences, and holds the Alexander W. Dreyfoos, Jr. (1954) Professorship at the

Media Lab. Formerly Dean of the School of Architecture and Planning at MIT, he also directs the Media Lab's Smart Cities research group, and serves as architectural adviser to the President of MIT. Mitchell is currently chair of The National Academies Committee on Information Technology and Creativity.

Erkki Liikanen born in Mikkeli, Finland in 1950. Has a Master in political and economical sciences by the University of Helsinki. Since July 2004 he is Governor of the Bank of Finland. Between 1999 and 2004 he was a member of the European Commission for Enterprises and Information Society.

Pekka Himanen divides his time between the Helsinki Institute for Information Society and the University of California at Berkeley. He has also acted as an advisor on the information society to the Finnish President, Government and Parliament. His books on the network society have been published in twenty languages. They include *The Hacker Ethic and the Spirit of the Information Age* (2001) and (with Manuel Castells) *The Information Society and the Welfare State: The Finnish Model* (2001).

Carlos Alvarez is Secretary of State for the Economy in the Chilean Government. Born in Punta Arenas, in 1962. He is an civil engineer and has a Master in Public Administration from Harvard University. He taught economy at the Universidad de Chile between 1989 and 1993.

Maria João Rodrigues is a Full Professor of Economics at the University of Lisbon, Instituto Superior de Ciências do Trabalho e da Empresa (ISCTE), University of Lisbon. Other current activities are: President of the European Commission's Advisory Group for Social Sciences (6th Framework Programme of R&D); Special Adviser to the Luxembourg Presidency of the European Union, in charge of the Mid-term Review of the Lisbon Strategy; Member of the Board of the European Policy Centre Council, Brussels;Member of the Board of *"Notre Europe,"* Paris. recent activities developed in the last five years include being a Member of the Group of Economic Analysis supporting the President of the European Commission (2003-2004); Member of the High Level Group on the Future of European Social Policies, European Union (2003-2004); Member of the High Level Group on Information Society, European Union (2003-2004); Member of the European Employment Task Force, European Union (2003); General rapporteur for the *Global Employment Forum*, ILO, United Nations (2001); Member of OECD network of government long-term strategists (2000).

Acknowledgements

Although dealing with the wide-ranging and manifold tasks and duties that are part of the everyday work of the President of the Portuguese Republic, I have continued to reflect, in recent years, on the nature and direction of the movement that interlinks the information society, the knowledge economy and the network society. Where is it taking us? What demands does it make of the economic agents and political decision makers? How does it affect our daily lives and the way in which we define the everyday horizons of our citizens?

It so happens that the speed at which these developments are taking place is so vertiginous and the work carried out by analysts to come to a proper understanding of what is going on are so intense, that complying with the duty of the President of the Republic—i.e., accompanying and trying to understand the changes going on around us—is not easily compatible with the performance of the normal tasks and duties that come with the office.

In these conditions, taking time out to think is a necessity that makes good common sense. This thinking will be all the more profitable done in the company of those who are best prepared to reflect, with the support of solid theoretical and empirical foundations, on social transformation.

Indeed: stopping to think, one more time, on the limitations and opportunities of our societies in the global context of network societies, was what I decided to do. In this, I have been truly privileged to be able to rely on the support of Professor Manuel Castells, who is, without doubt, one of the most brilliant and acknowledged theorists on social change in the digital era.

During the two days of intense work at the conference organized by Professor Castells, with the support of Professor Gustavo Cardoso, it was possible, thanks to the quality of the national and foreign specialists attending—and I would like to take the occasion of the publication of their contributions to thank them once again for their participation—to present and discuss updated perspectives on the main trends towards development of the network society and its policy dimension. This was achieved without neglecting the fact that these trends are realized at different speeds and in very different patterns in different countries and areas of social life.

From the contributions made and debates held at the conference, and now published in this volume, it is reasonable to conclude that some of the perplexities aroused in this respect by the Portuguese, North American, Finnish, Chilean, Brazilian, UK, Spanish and Catalonian, Dutch, Belgium and other European and Worldwide cases here addressed are common to other societies, albeit at different levels. Sharing this knowledge and comparing different realities is a necessary condition to the development of policies and their implementation in the world we live in. I hope this book might contribute to a better policy making in the network society and knowledge economy.

Jorge Sampaio, President of the Portuguese Republic

Editor's Preface

This volume explores the patterns and dynamics of the network society in its policy dimension, ranging from the knowledge economic, based in technology and innovation, to the organizational reform and modernization in the public sector, focusing also the media and communication policies. The Network Society is our society, a society made of individuals, businesses and state operating from the local, national and into the international arena. Although our societies have many things in common they are also the product of different choices and historical identities. In this volume we chose to focus both what we have considered to be already network societies and also those who are going through a transition process. Accepting the invitation from President Jorge Sampaio to discuss the knowledge economy and the network society from a policy point of view was a challenge that we and the different authors that have contributed to this book believe was worth it.

Policy is usually a strategic choice in order to deal either with uncertainty or with the reality already faced by populations or countries, in our times policy making is becoming increasingly important and at the same time more difficult.

What defines the collective research effort presented in this book is the conviction that the difficulty is probably more a result of the change, and consequently the need to understand what that change is, rather than of an increasingly difficulty of issues and problems. This volume is a small contribution for a better understanding of our societies, both those in transition and those already on the doorsteps of a network society.

The perspective of this book is cross cultural. A perspective drawn, not just by the diversity of geographical origins of its participants, but due to the very own thematic and the geographical scope that we tried to achieve. This is a book that focus on the transition societies of Portugal, Spain—and its different autonomies, Italy, Greece, Poland, Hungary, Czech Republic, Slovakia, Brazil, Argentina, Uruguay and Chile. This is also a book where the comparison of those transition societies with societies, where the network relations that characterize informational societies, is present. So this book focuses on informational societies like the US, Finland, UK and several other members of the more developed countries in the European Union and how policy is being developed.

The volume begins with Manuel Castells and Gustavo Cardoso contextualization of the network society in its different dimensions, from knowledge to policy and from those societies in transition to the Network Society to the already advanced informational societies. Part II analyzes the knowledge economy, technology, innovation, productivity, competitiveness: the new productive economy. Dale W. Jorgenson and Khuong Vu focus on the information technology and its relationship with the world economy, analyzing the impact of investment in information technology (IT) equipment and software on the world economy. Following Dale Jorgenson's detailed overview of the evidence on international comparisons among the G-7 nations in productivity growth, Luc Soete tries to answer why "Europe Lags Behind the United States and Why Various European Economies Differ in Innovation and Productivity," focusing on the need to better understand the precise relationship between ICT and the overall policy framework for the European economies.

Part III focuses on organizational reform and technological modernization in the public sector. The chapter starts with Jane Fountain's analysis of the Virtual State, a term that is a metaphor meant to draw attention to the structures and processes of the state that are becoming more and more deeply designed with digital information and communication systems. Jane Fountain focuses her approach on the discussion of the technology enactment framework, an analytical framework to guide exploration and examination of information-based change in governments focusing on current initiatives in the U.S. federal government to build crossagency relationships and systems. In a different policy domain, James Katz analyses the role of the Internet in providing an opportunity to the public and healthcare professionals to access medical and health information, improve the efficiency and effective, timely healthcare stressing that important empirical questions remain to be answered at every level about how effective these systems are, how people in various socio-demographic sectors actually use these systems, what their different effects are on those sectors, and whether their expense justifies the efforts involved. Betty Collis' analysis of education is another contribution to this chapter where she stresses the major changes that are occurring in society in the ways in which we work and interact with each other, focusing on several of the main characteristics of functioning productively in a knowledge economy and giving some examples of how these characteristics can relate to transformations in educational processes in the corporate setting, for ongoing professional education, and in higher education. This chapter ends with Geoff Mulgan's account of both international and UK experience in policy making in the information age and aims to show that the question of e-government is inseparable from broader questions of government: how it is evolving, in response to what forces, with what tools, and taking what shapes, suggesting a framework for assessing impacts in terms of public value.

Part IV deals with another area of policy, that of media, communication, wireless and policies in the network society. In this chapter Jonathan Taplin outlines the critical transition from a media world of analogue scarcity (a limited number of broadcast channels) to the coming world of digital abundance where any maker of content (films, music, video games) could have access to the world's audience through a server based on demand media environment. His analysis seeks to clarify what the new environment would look like and how the transition to IPTV could aid all of the existing media stakeholders. Taplin suggests that the new environment would also enable an explosion of creativity as the distribution bottleneck that has existed for one hundred years of media history could be unlocked.

Focusing on Identity, another dimension of the media policies, Imma Tubella suggests that while traditional media, in special television, play an enormous role in the construction of collective identity, Internet influences the construction of individual identity, as individuals increasingly rely on their own resources to construct a coherent identity for themselves in an open process of self formation as a symbolic project through the utilization of symbolic materials available to them. The logic of Internet suggests a definition of self whose key quality is not so much being closed and isolated as being connected.

Bringing into the discussion the need to address the choices of technology at the policy level, François Bar and Hernan Galperin focus on the infrastructure dimension and its social implications while analyzing the deployment of wireless communication infrastructure, stressing the differences between the wireless and the traditionally big infrastructures investment programs undertaken by large entities such as telecommunications operators and government agencies. They suggest that three parallel trends are converging to permit departure from that tradition: the emergence of more flexible spectrum policies, which has removed regulatory barriers to entry; the advent of new wireless technologies, which has fundamentally changed the cost equation in favour of wireless solutions; and the entrance of many small business and non-profit actors eager to play new roles in the creation and management of wireless communication networks.

The chapter ends with another policy area, that of software, where Marcelo Branco analyzes free software role on our societies and the implications of following just one trend: that towards universal access of the population to the worldwide computer network with technologies we do not master and contents we have no influence on guarantees neither digital democratization nor the socialization of the economic and social benefits provided by the technological advances. Marcelo Branco argues that the high cost of the software used in computers and the barrier to free scientific and technological knowledge imposed by proprietary licences have hindered and even prevented some regions of the world from benefiting from this revolution in order to provide better quality of life for their citizens.

Part V focuses the need to network knowledge both at the global and local level in order to achieve better policies. Jeff Cole, coordinator of *The World Internet Project* (WIP), argues that since television was the one mass medium expected to be a mass medium, a panel study should have commenced in the late 1940s as the United States and much of Western Europe and Asia acquired television. A long-term study of individuals as they became television users would have done much to answer some fundamental questions about the rise of television and its effects on the audience. Such a study also could have documented television's effects on consumer behavior to determine whether and how it affected consumer purchases, connection to the civic process, desire to travel, career aspirations and much else. Cole argues that we currently need to focus on the uses of Internet in order to understand better our present and consequently be able to design more coherent and social and economic policies adapted to the communalities and differences that cross our societies. William Mitchell, in a different, but complementary approach, focuses on the local, ana-lyzing what kinds of buildings are required by the network economy and the knowledge society. How should these be distributed spatially within a city?

The final chapter of the book focuses on the policies of transition to the network society. Pekka Himanen looks at the challenges that are going on in the information society and their future evolution on a medium term trend, giving particular emphasis on the situation in Finland and Europe. For Himanen, the most critical aspect in the development of the information *society* is the development of the deep-set structures of society, to which we must now pay close attention, stressing that the development of technology will help only when it is combined with changes in the underlying structures.

Erkki Liikanen's contribution focuses on the European Union poli-cies, namely, why it is important to increase productivity and innova-tion in Europe across all industry and service sectors, what is the key role ICTs play in improving Europe's economy and how the European Union stimulates this through the eEurope 2005 Action Plan and what should be the political approach to sustain the development of the broadband market. Focusing on South America, namely Chile, Carlos Alvarez analyzes the incorporation of Information and Communications Technologies (ICTs) as a key component of Chile´s strategy for economic growth and social development, giving a con-text of the global impact of ICT to later concentrate on how ICTs have been embraced as a government initiative in Chile. We then return again our attention to Europe with a contribution by Maria João Rodrigues that asks, "What Europe do we want and for what?" Her argument is that the traditional discourses focusing on the need to ensuring peace within borders are no longer working, namely for the younger generations who take this for granted. Given that, we need a more forward-looking approach to the European citizens aspi-rations by focusing on sustaining their living conditions in a global economy, making Europe a stronger player in improving global gov-ernance and creating a more democratic and effective political system. The paths and objectives for Europe are here discussed under the framework of the Lisbon Strategy.

Finally, Jorge Sampaio, President of the Portuguese Republic, responsible for the fostering of this book by inviting the different scholars and politicians that contributed to this fruitful exchange of ideas and analysis, provides what he suggests to be guidelines for enacting policies in the Information Age. For Jorge Sampaio, in this context, the clear formulation of strategic guidelines and, above all, making decisions at the right time and on the basis of knowledge of the current economic and social trends are absolutely crucial for stimulating and monitoring the necessary changes. In other words: full exploitation of the information technologies with a view to modernizing companies, the public administration and the state itself can only be achieved if, before this, in each one of the principal fields of economic and social life, the main barriers associated with the conventional organizational models and modes of operation are examined. Without organizational innovation, technological innovation will never constitute a development factor and effective source of competitiveness. Jorge Sampaio argues that in countries characterized by high degrees of dualism and asymmetry, the role of the state in creating the infrastructural and support conditions for industrial activity, paying particular attention to the universe of the small and medium-sized enterprises, becomes perhaps even more indispensable than in other contexts. However, state intervention, though necessary, is far from enough. The role of the business community is indispensable in preparing any national economy for successful entry into the age of the information society and globalization. This is because, in the final analysis, it is the enterprises that, depending on a given institutional framework and the stock of skills available in the employment system, will actively contribute to adding vale to the wealth accumulated by an economy.

This is a book on knowledge and policy, two ends of the same process of managing our lives. Only their fruitful combination can allow a better understanding and a better life for our societies. That is the challenge of the network society.

Gustavo Cardoso and Manuel Castells

Part I:
The Network Society:
From Knowledge to Policy

Chapter 1

The Network Society:
From Knowledge to Policy

Manuel Castells

Understanding Social Transformation

Our world has been in a process of structural transformation for over two decades. This process is multidimensional, but it is associated with the emergence of a new technological paradigm, based in information and communication technologies, that took shape in the 1970s and diffused unevenly around the world. We know that technology does not determine society: it *is* society. Society shapes technology according to the needs, values, and interests of people who use the technology. Furthermore, information and communication technologies are particularly sensitive to the effects of social uses on technology itself. The history of the Internet provides ample evidence that the users, particularly the first thousands of users, were, to a large extent, the producers of the technology.

However, technology is a a necessary, albeit not sufficient condition for the emergence of a new form of social organization based on networking, that is on the diffusion of networking in all realms of activity on the basis of digital communication networks. This process can be likened to the role of electricity and the electrical engine in diffusing the organizational forms of the industrial society (eg. the large manufacturing factory, and its correlate the labor movement) on the basis of new technologies of energy generation and distribution. It can be argued that nowadays wealth, power, and knowledge generation are largely dependent on the ability to organize society to reap the benefits of the new technological system, rooted in microelectronics, computing, and digital communication, with its growing connection to the biological revolution and its derivative, genetic engineering. I have conceptualized as the network society the social structure resulting from the interaction between the new technological paradigm and social organization at large.

Often, the emerging society has been characterized as information society or knowledge society. I take exception with this terminology—not because knowledge and information are not central in our society, but because they have always been so, in all historically known societies. What is new is the microelectronics-based, networking technologies that provide new capabilities to an old form of social organization: networks. Networks throughout history had a major advantage and a major problem vis-a-vis other forms of social organization. On the one hand, they are the most adaptable and flexible organizational forms, so following very efficienctly the evolutionary path of human social arrangements. On the other hand, in the past they could not master and coordinate the resources needed to accomplish a given task or fulfill a project beyond a certain size and complexity of the organization required to perform the task. Thus, in the historical record, networks were the domain of the private life, while the world of production, power, and war was occupied by large, vertical organizations, such as states, churches, armies, and corporations that could marshall vast pools of resources around the purpose defined by a central authority. Digital networking technologies enable networks to overcome their historical limits. They can, at the same time, be flexible and adaptive thanks to their capacity to decentralize performance along a network of autonomous components, while still being able to coordinate all this decentralized activity on a shared purpose of decision making. Digital communication networks are the backbone of the network society, as power networks (meaning energy networks) were the infrastructure on which the industrial society was built, as it was demonstrated by historian Thomas Hughes. To be sure, the network society manifests itself in many different forms, according to the culture, institutions, and historical trajectory of each society, as the industrial society encompassed realities as different as the United States, and the Soviet Union, England or Japan, while still sharing some fundamental features that were recognized as defining industrialism as a distinct form of human organization—not determined by the industrial technologies, but unthinkable without these technologies.

Furthermore, because the network society is based on networks, and communication networks transcend boundaries, the network society is global, it is based on global networks. So, it is pervasive throughout the planet, its logic transforms extends to every country in the planet, as it is diffused by the power embedded in global networks of capital, goods, services, labor, communication, information, science, and technology. So, what we call globalization is another way to refer to the network society, although more descriptive and less analytical than what the concept of network society implies. Yet, because networks are selective according to their specific programs, because they can simultaneously communicate and incommunicate, the network society diffuses in the entire world, but does not include all people. In fact, in this early 21st century, it excludes most of humankind, although all of humankind is affected by its logic, and by the power relationships that interact in the global networks of social organization.

Understanding structural transformation in its morphological form, meaning the rise of the network society as a specific type of social structure, frees the analysis from its promethean underpinnings, and leaves open the value judgment on the meaning of the network society for the well being of humankind. We are mentally framed in an evolutionary view of human progress, coming from the Enlightenment and reinforced by Marxism, according to which humankind, led by Reason and equipped with Technology, moves from survival to agricultural societies, then to the industrial society, and finally to the post-industrial/information/knowledge society, the shining hill where Homo Sapiens will finally make his dignified dwelling. Yet, even a superficial look at the historical record belies this fairy tale of human progress, as the Nazi or Stalinist Holocausts are witness to the destructive potential of the industrial age, and as the wonders of the information technology revolution coexist with the self-destructive processes of global warming or the resurgence of pandemics on a planetary scale.

So, the issue is not how to reach the network society as a self-proclaimed superior stage of human development. The issue is to recognize the contours of our new historical terrain, meaning the world we live in. Only then it will be possible to identify the means by which specific societies in specific contexts can pursue their goals and realize their values by using the new opportunities generated by the most extraordinary technological revolution in humankind, the one transforming our capacities of communication and enabling to modify the codes of life, that is the one giving us the tools to actually master our own condition, with all the potentially destructive or creative implications of this capacity. This is why diffusing the Internet or putting more computers in the schools does not in itself amount to much social change. It depends where, by whom, for whom, and for what communication and information technologies are used. What we know is that this technological paradigm has superior performing capacity vis-a-vis previous technological systems. But to know how to use it to the best of its potential, and in accordance with the projects and decisions of each society, we need to know the dynamics, constraints and possibilities of the new social structure associated with it: the network society.

As for the actual content of the network society as a social structure, I will now turn to present what academic research knows on the subject.

The Network Society Beyond Myths: Findings of Scholarly Research (*)

In the early years of the 21st century, the network society is not the emerging social structure of the Information Age: it already configures the nucleus of our societies. Indeed, we have a considerable body of knowledge gathered in the last decade by academic researchers around the world on the fundamental dimesions of the network society, including studies that show the commonality of this nucleus across cultures, as well as the cultural and institutional differences of the network society in various contexts.

It is unfortunate that the media, politicians, social actors, business leaders, and decision makers continue to talk about the information society or the network society or whatever they want to call it, in terms that are those of futurology and uninformed journalism, as if the transformations were still in the future, and as if technology was an independent force that has either to be denounced or worshipped. Traditional intellectuals, increasingly unable to understand the world we live in, and thus undermined in their public role, are particularly critical of the advent of a new technological environment without actually knowing much about the processes on which they elaborate their discourses. In these views, new technologies destroy jobs, Internet isolates , we suffer from an overload of information, the digital divide increases social exclusion, Big Brother extends its surveillance thanks to more powerful digital technologies, technological development is controlled by the military, the tempo of our lives is relentlessly accelerated by technology, biotechnology leads to human cloning and to major environmental hazars, Third World countries do not need technology but the satisfaction of their human needs, children are increasinly ignorant because they are messaging and chatting instead of reading books, nobody knows who is whom in the Internet, work efficiency is hampered by technology that does not rely on human experience, crime and violence, and even terrorism use the Internet as a privileged medium, and we are rapidly losing the magic of the human touch. We are alienated by technology. Or else, you can reverse everything I just wrote in the opposite sense, and we will enter the paradise of human fulfillment and creativity induced by technological wonders, in the mirror version of the same mythology, this time propagated by consultants and futurologists, often on the payroll of technology companies.

And yet we know reasonably well the contours of the network society. There is in fact a big gap between knowledge and public consciousness, mediated by the communication system and the processing of information within our mental frames.

The network society, in the simplest terms, is a social structure based on networks operated by information and communication technologies based in microelectronics and digital computer networks that generate, process, and distribute information on the basis of the knowledge accumulated in the nodes of the networks. A network is a formal structure (see Monge and Contractor, 2004). It is a system of interconnected nodes. Nodes are, formally speaking, the points where the curve intersects itself. Networks are open structures that evolve by adding or removing nodes according to the changing requirements of the programs that assign performance goals to the networks. Naturally, these programs are decided socially from outside the network. But once they are inscripted in the logic of the network, the network will follow efficiently these instructions, adding, deleting, and reconfigurating, until a new program replaces or modifies the codes that command its operational system.

What the network society actually is cannot be decided outside the empirical observation of social organization and practices that embody this network logic. Thus, I will summarize the essence of what scholarly research (that is the production of knowledge recognized as such by the scientific community) has found in various social contexts.

Let us start with the economy. **The network economy** (known at one point as "the new economy") is a new, efficient form of organization of production, distribution, and management that is at the source of the substantial increase in the rate of productivity growth in the United States, and in other economies that adopted these new forms of economic organization. The rate of productivity growth in the U.S. during 1996-2005 more than doubled the rate of productivity growth in 1975-95. Similar observations can be applied to those European economies, such as Finland or Ireland, that quickly adopted a similar form of techno-economic organization, albeit in a very different institutional context (eg, the maintenance of the welfare state). Studies, including the research presented by Dale Jorgenson in this volume, show that the rate of productivity growth in other European economies and in Japan may have increased as well once statistical categories are adapted to the conditions of production in an economy that has gone beyond the industrial era under which these categories were created. Throughout the world, developing economies that articulate themselves to the dynamic nucleus of the global network economy display even higher rates of productivity growth (eg in the manufacturing sectors of China or India). Moreover, the increase of productivity is the most direct empirical indicator of the transformation of a productive structure. Researchers have found that productivity growth in this period has been largely associated to three processes, all of which are necessary conditions for productivity growth to take place: generation and diffusion of new microelectronics/digital technologies of information and communication, on the basis of scientific research and technological innovation; transformation of labor, with the growth of highly educated, autonomous labor that is able to innovate and adapt to a constantly changing global and local economy; diffusion of a new form of organization around networking. Only when the three conditions are fulfilled in a firm, a sector, a region, or a country, productivity rises substantially, and only this surge in productivity can sustain competitiveness in the long run.

Organizational networking is as critical today as was the process of vertical integration of production in the large scale organizations of the industrial era. Networking has proceeds through a number of processes that reinforced each other over the last 25 years: large corporations decentralize themselves as networks of semi-autonomous units; small and medium firms form business networks, keeping their autonomy and flexibility while making possible to pull together resources to attain a critical mass, enabling them to compete in the market; small and medium business networks become providers and subcontractors to a variety of large corporations; large corporations, and their ancillary networks, engage in strategic parnertships on various projects concerning products, processes, markets, functions, resources, each one of this project being specific, and thus building a specific network around such a project, so that at the end of the project, the network disolves and its components form other networks around other projects. Thus, at any given point in time, economic activity is peformed by networks of networks built around specific business projects. The firm continues to be the legal unit, and the unit for accumulation of capital, but the operational unit is the business network, what I call the network enterprise to emphasize the fact that is a network focusing on performing a project. Besides, since accumulation of capital actually takes place in the global financial market, that is also a network, the firm is simply the connecting node between the networks of production built around business projects and the networks of accumulation organized around global finance.

These networks are those that hire and fire workers on a global scale. It follows structural unstability in the labor markets everywhere, and a requirement for flexibility of employment, mobility of labor, and constant re-skilling of the workforce. The notion of a stable, predictable, professional career is eroded, as relationships between capital and labor are individualized and contractual labor conditions escape collective bargaining.

Together with the feminization of the labor force, we can say, summarizing numerous studies, that **we have evolved from "the organization man" to the "flexible woman."** However, this process of individualization and fragmentation of the labor force does not mean that long term contracts and stable jobs disappear. There is flexibility built into stability. And there are considerable differences for various categories of workers and levels of skill. **The key developments in the transformation of labor and work are:**

> Technological change does not induce unemployment in the aggregate labor market. Although some workers are displaced and some occupations are phased out (eg, traditional typist-secretaries), other occupations appear (eg. assistant managers

instead of secretaries), more jobs are created, and most displaced workers are re-employed, except for those too old to adapt, their fate being decided depending on public policies in each society. In fact, the least technologically advanced is a firm, region or country, and the more it is exposed to layoffs of its workers, since it cannot keep up with the competition. So, there is a correlation between technological innovation and employment, as well as between technological innovation, organizational innovation, and standards of living of workers.

Ability to work autonomously and be an active component of a network becomes paramount in the new economy. This is what I have conceptualized as **self-programmable labor.** Companies will seek to retain this type of labor as much as possible, because this is the main source for its productivity and innovation capacity. This runs against the notion of the unstability of the labor force. However, the self-programmable worker is the one that has bargaining power in the labor market. So, his/her contract may be a stable one, but his/her continuity in the job tends to be reduced vis-a-vis previous cohorts of workers, because he/she is always on the move, searching for new opportunities. And not necessarily to increase monetary gains but to enjoy greater freedom, flex-time, or more opportunity to create.

Most workers are still not employed at the best of their capacity, but as mere executants along the lines of traditional industrial discipline. In this case, they are generic labor, and they can be replaced by machines or by less expensive labor either in the country (immigrants, women, minorities) or across the globe. Under such conditions, companies tend to limit long term commitment to generic labor, thus opting for subcontracting, temporary employment, or part time work. On the other hand, these workers tend to strengthen their negotiation power through collective bargaining and unionization. But being the most vulnerable labor force, they increasingly face an uphill battle that is at the source of offshoring of manufacturing and routine service work.

There is a growing contradiction between the autonomy and innovation capacity required to work in the network enterprise, and the system of management/labor relations rooted in the institutions of the industrial age. The ability to reform this system conditions the organizational and social transition in all societies. More often than not, the necessary adaptation of the workforce to the new conditions of innovation and productivity is manipulated by companies to their advantage. It is a self-defeating strategy for management, as workers can only use their autonomy to be more productive if they have a vested interest in the competitiveness of the firm. This interest starts with their stability in their jobs, and their ability to make their own decisions in the operation of the network.

Trade unions do not disappear in the network society. But, depending on their strategies, they might become trenches of resistance to economic and technological change, or powerful actors of innovation on the new meaning of work and wealth creation in a production system based on flexibility, autonomy, and creativity. Organizing labor in a network of networks has very different requirements to organizing labor in the socialized process of work in the large corporation. While changes in the labor force and in the labor market are structural, linked to the evolution of the network society, changes in the role of social actors depend on their practice, and on their ability to situate the interests they defend in the new forms of production and management.

The network society is also manifested in **the transformation of sociability.** Yet, what we observe is not the fading away of face-to-face interaction or the increasing isolation of people in front of their computers. We know, from studies in different societies, that in most instances Internet users are more social, have more friends and contacts, and are more socially and politically active than non users. Moreover, the more they use the Internet, the more they also engage in face-to-face interaction in all domains of their lives. Similarly, new forms of wireless communication, from mobile phone voice communication to SMSs, WiFi and WiMax, substantially increase sociability, particularly for the younger groups of the population. The network society is a hypersocial society, not a society of isolation. People, by and large, do not fake their identity in the Internet, except for some teenagers experimenting with their lives. People fold the technology into their lives, link up virtual reality and real virtuality, they live in various technological forms of communication, articulating them as they need it.

[handwritten margin note: Major Change in Sociability]

However, there is a major change in sociability, not a consequence of Internet or new communication technologies, but a change that is fully supported by the logic embedded in the communication networks. This is the emergence of **networked individualism,** as social structure and historical evolution induce the emergence of individualism as the dominant culture of our societies, and the new communication technologies perfectly fit into the mode of building sociability along self-selected communication networks, on or off depending on the needs and moods of each individual. So, the network society is a society of networked individuals.

A central feature of the network society is **the transformation of the realm of communication, including the media.** Communication constitutes the public space, i.e. the cognitive space where people's minds receive information and form their views by processing signals from society at large. In other words, while interpersonal communication is a private relationship, shaped by the actors of the interaction, media communication systems sets the relationship between the institutions and organizations of society and people at large, not as individuals, but as a collective receiver of information, even if ultimately information is processed by each individual according to her personal characteristics. This is why the structure and dynamics of socialized communication is essential in the formation of consciousness and opinion, at the source of political decision making.

In this regard, **the new communication system is defined by three major trends:**

Communication is largely organized around media business conglomerates that are global and local at the same time, and that include television, radio, the print press, audiovisual production, book publishing, music recording and distribution, and on line commercial firms. These conglomerates are linked to media organizations around the world, under different forms of partnership, while engaging at the same time in fierce competition amongst themselves. Communication is both global and local, generic and customized, depending on markets and products.

The communication system is increasingly digitized, and gradually interactive. So, concentration of business does not mean a unified, unidirectional process of communication. Societies have moved from a mass media system to a customized and fragmented multimedia system, where audiences are increasingly segmented. Because the system is diversified and flexible, it is increasingly inclusive of every message sent in society. In other words, the technological malleability of the new media allows a much greater integration of all sources of communication into the same hypertext. So, digital communication becomes less centrally organized, but absorbs into its logic an increasing share of social communication.

As the network society diffuses, and new communication technologies expand their networks, there is an explosion of horizontal networks of communication, quite independent from media business and governments, that allows the emergence of what I call **self-directed mass communication.** It is mass communication because it is diffused throughout the Internet, so it potentially reaches the whole planet. It is self-directed because it is often initiated by individuals or groups by themselves, bypassing the media system. The explosion of blogs, vlogs, podding, streaming, and other forms of interactive, computer to computer communication sets up a new system of global, horizontal communication networks that, for the first time in history, allow people to communicate with each other without going through the channels set up by the institutions of society for socialized communication.

Thus, the network society constitutes socialized communication beyond the mass media system that characterized the industrial society. But it does not represent the world of freedom sung by the libertarian ideology of Internet prophets. It is made up both of an oligopolistic business multimedia system controlling an increasingly inclusive hypertext, and of an explosion of horizontal networks of autonomous local/global communication—and, naturally, of the interaction between the two systems in a complex pattern of connections and desconnections in different contexts. However, what results from this evolution is that the culture of the network society is largely shaped by the messages exchanged in the composite electronic hypertext made by the technologically linked networks of different communication modes. In the network society, virtuality is the foundation of reality through the new forms of socialized communication.

Since **politics is largely dependent on the public space of socialized communication, the political process is transformed under the conditions of the culture of real virtuality.** Political opinions, and political behavior, are formed in the space of communication. Not that whatever is said in this space determines what people think or do. In fact, the theory of the interactive audience, supported by research across cultures, has determined that receivers of messages process these messages in their own terns. Thus, we are not in an Orwellian universe, but in a world of diversified messages, recombining themselves in the electronic hypertext, and processed by minds with increasinly autonomous sources of information. However, the domination of the media space over people's minds works through a fundamental mechanism: presence/absence of a message in the media space. Everything or everyone that is absent from this space cannot reach the public mind, thus it becomes a non entity. This binary mode of media politics has extraordinary consequences on the political process and on the institutions of society. It also implies that presence in the media is essential for building political hegemony or counter-hegemony—and not only during the electoral campaigns.

Mainstream media, and particularly television, still dominate the media space, although this is changing fast. Because the language of television is based on images, and the simplest political image is a person, political competition is built around political leaders. Few people know the actual programs of political parties. And programs are built by pollsters focusing on what people would like, so they tend to be very similar at least in their wording. People think in metaphors, and built these metaphors with images. Trust and character are constructed around the image of a person. Because of this, character assassination becomes the political weapon of choice. Negative messages are much more effective than positive messages. And the most negative message is to undermine the trust of people in their potential leader by diffusing, fabricating, or manipulating damaging information. Media politics and image politics lead to scandal politics, the kind of politics at the forefront of the political process almost everywhere in the world.

There is an even deeper transformation of political institutions in the network society: **the rise of a new form of state** that gradually replaces the nation-states of the industrial era. This is related to globalization, that is the formation of a network of global networks than link selectively across the planet all functional dimensions of societies. Because the network society is global, the state of the network society cannot operate only or primarily in the national context. It has to engage in a process of global governance but without a global government. The reasons why there is not a global government, and it is unlikely it will be one in the foreseeable future, are rooted in the historical inertia of institutions, and of the social interests and values embedded in these institutions. Simply put, neither current political actors nor people at large want a world government, so it will not happen. But since global governance of some sort is a functional need, nation-states are finding ways to co-manage the global processes that affect most of the issues related to their governing practice. To do so, they increasingly share sovereignty while still proudly branding their flags. They form networks of nation-states, the most integrated and significant of which is the European Union. But they are around the world a number of state associations more or less integrated in their institutions and their practice that structure specific processed of transnational governance. In addition, nation-states have spurred a number of formal and informal international and supranational institutions that actually govern the world. Not only the United Nations, and verious military alliances, but also the International Monetary Fund and its ancillary agency, the World Bank, the G-8 club of leading countries in the world (with the permission of China), and a number of ad hoc groupings.

Furthermore, to connect the global and the local, nation-states have asserted or fostered a process of decentralization that reaches out to regional and local governments, and even to NGOs, often associated to political management. Thus, the actual system of governance in our world is not centered around the nation-state, although nation-states are not disappearing by any means. Governance is operated in a network of political institutions that shares sovereignty in various degrees an reconfigurates itself in a variable geopolitical geometry. This is what I have conceptualized as **the network state.** It is not the result of technological change, but the response to the structural contradiction between a global system and a national state. However, globalization is the form that takes the diffusion of the network society in its planetary reach, and new communication and transportation technologies provide the necessary infrastructure for the process of globalization. New communication technologies also help the actual operation of a complex network state, but this is a tool of performance rather than a determining factor. The transition from the nation-state to the network state is an organizational and political process prompted by the transformation of political management, representation and domination in the conditions of the network society.

Thus, the network society is not the future that we must reach as the next stage of human progress by embracing the new technological paradigm. It is our society, in different degrees, and under different forms depending on countries and cultures. Any policy, any strategy, any human project, has to start from this basic fact. It is not our destination, but our point of departure to wherever "we" want to go, be it heaven, hell, or just a refurbished home.

Key Policy Issues in the Network Society

People, social actors, companies, policy makers do not have to do anything to reach or develop the network society. **We are in the network society,** although not everything or everybody is included in its networks. Therefore, from a policy standpoint, the key question is how to proceed to maximize the chances for fulfilling the collective and individual projects that express social needs and values under the new structural conditions. For instance, a full deployment of broad band digital communication networks, wired or wireless, is certainly a conditioning factor for business to work on the model of the network enterprises or for virtual education to foster life long learning, a major asset in the knowledge-based social organization characteristic of the society. However, to introduce technology per se does not ensure productivity, innovation, or greater human development. Thus, when in 2000 the European Union approved a strategy known as the Lisbon Agenda to catch up with the United States in economic competitiveness, while strengthening the European social model, much of the emphasis was placed on technological upgrading and enhancement of research capabilities. The European technological infrastructure improved considerably, but effects on productivity, on learning, on creativity, and on entrepreneurialism, were very limited. This is because acting on the developmental potential specific to the network society requires a combination of initiatives in technology, business, education, culture, spatial restructuring, infraestructure development, organizational change, and institutional reform. It is the synergy between these processes that acts as a lever of change on the mechanisms of the network society.

With this perspective in mind, and observing both the European and international experience in the first years of the 21st century, there are some issues that appear to be conditioning the overall development of a productive, creative, and equitable network society. In other words, policies tackling these strategic issues seem to be the key policies to deliberately advance human well being in the new historical context. Being highly selective and certainly subjective, since we have now left the presentation of research findings to enter the policy debate, here then are what I consider to be the key issues:

- **The public sector is at present the decisive actor to develop and shape the network society.** Individual innovators, counter-cultural communities, and business firms have done their job at inventing a new society and diffusing it around the world. The shaping and guiding of this society is, as has always been the case in other societies, in the hands of the public sector, regardless of ideological discourses hiding this reality. And yet, the public sector is the sphere of society where new communication technologies are the least diffused and where organizational obstacles to innovation and networking are the most pronounced. Thus, **reform of the public sector commands everything else** in the process of productive shaping of the network society. This includes the diffusion of e-governance (a broader concept than e-government because it includes citizen participation and political decision-making); e-health; e-learning; e-security; and a system of dynamic regulation of the communication industry, adapting it to the values and needs of society. All these transformations require the diffusion of interactive, multilayered networking as the organizational form of the public sector. This is tantamount to the reform of the state. Indeed, the rational bureaucratic model of the state of the industrial era is in complete contradiction to the demands and processes of the network society.

- At the source of the entire process of social change there is a new kind of worker, the self-programmable worker, and a new type of personality, the values-rooted, flexible personality able to adapt to changing cultural models along the life cycle because of her/his ability to bend without breaking, to remain inner-directed while evolving with the surrounding society. This innovative production of human beings, under the conditions of the crisis of patriarchalism and the crisis of the traditional family, **requires a total overhauling of the school system,** in all its levels and domains. This refers certainly to new forms of technology and pedagogy, but also to the content and organization of the learning process. As difficult as it sounds, societies that will not be able to deal with this issue will encounter major economic and social problems in the current process of structural change. For instance, one of the major reasons for the success of the Finnish Model in the network society resides in the quality of its education system, in contrast to other areas in the world, for instance the United States, where much of the population is increasingly alien to the system of knowledge management that has been largely generated in their own country. Education policy is central to everything. But not any kind of education or any kind of policy: education based on the model of learning to learn along the life cycle, and geared towards stimulating creativity and innovation in the ways and goals of applying this learning capacity in all domains of professional and social life.

- Global development is now largely a function of enabling countries and their people to function productively in the global economy and the network society. This implies the diffusion of information and communication technologies througout the world, so that networks reach everywhere. But it also implies the production of the human resources necessary to operate this system, and the distribution of capacity to generate knowledge and manage information. **The new, informational model of development redefines the condition of shared growth in the world.** In fact, hundreds of millions of people have benefited from the global competition spurred by the dynamism of these networks. Large sections of China, India, East and Southeast Asia, the Middle East, and some Latin American areas (Chile certainly, but also some regions of other countries) are now integrated productively in the networked global economy. Yet, more people are switched off from these networks than fully incorporated to them. The global segmentation of the network society, precisely because of its dynamism and productivity, is placing a significant part of humankind under conditions of structural irrelevance. It is not just poverty, it is that the global economy and the network society work more efficiently without hundreds of millions of our co-inhabitants of this planet. Thus, a major contradiction: the more we develop a highly productive, innovative system of production and social organization, the less this core needs a substantial proportion of marginal population, and the more difficult it becomes for this population to catch up. The correction of this massive exclusionary process requires concerted international public policy acting on the roots of the new model of development (technology, infrastructure, education, diffusion and management of knowledge) rather than just providing for the needs arising from social exclusion in the form of charity.

- Creativity and innovation are the key drivers of value creation and social change in our societies—in fact in all societies. **In a world of digital networks, the process of interactive creativity is contradicted by the legislation of property rights inherited from the industrial era.** Moreover, because large corporations have built their wealth and power on the control of these property rights, regardless of the new conditions of innovation, companies and governments are making the communication of innovation even more difficult than in the past. The capture of innovation by an intellectually conservative business world may well stall the new waves of innovation on which the creative economy and a redistributive network society depend. Even more so at the global level, as intellectual property rights become the key issue for latecomers in the global competition. International agreements on the redefinition of intellectual property rights, starting with the well rooted practice of open source software, is a must for the preservation on innovation and the fostering of creativity on which depends human progress now and then.

Dilemmas of Our Time: Creativity versus Rentier Capitalism; Communication Democracy versus Political Control

In this early 21st century we are at the crossroads of the development of the network society. We are witnessing an increasing contradiction between current social relationships of production and the potential expansion of formidable productive forces. This may be the only lasting contribution from the classical Marxist theory. The human potential embedded in new communication and genetic technologies, in networking, in the new forms of social organization and cultural invention, is truly extraordinary. Yet, existing social systems stall the dynamics of creativity, and, if challenged with competition, tend to implode. This was the case of the statist system of the Soviet Union (Castells and Kiselyova, 1995). Now, rentier capitalism of the Microsoft type appears to be blocking the development of a new frontier of expansion of innovation, in contrast to other capitalist business models, eg. the newborn IBM. Thus, reform of capitalism is also possible in this domain, including new models of intellectual property rights, and a diffusion of technological development responsive to the human needs of the whole planet. This is why the issue of intellectual property rights is strategically so important.

But there is something else: the emergence of unfettered communication and self-organization at the socio-political level, bypassing the mass media, and challenging formal politics. This is the case of insurgent political campaigns, such as Howard Dean's campaign in the U.S. in 2003-04, or the exposure of Jose Maria Aznar's lies on terrorism by thousands of Spanish youth mobilized with their cell phones, and leading to the electoral defeat of Spanish conservatives in March 2004. This is why in fact governments are ambiguous vis-a-vis the uses of Internet and new technologies. They praise their benefits, yet they fear to lose the control of information and communication in which power has always been rooted.

Accepting democracy of communication is accepting direct democracy, something no state has accepted in history. Accepting a debate to redefine property rights goes to the heart of the legitimacy of capitalism. Accepting that the users are the producers of technology challenges the power of the expert. So, an innovative, yet pragmatic policy will have to find a middle way between what is socially and politically feasible in each context, and the enhancement of the cultural and organizational conditions for creativity on which innovation, thus power, wealth, and culture, are based in the network society.

* * *

(*) The analysis presented here is based on a very broad body of research that would overwhelm the thread of the argument if fully cited in this text. Therefore, I am taking the liberty to refer the reader to my recent works on the matter, not because I support my analysis with my own bibliography, but because my recent publications contain an extensive, and systematic bibliography from different areas in the world, that should be considered as the generic references of the analysis.

With this caveat, the interested reader may consult the sources included in the following books by Manuel Castells:

The Information Age: Economy, Society, and Culture, Oxford: Blackwell, 3 volumes, 2nd edition, 2000-2004; *The Internet Galaxy*, Oxford: Blackwell, 2001; *The collapse of Soviet Communism: the view from the Information Society*, Berkeley, International and Area Studies Press, 1995 (with Emma Kiselyova) (updated edition by Figueroa Press, Los Angeles, 2003); *La societat xarxa a Catalunya*, Barcelona: Random House, 2003 (with I.Tubella et alter); *The Information Society and the Welfare State: The Finnish Model*, Oxford: Oxford University Press, 2002 (with Pekka Himanen); *The Network Society: A Cross-Cultural Perspective*, Northampton, Massachussets: Edward Elgar, 2004 (editor and co-author); "Global Governance and Global Politics," *Political Science*, January 2005; *The Mobile Communication Society*, forthcoming (with M. Fernandez-Ardevol, JCL Qiu, and A. Sey). In addition, important references on specific points are the recent books by Peter Monge and Nosh Contractor, *A Theory of Communication Networks*, New York: Routledge, 2004; Frank Levy, *Computers and Work*, Cambridge, MA: MIT Press, 2005; and Ulrich Beck, *Power in the Global Age*, Cambridge: Polity Press, 2006.

Furthermore, the chapters in this book, and their references, have also been used in the elaboration of my analysis.

Chapter 2

Societies in Transition to the Network Society

Gustavo Cardoso

Several analysts have put forward the idea that societies are currently experiencing significant change characterized by two parallel trends that frame social behaviour: individualism and communalism (Castells, 2003b).

Individualism, in this context, denotes the construction of meaning around the realization of individual projects. Communalism, in turn, can be defined as the construction of meaning around a set of values defined by a restricted collective group and internalized by the group's members.

Various observers have looked at these two trends as potential sources of disintegration of current societies, as the institutions on which they are based lose their integrating capacity, i.e. they become increasingly incapable to giving meaning to the citizens: the patriarchal family model, the civic associations, companies and, above all, representative democracy and the nation state. These institutions have been, to some extent, fundamental pillars of the relationship between society and the citizens throughout the 20th century (Castells 2003; 2004, Giddens 2000).

However, another hypothesis is possible. Perhaps what we are witnessing is not the disintegration and fractioning of society, but the reconstruction of the social institutions and, indeed, of the structure of society itself, proceeding from autonomous projects carried out by society members. This independence (i.e. independence from society's institutions and organizations) can be regarded as individual or collective, in the latter case in relation to a specific social group defined by its autonomous culture.

In this perspective, the autonomization of individuals and groups is followed by the attempt to reconstruct meaning in a new social structure on the basis their self-defined projects. By supplying the techno-logical resources for the socialization of the projects of each individual in a network of similar subjects, the Internet, together with the mass media, becomes a powerful social reconstruction tool and not a cause of disintegration. This social (re)construction, giving rise to the new structure, will not have to follow the same values logic of the late industrial society.

However, as the Internet is a technology, its appropriation and domestication (Silverstone 1994) may also take place in a conservative way and thus act merely to perpetuate social life as it had already existed.

The examples are manifold. If we wish to expand our field of vision we can look at the Internet as, for example, an instrument for the maintenance of a patriarchal society rooted in a fundamentalist inter-pretation of Islam, when we see it being used for the recruitment of volunteers for al-Qaeda, or as an instrument for the perpetuation of old public administration models, when the websites of the ministries offer nothing more than the telephone numbers of the various serv-ices, in what amounts to the mere substitution of the yellow pages, in hardcopy form, by hypertext in a closed institutional circuit. Or when we limit ourselves to constructing a personal page in which we center content around our own personality and identity without any connec-tion to any entities to which we belong or are affiliated, thus rejecting the logic of sharing in a network of interests.

In other words, the hypothesis for the analysis of social develop-ment and the role of the Internet in that development is that the Internet is a tool for the construction of projects. However, if it is merely used as one more means of doing something we already do, then its use is limited and is not necessarily different from that of the other media (for example, television, as far as entertainment and news information are concerned).

As one can verify by means of the study of the reality of two soci-eties in transitions—Catalonia and Portugal (Castells et al.2003, Cardoso et al. 2005)—the Internet is appropriated in different ways by different people and not all of them effect uses that distinguish the Internet from what the other media could offer. This is a reality that is, perhaps, more perceptible in societies where the Internet utilization levels are still quite low. However, different studies conducted in different societies (Cole 2005) demonstrate that that is a reality that is not directly linked with the character of transition or affirmation as an information society, but with variables such as the education and generation dimensions.

Nevertheless, there is something in societies in transition that accentuates the differences more. In other words, in societies in transition, the divisions between those who use and those who do not use technologies such as the Internet are greater and tend to make utilization of them more a question of the generation to which one belongs: the younger the generation the greater the use and the higher the education level the greater the use.

If it is a recognized fact that societies such as the United States, Finland and Singapore can be classified as "informational societies" (Castells and Himanen 2002), how can we define those societies in transition towards the information society? In other words, societies in which the mark of networked social organization already asserts itself in broad segments of society?

In order to answer that question, we require a more in-depth analysis of a society whose characteristics, though profoundly European, also reveal similarities in terms of relations and values to countries of the American continent: Portugal.

The argument for the choice of Portugal as a typical example of a society in transition towards the network society is that Portugal is a country that shares, to varying degrees, development characteristics and historico-political values and conditioning factors with a group of other societies, for which the common denominator is the fact that they all experienced, in the last three decades, the democratization of their societies and, at the same time, have similar informational development rankings.

All of these societies are classified by different digitalization indexes (ITU 2003) in one and the same group: the high digital access countries. In the concrete case of the DAI (ITU 2003), the group is led by Spain, with Brazil bringing up the rear. It includes, amongst others, the countries we have chosen to study herein, i.e. those that were protagonists of waves of democratization in the last 30 years (Huntington

1991, Altman 2002) in Europe and South America[1]: Spain, the Czech Republic, Greece, Portugal, Hungary, Poland, Slovakia, Chile, Uruguay, Argentina and Brazil.

However, because it is necessary to compare this group of countries with a group of more informationally developed countries, we have also chosen to conduct a comparative analysis herein of Finland, the USA and Singapore. Finally, we will also analyse the case of Italy in this transition context, for, although it is a member of the G7, Italy has a proto-information model (Castells 2002) that is closer, on various levels, to a society in transition than a full informational society.

We will look at Portugal as a paradigmatic example of transition in progress, but at the same time we will seek to identify the characteristics that make societies that differ so much as Spain, Greece, the Czech Republic, Slovakia, Hungary and Poland, and also Argentina, Chile, Uruguay and Brazil, societies in transition towards the network society.

Societies in Transition in the Global Network

An analysis of the different information society models can have as its starting point the individualization of four dimensions (technology, economy, social well-being and values), through which one can better understand what each society's position is in relation to the global information society panorama (Castells and Himanen, 2001). On this basis one can consider that a society is an informational society if it possesses a solid information technology: infrastructure, production and knowledge (Castells and Himanen, 2001).

---

[1] Huntington suggests that, during the 1970s and 1980s there were transitions from non-democratic political systems to democratic systems and that those changes can be seen in the context of a greater trend towards transition to democracy. Without going into the various premises put forward by Huntington in more detail, I think that his contribution is of interest for the analysis of the societies in transition to the network society due to the fact that he establishes a link between different geographic zones and societies at the values level. In other words, all the societies studied herein have shared one common value in the last three decades—the search for democracy—and seek today integration in the global economy as informational societies, with most of the indicators placing them in a transition zone. Almost all of the countries analysed here as being in transition to the network society are referred to by Huntington as common examples of transition to democracy. Huntington defines three types of transition, which include all the countries analysed here: 1) transformation (for example, Spain, Hungary and Brazil), where elites in power took on the leadership of the transition processes; 2) substitution (as in Portugal and Argentina), where opposition groups led the democratization process; 3) transplacements (as in Poland and Czechoslovakia), where democratization occurred from joint action by government and opposition groups.

Finland, the United States and Singapore are advanced informational societies. They are also dynamic economies because they are internationally competitive, have productive companies and are innovative. But because "(…) technology and the economy are merely a part of the story" (Castells and Himanen, 2001: 31), one can say that a society is open if it is so politically, i.e., at the civil society level, and if it is receptive to global processes. Likewise, its social well-being can be assessed in terms of its income structure and the coverage offered to the citizens in terms of health and education.

When looked at in terms of the evolution of development models, Portugal is a country that is going through a transition process from the industrial society to the informational society. However, we are speaking of an industrial society, which, similar to the Italian and Spanish societies, is to a large extent made up of small and medium-sized enterprises but that has never asserted itself as a large-scale industrial producer (Castells, 2002). In the second half of the 20th century, Portugal assumed what can be termed proto-industrialism and is now seeking to achieve a proto-informationalism (Castells, 2002). As an example of a society in transition, the analysis of Portugal reveals that it is a country which, through its multiple affiliation networks (which range from membership of the European Union to the maintenance of good relations in terms of defence with the USA and to the establishment of partnership networks with Brazil, the former African and Asian colonies and the autonomous regions of neighbouring Spain), seeks to adapt to the conditions of global economic change. And that is a pattern common to all societies in transition.

Nowadays, one can frequently read, in documents produced within the European Union institutions or within the framework of the OECD or even UN, that the equation for the economic and social development of countries, cities and zones in the Information Age is the appropriation of the use of the technological tools and their introduction into the production and personal relational circuits, requiring for this that the whole of the country, city or zone in question realize their effective insertion both into the entrepreneurial fabric and at the State level (in the management of the republic, in education, in management and defence of the territory, etc.).

In the latter half of the 1990s, investment in information technologies as a source of GDP creation in countries such as the USA, United Kingdom and Canada equalled in percentage terms the isolated contribution made by labor or the investment in capital not coming from the information technologies (Jorgensen 2005). The trend towards the convergence of the investment contribution in information technologies with the contribution from other investments in capital or the labour contribution would seem to be a general one for all the more developed countries, albeit in varying degrees. Likewise, there is a trend in all countries towards an increase in the value added provided by the information technologies in the creation of value added in the services sector (OECD 2004).

To clarify this a little, one should add that, contrary to general perceptions, the productive fabric in the information age does not consist merely of the technology companies (the so-called "dotcom" companies) but also that of companies that are able to incorporate the information technologies in their productive, organizational, distribution and promotion processes.

Hence, the new economy is not only the likes of amazon.com, e-bay or the telecommunications companies, although these are indeed part of that economy, but also companies like INDITEX (a Spanish group that owns ZARA and other clothing brands) that have been able to use the Internet to achieve their economic objectives (Castells, 2004b).

Indeed, the new economy includes many more companies from traditional sectors than purely technological companies or those with a direct vocation for online business. It is normal for the productive fabric today, as has always been the case down through the centuries, to be led by one driving force sector, as well as others that will make use of that dynamism to innovate.

In order to triumph in this game, any country or geographic zone also requires a workforce with the capacity to use the new technology to innovate, be it in the private sector or in the state. Workforces that carry out repetitive—or not creative—work but with the use of the technologies, a telecommunications structure, an innovative entrepreneurial fabric, a state that is able to create the appropriate vocational training conditions, conversion of organizational and management models and establishes legislation on regulation, frameworks and incentives.

The data contained in the following tables compare Portugal and the other countries in transition to three information society models.

These models that can be given the names of Silicon Valley, an open society model guided by the market; Singapore, the authoritarian information regime model; and, finally, the Finnish model of an information-welfare society.

If classification of a society as an information society is based on a solid information technology at the infrastructure, production and knowledge levels, what position do these countries have in terms of these dimensions?

Table 2.1 Technological Achievement Index (2001)

Country	TAI Position	Group
Spain	19	Potential Leaders
Italy	20	Potential Leaders
Czech Republic	21	Potential Leaders
Hungary	22	Potential Leaders
Slovakia	25	Potential Leaders
Greece	26	Potential Leaders
Portugal	27	Potential Leaders
Poland	29	Potential Leaders
Argentina	34	Potential Leaders
Chile	37	Potential Leaders
Uruguay	38	Dynamic Adopters
Brazil	43	Dynamic Adopters

Source: UNDP, 2001.

Most of the countries classified here in terms of the technological development index in 2001 (UNDP, 2001) were in what we can call the second division of countries—the so-called potential leaders—whereby this second division is led by Spain (19th place) and Italy (20th). Brazil closed the list of countries in transition to the network society in analysis here.

However, Brazil is worthy of special attention, for, according to the IMD (2004), if we consider the competitiveness dimension for the whole of Brazil, the country occupies 53rd place. If we consider only the state of São Paulo, where a number of high-potential technological centers are centered around the University of Campinas, the contribution to the GDP in 1998 amounted to roughly to one third of the Brazilian total, then the position of São Paulo at the global level places it in 47th place. However, this is by no means a peculiarity of Brazil, as, as far as societies in transition are concerned, there would seem to be geographic differences in terms of integration in the global economy.

Table 2.2a   International comparisons in the field of technology

	Finland	USA	Singapore	Portugal	Spain	Italy	Czech Rep.	Advanced economies
Infrastructure								
Machines connected to the Internet (per 10,000 inh.)[1]	1707.25(3)	3714.01(1)	478.18	239.28	133.24	117.28	209.78	819.15
Mobile phone contracts (per 1,000 inh.)[2]	867	488	796	825	824	939	849	740
Production								
High technology exports as a percentage of the total exports[2]	24	32	60	7	7	9	14	21
Electronic commerce (secure servers per 100,000 inhabitants)[3]	14.9	33.28 (1)	17.31	2.34	3.2	2.2	3.8	16.3
Growth rate for secure servers, 1998-2001 (%)	656	397	527	600	358	460	796	555
Ratio between hosts and secure servers (2001)	1144	1139	357	1054	423	527	541	692
Knowledge								
Internet users (%) (2001)[4]	75.95	71.1	40.8	37.79	35.45	53.21	46.51	53
Ratio of participation of the higher education student population in sciences (%)*	37	13,9	24,2	31	31	28	34	25,0
Scientist and engineers in R&D (per thousand persons)[2]	7110	4099	4052	1754	1948	1128	1466	2778
PISA Test—mathematical literacy	544 (2)	483 (25)	–	466 (29)	485 (25)	466 (29)	516 (12)	504
PISA Test—scientific literacy	548 (1)	491 (20)	–	468 (31)	487 (22)	486 (22)	523 (5)	510

*UNESCO definition for the indicator in question: "gross enrollment in tertiary education—total enrolment in tertiary education regardless of age, expressed as a percentage of the population in the five-year age group following the secondary-school leaving age."

Source: 1 Values for all countries taken from World Indicators, ITU, http://www.itu.int/itunews/issue/2002/04/table4.html; 2 Values for all countries take from the UNDP Human Development Report 2004; 3 Values obtained by Netcraft in December 2001: http://www.atkearney.com/shared_res/pdf/Secure_servers_2002_S.pdf; 3 Host values taken from World Indicators, ITU http://www.itu.int/itunews/issue/2002/04/table4.html; 4 ESS Data 2003, WIP 2004 and http://www.internetworldstats.com/stats2.htm ; 5 Adapted from Castells and Himanen, 2002, except for data for Portugal, taken from the UNDP Human Development Report

Table 2.2b International comparisons in the information technology domain

	Slovakia	Hungary	Greece	Poland	Chile	Argentina	Uruguay	Brazil	Advanced economies
Infrastructure									
Machines connected to the Internet (per 10,000 inh.)[1]	134.29	168.04	135.18	126.82	79.20	124.14	210.93	95.31	819.15
Mobile phone contracts (per 1,000 inh.)[2]	544	676	845	363	428	178	193	201	740
Production									
High technology exports as a percentage of the total exports[2]	3	25	10	3	3	7	3	19	21
Electronic commerce (secure servers per 100,000 inhabitants)[3]	1,9	1,8	1,7	1,7	1,2	0,8	–	0,9	16,3
Growth rate for secure servers, 1998–2001 (%)	1040	936	765	1830	678	1000	–	429	555
Ratio between hosts and secure servers (2001)	697	941	813	743	645	1604	–	1303	692
Knowledge									
Internet users (%) (2001)[4]	–	46,21	25,87	38,68	34,8	14,9	34,5	9,9	53
Ratio of participation of the higher education student population in sciences (%)*	43	32	–	–	43	30	24	23	25,0
Scientist and engineers in R&D (per thousand persons)[2]	1774	1440		1473	419	684	276	323	2778
PISA Test—mathematical literacy	498 (19)	490 (22)	445 (32)	490 (22)	–	–	422 (34)	356 (38)	504
PISA Test—scientific literacy	495 (18)	503 (14)	481 (25)	498 (17)	–	–	438 (33)	390 (38)	510

*UNESCO definition for the indicator in question: "gross enrollment in tertiary education—total enrolment in tertiary education regardless of age, expressed as a percentage of the population in the five-year age group following the secondary-school leaving age."

Source: 1 Values for all countries taken from World Indicators, ITU, http://www.itu.int/itunews/issue/2002/04/table4.html; 2 Values for all countries take from the UNDP Human Development Report 2004; 3 Values obtained by Netcraft in December 2001: http://www.atkearney.com/shared_res/pdf/Secure_servers_2002_S.pdf; 3 Host values taken from World Indicators, ITU http://www.itu.int/itunews/issue/2002/04/table4.html; 4 ESS Data 2003, WIP 2004 and http://www.internetworldstats.com/stats2.htm ; 5 Adapted from Castells and Himanen, 2002, except for data for Portugal, taken from the UNDP Human Development Report

The selective inclusion to which Castells (2003) refers when analyzing the space of flows is a perceptible reality in the case of the relation established between Catalonia and Spain or Lombardy and Italy (IMD 2004) or between the Greater Buenos Aires area and Argentina (Amadeo 2005).

The more populous countries apparently seem to be incapable of effecting, or prefer not to effect, this transition to information and network societies for the whole of their territory and population, at least in this phase of history.

The similarity between the countries listed above is confirmed by other international indices such as that of the ITU (International Telecommunications Union), the DAI (2003). Namely, because the DAI (Digital Access Index) establishes identification categories, such as: infrastructure (relating to telephone lines, mobile phone and Internet subscriptions), cost (Internet access and use prices in comparison to the national income); knowledge (literacy and inclusion in the education system); quality (international bandwidth and broadband subscribers) and utilization of the Internet.

If we compare these categories in the leading countries (such as Finland, USA and Singapore) and the societies defined as transition societies, we see that it is not only the low levels of technology utilization in the latter that makes the difference. Indeed, in recent years we have come to understand that studies carried out by those involved in the technological processes themselves, such as the telecommunications operators, are beginning to accept that the communication infrastructure is not the only element that can explain the differences between countries and that income and education also play a very important role (ITU 2003). Only if we look at society in an integrated manner—taking into account the infrastructure, production and knowledge (Castells and Himanen, 2001)—can we identify the transition processes in progress in contemporary societies.

The analysis of international comparisons in the technological domain reveals an apparently converging reality amongst the different societies analyzed here. They all present figures for machines connected to the Internet that are approximately one quarter of the average for the advanced economies and also one third of the high technology exports achieved by the advanced economies (with the exception of Poland, Uruguay and Argentina), presenting, finally,

Internet utilization values of more than two-thirds of the average for the advanced economies (with the exception of Argentina and Brazil).

In general terms, the countries analyzed here always present better results and more balanced values in the technological "knowledge" dimension than in the "infrastructure" and "technology production" dimensions. However, the irregularity of the performance in these two latter categories would seem, in itself, to be a distinguishing mark of these societies and the fruit of the fact that, in the transition process, they have not yet been able to stabilize good results in all categories.

Examples of this irregularity in terms of results are the percentage values for Brazil (19) and Hungary (25) in relation to the average high technology export figures for the G7 (21) or the number of mobile phone contracts in Portugal, Spain, Italy, Greece and the Czech Republic, which are all above the G7 average, and also the growth rates for secure servers in Portugal, the Czech Republic, Slovakia, Hungary, Poland, Greece, Chile and Argentina, whose figures are close to, or above, those of the three information economies analyzed here (Finland, USA and Singapore).

However, we also have to take into account some peculiarities of the societies in transition, without which it would be difficult to explain some of their performances. By way of example, let us look at the question of secure server penetration. The fact that Portugal and Spain have higher ATMs per million inhabitants rates (AETIC 2004), with 1,047 and 1,230 machines compared to an EU average of 700, has allowed for the development of alternative systems to the use of credit cards and secure servers for online purchases. The fact that Portugal has a debit card system common to the whole banking system, the so-called "Multibanco" system, has made it possible to make online orders with payment through the ATM network, thus creating an alternative and more secure electronic channel for transactions. This is one example of many that help us to understand that, in addition to the common and individual traits, there are sometimes situations common to two or more countries that allow for the identification of some characteristic sub-groups in the context of the transition analyzed here.

If there is something that brings the different societies from two continents analyzed here closer together then it is, as mentioned above, the technological knowledge dimensions. Hence, the figures for the number of tertiary education students in the sciences is clearly higher than the average for the G7 in almost all of the countries included in the study (Uruguay and Brazil are the exceptions), and the figures for scientists and investigators in R&D are higher than the half of the values for the G7 countries (with only the four South American countries below that average). As far as the PISA literacy test results for mathematics and the sciences are concerned, only Uruguay and Brazil present values lower than 90% of those presented by the advanced economies.

It is also in the knowledge dimension, in this case not merely technological knowledge, that the generational mark that seems to be common to all these societies manifests itself most. The question of education is fundamental for analyzing the transition to the network society with an informational economic organization because, as we shall see, there is a strong correlation in all the societies between the educational competences given and the number of users of the basic network society technology: the Internet.

The Internet use figures constitute one reference value for characterizing the transition of a society to the network society because they reflect both the dimension of use in the socialization context and the market potential. Indeed, without a high number of users, there would also be no incentive for increasing electronic commerce (be it at the inter-company level or with private persons).

An analysis of the preceding table shows that the relation between access and use is dependant on a fundamental conditioning factor, the education level. Age is also a mobilizing factor, as it facilitates use via the group affiliation and practices amongst populations attending school (Table 2.3). However, different studies show that the stronger direct relationship is established between the education level and effective use of the Internet.

As far as the comparative analysis of the countries is concerned, the figures show that in the information societies use of the Internet by persons who have completed secondary education is between 60% and 90% of the users with higher education, while in the societies in transition, these values are less than 50%. The exception here is Portugal, with values of around 90%, as the number of Portuguese citizens who have completed secondary education is relatively low and, consequently, is closer in percentage terms to the numbers who have concluded higher education.

Table 2.3   Use of the Internet per country according to user's highest education level (%)

Country	Not completed primary education*	Primary or first stage of basic*	Lower secondary or second stage of basic*	Upper secondary*	Post secondary, non-tertiary*	First stage of tertiary*	Second stage of tertiary*
Portugal	21.10	18.86	37.24	48.87	–	48.61	50.00
Austria	16.66	–	33.88	51.45	77.09	–	76.62
Belgium	7.69	10.61	29.94	45.22	61.53	–	77.39
Switzerland	35.29	–	39.78	52.88	73.91	82.89	90.47
Czech Rep.	30.00	–	14.28	23.74	47.61	62.50	60.00
Germany	–	–	–	–	–	–	–
Denmark	–	20	46.07	61.08	73.46	84.50	100
Spain	0.91	1.69	16.63	31.68	44.64	61.79	68.42
Finland	25	15.18	55.55	63.94	–	79.20	100
France	6.08	8.93	25.10	24.16	49.57	67.06	77.04
U.K.	–	–	26.34	66.60	57.21	74.71	91.83
Greece	0.90	0.431	6.04	14.12	31.81	47.00	60
Hungary	1.51	16.58	6.63	23.49	–	40	58.69
Ireland	–	9.09	28.94	46.47	65.38	77.77	75.00
Israel	–	5.40	24.59	30.61	37.25	64.07	67.44
Italy	–	0.88	21.83	50.35	55.40	59.27	85.96
Luxembourg	–	20.00	50.00	61.53	–	100	100.00
Netherlands	–	21.875	38.57	66.02	71.79	79.40	80.00
Norway	–	–	25.49	60.75	77.77	80.51	90.00
Poland	–	3.70	5.63	12.40	18.79	42.95	43.64
Sweden	88.88	37.43	57.44	83.33	–	83.01	89.74
Slovenia	–	–	19.51	15	53.84	55.55	85.71

Source: European Social Survey 2002/2003. *Note: given the different names for education levels in the European context we opted to use the original ESS terms.

Although the analysis has thus far practically made reference to European countries only, a more geographically comprehensive study, such as that proposed by the World Internet Project (2005), establishes the same relationship between Internet use and education.

Table 2.4 Internet use rates in the population with secondary and higher education (%)

	Secondary	University
United Kingdom	64.4	88.1
Portugal	64.8	75.1
Germany	66.0	62.6
Hungary	14.6	45.5
Italy	53.5	77.3
Japan	45.7	70.1
Korea	44.9	77.7
Macao	49.5	76.7
Singapore	66.3	92.2
Spain	47.6	80.5
Sweden	76.4	83.8
Taiwan	18.2	54.9
USA	61.0	87.1

Source: CIES, Network Society in Portugal Survey, 2003 for Portugal; for all other countries the WIP (World Internet Project).

In characterizing societies in transition, the similarities are crossed with the exceptions and the question of Internet access offers a new example for the affirmation of singularities.

Although it is possible to establish similarities between the access rates in some of the countries studied here (Portugal, Poland, Spain), we also immediately find differences as to the effective use of that access. Indeed, if we establish a ratio between access and use, we see that Portugal is one of the countries that makes most use of the existing availability, putting it on a par with leading countries such as Norway, the Netherlands and Finland and ahead of other societies in transition such as the Czech Republic, which has high access figures but very low effective use by its populations.

What this use of the existing access availability ratio measures is the effective use of the technology, demonstrating that there must be other factors endogenous to each society that could explain why there are differences in the use of a technology even when the access is equally high to begin with.

Analysis of the values for Portugal and the other European countries shows that, in certain conditions, even when the access rate increases, that increase is not necessarily directly reflected in an increase in use, for there are dynamics peculiar to each country at play that can explain the different socialization rates for the technology.

Table 2.5—Internet access/use of access ratio

Country	Has Internet access at home or at work* %	Uses the Internet** %	Access availability usage ratio
Portugal	37.79	29.72	0.79(4)
Austria	67.22	54.37	0.81(3)
Belgium	67.14	43.70	0.65
Switzerland	72.89	57.85 (3)	0.79(4)
Czech Republic	46.51	27.56	0.59
Germany	–	–	–
Denmark	76.61 (3)	62.39(2)	0.81(3)
Spain	35.45	22.20	0.63
Finland	75.95 (4)	56.19	0.74
France	50.00	37.28	0.75
United Kingdom	57.55	45.21	0.79 (4)
Greece	25.87	13.40	0.52
Hungary	46.21	19.63	0.42
Ireland	66.12	40.39	0.61
Israel	54.25	39.22	0.72
Italy	53.21	30.51	0.57
Luxembourg	68.57	51.43	0.75
Netherlands	73.05	55.88	0.76
Norway	75.29 (5)	62.07(4)	0.82(2)
Poland	38.68	23.88	0.62
Sweden	77.96 (2)	66.94(1)	0.86 (1)
Slovenia	78.92 (1)	36.14	0.46

Source: European Social Survey 2002/2003. *Note: the figures refer to the aggregated sum of all those who responded that they at least have access regardless of the degree of utilization. **Note: the figures refer to the aggregated sum of those who make effective personal use of the Internet (whereby personal use is defined as: private or recreational use that has nothing to do with the professional occupation of the user).

Table 2.6   Percentage of citizens per age group that have completed secondary and tertiary education in selected countries

	Finland	USA	Portugal	Spain	Italy	Czech Rep.	Slovakia	Advanced Economies
Secondary >55 years	52	84	8	18	24	80	68	60
Secondary 25–34	88	87	35	58	60	88	93	80
Growth rate	69.23%	3.57%	337.50%	222.22%	150.00%	10.00%	36.76%	
Tertiary > 55	23.4	33.2	4.6	10.5	6.7	10.6	8.6	18
Tertiary	39	39	15	37	12	12	12	27
Growth rate	66.67%	17.47%	226.09%	252.38%	79.10%	13.21%	39.53%	

	Hungary	Greece	Poland	Chile	Argentina	Uruguay	Brazil	Advanced Economies
Secondary >55 years	48	28	37	28	28	23	15	60
Secondary 25–34	82	72	53	61	52	38	32	80
Growth rate	70.83%	157.14%	43.24%	117.86%	85.71%	65.22%	113.33%	
Tertiary > 55	12.6	10.2	10.5	6	9	7	6	18
Tertiary	15	24	16	12	15	9	14	27
Growth rate	19.05%	135.29%	52.38%	100.00%	66.67%	28.57%	133.33%	

Sources: Secondary education figures: Education Outlook OECD 2004; tertiary education figures: Education Outlook OECD 2003

If the relationship between use of the Internet and education seems to be transversal to all countries, there is also a characteristic in the education dimension that seems to be common to almost all countries analyzed her: all of them, with the exception of the Czech Republic, reveal strong generational differences in terms of the completion of secondary education and tertiary education. The countries under analysis can be grouped into three distinct groups. The first group includes most of the countries: all those which present growth rates for completion of the education level ranging from 300% to 50% between the generations. This first group is also heterogeneous, for though countries such as Greece and Hungary present values in the younger generations that place them above 70% completion of secondary education, Portugal, Brazil and Uruguay are below 40%. Also in this group, in an intermediate position, are Spain, Poland, Argentina and Chile, which all have values close to 60% of the population with secondary education completed in the younger generations. This first group (with the exception of Greece) is also characterized by figures for the completion of higher education that are clearly below the average for the G7 countries.

A second group of countries, made up of the Czech Republic and Slovakia, seems to be in a better position, presenting diminutive generational differences in terms of education, given that even in the older generations completion of secondary education was close to or above 70%.

Finally, we have a third group made up by Italy alone, a country characterized by high growth rates for the completion of secondary education in the younger generations and values very close to those of Finland as far as investment in tertiary education by the younger generations is concerned. Italy presents itself, once more, as a dual society: simultaneously an information society and one in transition.

The generation analysis focusing on the question of education can also be observed when we look at the relationship between age and use of the Internet.

Table 2.7 Use of the Internet by age interval per country (%)

Country	15-24	25-34	35-54	over 55
Austria	81.81	75.28	65.73	21.02
Belgium	75.60	63.35	48.18	12.69
Switzerland	88.00	76.82	71.48	29.14
Czech Republic	73.07	39.82	38.46	10.31
Denmark	91.66	81.33	72.95	33.33
Spain	50.15	35.98	28.81	3.78
Finland	91.93	82.53	63.94	22.29
France	62.67	53.90	45.00	13.28
UK	73.34	62.05	59.49	20.01
Greece	32.60	25.71	15.73	1.95
Hungary	63.55	27.55	15.24	4.15
Ireland	62.79	56.60	46.78	16.34
Israel	55.68	52.631	37.93	18.69
Italy	48.87	52.83	33.28	8.67
Luxembourg	85.71	80.00	54.54	18.18
Netherlands	87.09	76.26	67.30	29.97
Norway	85.71	80.00	74.28	30.70
Poland	53.32	34.25	18.81	3.43
Sweden	66.30	65.45	50.97	21.21
Slovenia	67.85	53.57	38.33	7.54
Average	68.91	57.56	46.56	16.61

Source: European Social Survey 2002/2003.

Another characteristic common to the societies in transition, in this case with bearing on our analysis of European societies, is the fact that there is a considerable difference between the use rates for the older and younger generations.

For all societies in transition for which there are comparative data (Portugal, Spain, Czech Republic, Greece, Hungary and Poland), one can verify that the older citizens using the Internet correspond to only 10% of the younger users. In the case of other European countries, the figures are almost always somewhat above 20%.

Table 2.8 International comparison of Internet use per age group (%)

	United Kingdom	Portugal	Germany	Hungary	Italy	Japan	Korea	Spain	USA
16 to 24 yrs	80.1	58.8	59.6	45.1	66.4	80.6	95.1	70.2	90.8
35 to 44 yrs	72.8	30.4	55.6	13.7	37.4	63.0	49.5	31.7	74.5
55 to 64 yrs	38.7	5.4	31.6	4.3	9.0	22.2	11.5	11.7	67.3

Source: CIES, Network Society in Portugal Survey, 2003 for Portugal; for all other countries: WIP (World Internet Project)

The age dimension also can be used for comparison not only at the European level, for European, American and Asian societies all offer the possibility of comparative inter-generational analyses. Italy figures as a country in an intermediate position between information societies such as Germany, the United Kingdom, Japan and the USA and other societies in transition such as Portugal, Spain and Hungary.

The explanation for these differences between the generations in using the Internet seems, for the societies in transition, to lie mostly in the difference in the possession of basic forms of literacy, whereas in the more developed information societies the differences probably have more to do with the availability of contents that adapt to the interests of all generations and, furthermore, the dimension of the sociability networks that the technology can offer to more senior citizens.

All the factors analyzed so far in the infrastructure, production and knowledge dimensions and also those relating to acquired skills, employment structure and predominance of low and medium technology areas in the economy, are also reflected in the economies' compared productivity levels and their GDP *per capita.*

On a competitiveness index of 0-100, where the average for the advanced economies is 74 points, the societies in transition under analysis here occupy varied positions. Chile (26th), Spain (31st), Portugal (39th) and Slovakia (40th) are amongst the top forty countries or regions, while the remaining countries occupy positions between 42nd (Hungary) and 59th (Argentina).

Whereas the Portuguese GDP *per capita* represents 67% of the average for the advanced economies, placing it amongst the top thirty countries in an international comparison (together with Spain, Italy and Greece), the other countries (with the exception of the Czech Republic, Slovakia and Hungary) present values below 30% of the GDP *per capita* of the G7 economies.

Table 2.9 International comparison of informational development indicators

	Finland	USA	Singapore	Chile	Spain	Portugal	Slovakia	Hungary
Competitiveness (scale 0-100)[1]	83 (8)	100 (1)	89 (2)	69 (26)	67 (31)	58 (39)	57 (40)	57 (42)
GDP per capita (US $)[2]	26,190	35,750	24,040	9,820	21,460	18,280	12,840	13,400
Stock market capitalization growth, 1996-2000 (%)[3]	894	429	n.d.	70.7	70.4	35.1	7.9	20.2
Investment in R&D as a % of GDP (2001)[4]	3.4(2)	2.8	2.1	0.5	1.0	0.8	0.6	0.9
Investment in knowledge as a % of GDP (2000)[5]	6.2	6.8	–	–	2.5	2.2	2.4	3.1
Revenue derived from intellectual property and licences (US $ per 1,000 inh.)[4]	107.5 (5)	151.7 (4)	–	0.4	9.0	3.1	–	35.3

Table 2.9 International comparison of informational development indicators (continued)

	Czech Rep.	Greece	Italy	Brazil	Portugal	Argentina	Uruguay	Advanced Economies
Competitiveness (scale 0-100)[1]	56 (43)	56 (44)	50 (51)	48 (53)	41 (57)	36 (59)	–	74
GDP per capita (US $)[2]	15,780	18,720	20,528	7,770	10,560	10,880	7,830	27009
Stock market capitalization growth, 1996-2000 (%)[3]	21.6	51.7	40.2	26.9	15.0	100.9	0.8	71.44
Investment in R&D as a % of GDP (2001)[4]	1.3	0.7	1.1	1.1	0.7	0.4	0.2	2.0
Investment in knowledge as a % of GDP (2000)[5]	3.7	1.6	2.3	–	1.9	–	–	4.7
Revenue derived from intellectual property and licences (US $ per 1,000 inh.)[4]	4.4	1.1	9.4	0.6	0.7	0.5	0.2	26

Source: 1 Figures obtained directly from the source cited in Castells and Himanen (2002); i.e. the IMD (2004); 2 Values for all countries taken from the UNDP Human Development Report 2004; 3 Adapted from Castells and Himanen 2002, except the data for Portugal, which were supplied by the Portuguese Securities Exchange Commission (CMVM)—http://www.cmvm.pt/consulta_de_dados_e_registos/indicadores/indicadores.asp— whereby the figures for Portugal refer to 1997-2000 (Shares—BVL 30); 4 Adapted from Castells and Himanen (2002) for Finland, USA and Singapore; remaining data taken from the World Development Indicators Report of the World Bank 2002 (capitalization 1990-2000); 5 Investment in knowledge is defined as the sum of expenditure on R&D, higher education and software (OECD Factbook 2005). Note: (*) relative position.

A comparison of the societies in transition in terms of the informational development indicators reveals more differences than common traits. Nevertheless, as far as investment in R&D and knowledge are concerned, it is possible to present two different transition stages.

Thus, Italy, Brazil,[2] Spain, Portugal, the Czech Republic, Hungary and Slovakia are representative of a stage in which the countries invest approximately 50% of the values of the advanced economies in R&D and knowledge. A second group of countries—led by Greece, Poland, Chile, Argentina and Uruguay—presents values below 0.7% of the GDP.

Still in the context of the international comparison of development we can also analyze the economies in transition according to two other classification levels: the readiness of economies for an informational development model and their growth and competitiveness rates.

In terms of the incorporation of technology into the society and economy, The Economist's e-readiness report for 2004 proposes an index that measures the readiness and receptiveness of economies for an informational development model, basing its ranking on six dimensions: connectivity and information technologies, business environment, business and consumer adoption, legal and policy environment, social and cultural environment and supporting e-services.

For example, Portugal achieves good results in the "business environment," "business and consumer adoption" and "legal and policy environment" dimensions, on the basis of which one can conclude that, in terms of business infrastructure and state actions, the conditions are given for the national economy developing in that informational context.

However, the informational model does not consist of these conditions alone. It needs technological infrastructure conditions, specialized support services, sufficient user numbers and also a technically qualified workforce.

The countries and regions that lead the first half of the e-readiness ranking, namely Scandinavia, the UK, the USA and the Netherlands, achieve good results in all of the fields analyzed. The societies in transition essentially show bad performances in terms of the use of the basic telephone network, the mobile network, the Internet and the use of com-

---

[2] For Brazil, the analysis refers only to the R&D value.

Table 2.10 Position of the information economies under analysis

	Connectivity	Business environment	Consumer and business adoption	Legal and policy	Social and cultural environment	Supporting e-services	Overall score
Category weight	0.25	0.20	0.20	0.15	0.15	0.05	–
Finland	6.06	8.51	8.45	9.05	9.00	9.25	8.08 (5)
USA	6.25	8.50	8.22	8.45	9.30	9.40	8.04 (6)
Singapore	6.70	8.44	8.14	8.31	9.00	8.75	8.02 (7)
Spain	5.18	7.96	7.49	8.58	7.50	8.00	7.20 (21)
Italy	5.40	7.29	6.80	8.49	8.00	8.25	7.05 (23)
Portugal	4.98	7.49	7.65	8.52	7.25	7.50	7.01 (24)
Greece	4.49	6.77	6.91	8.19	6.75	7.50	6.47 (27)
Czech Rep.	4.74	7.37	6.81	6.73	7.25	7.00	6.47 (27)
Chile	3.82	8.00	6.26	7.69	6.88	7.13	6.35 (29)
Hungary	4.08	7.18	6.49	6.87	7.25	7.00	6.22 (30)
Brazil	3.21	6.36	6.95	6.05	5.88	6.13	5.56 (35)
Poland	3.01	7.10	5.32	5.88	6.50	6.25	5.41 (36)
Argentina	3.32	5.91	5.95	5.54	6.88	6.38	5.38 (37)

Source: The Economist e-readiness report, 2004. Note: The countries leading the ranking are Denmark, United Kingdom, Norway and Sweden.*

*Connectivity and information technologies: measures the use of the basic telephone network, the mobile network, the Internet and the use of computers, as well as the cost, quality and reliability of services. Business environment: evaluate the general business climate in a country, including the strength of the economy, political stability, the regulatory environment, taxation, competition policy, the labour market, the quality of infrastructure and openness to trade and investment. Consumer and business adoption: assesses how prevalent e-business practices are in each country, i.e. how the Internet is used to auto- mate traditional business processes and how companies are helped by the development of logistics and online payment systems and the availability of finance and state investment in information technologies. Legal and policy environment: assesses a country's legal framework and the specific laws governing Internet use—how easy is it to register new businesses, how strong is protection of private property, and whether the governments support the creation of an Internet-conducive legal environment or are more concerned with censoring content and controlling access. Social and cultural environment: evaluates the literacy and basic education, which are preconditions for being able to use the new technologies, experience using the Internet and receptivity to it and the technical skills of the workforce. Finally, the existence of supporting e-services: the existence of consulting and IT services, the existence of back- office solutions and consistent industry-wide standards for platforms and programming languages.

puters, as well as the cost, quality and reliability of service.[3] These data are corroborated by other sources such as the OECD figures (Figure 1) or the World Economic Forum, whose ranking is analyzed below.

Continuing with the comparisons in terms of competitiveness, the Global Competitiveness Report (2004) produced by the World Economic Forum employs a ranking system based on three indexes: technology, quality of public institutions and macro-economic environment.[4] The GCI index reflects the balance between technological development and adoption and the reliability of the public institutions and macroeconomic environment.

---

[3] *Connectivity and information technologies*: measures the use of the basic telephone network, the mobile network, the Internet and the use of computers, as well as the cost, quality and reliability of services. *Business environment:* evaluate the general business climate in a country, including the strength of the economy, political stability, the regulatory environment, taxation, competition policy, the labour market, the quality of infrastructure and openness to trade and investment. *Consumer and business adoption:* assesses how prevalent e-business practices are in each country, i.e. how the Internet is used to automate traditional business processes and how companies are helped by the development of logistics and online payment systems and the availability of finance and state investment in information technologies. *Legal and policy environment:* assesses a country's legal framework and the specific laws governing Internet use—how easy is it to register new businesses, how strong is protection of private property, and whether the governments support the creation of an Internet-conducive legal environment or are more concerned with censoring content and controlling access. *Social and cultural environment:* evaluates the literacy and basic education, which are preconditions for being able to use the new technologies, experience using the Internet and receptivity to it and the technical skills of the workforce. Finally, the existence of *supporting e-services:* the existence of consulting and IT services, the existence of back-office solutions and consistent industry-wide standards for platforms and programming languages.

[4] The *technology index* is obtained using a set of data with differentiated weighting. The measured variables are Internet access in schools, whether the state of competition between ISPs is sufficient for guaranteeing high quality, low failure rates and low prices, whether the government programmes are successful or not in promoting the use of the information technologies and whether the legislation on e-commerce, digital signatures, consumer protection are developed and enforced. Furthermore, mobile phone penetration and the number Internet users, Internet hosts, telephone lines and personal computers are also measure; the *public institutions index* is measured on the independence of the judicial system in relation to political power, citizens and companies, whether the property rights, including movable goods, are well defined and protected by law, whether the state is impartial in awarding public contracts and whether or not organized crime constitutes a high cost to economic activity. Also measured are corruption dimensions, in particular to what extent bribery is common for achieving import and export authorizations, access to public assets and avoiding taxation; the *macro-economic environment index* is based the probability of the economy experiencing recession in the coming year and to what extent access to credit for companies is more or less difficult than the previous year. Also assessed are the state debts or surpluses in the preceding year, as well as the savings, inflation and exchange rates and the spread for loans and financial applications. Two further factors assessed are the country's rating in terms of international credit and to what extent the state supplies necessary goods and services not supplied by the market and distortive government subsidies.

Figure 2.1   Businesses using the Internet and businesses receiving orders over the Internet, percentage of businesses with ten or more employees, 2002 and 2003 or latest available year[1]

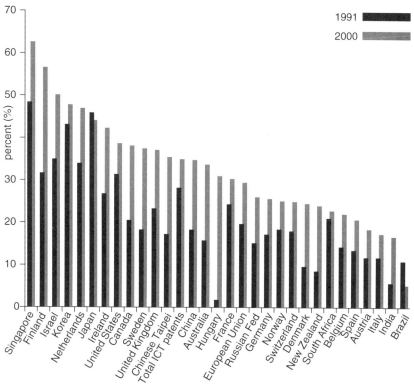

1. The provisional definition of ICT patents is presented in Annex B of the compendium.
2. Cut-off point: countries with more than 100 EPO applications in 2000.
Source: OECD, Patent Database, September 2004.

In a table led by Finland and the USA, Portugal occupied 24th place in 2004, having climbed one place in relation to 2003. Indeed, Portugal is accompanied in its leadership of the societies in transition by two other countries that have also climbed the table: Spain and Chile.

Despite presenting high figures at the technological level, the second group of countries analyzed here, consisting of Greece, Hungary, the Czech Republic, Slovakia and Italy, has lower scores in terms of their public institutions. The third group, which includes Uruguay, Brazil, Poland and Argentina, is penalized essentially by the negative scores for the macro-economic index.

Table 2.11 Growth Competitiveness Index (GCI)

	Finland	USA	Singapore	Chile	Spain	Portugal	Slovakia	Hungary
GCI Ranking (2004)	2	1	7	22	23	24	37	39
GCI Ranking (2003)	2	1	6	28	23	25	35	33
GCI Rating 2004	5.82	5.95	5.56	5.01	5.00	4.96	4.56	4.56
Technology index	6.24 (1)	5.92 (3)	5.11 (11)	4.55 (32)	4.86 (20)	4.78 (23)	4.42 (38)	4.66(29)
Quality of public institutions index	6.48 (3)	5.74 (21)	6.21 (11)	5.77 (20)	5.16 (34)	5.69 (23)	4.74 (44)	5.07 (37)
Macro-environment index	5.04 (15)	5.47 (3)	5.79 (1)	4.71 (27)	4.99 (16)	4.42 (34)	4.52 (31)	3.95 (55)

	Czech Rep.	Slovakia	Italy	Uruguay	Brazil	Poland	Argentina
GCI Ranking (2004)	40	43	47	54	57	60	74
GCI Ranking (2003)	39	43	41	50	54	45	78
GCI Rating 2004	4.55	4.43	4.27	4.08	4.05	3.98	3.54
Technology index	4.88 (19)	4.67 (28)	4.08 (50)	3.92 (56)	4.24 (42)	4.19 (45)	3.87 (57)
Quality of public institutions index	4.56 (51)	4.64 (49)	4.64 (48)	5.23 (32)	4.62 (50)	3.70 (80)	3.77 (79)
Macro-environment index	4.22 (41)	3.98 (54)	4.27 (38)	3.10 (90)	3.28 (80)	4.05 (51)	2.96 (94)

Source: The Global Competitiveness Report 2004, World Economic Forum.

Societies in Transitions, Values and Social Well-being

The information societies are characterized not only by the appropriation of technology but also their internal openness and social well-being.

None of the countries in transition analyzed have an authoritarian regime and the dominating values in those societies today are those of an open society. The openness of a society can be measured by various dimensions, such as the ratio between the population in prison and the total population.

As one can see in the following table (Table 3.14), whereas the Finnish model is characterized by a ratio twice as low as that for the USA, Portugal registers figures that are twice those for Finland, with values that are very close to the average for the G7 societies. However, if we look at the total number of countries in transition in terms of their prison inmate figures, we find that, with the exception of Italy and Greece, all of the remaining countries have an inmate population above the average for the advanced economies.

In terms of gender equality, the majority of societies in transition are below the average for the advanced economies (661), representing societies that are still very unequal in terms of gender. Only Spain and Argentina achieve better gender equality scores, bringing them closer to the egalitarian model in terms of gender relations: Finland (820).

To add a further dimension, we can also compare the well-being of the populations of the societies in transition to the well-being models associated with the three information society models under analysis (Finland, Singapore and Silicon Valley), by looking at the income structures.

Hence, measured by the ratio of the 20% richest to the 20% poorest is concerned, the Finnish model of an information welfare society presents the greatest equality of income (3.8). At the other end, the market-governed information society model (Silicon Valley) and the authoritarian model (Singapore) show much greater unbalance in terms of income distribution, occupying third and second place in the ranking of the advanced economies with the worst ratios between the income of the richest and that of the poorest (8.3 and 9.7 respectively).

Table 2.12   International comparison of citizenship indicators

	Finland	USA	Singapore	Portugal	Spain	Italy	Czech Rep.	Slovakia	Advanced Economies
Freedom of the press (index 0-100; 0 = free)[1]	9 (free)	13 (free)	64 (not free)	14 (free)	19 (free)	33 (partially free)	23 (free)	21 (free)	17 (free)
Gender equality (0-1,000, 0 = unequal)[2]	820 (4)	769 (14)	648 (20)	644 (23)	716 (15)	583 (32)	586 (30)	607 (26)	661
Membership of at least one association (%)[3]	80	90	–	29	29	40	60.5	65	53
Social trust (%)[7]	56	35.5	–	12	35	31.5	24	15.5	31
Inmate population (per 100,000 inh.)[4]	71 (−157)	714 (−1)	392	128	140	98	184	165	126
Foreigners or persons born abroad (% of population)[5]	2.6	12.4	33.6	2.3	3.2	2.8	2.3	0.6	8.8
Environment: CO_2 emission (metric tons per capita)[2]	10.3	19.8	14.7	5.9	5.3	6.6	11.6	6.6	10.4

Source: 1 Adapted from Castells and Himanen (2002), all data from the Press Freedom Survey 2004: http://www.freedomhouse.org/; 2 Adapted from Castells and Himanen (2002), except data for Portugal, which are taken from the UNDP Human Development Report 2001; 3 Adapted from Castells and Himanen (2002) and Norris, Pippa "Gender and Social Capital" 1999-2001 World Values Survey; 4 For all countries: International Centre for Prison Studies, King's College http://www.kcl.ac.uk/depsta/rel/icps/worldbrief/highest_to_lowest_rates.php; 5 Adapted from Castells and Himanen 2002, http://www.un.org/esa/population/publications/ittmig2002/WEB_migration_wallchart.xls 3. Note: (*) relative position. Based on Norris, Pippa "Gender and Social Capital" 1999-2001 World Values Survey (% of the population that responded that it generally trust others).

Table 2.12 International comparison of citizenship indicators

	Hungary	Greece	Poland	Chile	Argentina	Uruguay	Brazil	Advanced Economies
Freedom of the press (index 0-100; 0 = free)[1]	20 (free)	28 (free)	19 (free)	23 (free)	35 (partially free)	26 (free)	36 (partially free)	94
Gender equality (0-1,000, 0 = unequal)[2]	529 (39)	523 (43)	606 (27)	460 (58)	645 (21)	511 (46)	–	83
Membership of at least one association (%)[3]	29	57	25	50	42.5	–	–	53
Social trust (%)[7]	22	21	18	22.5	15.5	–	–	32
Inmate population (per 100,000 inh.)[4]	165	82	209	204	148	209	183	126
Foreigners or persons born abroad (% of population)[5]	3	5	5.4	1	3.8	2.7	0.3	8.8
Environment: CO_2 emission (metric tons per capita)[2]	5.4	8.5	7.8	3.9	3.9	1.6	1.8	10.6

Source: 1 Adapted from Castells and Himanen (2002), all data from the Press Freedom Survey 2003 : http://www.freedomhouse.org/; 2 Adapted from Castells and Himanen (2002), except data for Portugal, which are taken from the UNDP Human Development Report 2001; 3 Adapted from Castells and Himanen (2002), except data on Portugal, which are taken from Cardoso et Al., 2004, *A Sociedade em Rede em Portugal* (*The Network Society in Portugal*), CIES; 4 For all countries: International Centre for Prison Studies, King's College: http://www.kcl.ac.uk/depsta/rel/icps/worldbrief/highest_to_lowest_rates.php; 5 Adapted from Castells and Himanen 2002, except data for Portugal which were taken from the National Statistics Office's (INE) population report. Note: (*) relative position.

Table 2.13   International comparison of social well-being indicators

	Finland	USA	Singapore	Portugal	Spain	Italy	Czech Rep.	Slovakia	Advanced Economies
Combined rate of students of the first, second and third cycles[1]	106 (1)	92	87	93	92	82	78	74	94
Functional literacy (%)[2]	89.6 (2)	79.3	92.5	52	–	–	84.3	–	83
Life expectancy at birth (years)[1]	77.9	77.0	78.0	76.1	79.2	78.7	75.3	73.6	78
Health care coverage (%)[3]	100	82	–	100	100	100	–	–	n.d.
Number of working hours per annum per person[7]	1713	1792	–	1676	1800	1591	1972	1814	1636
Ratio of the 20% richest to the 20% poorest[4]	3.8 (3)	8.4	9.7	8.0	5.4	6.5	3.5	4.0	5.8
Percentage of population below the poverty line[5]	3.8 (4)	14.1	–	21	–	–	–	–	10.6
Gini coefficient[6]	26.9	40.8	42.5	38.5	32.5	36	25.4	25.8	28.57

Source: 1 Adapted from Castells and Himanen (2002), except data for Portugal, which were taken from the UNDP Human Development Report 2001; 2 Adapted from Castells and Himanen (2002), except data for Portugal, which were taken from the UNDP Human Development Report 2003, calculated on the basis of the "Lacking functional literacy skills" indicator, http://hdr.undp.org/reports/global/2003/pdf/hdr03_HDI.pdf; 3 Adapted from Castells and Himanen (2002), except data for Portugal. Given the existence of a universal National Health Service, one can presume total coverage of the Portuguese population; 4 Adapted from Castells and Himanen 2002, except data for Portugal, taken from http://www.worldbank.org/poverty/wdrpoverty/; 5 Adapted from Castells and Himanen 2002. The value for Portugal was taken from Capucha (2004), *Desafios da Pobreza (The Challenges of Poverty)*, Lisbon, ISCTE, p.131 (Doctoral Thesis). Relative poverty measurement referenced to a threshold of 60% of the average of the income available to households; 6 Data for all countries based on UNDP 2004.

Table 2.13   International comparison of social well-being indicators

	Hungary	Greece	Poland	Chile	Argentina	Uruguay	Brazil	Advanced Economies
Combined rate of students of the first, second and third cycles[1]	86	86	90	79	94	85	92	94
Functional literacy (%)[2]	66.8	–	57.4	95.9	96.9	97.6	87.3	83
Life expectancy at birth (years)[1]	71.7	78.2	73.8	76.0	74.1	75.2	68.0	78
Health care coverage (%)[3]	–	–	–	–	–	–	–	–
Number of working hours per annum per person[7]	–	1938	1956	–	–	–	–	1636
Ratio of the 20% richest to the 20% poorest[4]	4.9	6.2	5.8	18.7	18.1	10.4	31.5	5.8
Percentage of population below the poverty line[5]	14.5	–	23.8	19.9	28.4	–	23.9	10.6
Gini coefficient[6]	24.4	35.4	31.6	57.1	52.2	44.6	59.1	28.57

Source: 1 Adapted from Castells and Himanen (2002), except data for Portugal, which were taken from the UNDP Human Development Report 2001; 2 Adapted from Castells and Himanen (2002), except data for Portugal, which were taken from the UNDP Human Development Report 2003, calculated on the basis of the "Lacking functional literacy skills" indicator, http://hdr.undp.org/reports/global/2003/pdf/hdr03_HDI.pdf; 3 Adapted from Castells and Himanen (2002), except data for Portugal. Given the existence of a universal National Health Service, one can presume total coverage of the Portuguese population; 4 Adapted from Castells and Himanen 2002, except data for Portugal, taken from http://www.worldbank.org/poverty/poverty/wdrpoverty/; 5 Adapted from Castells and Himanen 2002. The value for Portugal was taken from Capucha (2004), *Desafios da Pobreza* (*The Challenges of Poverty*), Lisbon, ISCTE, p.131 (Doctoral Thesis). Relative poverty measurement referenced to a threshold of 60% of the average of the income available to households; 6 Data for all countries based on UNDP 2004.

All of the South American societies in transition (Brazil, Chile, Argentina and Uruguay) reveal extremely high inequality figures, sometimes three times as much as the USA (Brazil) or twice as much (Chile and Argentina).

As for the European societies, there is a division into two large groups. The first is made up of Portugal, Italy, Greece and Poland, with inequality values close to the USA informational society model. The second group includes the Czech Republic, Slovakia, Hungary and Spain, which are closer to the Finnish information society model.

Highlighting once more some of the specificities of each society under analysis, when we refer to the education level, it is also worthwhile stating that the openness of an information society does not depend only on the combined rate of students in the three education cycles, for if we neglect the school drop-out dimension (which the figures do not take into account) we would have a situation that would place Portugal and other societies in transition on a level with the USA and Finland, which are countries with much lower drop-out rates.[5]

In the field of education, a comparison between the countries as far as functional literacy, i.e. the capacity to apply knowledge acquired in school in the society one lives in, shows that there are also great divides between the countries, even in the European context. Thus, Portugal, together with Poland, presents the worst results of the European countries studied—with a functional literacy rate of only 52% as compared to an average of 83% for the advanced economies and more than 80% for the USA and Finland.

The openness of a society can also be measured on the social involvement of the citizens in everyday life. Together with Spain, Hungary and Poland, Portugal has the lowest rates of participation in associations, whereas Argentina and Italy present intermediate figures of around 40% for participation in associations. The Czech Republic, Slovakia, Chile and Greece are countries with over 50% of the population participating in associations.

---

[5] The data show that the drop-out rates in the EU are relatively high, with an average of 22.5%. However, there are considerable differences between the Member States. The Northern European states achieve better results than the other members. Portugal (40.7 %), Italy (30.2 %), Spain (30.0 %) and the United Kingdom (31.4 %) present high rates, while Germany (13.2 %), Austria (11.5 %) and the Scandinavian countries (Sweden 9.6 % and Finland 8.5 %) present below-average values (European Union 2000).

The reasons for the low participation levels are varied, but it is possible to identify some guiding hypotheses if we focus on a specific reality such as the Portuguese one.

Of the reasons for this lack of civic engagement, we can list, first and foremost, the degree of public confidence in the politicians for Portugal. Although it can be considered a global phenomenon (Castells 2004), the development of the degree of trust of the citizens in politicians is not identical in all societies. Whereas Portugal is in 28th place in terms of public trust in the honesty of its politicians, sharing this level with a group of European countries—Belgium, France, Italy and Ireland—Finland, in 3rd place, is one of the countries with the highest degree of trust in the honesty of its politicians in the world.

The analysis of civic engagement levels in the different countries must also take into account historic conditioning factors of both a global and local nature. What is known as unconventional political participation has increasingly become the most common form of civic engagement in our developed societies. Petitions, boycotts and other forms of direct action have become more common. For this reason, we should pay more attention to these forms of engagement than to membership in parties or trade unions and participation in demonstrations.

However, in terms of civic engagement measures in these terms, Portugal has even lower scores. The engagement index measured on the basis of different forms of civic involvement and participation in organizations shows that Portugal occupies the last place in an international comparison of 22 European countries and Israel. Despite the cultural and geographic proximity to Portugal, countries such as Spain and Italy have much higher levels of civic engagement.

The historic context of each society can also help us to understand the participation levels a little more. For example, in his analysis of data gathered in more than 70 countries, referring to more than 80% of the world population, on participation in established democracies and new democracies, Inglehart (2001) has linked the scarce civic participation in some societies to the *post-honeymoon* effect. Periods of high civic participation levels are followed by decreases or stagnation in participation, but in the long term the trend is for growth in participation.

Table 2.14 Civic engagement in European countries (%)

Country	Contacted politician or government member in the last 12 months	Worked in a political party or activist group in the last 12 months	Worked in another organization in the last 12 months	Signed a petition in the last 12 months	Boycotted certain products in the last 12 months	Bought a product for political/ethical environmental reasons in the last 12 months	Engagement ranking
Portugal	11.16	3.89	5.24	6.80	3.16	7.53	23rd (−1)
Austria	17.35	9.39	17.52	27.72	21.92	29.18	9th
Belgium	17.73	5.42	23.25	33.92	12.79	26.98	10th
Switzerland	16.91	7.61	16.74	40.40	33.66	46.93	2nd
Czech Rep.	21.42	3.87	13.98	15.07	11.05	22.10	15th
Germany	12.98	3.83	18.18	31.32	24.60	39.69	6th
Denmark	17.93	4.13	17.28	28.27	22.98	43.67	5th
Spain	11.66	5.79	14.60	22.25	7.72	11.48	16th
Finland	24.28	3.56	30.71	24.04	26.73	41.90	4th
France	16.83	4.52	17.03	33.75	25.84	27.46	8th
U.K.	18.33	3.16	9.30	39.45	26.19	32.78	7th
Greece	14.46	4.97	5.67	4.63	8.52	6.62	19th
Hungary	14.65	2.85	2.85	4.21	4.83	10.43	22nd
Ireland	22.36	4.63	13.71	27.24	13.33	24.41	13th
Israel	11.59	5.89	6.98	16.92	12.96	16.41	17th
Italy	12.13	3.25	8.16	18.49	7.90	6.34	18th
Luxembourg	17.14	2.85	16.66	27.77	14.28	28.57	12th
Netherlands	14.66	3.28	22.84	22.74	10.98	27.11	14th
Norway	23.85	9.48	28.16	37.17	20.11	36.59	3rd
Poland	9.55	2.89	6.03	7.15	3.84	10.50	21st
Sweden	16.43	4.96	24.55	40.75	32.45	55.12	1st
Slovenia	12.19	3.63	2.42	11.58	4.87	9.75	20th
Average	14.59	4.12	13.61	25.74	17.17	24.53	–

Source: European Social Survey 2002/2003.

Table 2.15   Participation over time in established and new democracies

	During and before change of regime	After change of regime	Change
Argentina	34	29	−5
Brazil	25	25	0
Chile	38	25	−13
Mexico	32	22	−7
Bulgaria	28	18	−10
Czech Republic	24	23	−1
East Germany	75	63	−12
Hungary	20	24	4
Poland	20	26	6
Slovenia	27	30	3
Slovakia	28	15	−13

	1981/1991	1995/2001	Difference
Portugal	25	27	2
Spain	31	34	3
Italy	52	62	10
USA	68	79	11
Belgium	39	75	36
France	54	72	18
Denmark	55	68	13
Japan	49	55	6
West Germany	54	60	6
Switzerland	62	68	6
United Kingdom	71	80	9

Source: Adapted from Inglehart (2001) on the basis of 1981-2001 World Values Survey.

According to Inglehart (2001), the data show that in 21 countries studied between 1981 and 1990, although the people vote less regularly, they are not becoming more apathetic. On the contrary, they would seem to have become more interested in politics. This opinion is confirmed by the studies carried out by Castells (2003a) in Catalonia and Cardoso (2005) in Portugal.

As Table 3.18 shows, interest in politics increased in 16 countries and decreased in only 4. Portugal is in the group of countries where political participation is lowest and has stagnated, as is Spain. In both countries, a period of rapid increase in participation in the 1970s was followed by a process of democratic normalization.

Although Inglehart does not present data that allow one to compare the 1970s, the decade of revolution and transition to democracy in Spain and Portugal, one can observe this type of behavior in the new democracies in Eastern Europe, which are characterized by periods of a rapid surge in participation followed by periods of less civic involvement. What the data do allow us to infer is the relative proximity of the participation levels between all the countries that have gone through transition to democracy in the last thirty years, regardless of whether they are in Europe or South America.

The *post-honeymoon decline* is no doubt significant but the fact that these societies experienced authoritarian regimes, be they of the left or the right, for many years is also justification for the low levels of political participation.

A third factor one must take into account in analyzing participation is the relationship between participation and trust in others. The World Values Survey data (2001) furthermore shows that countries with geographical and cultural affinities with Portugal—such as Spain, France and Italy—present relatively homogeneous intermediate values for membership of associations.

In Spain, the figures, for men and women respectively, are 32% and 26%, for Italy 46% and 38% and for France 36% and 43%. Where the differences are clearly greater is in the *trust in others*, for Spain (35%), Italy (32%) and France (20%) are clearly above the Portuguese values. This mistrust in relation to others is also obviously a factor to be taken into account in analyzing the low levels of civic participation.

Continuing the analysis of the possible factors that condition political participation in the context of the informational development models, one must including one more explanatory factor—education.

An analysis of the participation dimensions must also make reference to the Putnam analyses (1993) on the relationship between reading newspapers and participation in civic associations. Putnam argues that there is a direct correlation between reading newspapers and membership of associations (other than religious associations) and that the regions with the highest readership levels are also those that, as a rule, have the strongest civic communities. If we test this hypothesis, we see that, at least in Europe, more than just influencing engage-

Table 2.16   Signed petition in the last 12 months, according to highest education level (%)

Country	Not completed primary education*	Primary or first stage of basic*	Lower secondary or second stage of basic*	Upper secondary*	Post secondary, non-tertiary*	First stage non-tertiary*	Second stage of tertiary*
Portugal	0.91	4.63	2.11	15.26	–	19.44	50
Austria	9.09	–	20	25.85	32.57	–	43.58
Belgium	15.38	13.39	26.06	36.65	43.10	–	50.89
Switzerland	35.29	–	29.03	38.03	50.74	52	60
Czech Rep.	–	–	5.55	14.72	22.72	25.64	46.66
Germany	–	1.70	21.00	30.34	37.34	40.46	60.75
Denmark	–	16.66	24.50	23.26	36.73	42.25	33.33
Spain	3.40	15.90	24.09	28.99	34.54	40.00	38.88
Finland	–	8.86	22.22	27.89	33.33	31.68	33.33
France	15.72	20.24	31.71	39.34	33.33	44.731	53.58
U.K.	–	15.15	32.13	46.54	44.44	51.64	61.22
Greece	1.75	2.56	2.68	4.51	7.46	12.93	20
Hungary	–	3.01	3.52	4.37	–	9.83	11.11
Ireland	7.69	11.11	24	31.42	38	38.88	38.09
Israel	–	5.26	14.75	12.92	13.46	27.45	29.26
Italy	–	6.84	16.06	25.47	21.91	30.53	64.91
Luxembourg	–	18.18	25	33.33	–	–	40
Netherlands	10	10.07	17.26	22.80	30.76	34.44	20
Norway	–	–	26	36.02	33.33	43.42	52.63
Poland	–	2.48	4.94	9.90	7.46	20.80	12.37
Sweden	–	31.28	40.57	44.51	7.46	47.61	46.49
Slovenia	–	12.5	7.31	7.69	17.64	11.11	21.42

Source: European Social Survey 2002/2003. *Note: given the different names for education levels in the European context we opted to use the original ESS terms.

Table 2.17—Contacted politicians/government members in the last year, by education level (%)

Country	Not completed primary education*	Primary or first stage of basic*	Lower secondary or second stage of basic*	Upper secondary*	Post secondary, non-tertiary*	First stage non-tertiary*	Second stage of tertiary*
Portugal	3.66	10.62	8.45	17.42	–	20.83	–
Austria	9.09	–	10.61	18.04	18.18	–	30.76
Belgium	14.28	11.50	10.24	17.94	25.86	–	26.54
Switzerland	17.64	–	4.34	14.89	25.37	30.26	23.80
Czech Rep.	10.00	–	9.60	23.27	18.18	30	20
Germany	–	1.70	5.71	11.14	22.28	20.44	39.24
Denmark	–	20	12.74	15.84	22.44	26.76	33.33
Spain	2.782	9.66	10.37	13.40	15.90	22.62	61.11
Finland	12.5	13.92	18.51	23.97	–	37.62	66.66
France	7.49	16.66	14.21	14.34	16.66	18.07	26.28
UK	–	42.42	12.96	15.22	23.11	29.40	46.93
Greece	10.52	12.82	13.42	12.99	19.40	20.68	40.0
Hungary	5.97	7.53	16	15.30	–	25	31.11
Ireland	23.07	20	22.36	21.42	25.49	22.22	28.57
Israel	–	7.89	11.29	7.43	13.46	14.70	21.95
Italy	–	7.74	7.89	17.12	16.43	21.23	42.10
Luxembourg	–	9.09	25	16.66	0	0	25.00
Netherlands	–	5.38	10.28	13.18	11.53	27.66	20.00
Norway	–	–	14.00	22.04	25.00	31.16	42.10
Poland	0.89	3.41	7.08	11.20	13.33	18	23.10
Sweden	11.11	10.76	14.18	14.74		23.58	25
Slovenia		12.5	7.31	7.89	15.38	11.11	26.66

Source: European Social Survey 2002/2003. *Note: given the different names for education levels in the European context we opted to use the original ESS terms.

ment, newspaper readership (and membership of associations) is directly correlated to the education level of the citizens. As seen below (Table 3.22), education, much more than newspaper readership or watching TV news, is a central element in the civic engagement options made by the different citizens.

Another indicator of an informational society is the relationship it has with its media, i.e. both the freedom of the media to report freely and give opinions and the relationship between the beneficiaries and producers of the information.

Of all the societies in transition under analysis here, only Italy, Argentina and Brazil are classified as partially free in terms of the freedom of the press.

In classifying the freedom of the press, factors such as the legal framework for journalism, political influence and economic pressures on the freedom of expression are taken into account. Between 2001 and 2003, Portugal improved its general score (going from 17 to 15), accompanying a trend similar to that of Finland, while the United Sates revealed an opposite trend (from 17 to 19) and Singapore continued to be classified as a country without freedom of the press.[6]

Positive development, such as in the case of Portugal, may conceal that the final value is due to a positive assessment of the evolution of the legislation and regulation that may influence the contents of the media. However, this is offset by an increase in the economic pressures on news content. To quote the Press Freedom Survey, 2003, "Most media outlets are independent of the government; however, print and broadcast ownership is concentrated in the hands of four main media companies." (Press Freedom Survey 2003).

The comparison of models of social openness and citizenship carried out here, as well as the analysis of the social well-being, reveals much more clearly the differences than the data common to all the societies dealt with herein.

---

[6] Identical positions emerge when one looks at the online presence analysis. Finland, Portugal and the USA are amongst the least restrictive of the media's freedoms and Singapore is included in the moderately free (*Press Freedom Survey 2001*).

Table 2.18   Relationship between watching TV news and reading newspapers, by education level/country (%)

Country		Not completed primary education*	Primary or first stage of basic*	Lower secondary or second stage of basic*	Upper secondary*	Post secondary, non-tertiary*	First stage non-tertiary*	Second stage of tertiary*
Portugal	Watches TV news	92.15	95.87	97.18	98.48	0	97.22	100
	Reads newspapers	9.25	48.38	63.88	70.67	-	82.19	50
Austria	Watches TV news	88.88	0	93.60	96.93	97.52	0	98.63
	Reads newspapers	58.33	-	83.51	86.53	87.21	-	88.60
Belgium	Watches TV news	71.42	93.75	90.18	93.06	96.49	0	96.22
	Reads newspapers	35.71	54.86	56.62	62.93	60.68	-	68.42
Switzerland	Watches TV news	93.33	-	92.13	95.40	96.82	95.38	100
	Reads newspapers	94.11	-	83.87	90.88	91.30	89.47	90.47
Czech Republic	Watches TV news	70	-	93.44	97.30	95.23	100	100
	Reads newspapers	44.44	-	69.84	82.75	86.36	92.5	93.75
Germany	Watches TV news	89.28	91.08	97.06	99.37	99.85	100	89.28
	Reads newspapers	57.26	71.41	84.72	84.93	90.76	93.67	57.26
Denmark	Watches TV news	100	100	93.87	98.5	100	98.59	100
	Reads newspapers	100	80	68.31	77.22	79.59	83.09	100
Spain	Watches TV news	82.35	92.46	88.88	92.07	91.78	96.07	100
	Reads newspapers	24.88	43.26	45.58	67.40	69.19	80.49	89.47
Finland	Watches TV news	100	96.10	98.70	98.60	-	98.98	100
	Reads newspapers	87.5	92.40	92.59	91.83	-	95.04	100
France	Watches TV news	90.66	91.15	92.77	97.43	96.24	96.65	96.14
	Reads newspapers	57.14	66.66	58.27	67.21	62.43	55.53	69.48
UK	Watches TV news	100	84.84	90.78	94.99	96.13	95.06	95.65
	Reads newspapers	-	21.21	74.53	78.58	78.53	77.80	71.42
Greece	Watches TV news	100	84.84	90.78	94.99	96.13	95.06	95.65
	Reads newspapers	6.14	22.97	38.00	42.69	52.23	62.93	80

Table 2.18 Relationship between watching TV news and reading newspapers, by education level/country (%)
(continued)

Country		Not completed primary education*	Primary or first stage of basic*	Lower secondary or second stage of basic*	Upper secondary*	Post secondary, non-tertiary*	First stage non-tertiary*	Second stage of tertiary*
Hungary	Watches TV news	100	84.84	90.78	94.99	96.13	95.06	95.65
	Reads newspapers	40.90	74.37	80.61	89.07		88.33	93.33
Ireland	Watches TV news	84.61	87.5	89.33	92.95	94.11	94.44	95.23
	Reads newspapers	76.92	85.45	84.21	88.88	82.69	94.44	90.00
Israel	Watches TV news	71.42	91.42	86.20	89.05	91.30	91.30	94.87
	Reads newspapers	22.22	47.36	64.51	72.29	75.00	72.81	80.95
Italy	Watches TV news	80.93	97.30	93.75	96.34	89.04	97.56	100
	Reads newspapers	16.20	51.61	68.28	82.64	94.52	92.79	100
Luxembourg	Watches TV news	90.90	100	91.66	100	100	100	90.90
	Reads newspapers	.	72.72	75.00	83.33	100	100	80.00
Netherlands	Watches TV news	90.90	94.48	96.82	97.75	98.70	99.65	100
	Reads newspapers	72.72	69.23	82.14	81.64	87.17	86.71	100
Norway	Watches TV news	-	-	98.03	97.82	100	100	95.00
	Reads newspapers	-	-	96.07	96.25	88.88	97.40	100
Poland	Watches TV news	89.47	94.34	95.49	97.40	97.69	100	99.64
	Reads newspapers	24.10	44.53	60.28	74.60	79.10	76	87.37
Sweden	Watches TV news	88.88	95.36	97.12	95.42	-	98.03	97.39
	Reads newspapers	88.88	90.30	93.57	89.10	-	88.67	93.96
Slovenia	Watches TV news	-	85.71	87.80	89.74	94	100	92.85
	Reads newspapers	44.44	73.17	79.48	88.23	88.88	92.85	44.44

Source: European Social Survey 2002/2003. *Note: given the different names for education levels in the European context we opted to use the original ESS terms.

However, this is to be expected, for although they share values such as democracy and the wish to adopt informational society models, each society has its individual history and own identity, as well as different well-being models.

Social Change in Network Societies

The characterization of the societies in transition that we have endeavoured to achieve in this chapter, with a more in-depth treatment of the Portuguese situation, reflects the transition of populations with lower education levels to a society in which the younger generations have already more consolidated educational competences. However, this analysis also reflects societies, which, though they have made great efforts in the area of knowledge, are still trying to assert themselves in the infrastructure and technology production dimensions.

This analysis also reflects a socio-political transition—first from dictatorships to a democratic institutional politization and then to a routinization of democracy. In a process that combines growing scepticism in relation to the political parties and the government institutions and an increase in civic engagement, using autonomous and, at times, individualized forms of expression on the part of civil society.

It is in this context that one produces a fundamental transition in these societies: technological transition. A transition expressed through the diffusion of the Internet and the appearance of the *network society* in the social structure and practice.

After reading the above data and analyses, there is one question still to be answered: is there a generation divide or not in all the societies analyzed here? Though it is true that the data for the Portuguese society confirm the existence of that divide, it is not present in all the societies analyzed. Some of the exceptions are Eastern European countries such as the Czech Republic, Slovakia and Hungary.

The generation divide is not the result of an option; it is, rather, the fruit of a society in which the necessary cognitive resources are distributed unequally amongst the generations, so that societies in which formal learning and literacy are historically better established present transition processes that accentuate the generational differences to a lesser degree.

Only thus can one explain, for Portugal for example, that amongst those who were born before 1967 we find a section of social agents that are similar, in certain practice dimensions and, at times, representations, of the younger Portuguese citizens. This similarity is visible in the fact that they have educational competences that are close to one another, for example in the use of the Internet or in their approach to professional improvement.

The society we live in is not a society in social division. It is a society based on an informational development model, in which some cognitive skills are more valued than others, namely: the highest education level, formal literacy and technological literacies. All these are acquired and not innate skills. As such, social division is not inevitable; there is, rather, a process of transition in which the protagonists are those who most easily master these skills.

At the same time as experiencing multiple transition processes, societies such as the Portuguese and Catalan societies preserve strong social cohesion via a dense network of social and territorial relations. They are societies that change and maintain their cohesion at the same time. They evolve at the global level, while maintaining local and personal control over that which gives meaning to life (Castells 2004c). In the societies in transition that balance between change and social cohesion could be one more common trait.

However, although they share global networks, each societal reality is unique and only a more in-depth analysis of each nation would show us the signs of future evolution in each of our societies. That is the challenge in understanding the transitions in progress in our societies as they become network societies.

References

AETIC (2004), Métrica de la sociedad de la información, Madrid.

ALTMAN, David (2002), Prospects for e-government in latin America, International review of public administration, 2002, vol. 7, nº2.

AMADEO, Belen (2005), Ciberpolítica en Argentina, Paper presented at Seminário Internacional, 12 e 13 de Maio, Lisboa, ISCTE.

CARDOSO, Gustavo, FIRMINO DA COSTA, António (2005), A Sociedade Rede em Portugal, Porto, Campo das letras.

CASTELLS, Manuel (2002), A Sociedade em Rede. A Era da Informação. Economia, Sociedade e Cultura, Volume I, Lisboa, Fundação Calouste Gulbenkian.

CASTELLS, Manuel (2003), O Poder da Identidade. A Era da Informação. Economia, Sociedade e Cultura, Volume II, Lisboa, Fundação Calouste Gulbenkian.

CASTELLS, Manuel (2003b), La Societat Xarxa a Catalunya, Barcelona, Editorial UOC.

CASTELLS, Manuel (2004b), A Galáxia Internet, Lisboa Fundação Calouste Gulbenkian.

CASTELLS, Manuel e Ince, Martin (2004c) Conversas com Manuel Castells, Porto, Campo das Letras.

COLE, Jeff (2005), Internet and Society in a Global Perspective: Lessons from Five Years in the Field, Castells M. and Cardoso C., The Network Society, From Knowledge to Policy, Brookings Institution Press.

ESS SURVEY (2003), Available *Online* HTTP: http://ess.nsd.uib.no/

GIDDENS, Anthony, HUTTON, Will (2000) On the edge: living with global capitalism. London: Vintage.

GLOBAL COMPETITIVENESS REPORT (2004), World Economic Forum, Geneva.

HIMANEN, Pekka, CASTELLS, Manuel (2001), *The Information Society and the Welfare State: The Finnish Model,Oxford, Oxford University Press.*

HUNTINGTON, Samuel P. (1991)The third wave: Democratization in the Late Twentieth Century, University of Oklahoma Press.

IMD (2004), World Competitiveness Yearbook, 2004, Lausanne, World Competitiveness Center.

INGLEHART, Ronald e Catterberg Gabriela (2001), Trends in Political Action: The Developmental Trend and the Post-Honeymoon Decline, Available *Online* HTTP: http://www.worldval-uessurvey.org/Upload/5_Partapsa.pdf

ITU (2003), Digital Access Index, International Telecommunications Union 2003, Disponível *Online* HTTP: http://www.itu.int/newsarchive/press_releases/2003/30.html

JORGENSEN, Dale W.(2005), Information, Technology and the World Economy, Castells M. and Cardoso C., The Network Society, From Knowledge to Policy, Brookings Institution Press.

OCDE (2004) Education Outlook, Paris, OCDE.

OCDE (2004), OECD PISA review Available *Online* HTTP: http://www.pisa.oecd.org/ .

OCDE (2004), Patent Database, September 2004, Paris, OCDE.

PRESS FREEDOM SURVEY (2003), Available *Online* HTTP: http://www.freedomhouse.org/ .

PUTNAM, Robert , (1993), Making Democracy Work, Princeton, N.J.: Princeton University Press.

SILVERSTONE, Roger (1994) Television And Everyday Life, London: Routledge.

UNDP (2001), Human Development Report 2001, Available *Online* HTTP:<http://www.undp.org/hdr2001/ >.

UNDP (2003), Human Development Report 2003, Available *Online* HTTP:<http://www.undp.org/hdr2003/ >.

Part II

The Knowledge Economy, Technology, Innovation, Productivity, Competitiveness: The New Productive Economy

Chapter 3

Information Technology and the World Economy*

Dale W. Jorgenson and Khuong Vu

Introduction

The purpose of this paper is to analyze the impact of investment in information technology (IT) equipment and software on the world economy. The resurgence of the U.S. economy during the 1990's and the crucial role of IT investment have been thoroughly documented and widely discussed.[1] Jorgenson (2001) has shown that the remarkable behavior of IT prices is the key to understanding the resurgence of American economic growth. This behavior can be traced to developments in semiconductor technology that are widely understood by technologists and economists.

Jorgenson (2003) has shown that the growth of IT investment jumped to double-digit levels after 1995 in all the G7 economies—Canada, France, Germany, Italy, Japan, and the United Kingdom, as well as the United States.[2] In 1995-2001 these economies accounted for nearly fifty percent of world output and a much larger share of world IT investment. The surge of IT investment after 1995 is a response to the sharp acceleration in the rate of decline of prices of IT

* Department of Economics, Harvard University, 122 Littauer Center, Cambridge, MA 02138-3001. The Economic and Social Research Institute provided financial support for work on the G7 economies from its program on international collaboration through the Nomura Research Institute. We are grateful to Jon Samuels for excellent research assistance and helpful comments. Alessandra Colecchia, Mun S. Ho, Kazuyuki Motohashi, Koji Nomura, Kevin J. Stiroh, Marcel Timmer, and Bart van Ark provided valuable data. The Bureau of Economic Analysis and the Bureau of Labor Statistics assisted with data for the U.S and Statistics Canada contributed the data for Canada. We are grateful to all of them but retain sole responsibility for any remaining deficiencies.

[1] See Jorgenson and Kevin Stiroh (2000) and Stephen Oliner and Daniel Sichel (2000).

[2] Nadim Ahmad, Paul Schreyer, and Anita Wolfl (2004) have analyzed the impact of IT investment in OECD countries. Bart van Ark, et al. (2003) and Francesco Daveri (2002) have presented comparisons among European economies.

equipment and software. Jorgenson (2001) has traced this acceleration to a shift in the semiconductor product cycle from three years to two years in 1995.

In Section 2 we describe economic growth during the period 1989-2001 for the world economy as a whole and 116 economies listed in Table 3.1 below.[3] We have allocated the 116 economies among seven regions of the world listed in the table. We have divided the period in 1995 in order to focus on the response of these economies to the acceleration in the IT price decline. The major developments during the first half of the 1990's were the dramatic rise of Developing Asia and the stunning collapse of Eastern Europe and the former Soviet Union. As shown in Table 3.1, world economic growth has undergone a powerful revival since 1995. The world growth rate jumped nearly a full percentage point from 2.53 percent during 1989-1995 to 3.51 percent in 1995-2001.

In Section 3 we present levels of output per capita, input per capita and productivity for the world economy, seven regions of the world and 116 economies. Our most remarkable finding is that output differences are primarily explained by differences in input, rather than variations in productivity. Taking U.S. output per capita in 2000 as 100.0, world output per capita was a relatively modest 22.6 in 2001. Using similar scales for input per capita and productivity, world input per capita in 2001 was a substantial 34.6 and world productivity a robust 65.4!

In Section 4 we allocate the growth of output between input growth and productivity. World input greatly predominates in the growth of world output. Of the world growth rate of 2.53 percent during 1989-1995, productivity accounts for 0.37 percent or less than fifteen percent, while input growth accounts for 2.16 percent or more than eighty-five percent. Similarly, the higher world growth rate of 3.51 percent from 1995-2001 can be divided between productivity growth of 0.77 percent, less than twenty-two percent of total growth, and input growth of 2.74 percent, more than seventy-eight percent of the total.

---

[3] We have included countries with more than one million in population and a complete set of national accounting data for the period 1989-2001 from World Bank Development Indicators Online (WBDI). These economies account for more that 96 percent of world output.

In Section 4 we allocate the growth of input between investments in tangible assets, especially IT equipment and software, and investments in human capital. We show that the world economy, all seven regions, and almost every one of the 116 economies experienced a surge in investment in IT after 1995. This was most striking in the G7 economies, led by a rush of IT investment in the U.S. However, the soaring level of IT investment in the U.S. after 1995 was paralleled by increases throughout the G7, the Non-G7 industrialized economies, and Developing Asia. Doubling of IT investment also occurred in Latin America, Eastern Europe, and North Africa and the Middle East with near doubling in Sub-Saharan Africa.

World Economic Growth, 1989-2001

Table 3.1 presents shares of world product and regional product for each of the seven regions and 116 economies included in our study. The G7 economies accounted for slightly under half of world product from 1989-2001. The growth rates of these economies—2.15 percent before 1995 and 2.78 percent afterward—were considerably below world growth rates. The growth acceleration of 0.60 percent between the two periods also lagged behind the acceleration of world economic growth. The G7 shares in world growth were 41.3 percent during 1989-1995 and 37.2 percent in 1995-2001, well below the G7 shares in world product.

During 1995-2001 the U.S. accounted for more than 22 percent of world product and somewhat less than half of G7 output. Japan fell to a third the size of the U.S., but remained the second largest of the G7 economies and the third largest economy in the world after China. Germany ranked behind the U.S., China, Japan, and India, but remained the leading European economy. France, Italy and the U.K. were similar in size, but less than half the size of Japan. Canada was the smallest of the G7 economies.

The U.S. growth rate jumped sharply from 2.36 percent during 1989-1995 to 3.58 percent in 1995-2001. We note that the period 1995-2001 includes the U.S. recession of 2001 as well as the boom of the last half of the 1990's. The U.S. accounted for more than half of G7 growth before 1995 and over 60 percent afterward. The U.S. share in world growth was less than its share in world product before

1995, but greater after 1995. By contrast Japan's share in world economic growth before 1995 exceeded its share in world product, but fell short of its world product share after 1995. The shares of the G7 economies in world growth during 1989-2001, except for the U.S. and Japan, fell below the G7 shares in world product.

The 16 economies of Developing Asia generated more than 20 percent of world output before 1995 and almost 25 percent afterward. The burgeoning economies of China and India accounted for more than 60 percent of Asian output.[4] China has surpassed Japan to rank as the world's second largest economy and India has outstripped Germany to rank fourth. Indonesia and Korea are similar in size, but together they are only half the size of India. Taiwan and Thailand are also similar in size, jointly about one-tenth the size of China.

The economies of Developing Asia grew at 7.53 percent before 1995, but only 5.66 percent afterward. These economies accounted for an astonishing 60 percent of world growth during 1989-1995. Slightly less than half of this took place in China, while a little more than a third occurred in India. In 1995-2001 the share of Developing Asia in world growth declined to just over 40 percent, still well above the region's share in world product. China accounted for more than half of this and India about a quarter.

The 15 Non-G7 industrialized economies generated more than eight percent of world output during 1989-2001, slightly above Japan. Australia, The Netherlands, and Spain accounted for almost half of this. However, none of these approached Canada, the smallest among the G7 economies, in size. The Non-G7 economies were responsible for lower shares in world economic growth than world product before and after 1995. However, Israel and Norway had larger shares in growth than product before 1995 and Finland and Spain had larger shares in growth after 1995. Australian and Irish shares in world growth exceeded the shares of these countries in world product in both periods. Irish growth rates—5.15 percent during 1989-1995 and 8.85 percent in 1995-2001—compared with the stratospheric growth rates of Developing Asia.

---

[4] Our data for China are taken from World Bank (2004) indicators and are based on official Chinese estimates. Alwyn Young (2003) presents persuasive evidence that these estimates may exaggerate the growth of output and productivity in China.

The 19 Latin American economies generated more than eight percent of world output with Brazil responsible for a third of the total. During 1995-2001 Brazil's economy ranked ninth in the world, only slightly smaller than France, Italy, and the U.K., but larger than the rapidly fading Russian economy. Mexico was a little over half the size of Brazil and comparable in size to Spain. Argentina was a bit more than half the size of Mexico and ranked with Australia. Argentina and Mexico, taken together, were slightly less than Brazil in size. The remaining sixteen Latin American economies, collectively, also ranked below Brazil.

During 1989-1995 the share of the Latin American economies in world growth of almost ten percent exceeded their eight-and-a-half percent share in world product. In 1995-2001 these economies had a substantially smaller share in world growth of only six percent, while retaining close to an eight-and-a-half share in world product. Brazil's share in world growth was substantially below its three percent share in world product before and after 1995, while Chile, one of the smaller Latin American economies, had a larger share in world growth than product in both periods.

Before the fall of the Berlin Wall and the collapse of the Soviet Union, the 18 economies of Eastern Europe and the former Soviet Union were comparable in size to Latin America, generating more than eight percent of world product. Collectively, these economies subtracted 24.7 percent from world growth during 1989-1995, dragging their share of world product below six percent. Before 1995 the Russian economy was comparable in size to France, Italy, or the U.K., but fell to tenth in the world after Brazil during 1995-2001. The 11 economies of North Africa and the Middle East, taken together, were also comparable in size to France, Italy, or the U.K., while the 30 economies of Sub-Saharan Africa, collectively, ranked with Canada.

Poland was the only economy in Eastern Europe with a positive growth rate during 1989-1995. In 1995-2001 Poland's share in world growth exceeded its share in world product, while Russia's share in growth fell below its share in world product. Growth in the sizeable economy of Ukraine continued to languish during 1995-2001. The economies of North Africa and the Middle East had shares in growth well above their shares in world product during 1989-1995, but this was reversed in 1995-2001. The economies of Sub-Saharan Africa had shares in world growth below their shares in world product during both periods.

World Output, Input, and Productivity

Table 3.2 presents levels of output per capita, input per capita, and productivity for the world economy, seven regions, and 116 economies. Following Jorgenson (2001), we have chosen GDP as a measure of output. We have revised and updated the U.S. data presented by Jorgenson (2001) through 2001. Comparable data on investment in information technology have been have been constructed for Canada by Statistics Canada.[5] Data on IT for France, Germany, Italy, and the U.K. have been developed for the European Commission by Bart van Ark, *et al*.[6] Finally, data for Japan have been assembled by Jorgenson and Kazuyuki Motohashi for the Research Institute on Economy, Trade, and Industry.[7] We have linked these data by means of the OECD's purchasing power parities for 1999.[8]

We have distinguished investments in information technology equipment and software from investments in other assets for all 116 economies included in our study. We have employed the World Bank (2004), *World Development Indicators Online*, as a data source on GDP for economies outside the G7,[9] including purchasing power parities.[10] We have relied on the WITSA *Digital Planet Report (1998, 2000, 2002, 2004)*, as the starting point for constructing data on IT investment for these economies.[11] Details are given in the Appendix.

A constant quality index of capital input uses weights that reflect differences in capital consumption, tax treatment, and the rate of decline

---

[5] See John Baldwin and Tarek Harchaoui (2003).

[6] See van Ark, Johanna Melka, Nanno Mulder, Marcel Timmer, and Gerard Ypma (2003).

[7] See Jorgenson and Motohashi (2004).

[8] See OECD (2002).

[9] Maddison (2001) provides estimates of national product and population for 134 countries for varying periods from 1820-1998 in his magisterial volume, The World Economy: A Millenial Perspective.

[10] See World Bank (2004). Purchasing power parities are also available from the Penn World Table. See Heston, Summers, and Aten (2002).

[11] WITSA stands for the World Information Technology and Services Alliance.

of asset prices. We have derived estimates of capital input and property income from national accounting data for each of the G7 economies. Similarly, a constant quality index of labor input is based on weights by age, sex, educational attainment, and employment status. We have constructed estimates of hours worked and labor compensation from labor force surveys for each of the G7 economies. We have extended these estimates of capital and labor inputs to the 109 Non-G7 countries using data sources and methods described in the Appendix.

In Table 3.2 we present output per capita for the G7 economies from 1989 to 2001. We use 1999 OECD purchasing power parities to convert outputs for the G7 economies from domestic prices into U.S. dollars. In Table 3.2 we also present input per capita for the G7 for 1989-2001, taking the U.S. as 100.0 in 2000. We express input per capita in U.S. dollars, including both capital and labor inputs, using purchasing power parities constructed by Jorgenson (2003).[12] Finally, we present productivity levels for the G7 over the period 1989-2001 in Table 3.2. Productivity is defined as the ratio of output to input.

We find that output differences were primarily due to differences in input, rather than variations in productivity. Taking U.S. output per capita in 2000 as 100.0, G7 output per capita was 83.0 in 2001. Using similar scales for input per capita and productivity, G7 input per capita in 2001 was 85.8 and G7 productivity was 96.7, very close to the U.S. level. The range in output was from 64.4 for France to 100.0 for the U.S., while the range in input was from 62.2 for France to 100.7 for the U.S. Productivity varied considerably less from 87.2 for Japan to 109.6 for Canada. We conclude that differences in output per capita are largely explained by differences in input per capita rather than variations in productivity.

The U.S. sustained its lead in output per capita among the G7 economies throughout the period 1989-2001. Canada was very close to the U.S. in 1989, but fell substantially behind by 1995. The U.S.-Canada gap widened further during the last half of the 1990's. Germany, Japan, Italy, and the U.K. had similar levels of output per capita throughout 1989-2001, but these economies languished considerably below North American levels. France lagged behind the rest of

---

[12] Purchasing power parities for inputs follow the methodology described in detail by Jorgenson and Yip (2001).

the G7 in output per capita in 1989 and failed to make up lost ground during the subsequent decade.

The U.S. was the leader among the G7 economies in input per capita throughout the period 1989-2001. In 2001 Canada ranked next to the U.S. with Germany third. France and Italy started at the bottom of the ranking and have remained there. Productivity in the G7 has remained close to U.S. levels, rising from 91.7 in 1989 to 93.9 in 1995 and 96.7 in 2001, with the U.S. equal to 100.0 in 2000. Canada was the productivity leader throughout 1989-2001 with Italy and France close behind. The U.S. occupied fourth place, only moderately above the United Kingdom. Japan made substantial gains in productivity, but lagged behind the other members of the G7 in productivity, while Germany also lagged, surpassing only Japan.

In the economies of Developing Asia output per capita rose spectacularly from 5.8 in 1989 to 8.3 1995 and 10.7 in 2001 with the U.S. equal to 100.0 in 2000. The range was enormous with Hong Kong outstripping the G7, except for the U.S. and Canada, after 1995 and Singapore approaching France. By contrast Asia's largest economies, China and India, remained at 12.0 and 7.3, respectively, in 2001. These vast differences are due mainly to differences in input per capita, rather than variations in productivity. Developing Asia's levels of input per capita were 17.2 in 1989, 20.4 in 1995, and 24.9 in 2001, while Asian productivity levels were 33.7, 40.7, and 43.1, respectively, in these years. Hong Kong's productivity levels of 85.8 in 1989 and 90.9 in 1995 exceeded the levels of Germany and Japan, while Taiwan's productivity level exceeded that of Japan in 1995.

China made extraordinary gains in output per capita, growing from 4.7 in 1989 to 7.9 in 1995 and 12.0 in 2001 with the U.S. equal to 100.0 in 2000. India had essentially the same output per capita in 1989, but grew less impressively to levels of 5.8 in 1995 and 7.3 in 2001. China's input per capita—20.3 in 1989, 20.3 in 1995, and 26.5 in 2001—exceeded India's throughout the period. India's 31.0 productivity level in 1989 considerably surpassed China's 27.6. China's productivity swelled to 38.9 in 1995, outstripping India's 33.4. China expanded its lead with a productivity level of 45.3 in 2001 by comparison with India's 35.7.

The 15 Non-G7 industrialized economies, taken together, had levels of output per capita comparable to Germany, Italy, Japan, and the U.K. during 1989-2001. Input per capita for the 15 Non-G7 economies was also very close to these four G7 economies, while productivity for the group was comparable to that of the United Kingdom. This group included a number of star performers: Norway's output per capita of 103.6 in 2001 surpassed that of the United States, while Switzerland's input per capita of 103.5 also topped the U.S. Ireland's productivity greatly outstripped the rest of the industrialized world in 2001 with a level of 125.0! In that year the productivity leaders in the world economy were Ireland, Canada, Norway, France, and Italy.

For the Latin American region output per capita rose from 18.7 to 21.3 during 1989-2001, input per capita rose somewhat more from 28.0 to 33.0, but productivity eased from 66.7 to 64.6. Argentina was the leading Latin American economy in terms of output per capita, achieving the level of 34.5 in 2001. Uruguay led in input per capita, reaching 52.0 in 2001. Argentina, Mexico and Venezuela had high initial levels of productivity, comparable to those of Germany and Japan in 1989. Argentina maintained a relatively high but unchanging level, while Mexico and Venezuela had experienced productivity declines by 2001.

Latin America's lagging output per capita was due chiefly to insufficient input per capita, rather than a shortfall in productivity. However, the decline in productivity from 1989-2001 was pervasive, contrasting sharply with the rise in productivity in the G7 economies, the Non-G7 industrialized economies, and Developing Asia. Brazil's economic performance has been anemic at best and acted as a drag on the growth of Latin America and the world economy. Chile was a rare bright spot with strong performance in input per capita and substantial advances in productivity.

Output per capita in Eastern Europe and the former Soviet Union was 30.0 in 1989, well above the world economy level of 18.5. The collapse between 1989 and 1995 affected every economy except Poland, reducing output per capita to 19.6 and bringing the region below the world economy level of 19.8. A modest recovery between 1995 and 2001 brought the region to 22.9, only slightly above the world economy level of 22.6. Input in the region was stagnant at 37.4 in 1989, 37.2 in 1995, and 37.6 in 2001. Productivity collapsed along with output per capita, declining from 80.2 in 1989 to 52.7 in 1995, before climbing back to 60.9 in 2001.

Polish output per capita and productivity experienced a steady advance, but by 2001 several East European countries had recovered from the debacle of the early 1990's.[13] In 2001 output per capita was highest in tiny Slovenia at 49.8. This reflected input per capita of 49.4 and a dazzling productivity level of 100.8, comparable to the levels of Western Europe. The Czech Republic was next with output per capita at 42.0 in 2001 and a level of input per capita of 51.4. However, the Czech productivity level of 81.6 lagged behind Hungary's 82.5 and Slovakia's 92.3.

The downturn in output per capita and productivity was especially severe in the economies of the former Soviet Union. Russia's level of output per capita fell from 32.2 in 1989 to 19.3 in 1995 before recovering feebly to 22.5 in 2001. Ukraine fell from a considerably higher level of 39.6 in 1989 to 17.6 in 1995 and 18.2 in 2001. Russian input per capita remained essentially unchanged throughout the period 1989-2001, while productivity mirrored the decline in output, falling from a West European level of 91.0 in 1989 to 55.9 in 1995 before improving to 65.5 in 2001. The most extreme forms of economic collapse, followed by very weak recoveries, can be seen in the small economies of Georgia, the Kyrgyz Republic, and Moldova.

Output per capita in Sub-Sahara Africa was the lowest in the world throughout the period 1989-2001. Only South Africa, tiny Mauritius, and Botswana exceeded world average levels throughout the period. South Africa's economy was largest in the region and generated more than 40 percent of regional product. However, South African output per capita fell slightly, input per capital remained stationary, and productivity slumped during the period 1989-2001. South African productivity in 1989 was 91.4, above the level of the Non-G7 industrialized economies, but fell to 79.4 in 1995 before climbing back to 84.6 in 2001.

All the economies of North Africa and the Middle East fell short of world average levels of output and input per capita, except for Tunisia, which closely tracked world averages. Output per capita grew slowly

---

[13] A comprehensive analysis of in impact of IT investment in Poland is presented by Piatkowski (2004).

but steadily for the region as a whole during 1989-2001, powered by impressive gains in input per capita, but with stagnant productivity. The region grew more rapidly than the world economy before 1995, but more slowly afterward.

Sources of World Economic Growth

Table 3.3 presents the sources of world economic growth, following the methodology of Jorgenson (2001). We have allocated growth to the contributions of capital and labor inputs and the growth of productivity for the world economy, seven regions, and 116 economies.

We measure the contribution of IT investment to economic growth by weighting the growth rate of IT capital input by the share of this input in the value of output. Similarly, the contribution of Non-IT investment is a share-weighted growth rate of Non-IT capital input. The contribution of capital input is the sum of these two components.

We have divided labor input growth between the growth of hours worked and labor quality, where quality is defined as the ratio of labor input to hours worked. This reflects changes in the composition of labor input, for example, through increases in the education and experience of the labor force. The contribution of labor input is the rate of growth of this input, weighted by the share of labor in the value of output. Finally, the contribution of total factor productivity is the difference between the rate of growth of output and the rate of growth of input, including both capital and labor inputs.

The contribution of capital input to world output before 1995 was 1.12 percent, a little more than 44 percent of the rate of economic growth of 2.53 percent. Labor input contributed 1.04 percent or slightly more than 41 percent of growth, while total factor productivity growth of 0.37 percent accounted for less than 15 percent. After 1995 the contribution of capital input climbed to 1.55 percent, but remained around 44 percent of output growth, while the contribution of labor input rose to 1.20 percent, around 34 percent. Productivity increased to 0.77 percent or nearly 22 percent of growth. We conclude that capital input was the most important source of world economic growth before and after 1995, labor input was next in importance, and productivity the least important of the three sources of growth.

We have divided the contribution of capital input between IT equipment and software and Non-IT capital input. Non-IT capital input was more important before and after 1995. However, the contribution of IT more than doubled, rising from 0.26 percent to 0.56 percent or from a little over 23 percent of the contribution of capital input to over 36 percent. Similarly, we have divided the contribution of labor input between hours worked and labor quality. Hours rose from 0.44 percent before 1995 to 0.71 after 1995, while labor quality declined from 0.60 percent to 0.48 percent. Labor quality was the predominant source of labor input growth before 1995, but hours was the major source after 1995.

The acceleration in the rate of growth of world output before and after 1995 was 0.98 percent, almost a full percentage point. The contribution of capital input explained 0.43 percent of this increase, while the productivity accounted for another 0.40 percent. Labor input contributed a relatively modest 0.16 percent. The substantial increase in hours worked of 0.31 percent was the most important component of labor input growth. The jump in IT investment of 0.30 percent was most important source of the increase in capital input. This can be traced to the stepped up rate of decline of IT prices after 1995 analyzed by Jorgenson (2001).

Table 3.3 presents the contribution of capital input to economic growth for the G7 nations, divided between IT and Non-IT. This is the most important source of growth, before and after 1995. The contribution of capital input before 1995 was 1.26 or almost three-fifths of the output growth rate of 2.15 percent. The next most important source of growth, labor input, accounted for 0.51 percent before 1995 and 0.74 percent afterward, about 24 percent and 27 percent of growth, respectively. Productivity was the least important source of growth, explaining 0.38 percent before 1995 and 0.45 percent after 1995 or less than 18 percent and slightly more than 16 percent of G7 growth in the two periods.

The powerful surge of IT investment in the U.S. after 1995 is mirrored in similar jumps in growth rates of the contribution of IT capital through the G7. The contribution of IT capital input for the G7 more than doubled from 0.37 during the period 1989-1995 to 0.77 percent during 1995-2001, jumping from 29 percent of the contribution of capital input to more than 48 percent. The contribution of

Non-IT capital input predominated in both periods, but receded slightly from 0.88 percent before 1995 to 0.82 percent afterward. This reflected the substitution of IT capital input for Non-IT capital input in response to rapidly declining prices of IT equipment and software.

Before 1995 the contribution of labor quality of 0.42 percent accounted for more than eighty percent of the contribution of G7 labor input, while after 1995 the contribution of hours worked of 0.50 percent explained almost seventy percent. The modest acceleration of 0.63 percent in G7 output growth after 1995 was powered by investment in IT equipment and software, accounting for 0.40 percent, and the contribution of hours worked of 0.41 percent. Productivity growth in the G7 rose by 0.07 percent, while the contribution of Non-IT investment dropped by 0.06 percent and the contribution of labor quality declined by 0.18 percent.

In Developing Asia the contribution of capital input increased from 1.75 percent before 1995 to 2.38 percent after 1995, while the contribution of labor input fell from 2.02 percent to 1.70 percent. This reversal of roles for capital and labor inputs had a slightly positive impact on growth, so that the significant slowdown in the Asian growth rate from 7.53 percent to 5.66 percent can be traced entirely to a sharp decline in productivity growth from 3.75 to 1.58 percent. Before 1995 productivity explained slightly over half of Asian growth, but productivity fell below both capital and labor inputs after 1995, accounting for less than 28 percent of growth.

The first half of the 1990's was a continuation of the Asian Miracle, analyzed by Paul Krugman (1994), Lawrence Lau (1999), and Young (1995). This period was dominated by the spectacular rise of China and India, and the continuing emergence of the Gang of Four—Hong Kong, Korea, Singapore, and Taiwan. However, all the Asian economies had growth rates considerably in excess of the world average of 2.53 percent with the sole exception of The Philippines. The second half of the 1990's was dominated by the Asian crisis, most evident in the sharp declines in growth rates in Indonesia and Thailand. This period conforms much more closely to the "Krugman thesis," attributing Asian growth to input growth rather than productivity.

Developing Asia experienced a powerful surge in investment in IT equipment and software after 1995. The contribution of IT investment to Asian growth more than doubled from 0.16 percent to 0.40 percent, explaining less than 10 percent of the contribution of capital input before 1995, but almost 17 percent afterward. The surge in IT investment was particularly strong in China, rising from 0.17 percent before 1995 to 0.59 percent afterward. India fell substantially behind China, but outperformed the region as a whole, increasing from 0.08 to 0.22 percent. The contribution of Non-IT investment in Asia greatly predominated in both periods and also accounted for most of the increase in the contribution of capital input after 1995. Both hours worked and labor quality declined after 1995 with hours worked dominating in both periods.

Economic growth in the fifteen Non-G7 industrialized economies accelerated much more sharply than G7 growth after 1995. The contribution of labor input slightly predominated over capital input before and after 1995. The contribution of labor input was 0.81 percent before 1995, accounting for about 40 percent of Non-G7 growth, and 1.26 after 1995, explaining 39 percent of growth. The corresponding contributions of capital input were 0.75 percent and 1.12 percent, explaining 37 and 34 percent of Non-G7 growth, respectively. Non-G7 productivity also rose from 0.47 before 1995 to 0.89 percent afterward, accounting for 23 and 27 percent of growth in the two periods.

The impact of investment in IT equipment and software in the Non-G7 economies doubled between the two periods, rising from 0.22 percent to 0.44 percent or from 29 percent of the contribution of Non-G7 capital input to 39 percent. This provided a substantial impetus, amounting to 0.22 percent, to the acceleration in Non-G7 growth of 1.25 percent. Australia, Ireland and Sweden emerged as star performances in IT investment, surpassing France, Germany, and Italy. Non-IT investment explained another 0.14 percent of the growth acceleration. However, the most important components of higher Non-G7 growth were the increased contribution of hours worked of 0.49 percent and improved productivity growth of 0.42 percent.

Latin America's growth decelerated slightly after 1995, falling from 2.95 to 2.52 percent. The contribution of labor input was 1.92 percent before 1995 and 1.89 percent afterward, accounting for the lion's share of regional growth in both periods. The contribution of capital input rose after 1995 from 0.72 percent to 0.99 percent, but remained relatively weak. Nonetheless the contribution of IT investment more than doubled, jumping from 0.15 percent before 1995 to 0.34 percent afterward or from 21 percent of the contribution of capital input to 34 percent. Productivity was essentially flat from 1989 to 2001, rising by 0.31 percent before 1995 and falling by 0.36 percent after 1995. Productivity contributed a little more than ten percent to growth before 1995, but acted as a drag on growth afterward.

The collapse of economic growth in Eastern Europe and the former Soviet Union before 1995 can be attributed almost entirely to a steep decline in productivity. This was followed by a revival in both growth and productivity after 1995. The contribution of capital input declined both before and after 1995, while IT investment jumped from 0.09 to 0.26. Hour worked also declined in both periods, but labor quality improved substantially.

Productivity in Sub-Saharan Africa collapsed during 1989-1995 but recovered slightly, running at—1.63 percent before 1995 and 0.36 percent afterward. The contribution of labor input predominated in both periods, but fell from 2.77 percent to 1.89 percent, while the contribution of capital input rose from 0.52 percent to 0.99 percent. Productivity in North Africa and the Middle East, like that in Latin America, was essentially stationary from 1989-2001, falling from a positive rate of 0.50 percent before 1995 to a negative rate of—0.46 percent afterward.

Summary and Conclusions

In summary, the world economy, led by the G7 economies and the Non-G7 industrialized economies performed at an outstanding level throughout the period 1989-2001. Latin America hovered around world average levels, while Eastern Europe and the former Soviet Union descended to closely comparable levels. Sub-Saharan Africa and North Africa and the Middle East languished considerably below the world average. Developing Asia accounted for an astonishing 60 percent of world economic growth before 1995 and 40 percent afterward, with China alone responsible for half of this. However, Developing Asia remained well below world average levels of performance.

We have considered the impact of IT investment and the relative importance of input growth and productivity in accounting for economic growth. We conclude that the trends most apparent in the U.S. have counterparts throughout the world. Investments in tangible assets, including IT equipment and software, are the most important sources of growth. However, Non-IT investment still predominates in the contribution of capital input. The contribution of labor input is next in magnitude with labor quality dominant before 1995 and hours worked afterward. Finally, productivity is the least important of the three sources of growth.

The leading role of IT investment in the acceleration of growth in the G7 economies is especially pronounced in the U.S., where IT is coming to dominate the contribution of capital input. The contribution of labor input predominates in the Non-G7 industrialized economies, as well as Latin America, Eastern Europe, Sub-Saharan Africa, and North Africa and the Middle East. Productivity growth was important in Developing Asia before 1995, but assumed a subordinate role after 1995. Productivity has been stagnant or declining in Latin America, Eastern Europe, Sub-Saharan Africa, and North Africa and the Middle East.

All seven regions of the world economy, as well as 112 of the 116 economies we consider,[14] experienced a surge in investment in IT equipment and software after 1995. The impact of IT investment on economic growth has been most striking in the G7 economies. The rush in IT investment was especially conspicuous in the U.S., but the increases in the contribution of IT capital input in Canada, Japan, and the U.K. were only slightly lower. France, Germany, and Italy also experienced a surge in IT investment, but lagged considerably behind the leaders. While IT investment followed similar patterns in all the G7 nations, Non-IT investment varied considerably and helped to explain important differences in G7 growth rates.

Although the surge in investment in IT equipment and software is a global phenomenon, the variation in the contribution of IT investment has increased considerably since 1995. Following the G7, the next most important increase was in Developing Asia, but the contri-

---

[14] Indonesia, Mexico, Nigeria, and Pakistan are the exceptions.

bution of IT investment after 1995 ranged from China's 0.59 percent to only 0.06 percent in Bangladesh. Developing Asia was followed, in turn, by the Non-G7 industrialized economies, which encompass outstanding performers such as Australia, Ireland, and Sweden, as well as low-performing economies like Austria, Greece, and Spain. The role of IT investment more than doubled in Latin America, Eastern Europe, and North Africa and the Middle East, and nearly doubled in Sub-Saharan Africa.

Appendix

To measure capital and labor inputs and the sources of economic growth, we employ the production possibility frontier model of production and the index number methodology for input measurement presented by Jorgenson (2001). For the G7 economies we have updated and revised the data constructed by Jorgenson (2003). For the remaining 109 economies, we rely on two primary sources of data[15]: *World Bank Development Indicators Online* (2004) provides national accounting data for 1960-2002 for all economies in the world except Taiwan. WITSA's *Digital Planet Report* (2002, 2004) gives data on expenditures on IT equipment and software for 50 major economies, including the G7.

U.S. data on investment in IT equipment and software, provided by the Bureau of Economic Analysis (BEA) are the most comprehensive.[16] We use these data as a benchmark in estimating IT investment data for other economies. For the economies included in the *Digital Planet Report* we estimate IT investment from IT expenditures. The *Digital Planet Report* provides expenditure data for computer hardware, software, and telecommunication equipment on an annual basis, beginning in 1992.

Expenditure data from the *Digital Planet Report* are given in current U.S. dollars. However, data are not provided separately for investment and intermediate input and for business, household, and government

---

[15] Other important sources of data include the Penn World Table, the International Telecommunication Union (ITU) telecommunications indicators, and the UNDP Human Development reports.

[16] The BEA data are described by Grimm, Moulton, and Wasshausen (2004).

sectors. We find that the ratio of BEA investment to WITSA expenditure data for the U.S. is fairly constant for the periods 1981-1990 and 1991-2001 for each type of IT equipment and software. Further, data on the global market for telecommunication equipment for 1991-2001, reported by the International Telecommunication Union (ITU), confirms that the ratio of investment to total expenditure for the U.S. is representative of the global market.

We take the ratios of IT investment to IT expenditure for the U.S. as an estimate of the share of investment to expenditure from the *Digital Planet Report*. We use the penetration rate of IT in each economy to extrapolate the investment levels. This extrapolation is based on the assumption that the increase in real IT investment is proportional to the increase in IT penetration.

Investment in each type of IT equipment and software is calculated as follows:

$$I_{c,A,t} = \eta_{c,A,t} {}^* E_{c,A,t}$$

where $I_{c,A,t}$, $\eta_{c,A,t}$, and $E_{c,A,t}$ are investment, the estimated investment-to-expenditure ratio, and the *Digital Planet Report* expenditures, respectively, for asset A in year t for country c.[17]

Given the estimated IT investment flows, we use the perpetual inventory method to estimate IT capital stock. We assume that the geometric depreciation rate is 31.5% and the service life is 7 years for computer hardware, 31.5% and 5 years for software, and 11% and 11 years for telecommunication equipment. Investment in current U.S. dollars for each asset is deflated by the U.S. price index to obtain investment in constant U.S. dollars.

To estimate IT investment for the 66 economies not covered by the *Digital Planet Reports*, we extrapolate the levels of IT capital stock per capita we have estimated for the 50 economies included in these

---

[17] The IT expenditures for years prior to 1992 are projected by means of the following model:

$$\ln(Ec_{i,t-1}) = \beta_0 + \beta_1 \ln(Ec_{i,t}) + \beta_2 \ln(y_{i,t-1})$$

where $Ec_{i,t}$ represents expenditure on IT asset c and the subscripts i and t indicate country i in year t, and $y_{i,t}$ is GDP per capita. The model specifies that, for a country i, spending on IT asset c in year t-1 can be projected from GDP per capita in that year and the spending on the asset c in period t.

Reports. We assume that IT capital stock per capita for the 66 additional economies is proportional to the level of IT penetration. The details are as follows:

For computers we divide the 50 economies included in the *Digital Planet Reports* into 10 equal groups, based on the level of personal computer (PC) penetration in 2001. We estimate the current value of computer stock per capita in 2001 for an economy i as:

$$s^i_{HW} = \bar{s}^I_{HW} * (P^i_{HW} / \bar{P}^I_{HW}),$$

where $\bar{s}^I_{HW}$ is the average value of computer capital per capita in 2001 of group I for countries included in the *Digital Planet Report*, P^i_{HW} and $\bar{P}^I_{HW}$ are the PC penetration rates of economy i and the average PC penetration of group I, respectively.

For the economies with data on PC penetration for 1995, we use the growth rates of PC penetration over 1989-2001 to project the current value of computer capital stock per capita backwards. We estimate computer capital stock for each year by multiplying capital stock per capita by population. For economies lacking the data of PC penetration in 1995 and 1989, we estimate computer capital stock by assuming that the growth rates in the two periods, 1995-2001 and 1989-1995, are the same as those for the group to which it belongs.

For software capital stock, we divide the 116 countries into 10 categories by level of PC penetration in 2001. We sub-divide each of these categories into three categories by degree of software piracy[18], generating 30 groups. We assume that the software capital stock-to-hardware capital stock ratio is constant in each year for each of the 30 groups:

$$s^i_{SW} = \bar{s}^I_{SW} * (s^i_{HW} / \bar{s}^I_{HW})$$

where $\bar{s}^I_{SW}$ is the average software capital stock per capita of subgroup I in 2001. Since the value of computer stock per capita has been estimated for 1995 and 1989, this enables us to estimate the software capital stock per capita for these two years.

---

[18] The information on software piracy is based on study conducted by the Business Software Alliance (2003).

Finally, we define the penetration rate for telecommunications equipment as the sum of main-line and mobile telephone penetration rates. These data are available for all 116 economies in all three years—1989, 1995, and 2001. We have divided these into 10 groups by the level of telecommunications equipment penetration for each year. The current value of telecommunications capital stock per capita is estimated as:

$$s_{TLC}^{it} = \bar{s}_{TLC}^{It} * (P_{TLC}^{it} / \bar{P}_{TLC}^{It})$$

where $\bar{s}_{TLC}^{It}$ is the average current of telecommunications equipment capital stock per capita in year t of group I for economies included in the *Digital Planet Reports* and P_{TLC}^{it} and $\bar{P}_{TLC}^{It}$ are the telecommunications equipment penetration rates of economy i and the average penetration rate of group I in year t.

We employ Gross Fixed Capital Formation for each of the 109 economies provided by the World Bank, measured in current U.S. dollars, as the flow of investment. We use the World Bank investment deflators to convert these flows into constant U.S. dollars. The constant dollar value of capital stock is estimated by the perpetual inventory method for each of the 109 economies for 1989 and the following years. We assume a depreciation rate of 7% and a service life of 30 years.

The current value of the gross capital stock at a year is the product of its constant dollar value and the investment deflator for that year. We estimate the current value of Non-ICT capital stock of an economy for each year by subtracting the current value of IT stock from the current value of capital stock in that year. Given the estimates of the capital stock for each type of asset, we calculate capital input for this stock, using the methodology presented of Jorgenson (2001).

Finally, labor input is the product of hours worked and labor quality:

$$L_t = H_t * q_t$$

where L_t, H_t, and q_t, respectively, are the labor input, the hours worked, and labor quality. A labor quality index requires data on education and hours worked for each of category of workers.

We extrapolate the labor quality indexes for the G7 economies by means of the following model:

$q_{i, t} = \beta_0 + \beta_1$ Education$_{i, t}$ + β_2 Institution1$_i$ + β_3 Institution2$_i$ + β_4 Income1989$_i$ + β_5T

where subscripts i and t indicate economy i in year t. Education is the educational attainment of the population aged 25 or over from the data set constructed by Robert Barro and Jong-Wha Lee (2001). Institution1 = "Rule of Law" and Institution2 = "Regulatory Quality" are constructed by Daniel Kaufmann, Aart Kraay, and Massimo Mastruzzi (2004) for the World Bank; Income1990 is GDP per capita for 1990 from World Bank Development Indicators; and T is a time dummy.

Labor quality is largely explained by educational attainment, institutional quality and living conditions. The model fits well ($R^2 = 0.973$) and all the explanatory variables are statistically significant. We assume that hours worked per worker is constant at 2000 hours per year, so that growth rates of hours worked are the same as employment.

In order to provide a global perspective on the impact of IT investment on economic growth, we have been able to exploit the excellent work on development indicators by the World Bank (2004), as well as information technology expenditures by WITSA (2002, 2004). However, it is important to note that the resulting estimates are far below the quality standards of Bureau of Economic Analysis or research on OECD and EU economies. The next objective should be to develop data on IT expenditures and IT investment within a national accounting framework for the major economies of the world, both industrialized and developing.

Appendix to Chapter 3
Tables and Figures

Table 3.1 The World Economy: Shares in Size and Growth by Region and Individual Economy

Notes: Numbers for growth and shares are in percentage, the shares are weighted by nominal share in the GDP of each country and averaged for each period.

Group Summaries

Group	Period 1989-1995			Period 1995-2001		
	GDP Growth	Average Share		GDP Growth	Average Share	
		Size	Growth		Size	Growth
World (116 Economies)	**2.53**	**100.00**	**100.00**	**3.51**	**100.00**	**100.00**
G7	2.15	47.82	40.72	2.78	46.24	36.62
Developing Asia	7.53	20.29	60.62	5.66	24.85	40.13
Non-G7	2.03	8.94	7.19	3.27	8.76	8.16
Latin America	2.95	8.48	9.90	2.52	8.33	5.97
Eastern Europe	-7.13	8.67	-25.15	2.09	5.98	3.56
Sub-Sahara Africa	1.65	2.47	1.61	3.24	2.38	2.19
North Africa and Middle-East	3.87	3.33	5.11	3.43	3.46	3.38

G7 (7 Economies)

Economy	Period 1989-1995					Period 1995-2001				
	GDP Growth	GDP Share Group	GDP Share World	Growth Share Group	Growth Share World	GDP Growth	GDP Share Group	GDP Share World	Growth Share Group	Growth Share World
Canada	1.39	4.91	2.35	3.17	1.29	3.34	4.86	2.25	5.84	2.14
France	1.30	6.93	3.32	4.19	1.71	2.34	6.65	3.08	5.60	2.05
Germany	2.34	10.81	5.17	11.76	4.79	1.18	10.37	4.80	4.40	1.61
Italy	1.52	7.42	3.55	5.24	2.13	1.90	7.07	3.27	4.83	1.77
Japan	2.56	16.23	7.76	19.31	7.86	1.85	15.98	7.39	10.63	3.90
United Kingdom	1.62	7.44	3.56	5.60	2.28	2.74	7.30	3.38	7.20	2.64
United States	2.36	46.25	22.12	50.73	20.66	3.58	47.76	22.07	61.49	22.51
All Group	**2.15**	**100.00**	**47.82**	**100.00**	**40.72**	**2.78**	**100.00**	**46.24**	**100.00**	**36.62**

Developing Asia(16 Economies)

Economy	Period 1989-1995					Period 1995-2001				
	GDP Growth	GDP Share		Growth Share		GDP Growth	GDP Share		Growth Share	
		Group	World	Group	World		Group	World	Group	World
Bangladesh	4.54	2.23	0.45	1.35	0.80	5.09	2.00	0.50	1.80	0.72
Cambodia	7.48	0.26	0.05	0.26	0.15	6.27	0.26	0.07	0.29	0.12
China	10.14	36.58	7.50	49.27	30.10	7.79	42.12	10.51	57.96	23.31
Hong Kong	4.90	1.87	0.38	1.22	0.73	3.22	1.59	0.39	0.91	0.36
India	5.13	23.90	4.80	16.29	9.74	5.66	22.15	5.50	22.15	8.87
Indonesia	7.75	7.27	1.48	7.49	4.53	1.14	6.46	1.59	1.30	0.52
Malaysia	8.98	1.87	0.38	2.23	1.36	3.89	1.86	0.46	1.28	0.51
Nepal	4.99	0.31	0.06	0.21	0.12	4.70	0.28	0.07	0.23	0.09
Pakistan	4.50	3.66	0.73	2.18	1.30	3.09	3.09	0.76	1.69	0.67
Philippines	2.28	3.54	0.70	1.08	0.64	3.49	2.83	0.70	1.75	0.70
Singapore	8.70	0.80	0.16	0.92	0.56	4.77	0.80	0.20	0.68	0.27
South Korea	7.42	6.82	1.38	6.73	4.06	4.47	6.58	1.63	5.19	2.08
Sri Lanka	5.41	0.68	0.14	0.49	0.29	3.83	0.61	0.15	0.41	0.16
Taiwan	6.58	4.39	0.89	3.84	2.31	3.05	3.96	0.98	2.13	0.85
Thailand	8.68	4.43	0.90	5.11	3.11	0.64	4.00	0.99	0.45	0.18
Vietnam	7.35	1.36	0.28	1.33	0.80	7.14	1.40	0.35	1.77	0.71
All Group	**7.53**	**100.00**	**20.29**	**100.00**	**60.62**	**5.66**	**100.00**	**24.85**	**100.00**	**40.13**

Non-G7 (15 Economies)

Economy	Period 1989-1995					Period 1995-2001				
	GDP Growth	GDP Share		Growth Share		GDP Growth	GDP Share		Growth Share	
		Group	World	Group	World		Group	World	Group	World
Australia	2.74	12.93	1.16	17.42	1.25	3.70	13.34	1.17	15.09	1.23
Austria	2.46	6.12	0.55	7.41	0.53	2.29	6.02	0.53	4.21	0.34
Belgium	1.69	7.55	0.68	6.27	0.45	2.53	7.29	0.64	5.64	0.46
Denmark	1.79	4.32	0.39	3.79	0.27	2.34	4.17	0.37	2.99	0.24
Finland	-0.56	3.54	0.32	-0.97	-0.07	4.23	3.33	0.29	4.31	0.35
Greece	1.03	4.82	0.43	2.45	0.18	3.47	4.70	0.41	4.98	0.41
Ireland	5.15	2.08	0.19	5.27	0.38	8.85	2.71	0.24	7.32	0.60
Israel	6.40	2.93	0.26	9.22	0.66	3.34	3.31	0.29	3.38	0.28
Netherlands	2.41	11.34	1.01	13.42	0.97	3.20	11.43	1.00	11.17	0.91
New Zealand	2.40	2.12	0.19	2.50	0.18	2.78	2.11	0.18	1.79	0.15
Norway	3.34	4.02	0.36	6.61	0.48	2.74	4.18	0.37	3.51	0.29
Portugal	2.17	4.55	0.41	4.85	0.35	3.38	4.57	0.40	4.72	0.39
Spain	1.72	21.33	1.91	18.07	1.30	3.56	21.36	1.87	23.27	1.90
Sweden	0.67	6.12	0.55	2.02	0.15	2.63	5.80	0.51	4.67	0.38
Switzerland	0.55	6.23	0.56	1.68	0.12	1.70	5.66	0.50	2.95	0.24
All Group	**2.03**	**100.00**	**8.94**	**100.00**	**7.19**	**3.27**	**100.00**	**8.76**	**100.00**	**8.16**

Latin America(19 Economies)

Economy	Period 1989-1995					Period 1995-2001				
	GDP Growth	GDP Share Group	GDP Share World	Growth Share Group	Growth Share World	GDP Growth	GDP Share Group	GDP Share World	Growth Share Group	Growth Share World
Argentina	4.88	12.16	1.03	20.15	2.00	1.37	12.44	1.04	6.79	0.41
Bolivia	4.10	0.53	0.05	0.74	0.07	3.03	0.56	0.05	0.67	0.04
Brazil	1.84	37.50	3.18	23.41	2.32	2.09	35.80	2.98	29.69	1.77
Chile	7.55	3.20	0.27	8.19	0.81	4.01	3.81	0.32	6.07	0.36
Colombia	4.35	7.64	0.65	11.27	1.12	0.96	7.61	0.63	2.91	0.17
Costa Rica	5.02	0.84	0.07	1.43	0.14	4.19	0.94	0.08	1.57	0.09
Ecuador	2.64	1.70	0.14	1.52	0.15	1.61	1.64	0.14	1.05	0.06
El Salvador	5.78	0.70	0.06	1.37	0.14	2.79	0.76	0.06	0.85	0.05
Guatemala	4.00	1.17	0.10	1.59	0.16	3.61	1.25	0.10	1.79	0.11
Honduras	2.92	0.39	0.03	0.39	0.04	2.92	0.40	0.03	0.46	0.03
Jamaica	2.29	0.31	0.03	0.24	0.02	0.22	0.29	0.02	0.03	0.00
Mexico	2.09	22.41	1.90	15.87	1.57	4.37	23.10	1.92	40.12	2.39
Nicaragua	1.20	0.34	0.03	0.14	0.01	5.95	0.36	0.03	0.86	0.05
Panama	5.76	0.39	0.03	0.76	0.08	3.88	0.44	0.04	0.68	0.04
Paraguay	3.16	0.98	0.08	1.05	0.10	1.03	0.94	0.08	0.39	0.02
Peru	3.56	4.28	0.36	5.17	0.51	2.06	4.30	0.36	3.52	0.21
Trinidad and Tobago	1.40	0.30	0.03	0.14	0.01	4.58	0.30	0.03	0.55	0.03
Uruguay	3.27	0.95	0.08	1.05	0.10	1.17	0.92	0.08	0.43	0.03
Venezuela	3.87	4.20	0.36	5.51	0.55	0.97	4.13	0.34	1.59	0.09
All Group	**2.95**	**100.00**	**8.48**	**100.00**	**9.90**	**2.52**	**100.00**	**8.33**	**100.00**	**5.97**

Eastern Europe (18 Economies)

Economy	Period 1989-1995					Period 1995-2001				
	GDP Growth	GDP Share Group	GDP Share World	Growth Share Group	Growth Share World	GDP Growth	GDP Share Group	GDP Share World	Growth Share Group	Growth Share World
Albania	-3.83	0.33	0.03	0.18	-0.04	7.69	0.44	0.03	1.62	0.06
Armenia	-10.76	0.29	0.03	0.44	-0.11	5.71	0.30	0.02	0.82	0.03
Bulgaria	-3.80	2.14	0.18	1.14	-0.27	-0.04	2.20	0.13	-0.04	0.00
Croatia	-5.18	1.65	0.14	1.20	-0.29	3.41	1.83	0.11	2.99	0.11
Czech Republic	-0.97	5.12	0.42	0.69	-0.16	1.52	5.93	0.36	4.30	0.15
Estonia	-6.38	0.47	0.04	0.42	-0.10	5.06	0.53	0.03	1.28	0.05
Georgia	-22.03	0.76	0.07	2.35	-0.64	5.48	0.49	0.03	1.28	0.05
Hungary	-2.59	4.01	0.33	1.46	-0.34	3.90	4.80	0.29	8.96	0.32
Kyrgyz Republic	-11.79	0.54	0.05	0.89	-0.23	5.41	0.51	0.03	1.32	0.05
Latvia	-12.06	0.69	0.06	1.17	-0.30	5.56	0.65	0.04	1.74	0.06
Lithuania	-9.45	1.01	0.09	1.34	-0.33	4.46	1.05	0.06	2.23	0.08
Moldova	-16.70	0.55	0.05	1.29	-0.34	-1.11	0.36	0.02	-0.19	-0.01
Poland	2.17	10.51	0.84	-3.21	0.72	4.33	14.28	0.85	29.60	1.05
Romania	-2.77	5.52	0.46	2.15	-0.51	-0.45	5.78	0.35	-1.25	-0.04
Russian Federation	-8.44	46.04	4.04	54.53	-13.48	1.86	44.14	2.64	39.33	1.40
Slovakia	-2.98	2.04	0.17	0.85	-0.20	4.31	2.39	0.14	4.94	0.18
Slovenia	-0.59	1.00	0.08	0.08	-0.02	4.02	1.26	0.08	2.43	0.09
Ukraine	-13.59	17.32	1.58	33.03	-8.51	-0.22	13.06	0.78	-1.37	-0.05
All Group	**-7.13**	**100.00**	**8.67**	**100.00**	**-25.15**	**2.09**	**100.00**	**5.98**	**100.00**	**3.56**

Sub-Sahara Africa (30 Economies)

Economy	Period 1989-1995					Period 1995-2001				
	GDP Growth	GDP Share Group	GDP Share World	Growth Share Group	Growth Share World	GDP Growth	GDP Share Group	GDP Share World	Growth Share Group	Growth Share World
Benin	3.99	0.56	0.01	1.35	0.02	5.15	0.64	0.02	1.01	0.02
Botswana	4.40	1.25	0.03	3.32	0.05	5.93	1.47	0.03	2.69	0.06
Burkina Faso	2.85	1.18	0.03	2.04	0.03	4.25	1.26	0.03	1.66	0.04
Cameroon	-2.64	3.22	0.08	-5.15	-0.08	4.72	2.94	0.07	4.29	0.09
Central African Rep.	0.45	0.46	0.01	0.13	0.00	2.16	0.43	0.01	0.29	0.01
Chad	0.83	0.81	0.02	0.41	0.01	3.36	0.80	0.02	0.83	0.02
Congo, Rep.	0.69	0.36	0.01	0.15	0.00	2.60	0.34	0.01	0.27	0.01
Cote d'Ivoire	1.03	2.85	0.07	1.78	0.03	2.84	2.76	0.07	2.43	0.05
Ethiopia	1.41	4.38	0.11	3.75	0.06	5.64	4.69	0.11	8.16	0.18
Gabon	3.36	1.00	0.02	2.03	0.03	1.79	1.01	0.02	0.56	0.01
Gambia, The	2.31	0.22	0.01	0.31	0.01	4.84	0.24	0.01	0.36	0.01
Ghana	4.04	3.57	0.09	8.73	0.14	4.21	3.94	0.09	5.13	0.11
Guinea	3.76	1.78	0.04	4.06	0.07	4.03	1.94	0.05	2.42	0.05
Kenya	2.00	3.20	0.08	3.87	0.06	1.66	3.09	0.07	1.59	0.03
Madagascar	0.24	1.34	0.03	0.19	0.00	4.11	1.31	0.03	1.67	0.04
Malawi	3.37	0.57	0.01	1.16	0.02	2.47	0.59	0.01	0.45	0.01
Mali	2.08	0.99	0.02	1.24	0.02	5.19	1.06	0.03	1.70	0.04
Mauritius	5.11	1.13	0.03	3.49	0.06	5.36	1.33	0.03	2.21	0.05
Mozambique	2.85	1.05	0.03	1.81	0.03	8.38	1.28	0.03	3.32	0.07
Namibia	4.39	1.29	0.03	3.43	0.06	3.25	1.40	0.03	1.40	0.03
Niger	0.40	0.84	0.02	0.20	0.00	3.48	0.82	0.02	0.88	0.02
Nigeria	3.36	10.57	0.26	21.46	0.35	2.80	10.97	0.26	9.49	0.21
Senegal	1.87	1.56	0.04	1.76	0.03	5.21	1.67	0.04	2.68	0.06
South Africa	0.66	43.68	1.08	17.50	0.28	2.64	41.64	0.99	33.93	0.74
Swaziland	3.74	0.52	0.01	1.18	0.02	2.98	0.55	0.01	0.51	0.01
Tanzania	2.62	1.22	0.03	1.92	0.03	4.43	1.30	0.03	1.78	0.04
Togo	0.02	0.80	0.02	0.01	0.00	1.79	0.73	0.02	0.40	0.01
Uganda	6.69	2.85	0.07	11.52	0.19	6.05	3.58	0.09	6.69	0.15
Zambia	-1.26	1.12	0.03	-0.86	-0.01	3.10	1.02	0.02	0.98	0.02
Zimbabwe	2.12	5.61	0.14	7.20	0.12	0.14	5.21	0.12	0.23	0.00
All Group	**1.65**	**100.00**	**2.47**	**100.00**	**1.61**	**3.24**	**100.00**	**2.38**	**100.00**	**2.19**

North Africa and Middle-East (11 Economies)

Economy	Period 1989-1995					Period 1995-2001				
	GDP Growth	GDP Share Group	GDP Share World	Growth Share Group	Growth Share World	GDP Growth	GDP Share Group	GDP Share World	Growth Share Group	Growth Share World
Igeria	0.35	13.54	0.45	1.21	0.06	3.03	11.96	0.41	10.56	0.36
Egypt	3.70	14.16	0.47	13.56	0.69	4.87	14.71	0.51	20.88	0.70
Iran	5.41	25.80	0.86	36.11	1.85	3.93	27.39	0.95	31.38	1.06
Jordan	5.88	1.25	0.04	1.90	0.10	3.27	1.32	0.05	1.26	0.04
Lebanon	13.51	0.83	0.03	2.89	0.15	2.10	1.02	0.04	0.62	0.02
Mauritania	3.38	0.43	0.01	0.38	0.02	3.98	0.43	0.01	0.50	0.02
Morocco	1.42	8.61	0.29	3.17	0.16	3.94	8.10	0.28	9.31	0.31
Syrian Arab Rep.	7.60	2.96	0.10	5.82	0.30	3.14	3.26	0.11	2.98	0.10
Tunisia	4.45	4.16	0.14	4.79	0.24	5.33	4.49	0.16	6.98	0.24
Turkey	4.10	27.65	0.92	29.29	1.49	1.86	26.63	0.92	14.41	0.49
Yemen, Rep.	5.45	0.62	0.02	0.88	0.04	5.57	0.69	0.02	1.13	0.04
All Group	**3.87**	**100.00**	**3.33**	**100.00**	**5.11**	**3.43**	**100.00**	**3.46**	**100.00**	**3.38**

Table 3.2: Levels of Output and Input per Capita and Productivity (U.S. in 2000 = 100)

Group Summaries

Group	Output Per Capita			Input Per Capita			Productivity		
	1989	1995	2001	1989	1995	2001	1989	1995	2001
World (116 Economies)	**18.5**	**19.8**	**22.6**	**28.4**	**30.7**	**34.6**	**65.2**	**64.4**	**65.4**
G7	66.9	72.8	83.0	73.0	77.6	85.8	91.7	93.9	96.7
Developing Asia	5.8	8.3	10.7	17.3	20.4	24.9	33.7	40.7	43.1
Non-G7	54.4	59.3	69.7	60.7	65.4	73.9	89.6	90.7	94.2
Latin America	18.7	20.0	21.3	28.0	29.9	33.0	66.7	67.0	64.6
Eastern Europe	30.0	19.6	22.9	37.4	37.2	37.6	80.2	52.7	60.9
Sub-Sahara Africa	5.8	5.4	5.7	15.0	15.6	16.6	38.5	34.8	34.1
North Africa & Middle East	11.6	12.8	14.1	21.9	23.9	27.3	52.7	53.5	51.6

G7 (7 Economies)

Group	Output Per Capita			Input Per Capita			Productivity		
	1989	1995	2001	1989	1995	2001	1989	1995	2001
Canada	79.4	80.2	92.5	75.0	75.7	84.4	105.9	105.9	109.6
France	54.5	57.4	64.4	53.7	57.4	62.2	101.5	100.0	103.5
Germany	59.0	65.5	69.7	71.6	74.3	79.5	82.4	88.2	87.7
Italy	57.7	62.5	69.3	55.9	59.2	67.6	103.2	105.6	102.5
Japan	56.3	64.4	71.1	72.5	78.3	81.5	77.7	82.2	87.2
United Kingdom	56.9	61.8	71.8	61.7	67.5	74.2	92.2	91.6	96.8
United States	80.6	86.3	100.0	84.4	89.1	100.7	95.5	96.9	99.3
All Group	**66.9**	**72.8**	**83.0**	**73.0**	**77.6**	**85.8**	**91.7**	**93.9**	**96.7**

Developing Asia (16 Economies)

Group	Output Per Capita			Input Per Capita			Productivity		
	1989	1995	2001	1989	1995	2001	1989	1995	2001
Bangladesh	3.5	4.1	5.0	14.2	16.6	20.4	24.6	24.8	24.5
Cambodia	4.5	5.8	7.0	16.9	19.6	23.0	26.5	29.7	30.4
China	4.7	7.9	12.0	16.9	20.3	26.5	27.6	38.9	45.3
Hong Kong	54.9	67.8	74.0	64.0	74.6	85.9	85.8	90.9	86.1
India	4.7	5.8	7.3	15.3	17.3	20.3	31.0	33.4	35.7
Indonesia	6.4	9.2	9.1	17.8	21.8	26.1	35.8	42.2	34.9
Malaysia	15.6	23.0	25.1	27.5	35.1	41.3	56.9	65.6	60.9
Nepal	2.9	3.4	3.9	16.0	17.6	19.8	18.3	19.5	19.9
Pakistan	5.8	6.6	6.9	15.5	17.0	18.4	37.6	38.7	37.3
Philippines	10.6	10.6	11.6	19.9	21.3	22.9	53.2	49.9	50.5
Singapore	40.7	56.8	64.1	65.7	74.8	84.8	62.0	76.0	75.6
South Korea	24.9	36.6	45.5	37.7	50.0	60.4	66.2	73.1	75.4
Sri Lanka	7.0	9.0	10.4	22.1	25.7	30.8	31.6	35.0	33.9
Taiwan	34.9	48.8	55.5	45.0	56.2	67.7	77.5	86.9	81.9
Thailand	12.1	19.0	19.0	28.8	37.0	41.2	42.0	51.2	46.1
Vietnam	3.3	4.5	6.2	12.3	14.2	17.5	26.5	31.7	35.4
All Group	**5.8**	**8.3**	**10.7**	**17.3**	**20.4**	**24.9**	**33.7**	**40.7**	**43.1**

Non-G7 (15 Economies)

Group	Output Per Capita			Input Per Capita			Productivity		
	1989	1995	2001	1989	1995	2001	1989	1995	2001
Australia	61.2	66.8	78.0	68.9	72.4	81.9	88.9	92.2	95.3
Austria	64.2	71.5	81.6	71.1	77.3	84.7	90.4	92.5	96.3
Belgium	62.0	67.8	77.1	59.7	66.1	73.2	103.9	102.6	105.4
Denmark	68.8	75.1	84.9	84.5	89.1	97.4	81.4	84.4	87.2
Finland	62.3	58.6	73.4	75.8	71.4	76.5	82.2	82.0	96.0
Greece	39.9	41.0	49.9	43.1	45.2	49.1	92.6	90.7	101.6
Ireland	43.6	57.9	91.0	49.5	57.0	72.8	88.2	101.6	125.0
Israel	45.8	54.7	57.6	48.4	55.5	62.2	94.5	98.6	92.5
Netherlands	61.2	68.0	79.6	69.5	75.9	84.8	88.1	89.5	93.9
New Zealand	49.8	53.6	59.7	65.1	68.8	75.1	76.5	78.0	79.5
Norway	73.8	88.2	103.6	80.7	85.3	95.3	91.5	103.4	108.7
Portugal	37.1	41.9	50.6	48.8	54.1	63.4	76.1	77.5	79.8
Spain	44.8	49.6	59.2	45.1	50.3	60.2	99.4	98.6	98.3
Sweden	60.7	61.0	71.9	79.7	81.1	91.0	76.2	75.3	79.0
Switzerland	79.4	77.5	83.3	91.4	96.7	103.5	86.9	80.1	80.5
All Group	**54.4**	**59.3**	**69.7**	**60.7**	**65.4**	**73.9**	**89.6**	**90.7**	**94.2**

Latin America (19 Economies)

Group	Output Per Capita			Input Per Capita			Productivity		
	1989	1995	2001	1989	1995	2001	1989	1995	2001
Argentina	26.8	33.7	34.5	35.1	35.2	40.0	76.5	95.8	86.2
Bolivia	6.0	6.6	6.8	21.3	23.2	25.8	28.0	28.3	26.5
Brazil	19.9	20.3	21.3	29.8	31.1	33.4	66.8	65.4	63.7
Chile	16.0	22.9	26.8	29.0	34.6	41.0	55.3	66.1	65.4
Colombia	16.0	18.4	17.5	23.9	26.8	27.5	66.9	68.7	63.8
Costa Rica	19.9	23.3	26.5	39.3	44.1	50.7	50.7	52.8	52.3
Ecuador	12.8	13.2	13.2	25.4	27.4	28.5	50.5	48.2	46.1
El Salvador	9.5	11.9	12.7	26.2	30.0	34.7	36.3	39.8	36.5
Guatemala	9.9	10.8	11.5	23.3	24.7	27.0	42.6	43.8	42.5
Honduras	6.2	6.2	6.3	16.4	18.3	20.9	37.7	33.9	30.0
Jamaica	10.1	11.1	10.8	25.9	29.6	33.3	39.0	37.6	32.3
Mexico	21.1	21.4	25.5	26.6	29.8	34.6	79.1	71.8	73.7
Nicaragua	7.3	6.6	8.0	21.5	20.8	24.2	33.8	31.7	33.1
Panama	11.4	14.4	16.5	29.5	33.3	39.1	38.7	43.2	42.3
Paraguay	18.0	18.7	17.4	28.8	31.5	32.8	62.5	59.4	53.0
Peru	14.9	16.3	16.7	28.0	31.0	34.9	53.1	52.7	47.8
Trinidad and Tobago	19.3	20.1	25.8	35.0	39.6	49.3	55.0	50.9	52.3
Uruguay	22.8	26.6	27.4	45.7	48.4	52.0	49.9	54.8	52.7
Venezuela	16.1	17.6	16.6	19.6	20.3	20.7	82.2	87.0	79.9
All Group	**18.7**	**20.0**	**21.3**	**28.0**	**29.9**	**33.0**	**66.7**	**67.0**	**64.6**

Eastern Europe (18 Economies)

Group	Output Per Capita			Input Per Capita			Productivity		
	1989	1995	2001	1989	1995	2001	1989	1995	2001
Albania	9.2	7.5	12.0	23.8	27.2	32.9	38.8	27.4	36.6
Armenia	8.9	5.3	8.0	26.3	32.2	32.3	34.0	16.4	24.7
Bulgaria	21.5	18.1	19.2	29.6	27.9	29.2	72.7	64.8	65.8
Croatia	32.0	24.7	31.5	41.1	46.5	55.9	77.9	53.1	56.2
Czech Republic	40.1	37.9	42.0	47.1	48.4	51.4	85.0	78.4	81.6
Estonia	29.3	21.8	31.1	57.0	56.4	59.8	51.4	38.6	52.0
Georgia	19.6	5.3	7.6	27.2	27.0	28.3	72.3	19.7	26.8
Hungary	33.1	28.8	36.6	38.3	39.0	44.3	86.6	73.9	82.5
Kyrgyz Republic	14.0	6.5	8.3	23.7	25.5	25.6	59.0	25.5	32.6
Latvia	29.3	15.2	22.6	46.2	45.7	54.1	63.4	33.2	41.7
Lithuania	28.2	17.4	23.7	49.7	50.8	56.4	56.8	34.2	42.0
Moldova	16.1	5.9	5.6	28.3	29.2	28.5	57.0	20.3	19.8
Poland	20.0	22.4	29.1	31.7	31.8	36.9	63.1	70.4	78.8
Romania	20.6	17.8	17.6	24.6	24.5	25.2	83.6	72.7	69.7
Russian Federation	32.2	19.3	22.5	35.4	34.6	34.3	91.0	55.9	65.5
Slovakia	33.5	27.7	34.3	36.2	36.3	37.2	92.6	76.1	92.3
Slovenia	40.0	38.8	49.8	47.0	45.6	49.4	85.3	85.2	100.8
Ukraine	39.6	17.6	18.2	54.3	53.8	49.1	72.9	32.7	37.2
All Group	**30.0**	**19.6**	**22.9**	**37.4**	**37.2**	**37.6**	**80.2**	**52.7**	**60.9**

Sub-Sahara Africa (30 Economies)

Group	Output Per Capita			Input Per Capita			Productivity		
	1989	1995	2001	1989	1995	2001	1989	1995	2001
Benin	2.6	2.7	3.2	14.8	14.5	16.9	17.4	18.8	18.9
Botswana	21.0	22.6	28.4	32.6	37.1	44.7	64.4	60.8	63.5
Burkina Faso	3.0	3.1	3.4	13.6	14.8	16.9	21.8	20.7	20.2
Cameroon	7.3	5.2	6.0	15.4	15.5	15.8	47.2	33.7	38.1
Central African Republic	3.8	3.3	3.4	17.3	17.7	18.1	21.7	18.9	18.7
Chad	3.3	2.9	3.0	16.3	16.1	18.8	20.5	18.3	15.9
Congo, Rep.	3.4	2.9	2.8	13.0	13.2	13.4	26.5	22.3	21.3
Cote d'Ivoire	5.8	5.0	5.1	19.0	18.0	17.8	30.3	27.9	28.7
Ethiopia	2.0	1.9	2.3	11.4	11.7	12.3	17.8	16.4	18.8
Gabon	23.3	23.7	22.7	36.9	34.6	34.6	63.2	68.4	65.7
Gambia, The	5.6	5.1	5.7	15.0	16.4	17.9	37.4	31.2	31.6
Ghana	5.0	5.5	6.3	16.7	17.8	21.9	30.1	30.7	29.0
Guinea	6.8	7.2	7.9	19.9	20.6	21.9	34.0	34.9	36.3
Kenya	3.2	3.0	2.9	13.2	14.2	16.3	23.9	21.3	17.8
Madagascar	2.8	2.4	2.6	14.4	14.7	15.7	19.3	16.3	16.3
Malawi	1.5	1.6	1.7	14.2	14.0	13.0	10.5	11.7	12.7
Mali	2.7	2.6	3.1	14.6	15.0	16.0	18.3	17.2	19.1
Mauritius	21.9	27.8	35.8	35.8	43.3	50.4	61.0	64.2	71.0
Mozambique	1.6	1.7	2.5	9.4	10.2	12.3	17.3	16.8	20.2
Namibia	19.9	21.2	21.8	36.4	34.5	32.3	54.7	61.4	67.6
Niger	2.7	2.2	2.3	12.5	11.8	11.6	21.4	19.0	19.4
Nigeria	2.4	2.5	2.5	9.3	9.9	11.6	26.1	25.1	21.8
Senegal	4.9	4.7	5.5	17.0	18.0	20.2	28.9	26.2	27.2
South Africa	29.5	27.1	27.7	32.3	34.1	32.7	91.4	79.4	84.6
Swaziland	14.8	15.3	15.5	26.9	28.7	31.3	55.0	53.4	49.3
Tanzania	1.1	1.1	1.2	10.9	11.6	12.0	9.9	9.1	9.9
Togo	5.6	4.9	4.6	16.7	16.7	16.6	33.7	29.6	27.3
Uganda	3.3	4.0	4.9	16.6	17.6	19.4	19.8	22.9	25.3
Zambia	3.7	2.9	3.1	18.7	16.7	16.2	19.6	17.3	19.0
Zimbabwe	12.6	12.4	11.2	24.4	27.8	28.8	51.7	44.5	38.8
All Group	5.8	5.4	5.7	15.0	15.6	16.6	38.5	34.8	34.1

North Africa and Middle East (11 Economies)

Group	Output Per Capita			Input Per Capita			Productivity		
	1989	1995	2001	1989	1995	2001	1989	1995	2001
Algeria	17.5	15.6	17.0	26.2	26.2	28.6	67.0	59.4	59.4
Egypt	7.9	8.7	10.4	15.4	15.7	17.9	51.5	55.6	58.2
Iran	13.2	16.5	19.1	26.6	29.4	34.5	49.7	56.1	55.3
Jordan	11.0	11.4	11.6	22.4	23.6	25.5	49.1	48.4	45.4
Lebanon	4.8	9.6	9.9	27.0	26.8	28.9	17.7	35.6	34.3
Mauritania	6.3	6.6	7.6	17.9	18.1	20.9	35.2	36.8	36.1
Morocco	11.2	10.9	12.5	21.0	21.6	24.2	53.5	50.6	51.5
Syrian Arab Republic	6.4	8.3	8.6	23.5	24.3	25.9	27.3	34.3	33.3
Tunisia	14.7	17.0	21.7	28.6	31.7	36.3	51.3	53.8	59.8
Turkey	14.3	16.3	16.4	23.6	28.8	34.0	60.6	56.4	48.4
Yemen, Rep.	1.5	1.5	1.8	7.6	8.8	10.4	19.4	17.6	17.5
All Group	**11.6**	**12.8**	**14.1**	**21.9**	**23.9**	**27.3**	**52.7**	**53.5**	**51.6**

Table 3.3: Sources of Output Growth: 1995-2001 vs. 1989-1995 Group Summaries

Economy	Period 1989-1995						Period 1995-2001					
	GDP Growth	Sources of Growth (% points per annum)					GDP Growth	Sources of Growth (% points per annum)				
		Capital		Labor		TFP		Capital		Labor		TFP
		ICT	Non-ICT	Hours	Quality			ICT	Non-ICT	Hours	Quality	
World (116 Economies)	2.53	0.26	0.86	0.44	0.60	0.37	3.51	0.56	0.99	0.71	0.48	0.77
G7	2.15	0.37	0.88	0.09	0.42	0.38	2.78	0.77	0.82	0.50	0.24	0.45
Developing Asia	7.53	0.16	1.59	1.19	0.84	3.75	5.66	0.40	1.98	0.94	0.75	1.58
Non-G7	2.03	0.22	0.54	0.38	0.42	0.47	3.27	0.44	0.68	0.87	0.40	0.89
Latin America	2.95	0.15	0.57	1.18	0.74	0.31	2.52	0.34	0.66	1.22	0.67	-0.36
Eastern Europe	-7.13	0.09	-0.18	-0.80	0.75	-7.00	2.09	0.26	-0.81	-0.22	0.73	2.14
Sub-Saharan Africa	1.65	0.15	0.37	1.67	1.10	-1.63	3.24	0.29	0.69	1.08	0.81	0.36
N. Africa & Middle East	3.87	0.11	0.74	1.40	1.13	0.50	3.43	0.28	1.02	1.59	1.00	-0.46

G7 Economies (7 Economies)

Economy	Period 1989-1995						Period 1995-2001					
	GDP Growth	Sources of Growth (% points per annum)					GDP Growth	Sources of Growth (% points per annum)				
		Capital		Labor		TFP		Capital		Labor		TFP
		ICT	Non-ICT	Hours	Quality			ICT	Non-ICT	Hours	Quality	
Canada	1.39	0.49	0.27	0.08	0.55	0.00	3.34	0.86	0.81	0.91	0.18	0.58
France	1.30	0.19	0.93	-0.17	0.61	-0.26	2.34	0.42	0.73	0.40	0.19	0.60
Germany	2.34	0.26	1.05	-0.42	0.33	1.12	1.18	0.46	0.65	-0.06	0.23	-0.10
Italy	1.52	0.26	0.86	-0.35	0.38	0.37	1.90	0.49	0.98	0.57	0.35	-0.49
Japan	2.56	0.31	1.16	-0.39	0.54	0.94	1.85	0.75	0.35	-0.44	0.21	0.98
United Kingdom	1.62	0.27	1.69	-0.72	0.49	-0.11	2.74	0.76	0.18	0.59	0.30	0.91
United States	2.36	0.47	0.68	0.62	0.36	0.23	3.58	0.93	1.11	0.89	0.23	0.42
All Group	**2.15**	**0.37**	**0.88**	**0.09**	**0.42**	**0.38**	**2.78**	**0.77**	**0.82**	**0.50**	**0.24**	**0.45**

Developing Asia (16 Economies)

Economy	Period 1989-1995						Period 1995-2001					
	GDP Growth	Sources of Growth (% points per annum)					GDP Growth	Sources of Growth (% points per annum)				
		Capital		Labor		TFP		Capital		Labor		TFP
		ICT	Non-ICT	Hours	Quality			ICT	Non-ICT	Hours	Quality	
Bangladesh	4.54	0.03	1.64	1.67	1.07	0.13	5.09	0.06	2.57	1.66	0.96	-0.17
Cambodia	7.48	0.05	2.61	1.77	1.11	1.94	6.27	0.17	3.16	1.60	0.95	0.39
China	10.14	0.17	1.74	0.87	0.89	6.46	7.79	0.59	2.46	0.56	0.79	3.38
Hong Kong	4.90	0.37	1.54	0.78	0.44	1.76	3.22	0.58	1.45	1.11	0.35	-0.27
India	5.13	0.08	1.17	1.27	0.89	1.72	5.66	0.22	1.66	1.35	0.84	1.58
Indonesia	7.75	0.11	1.60	1.64	0.85	3.54	1.14	0.10	1.71	1.48	0.81	-2.97
Malaysia	8.98	0.32	2.14	2.11	0.81	3.60	3.89	0.47	1.78	1.88	0.52	-0.76
Nepal	4.99	0.10	1.52	1.31	1.00	1.06	4.70	0.16	1.79	1.53	0.89	0.33
Pakistan	4.50	0.13	1.42	1.46	1.02	0.47	3.09	0.09	1.10	1.59	0.91	-0.60
Philippines	2.28	0.12	0.65	1.60	0.70	-0.79	3.49	0.21	0.79	1.38	0.65	0.47
Singapore	8.70	0.47	1.58	1.81	0.54	4.30	4.77	0.71	1.79	1.15	0.35	0.75
South Korea	7.42	0.33	2.13	1.45	0.63	2.89	4.47	0.49	1.70	0.82	0.52	0.95
Sri Lanka	5.41	0.03	1.56	1.42	0.70	1.70	3.83	0.15	1.69	1.81	0.68	-0.50
Taiwan	6.58	0.23	1.92	0.91	0.53	2.98	3.05	0.45	2.11	0.37	0.50	-0.38
Thailand	8.68	0.12	2.22	1.19	0.67	4.47	0.64	0.14	0.93	0.55	0.62	-1.61
Vietnam	7.35	0.19	1.05	1.27	1.29	3.55	7.14	0.51	2.21	1.03	0.92	2.47
All Group	**7.53**	**0.16**	**1.59**	**1.19**	**0.84**	**3.75**	**5.66**	**0.40**	**1.98**	**0.94**	**0.75**	**1.58**

Non-G7 (15 Economies)

Economy	Period 1989-1995						Period 1995-2001					
	GDP Growth	Sources of Growth (% points per annum)					GDP Growth	Sources of Growth (% points per annum)				
		Capital		Labor		TFP		Capital		Labor		TFP
		ICT	Non-ICT	Hours	Quality			ICT	Non-ICT	Hours	Quality	
Australia	2.74	0.32	0.43	0.69	0.39	0.92	3.70	0.61	0.77	0.99	0.38	0.96
Austria	2.46	0.15	0.70	0.52	0.36	0.72	2.29	0.26	0.66	0.11	0.37	0.89
Belgium	1.69	0.24	0.63	0.29	0.38	0.14	2.53	0.35	0.63	0.46	0.37	0.72
Denmark	1.79	0.18	0.25	0.32	0.32	0.72	2.34	0.41	0.64	0.13	0.34	0.82
Finland	-0.56	0.14	0.08	-1.17	0.40	-0.01	4.23	0.54	0.04	0.64	0.36	2.65
Greece	1.03	0.10	0.19	0.48	0.55	-0.28	3.47	0.25	0.44	0.17	0.52	2.08
Ireland	5.15	0.30	0.54	1.27	0.42	2.62	8.85	0.65	1.43	2.14	0.39	4.24
Israel	6.40	0.37	1.31	2.85	0.42	1.44	3.34	0.56	1.14	1.72	0.42	-0.50
Netherlands	2.41	0.30	0.43	0.77	0.37	0.53	3.20	0.59	0.51	0.68	0.35	1.07
New Zealand	2.40	0.32	0.13	1.16	0.35	0.43	2.78	0.53	0.52	0.71	0.36	0.67
Norway	3.34	0.18	0.07	0.57	0.45	2.07	2.74	0.40	0.38	0.61	0.32	1.03
Portugal	2.17	0.19	0.77	0.06	0.47	0.67	3.38	0.47	0.98	0.61	0.46	0.86
Spain	1.72	0.14	0.83	-0.05	0.51	0.30	3.56	0.25	0.96	1.63	0.49	0.24
Sweden	0.67	0.22	0.28	-0.32	0.48	0.01	2.63	0.70	0.19	0.46	0.34	0.94
Switzerland	0.55	0.25	0.54	0.46	0.32	-1.01	1.70	0.44	0.31	0.40	0.31	0.25
All Group	**2.03**	**0.22**	**0.54**	**0.38**	**0.42**	**0.47**	**3.27**	**0.44**	**0.68**	**0.87**	**0.40**	**0.89**

Latin America (19 Economies)

Economy	Period 1989-1995						Period 1995-2001					
	GDP Growth	Sources of Growth (% points per annum)					GDP Growth	Sources of Growth (% points per annum)				
		Capital		Labor		TFP		Capital		Labor		TFP
		ICT	Non-ICT	Hours	Quality			ICT	Non-ICT	Hours	Quality	
Argentina	4.88	0.20	0.41	-0.19	0.61	3.86	1.37	0.21	0.26	1.99	0.56	-1.65
Bolivia	4.10	0.05	0.76	2.35	0.77	0.17	3.03	0.43	1.58	1.45	0.70	-1.12
Brazil	1.84	0.10	0.25	0.99	0.79	-0.29	2.09	0.44	0.47	0.69	0.72	-0.23
Chile	7.55	0.28	1.53	1.52	0.52	3.69	4.01	0.51	1.91	0.65	0.47	0.47
Colombia	4.35	0.16	0.87	1.79	0.75	0.78	0.96	0.53	0.42	0.28	0.70	-0.97
Costa Rica	5.02	0.35	1.75	1.62	0.60	0.70	4.19	0.81	1.53	1.47	0.56	-0.17
Ecuador	2.64	0.07	0.52	2.01	0.84	-0.79	1.61	0.11	0.26	1.21	0.76	-0.73
El Salvador	5.78	0.08	1.27	2.17	0.76	1.52	2.79	0.23	1.38	1.90	0.71	-1.44
Guatemala	4.00	0.04	0.65	1.97	0.88	0.46	3.61	0.14	1.34	1.81	0.84	-0.52
Honduras	2.92	0.05	1.31	2.35	1.00	-1.79	2.92	0.14	1.76	2.16	0.91	-2.05
Jamaica	2.29	0.10	1.11	0.98	0.73	-0.62	0.22	0.32	0.91	0.83	0.67	-2.52
Mexico	2.09	0.20	0.88	1.48	0.74	-1.21	4.37	0.19	0.87	1.85	0.64	0.81
Nicaragua	1.20	0.18	-0.24	1.32	1.00	-1.06	5.95	0.28	1.07	2.97	0.91	0.73
Panama	5.76	0.05	1.23	1.95	0.66	1.85	3.88	0.14	2.07	1.46	0.58	-0.38
Paraguay	3.16	0.04	1.38	1.86	0.71	-0.84	1.03	0.26	0.66	1.38	0.64	-1.91
Peru	3.56	0.08	0.94	1.86	0.80	-0.12	2.06	0.21	1.18	1.63	0.67	-1.62
Trinidad and Tobago	1.40	0.05	0.39	1.60	0.67	-1.31	4.58	0.17	1.78	1.57	0.62	0.45
Uruguay	3.27	0.13	0.50	0.52	0.55	1.57	1.17	0.42	0.83	0.04	0.55	-0.66
Venezuela	3.87	0.13	0.03	1.91	0.86	0.94	0.97	0.27	0.05	1.26	0.78	-1.39
All Group	**2.95**	**0.15**	**0.57**	**1.18**	**0.74**	**0.31**	**2.52**	**0.34**	**0.66**	**1.22**	**0.67**	**-0.36**

Eastern Europe (18 Economies)

	Period 1989-1995						Period 1995-2001					
		Sources of Growth (% points per annum)						Sources of Growth (% points per annum)				
		Capital		Labor				Capital		Labor		
Economy	GDP Growth	ICT	Non-ICT	Hours	Quality	TFP	GDP Growth	ICT	Non-ICT	Hours	Quality	TFP
Albania	-3.83	0.03	1.58	-0.44	0.78	-5.78	7.69	0.45	2.82	-1.16	0.78	4.80
Armenia	-10.76	0.00	1.13	-0.54	0.85	-12.21	5.71	0.04	-1.70	-0.47	0.95	6.89
Bulgaria	-3.80	0.11	-0.36	-2.24	0.79	-2.10	-0.04	0.26	-0.63	-0.40	0.69	0.04
Croatia	-5.18	0.20	1.29	-1.08	0.80	-6.40	3.41	0.83	1.31	-0.43	0.73	0.97
Czech Republic	-0.97	0.18	-0.17	0.00	0.47	-1.44	1.52	0.44	0.15	-0.35	0.48	0.79
Estonia	-6.38	0.19	-0.48	-1.82	0.50	-4.76	5.06	0.77	-0.60	-0.61	0.55	4.96
Georgia	-22.03	0.12	-1.11	-0.25	0.85	-21.64	5.48	0.55	-1.03	0.01	0.85	5.09
Hungary	-2.59	0.25	0.07	-0.84	0.53	-2.60	3.90	0.48	0.36	0.45	0.55	2.05
Kyrgyz Republic	-11.79	0.09	0.63	0.65	0.81	-13.98	5.41	0.20	-0.67	0.97	0.81	4.10
Latvia	-12.06	0.09	0.03	-1.95	0.56	-10.79	5.56	1.11	-0.22	0.20	0.66	3.81
Lithuania	-9.45	0.10	0.33	-2.05	0.61	-8.44	4.46	0.55	0.09	-0.27	0.70	3.40
Moldova	-16.70	0.10	-0.19	-0.09	0.67	-17.18	-1.11	0.58	-1.45	-0.48	0.71	-0.46
Poland	2.17	0.12	0.09	-0.50	0.61	1.86	4.33	0.48	1.00	-0.07	0.56	2.36
Romania	-2.77	0.03	-0.55	-0.60	0.88	-2.53	-0.45	0.12	-0.32	-0.19	0.76	-0.82
Russian Federation	-8.44	0.08	-0.12	-1.02	0.80	-8.18	1.86	0.11	-1.44	-0.14	0.80	2.53
Slovakia	-2.98	0.16	-0.13	-0.29	0.60	-3.31	4.31	0.42	0.18	-0.21	0.61	3.31
Slovenia	-0.59	0.13	-0.63	-0.40	0.58	-0.26	4.02	0.35	0.17	0.11	0.53	2.87
Ukraine	-13.59	0.05	-0.59	-0.52	0.82	-13.36	-0.22	0.19	-2.56	-0.88	0.92	2.12
All Group	**-7.13**	**0.09**	**-0.18**	**-0.80**	**0.75**	**-7.00**	**2.09**	**0.26**	**-0.81**	**-0.22**	**0.73**	**2.14**

Sub-Sahara Africa (30 Economies)

Economy	Period 1989-1995 GDP Growth	Sources of Growth (% points per annum) Capital ICT	Non-ICT	Labor Hours	Quality	TFP	Period 1995-2001 GDP Growth	Sources of Growth (% points per annum) Capital ICT	Non-ICT	Labor Hours	Quality	TFP
Benin	3.99	0.03	0.15	1.68	0.84	1.30	5.15	0.10	2.60	1.69	0.72	0.04
Botswana	4.40	0.04	2.66	2.01	0.65	-0.96	5.93	0.18	2.30	2.09	0.61	0.75
Burkina Faso	2.85	0.03	1.49	1.11	1.07	-0.86	4.25	0.06	2.42	1.20	0.97	-0.41
Cameroon	-2.64	0.03	-0.17	1.72	1.39	-5.61	4.72	0.08	-0.12	1.51	1.23	2.02
Central African Republic	0.45	0.03	0.56	1.28	0.90	-2.32	2.16	0.06	0.33	1.10	0.82	-0.14
Chad	0.83	0.04	0.18	1.62	0.88	-1.89	3.36	0.07	2.82	1.91	0.84	-2.28
Congo, Rep.	0.69	0.02	0.40	1.84	1.32	-2.88	2.60	0.09	0.26	1.91	1.17	-0.82
Cote d'Ivoire	1.03	0.02	-0.85	2.31	0.91	-1.36	2.84	0.16	-0.36	1.74	0.85	0.46
Ethiopia	1.41	0.05	0.37	1.16	1.18	-1.35	5.64	0.10	1.01	1.34	0.96	2.22
Gabon	3.36	0.01	-0.51	1.47	1.06	1.32	1.79	0.09	0.25	1.10	1.01	-0.67
Gambia, The	2.31	0.10	1.68	2.35	1.17	-2.99	4.84	0.50	1.26	1.84	1.06	0.18
Ghana	4.04	0.06	1.20	1.62	0.89	0.28	4.21	0.14	2.73	1.47	0.78	-0.91
Guinea	3.76	0.03	0.99	1.39	0.95	0.40	4.03	0.08	1.02	1.28	0.95	0.70
Kenya	2.00	0.05	0.67	2.06	1.15	-1.93	1.66	0.19	0.72	2.67	1.02	-2.93
Madagascar	0.24	0.06	0.47	1.55	0.98	-2.82	4.11	0.14	1.06	1.96	0.94	0.01
Malawi	3.37	0.03	-0.27	0.93	0.90	1.78	2.47	0.08	-1.14	1.25	0.82	1.46
Mali	2.08	0.02	0.84	1.32	0.90	-1.01	5.19	0.06	1.20	1.36	0.82	1.74
Mauritius	5.11	0.24	2.36	1.00	0.65	0.85	5.36	0.46	1.95	0.64	0.61	1.69
Mozambique	2.85	0.13	0.65	0.99	1.54	-0.45	8.38	0.22	2.47	1.30	1.33	3.06
Namibia	4.39	0.08	-0.01	1.84	0.55	1.93	3.25	0.26	1.16	-0.31	0.55	1.59
Niger	0.40	0.02	-0.83	1.74	1.45	-1.98	3.48	0.03	-0.09	1.94	1.27	0.34
Nigeria	3.36	0.26	0.54	1.60	1.63	-0.67	2.80	0.18	0.93	2.63	1.42	-2.35

Continued next page

Sub-Sahara Africa (30 Economies) (continued)

	Period 1989-1995						Period 1995-2001					
		Sources of Growth (% points per annum)						Sources of Growth (% points per annum)				
		Capital		Labor				Capital		Labor		
Economy	GDP Growth	ICT	Non-ICT	Hours	Quality	TFP	GDP Growth	ICT	Non-ICT	Hours	Quality	TFP
Senegal	1.87	0.09	0.98	1.52	0.91	-1.63	5.21	0.57	1.71	1.46	0.86	0.60
South Africa	0.66	0.22	-0.02	1.74	1.04	-2.32	2.64	0.44	0.20	0.28	0.54	1.18
Swaziland	3.74	0.04	1.19	2.25	0.77	-0.51	2.98	0.18	1.34	2.09	0.69	-1.31
Tanzania	2.62	0.09	1.08	1.81	1.06	-1.42	4.43	0.17	0.40	1.53	0.97	1.36
Togo	0.02	0.06	-0.04	1.19	1.00	-2.20	1.79	0.59	-0.26	1.88	0.87	-1.30
Uganda	6.69	0.06	1.51	1.72	0.95	2.45	6.05	0.18	2.47	0.92	0.86	1.63
Zambia	-1.26	0.07	-1.68	1.43	0.98	-2.06	3.10	0.14	-0.79	1.56	0.66	1.53
Zimbabwe	2.12	0.05	1.79	1.66	1.11	-2.49	0.14	0.38	0.01	1.07	0.98	-2.30
All Group	1.65	0.15	0.37	1.67	1.10	-1.63	3.24	0.29	0.69	1.08	0.81	0.36

North Africa and Middle-East (11 Economies)

	Period 1989-1995						Period 1995-2001					
	GDP Growth	Sources of Growth (% points per annum)					GDP Growth	Sources of Growth (% points per annum)				
		Capital		Labor		TFP		Capital		Labor		TFP
Economy		ICT	Non-ICT	Hours	Quality			ICT	Non-ICT	Hours	Quality	
Algeria	0.35	0.03	0.11	0.97	1.24	-2.00	3.03	0.03	0.17	1.75	1.09	-0.01
Egypt	3.70	0.11	0.21	1.15	0.90	1.33	4.87	0.26	0.62	2.10	0.85	1.03
Iran	5.41	0.19	0.19	1.26	1.74	2.04	3.93	0.40	0.80	1.48	1.50	-0.24
Jordan	5.88	0.05	1.28	3.93	0.89	-0.26	3.27	0.23	0.77	2.55	0.79	-1.07
Lebanon	13.51	0.17	-1.08	1.89	0.85	11.67	2.10	0.32	0.12	1.57	0.73	-0.64
Mauritania	3.38	0.04	-0.09	1.51	1.17	0.75	3.98	0.27	1.20	1.76	1.04	-0.29
Morocco	1.42	0.06	0.84	0.65	0.81	-0.94	3.94	0.28	1.00	1.59	0.76	0.31
Syrian Arab Rep.	7.60	0.10	0.14	2.19	1.34	3.84	3.14	0.20	0.17	2.17	1.10	-0.49
Tunisia	4.45	0.03	0.97	1.80	0.83	0.81	5.33	0.09	1.22	1.48	0.78	1.76
Turkey	4.10	0.11	1.83	1.77	0.75	-0.36	1.86	0.34	1.93	1.23	0.64	-2.28
Yemen, Rep.	5.45	0.08	2.19	3.41	1.39	-1.62	5.57	0.12	2.65	1.73	1.21	-0.14
All Group	**3.87**	**0.11**	**0.74**	**1.40**	**1.13**	**0.50**	**3.43**	**0.28**	**1.02**	**1.59**	**1.00**	**-0.46**
The World (116 Economies)\	2.53	0.26	0.86	0.44	0.60	0.37	3.51	0.56	0.99	0.71	0.48	0.77

Figure 3.1A   Sources of Output Growth by Group of Economies

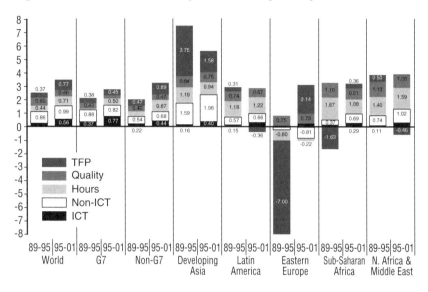

Figure 3.1B Capital Input Contribution to Growth by Group of Economies

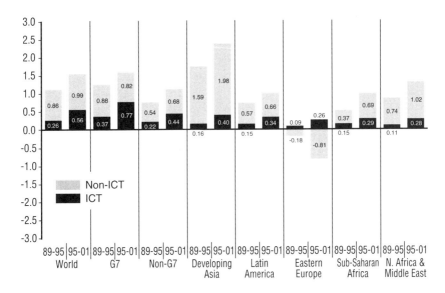

References

Ahmad, Nadim, Paul Schreyer, and Anita Wolfl (2004), "ICT Investment in OECD Countries and Its Economic Impact," Chapter 4 in OECD, The Economic Impact of ICT: Measurement, Evidence, and Implications, Paris: Organization for Economic Co-operation and Development.

Baldwin, John R., and Tarek M. Harchaoui (2003), Productivity Growth in Canada—2002, Ottawa: Statistics Canada.

Barro, Robert J., and Jong-Wha Lee (2001), "International Data on Educational Attainment: Updates and Implications," Oxford Economic Papers, Vol. 53, No. 4, July, pp. 541-563.

Business Software Alliance (2003), Global Software Piracy Study: Trends in Piracy, 1994-2002, Washington, DC: Business Software Alliance USA, June. See:

http://www.bsa.org/usa/research/loader.cfm?url=/commonspot/utilities/handle-link.cfm&thelink=CP___PAGEID=16808,index.cfm,443.

Daveri, Francesco (2002), "The New Economy in Europe: 1992-2001," Oxford Review of Economic Policy, Vol. 18, No. 4, September, pp. 345-362.

Grimm, Bruce, Brent Moulton, and David Wasshausen (2004), "Information Processing Equipment and Software in the National Accounts," in Carol Corrado, John Haltiwanger, and Daniel Sichel, eds., Measuring Capital in the New Economy, Chicago, IL: University of Chicago Press, forthcoming. See: http://www.nber.org/books/CRIW02/grimm-et-al7-22-04.pdf.

Heston, Alan, Robert Summers, and Bettina Aten (2002), Penn World Table Version 6.1, Philadelphia, PA: Center for International Comparisons at the University of Pennsylvania (CICUP), October. See: http://pwt.econ.upenn.edu/aboutpwt.html.

International Telecommunications Union (2004), World Telecommunications Indicators, Geneva: International Telecommunications Union, October. See: http://www.itu.int/ITUD/ict/publications/world/world.html.

Jorgenson, Dale W. (2001), "Information Technology and the U.S. Economy," American Economic Review, Vol. 91, No. 1, March, pp. 1-32.

_____ (2003), "Information Technology and the G7 Economies," World Economics, Vol. 4, No. 4, October-December, pp. 139-170.

Jorgenson, Dale W., and Kazuyuki Motohashi (2004), "Information Technology and the Japanese Economy," Tokyo: 17th Annual Trio Conference, December. See:

http://www.nber.org/~confer/2004/triof04/motohashi.pdf.

Jorgenson, Dale W., and Kevin J. Stiroh (2000), "Raising the Speed Limit: U.S. Economic Growth in the Information Age," Brookings Papers on Economic Activity, 1, pp. 125-211.

Jorgenson, Dale W., and Eric Yip (2000), "Whatever Happened to Productivity Growth?" in Charles R. Hulten, Edwin R. Dean, and Michael J. Harper, eds., New Developments in Productivity Analysis, Chicago, IL: University of Chicago Press, pp. 509-540.

Kaufmann, Daniel, Aart Kray, and Massimo Mastruzzi (2004), "Governance Matters III: Governance Indicators for 1996-2002," Washington, DC: World Bank, April. See: http://www.worldbank.org/wbi/governance/pdf/govmatters3_wber.pdf.

Krugman, Paul (1994), "The Myth of Asia's Miracle," Foreign Affairs, Vol. 73, No. 6, November/December, pp. 62-78.

Lau, Lawrence J. (1999), "The Sources of East Asian Economic Growth," in Gustav Ranis, Sheng-Cheng Hu, and Yun-Peng Chu, The Political Economy of Comparative Development in the 21st Century, Northampton, MA: Edward Elgar, pp. 45-75.

Maddison, Angus (2001), The World Economy: A Millenial Perspective, Paris, Organization for Economic Co-operation and Development.

Organization for Economic Co-operation and Development (2002), Purchasing Power Parities and Real Expenditures, 1999 Benchmark Year, Paris, Organization for Economic Co-operation and Development. See: http://www.sourceoecd.org.

Oliner, Stephen D., and Daniel J. Sichel (2000), "The Resurgence of Growth in the Late 1990's: Is Information Technology the Story?" Journal of Economic Perspectives, Vol. 14, No. 4, Fall, pp. 3-22.

Piatkowski, Marcin (2004), "Information Society in Poland: A Prospective Analysis," Warsaw: Transformation, Integration, and Globalization Economic Research, August. See:

http://www.tiger.edu.pl/onas/piatkowski/Information_Society_in_Pol and_A_Prospective_Analysis.pdf.

van Ark, Bart, Johanna Melka, Nanno Mulder, Marcel Timmer, and Gerard Ypma (2003), ICT Investment and Growth Accounts for the European Union, 1980-2000, Brussels, European Commission, March. See: http://www.ggdc.net/pub/online/gd56-2(online).pdf.

United Nations (2004), Human Development Report 2004, New York, NY: United Nations. See: http://hdr.undp.org/.

World Bank (2004), World Development Indicators 2004, Washington, DC: World Bank. See: http://www.worldbank.org/data/wdi2004/index.htm.

World Information Technology and Services Alliance, Digital Planet Report (2002, 2004), Washington, DC, World Information Technology and Services Alliance. See: http://www.witsa.org/.

Young, Alwyn (1995), The Tyranny of Numbers: Confronting the Statistical Realities of the East Asian Growth Experience," Quarterly Journal of Economics, Vol. 106, No. 1, August, pp. 641-680.

_____ (2003), "Gold into Base Metals: Productivity Growth in the People's Republic of China during the Reform Period," Journal of Political Economy, Vol. 111, No. 6, December, pp. 1220-1261.

Chapter 5

Innovation, Technology and Productivity: Why Europe Lags Behind the United States and Why Various European Economies Differ in Innovation and Productivity[1]

Luc Soete

Introduction

It seems particularly appropriate to discuss in more detail the core of what has become known in the European debate as the Lisbon challenge. As the most recent Economist Intelligence Unit report[2] argues, "The new economy story linked with ICT appears to come nearest to explaining divergent trends in the US and euro zone, although it is not definitive and important issues remain unclear, including the precise relationship between ICT and the overall policy framework." Following Dale Jorgenson's detailed overview of the evidence on international comparisons among the G-7 nations in productivity growth, I will focus here on some of the underlying main underlying policy issues for the European economies.

If there is any general policy slogan that might be appropriate in describing the challenge European countries face today in trying to achieve the Lisbon knowledge agenda[3] it would be, I submit, the need for policies *"activating knowledge."* The most relevant comparison to

---

[1] Paper presented at the Conference: "The Network Society and the Knowledge Economy: Portugal in the global context" Lisbon, March 5˜6, 2005.

[2] EIU executive briefing, *US/EU economy: Is it a "new economy" story after all?* February 22, 2005, http://eb.eiu.com/index.asp?layout=show_article_print&article_id=6

[3] In the following paragraphs, I limit myself to that part of the Lisbon agenda dealing with policies aimed at strengthening incentives for knowledge investments, not the social dimension.

be made here is with policies for "activating labor," which rose to popularity in Europe, and the UK in particular, in the early 1990s and were instrumental in reducing long term, structural unemployment.[4] Such policies focused on the many "passive" features of the highly regulated European labor markets, and the way these features had contributed to a rise in the structural component of long-term unemployment. "Active labor" market reforms aimed in the first instance at reducing labor market entry barriers, and in particular low wage unemployment traps, and increasing labor market flexibility, without putting in jeopardy the essence of the social security protection model typical of most European countries' welfare systems. In countries which went furthest ahead in such "active labor" market reforms such as the UK, the Scandinavian countries and The Netherlands, the result was not only a significant reduction in unemployment, but also sometimes impressive increases in employment participation rates of particular, underrepresented groups in the labor market which had become "activated" such as women and youngsters. Over time and with the formal assessment at the European level of such labor market reform policies—the so-called Luxembourg process—active labor market policies became a full and integral part of employment policies in most European countries.

The challenge today appears more or less similar, but this time with respect to the need for "activating knowledge," the essential ingredient for any policy aimed at increasing growth incentives in Europe.

As noted in the Sapir report,[5] since Lisbon (March 2000) European growth performance has been, contrary to expectations, weak, highlighting in particular the failure of the current European Union policy framework to provide sufficient national as well as EU-wide growth inducing incentives. This holds both for the Growth and Stability Pact as well as for structural, sector specific EU policies such as the Common Agricultural Policy or Social Cohesion Policy, which have been poor in bringing about structural growth enhancing reform. Also with respect to ICT use, research and development, innovation and

---

[4] See in particular the OECD's so-called *Job Study* (1994), which became a staunch defender of the need for such policies in Europe.

[5] See Sapir, A. et al. *An Agenda for a Growing Europe, The Sapir Report*, Oxford University Press, 2004.

knowledge more generally, policies pursued both in member countries and at the EU level seem to have been dominated by the old scale intensive industrial type, too much based on strengthening the competitiveness of existing firms and sectors and too little of the growth enhancing, innovation and creative destruction type.

Without such specific growth enhancing policies, the restrictive macro-economic policies introduced within the framework of the Growth and Stability pact in the euro zone countries have, if anything, exacerbated the "*non-active*" nature of knowledge activities. Under this low growth, restrictive fiscal scenario, public knowledge funding activities such as the delivery of (highly) skilled youngsters from universities, professional and technical high schools, or the research carried out within universities and public research laboratories, have remained by and large passive. Because of the lack of growth opportunities, public research output has remained by and large unused and unexploited in the rest of the economy and in particular the private sector. In the best (some might say worst) case they have only contributed to efforts abroad, i.e. to other countries through migration or through the transfer of knowledge to foreign firms and universities. Private knowledge funding activities on the other hand, due to lack of domestic growth opportunities, have been cut, rationalized, outsourced to foreign countries, or simply frozen. The Lisbon knowledge growth challenge is more than ever a real one: many countries particularly in continental Europe are in danger of a long term downward adjustment to a low knowledge intensive, low growth economy.[6]

Notwithstanding what was noted above about the particular need in continental Europe for innovative, creative destruction renewal, a policy of "*activating knowledge*" should, and probably first, build on existing strengths in knowledge creation and use. At the same time it should, however, aim at activating competencies, risk taking and readiness to innovate. In short, a policy aimed at activating knowledge should be directed towards the activation of unexploited forms of knowledge.

---

[6] In a recent Dutch article, two civil servants from the Ministry of Finance actually made the claim that the Dutch economy has, and I quote: "no comparative advantage in high tech goods." Furthermore, by importing high tech goods, the Dutch economy would actually benefit much more from those foreign productivity gains. See Donders, J. en N. Nahuis "De risico's van kiezen," ESB, 5 maart 2004, p.207. Similar arguments have been made at the EU level by John Kay.

The claim made here is that there are many of such forms, covering the full spectrum of knowledge creation, knowledge application and knowledge diffusion. ICT plays a crucial role in each of these areas. Furthermore, such policies should be directed towards public knowledge institutions, including higher education institutions; financial institutions not just venture capital providers; private firms in manufacturing as well as services; and last but not least individuals, as entrepreneurs, employee or employer, producer or consumer.

In this short contribution, the focus is very much on the first of these areas, the one governments have actually the biggest latitude for intervention and attempting at least to activate knowledge: public knowledge institutions. Five aspects of such knowledge investments, which are at the heart of the Lisbon agenda, will be discussed.

First is the issue of public investments in research and development. In most member countries public research institutions including universities have become increasingly under funded. "Activating" national budgets so as to free more money for public investment in such knowledge investments appears the easiest and most straightforward policy measure to be implemented given the commitment EU member countries already took in Barcelona.

Second, there is the need for improving the matching between private and public knowledge investment efforts. Increasingly, I would argue, European countries are confronted with a growing mismatch between private and public research investments.

Third, there appears also an urgent need for activating research in universities and other public research institutions in Europe. If there is one reservoir of unused knowledge potential it is likely to be found in those institutions.

Fourth, policies should be designed to activate human capital and knowledge workers. Shortages of research personnel loom large on the European horizon.

Fifth and foremost, there is in Europe a need for policies activating innovation.

Maybe there is a trade-off between innovation and creative destruction on the one hand and social security and stability on the other hand. But maybe existing social security policies can also become "activated" towards innovation, creative destruction, and entrepreneurship.

1. *"Activating Lisbon": beyond the simple Barcelona targets*

It was the growing awareness of Europe's falling behind in knowledge creation and knowledge diffusion which induced European heads of state to set the objective at the Lisbon summit in March 2000 to become the world's most competitive and dynamic knowledge economy by 2010. The Lisbon knowledge objective were translated into the so-called Barcelona target in the spring of 2002, whereby European countries would aim to spend approximately 3% of their Gross Domestic Product on investment in research, development, and innovation by 2010, a figure comparable to the current investment percentages in the United States and Japan.

It is unfortunate that the European Lisbon target was so explicitly translated into the Barcelona objective of 3%, an investment cost objective. Equally important, if not more so, is the question what the results—in terms of efficiency and effectiveness—of these investments would be. Furthermore, the separation of the 3% norm into a public component set at 1% of GDP, and a private component set at 2% of GDP, ignored some of the more fundamental differences between the United States (on which this separation was based) and most European countries' taxing regimes (neutral versus progressive) and the implications thereof for private and public parties, and in particular the role of public authorities in the funding of research and development. Particularly in continental European countries, it can be expected that both enterprises and individual citizens will, given the progressiveness of their income taxes, expect a higher contribution of public authorities in the financing of higher education and research. Their relatively "passive" attitude towards private investments in knowledge (most European citizens are perfectly happy to increase their indebtedness to acquire private property, and have large parts of their income spent most of their working life on mortgage repayments, but not to invest in their or their children's education and schooling) is to some extent the direct consequence of the progressive tax regimes most middle and high income families are confronted with over their working and family life.

To aim for a double effort of the private sector compared to the public one in knowledge investment is to ignore the different role of public authorities in Europe as opposed to the U.S. Furthermore, given the relatively limited leeway European public authorities have in inducing private firms to increase their R&D investments (the only feasible instrument: national R&D tax advantages contains substantial beggar-thy-neighbour elements in it and is likely to become increasingly challenged at the European court level), the Barcelona target appears ultimately a rather weak policy "focusing device" on the road to Lisbon.

Nevertheless, attainment of the public funding target of 1% of GDP in so far as it is something practical governments can do, could be elevated to an absolute minimum policy priority. How to achieve this within the current, highly restrictive budgetary framework conditions of most EU member countries? By "activating national budgets" in a growth enhancing direction, one could argue, redirecting government expenditures towards such knowledge investments, just as the Sapir report forcefully argued with respect to the EU budget.

But as will also be clear from what was said before, the setting of simplistic target objectives in the area of knowledge dynamics and innovation, even limited to the public sector, raises many questions.

First and foremost, there are factual questions. How real is the knowledge gap? The Barcelona target only addressed one highly imperfect, knowledge input indicator: R&D expenditures. Firms are not interested in increasing R&D expenditures just for the sake of it but because they expect new production technology concepts, new products responding to market needs, to improve their own efficiency or strengthen their competitiveness. If at all possible, firms will actually try to license such technologies or alternatively outsource at least part of the most expensive knowledge investments to suppliers of machinery, rather than have to forego themselves those costly investments. Today most firms are actually keen on increasing the efficiency of R&D by rationalizing, or reducing the risks involved in carrying out R&D, outsourcing it to separate small high tech companies which operate at arms length but can be taken over, once successful. Furthermore industrial R&D investment on which the Barcelona targets are based is heavily biased in favour of industrial production. Service sectors but also more engineering based activities are likely to be strongly underrepresented. As a result, the question about the "real" knowledge gap of Europe with respect to the U.S. remains very much subject to debate.

Central in this debate is the extent to which the commercial benefits of knowledge investments can be appropriated and by whom—the firm within the sector having made the R&D efforts, or a firm upstream or downstream? Or the final consumer, imitation taking place so quickly that none of the new product rents could be appropriated by the innovator?

It might well be that sectors and activities with little registered R&D-effort have a complex and actually deep knowledge base. Some of the most competitive European industries e.g., the offshore and dredge industry, the food processing, finance or insurance industry, carry out little if no R&D. According to OECD classifications, these are typically medium to low-technology industries. The knowledge bases appropriate to these industries display, however, great technical depth and variety. The list of institutions providing support and development of these different knowledge bases is similarly long and diverse. Thus a low-R&D industry may well be a major user of knowledge generated elsewhere. The same holds of course for many service sectors, where the introduction of new process or organizational structures as well as new product innovations, is unlikely to involve much formal R&D investment. But here too, the crucial question will be the extent to which such innovations can be easily imitated or can be formally protected through trademarks, copyrights or other forms of intellectual property, or kept secret.

The same argument holds at the international level. Again the central question will be whether the commercial benefits of knowledge investments can be appropriated domestically or are "leaking" elsewhere, to other countries. In the economic growth literature, the phenomenon of catching-up growth is typically characterized by lagging countries benefiting from the import, transfer of technology and knowledge, formally and particularly informally. In the current, increasingly global world economy, increasing R&D investment is hence unlikely to benefit only the domestic economy. This holds *a fortiori* for the EU with its twenty five independent member countries.

Thus, as highlighted by Meister and Verspagen (2003), achieving the 3% Barcelona target by 2010 is not really going to reduce the income gap with the U.S., the benefits of the increased R&D efforts not only accruing to Europe but also to the U.S. and the rest of the world.

In a similar vein, Griffith, Harrison and Van Reenen (2004) have illustrated how the U.S. innovation boom of the 1990s had major benefits for the UK economy, and in particular for UK firms that had shifted their R&D to the U.S. A UK firm shifting 10% of its innovative activity to the U.S. from the UK while keeping its overall level the same, would be associated with an additional increase in productivity of about 3%. "This effect is of the same order of magnitude as that of a doubling in its R&D stock" (Griffith et al. 2004, p.25).

In short, the link between the location of "national" firms' private R&D activities and national productivity gains is, in the current, increasingly global R&D world, at best tenuous.

To conclude this first section: achieving the Barcelona target should be brought back to what governments can practically achieve in the area of knowledge investment. Setting a common European target, such as the Barcelona one, can be useful if, but only if, it sharpens policy priorities. The current translation of those targets in public and private targets does anything but sharpen policy priorities. On the contrary, the debate on government expenditures in the euro zone countries is completely dominated by the other European 3% fiscal norm. That norm provides, however, no incentive to redirect public funding in the direction of knowledge enhancing investments. The most immediate measure policy makers should take is to reform their budget priorities in the direction of knowledge enhancing growth activities by raising as a minimum the public funding of R&D to the 1% of GDP level.

2. Activating the "joint production" of knowledge: attracting private R&D

Knowledge production is typically characterized by so-called "joint production" features: what modern growth economists have described as the increasing returns features of knowledge growth accumulation. In more down to earth terminology, knowledge investments by both private and public authorities have been characterized by strong complementarities and from a geographical perspective strong agglomeration features. In most continental European countries this led over the postwar period to a rapid catching up in public and private R&D[7] investments, particularly by large domestic firms in their home country. Such investments were often rather closely in line with national public R&D investments. In the late 1970s and early 1980s most European countries had actually caught up with the U.S. in private R&D investment. Technical high schools and universities were often closely integrated in this privately led knowledge investment growth path. This "national champion" led R&D catching up process led actually to a strong "over-concentration" of domestic R&D investments of such firms in their country of origin, certainly when compared to their international production activities. Along with the further internationalization (and 'Europeanization' in the running up to the 1992 European single market) of production, R&D investments became also more subject to internationalization. Initially, this was limited to R&D activities strongly linked to the maintenance and adjustment of production processes and product technology to the foreign market conditions, later on it involved also more fundamental research activities.

In short, a sheer natural trend towards the international spread of private R&D of the large European multinationals took place, on which much of individual member countries' knowledge strength had been built. By the same token, many of the close domestic connections between private and local public research institutions became weaker. This process is far from over, given the still wide disparities in the concentration of domestic R&D versus international sales. At the same time the renewal rate of R&D intensive firms in Europe was particularly poor. The rapid growth in the gap in the 1990s between the total amount of R&D spent by private firms in Europe and by private firms in the U.S., is a reflection of this lack in renewal of high growth firms in Europe as compared to the U.S., as illustrated in Figure 4.1 below.

---

[7] The UK's R&D spending remained in the early postwar period at a much higher level, more or less in line with that of the U.S., than that of most continental European countries primarily as a result of the large government spending in the military, aerospace industries and other public utilities sectors.

Figure 4.1   EU and US firms' renewal in the post-war period

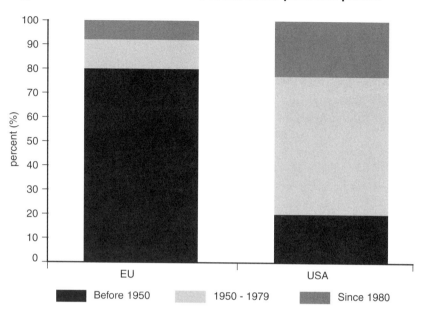

It is worthwhile noting that the gap between Europe and the U.S. in privately *financed* R&D, as illustrated in Figure 4.2a, is first and foremost a gap in R&D *performed* in the private sector (Figure 4.2b), i.e. R&D carried out in the private sector but funded both by private as well as public funds (including in the latter case in the U.S. primarily military R&D). Actually with respect to R&D *performed* in the public sector, there is no gap between Europe and the U.S., yet there remains a substantial gap in publicly *financed* R&D. The widening of the EU-U.S. gap over the 1990s between privately *performed* R&D suggests that firms under the pressure of internationalization increasingly turned their back on national European public research institutes and concentrated rather their R&D activities elsewhere in the world, and particularly in the U.S. Surprisingly since 2000, the gap between the U.S. and the EU has actually declined significantly. However, this decline is first and foremost the result of a decline in the R&D performed in the business sector in the U.S.

Universities and other public research institutes in Europe, under funded, failed by and large, and in contrast to their counterparts in the U.S., to provide the attractor pole to European (and foreign) firms for joint knowledge production—a role they actually fulfilled for many years within their secure national "cocooning" borders. It seems hence reasonable to conclude that Europe suffered from the fragmentation of what were relatively closed national, joint production R&D systems, with national R&D champions internationalizing their R&D activities due to both internal EU pressures in the late 1980s and external competition pressures in the 1990s, while public research institutions remained incapable of providing sufficient private R&D renewal.

Figure 4.2A   Gap in EU25—US R&D spending

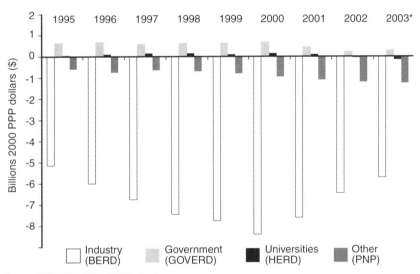

Source: OECD-MSTI. 2003* MERIT estimate

3. Activating university and fundamental research

The internationalization process described above has also been accompanied by a process of "*crowding out*" of fundamental, basic research from private firms' R&D activities. This process took place in most large firms in the 1980s and found its most explicit expression in the reorganization of R&D activities, from often autonomous laboratories directly under the responsibility of the Board of Directors in the 1960s to more decentralized R&D activities integrated and fully part of separate business units. Today only firms in the pharmaceutical sector and a couple of large firms outside of this sector are still involved in the funding and carrying out of fundamental research, as reflected e.g. in authorship of scientific publications. And even in those cases, firms rely heavily on outside, mostly public sources of fundamental research. For most firms the increased complexity of science and technology has meant a greater focus on applied and development research and a more explicit reliance on external, university or other, often public, knowledge centres for more fundamental research input. In line with what was discussed above, firms increasingly "shop" on the world market for access to basic and fundamental research and chose the best locations to locate their R&D laboratories. In doing so they will not only hope to make their own, in-house R&D more efficient, but also look to the efficiency, quality, and dynamics of the external, local knowledge institutions, such as universities and public R&D institutions.

Figure 4.2B   Gap in EU25—US R&D financing

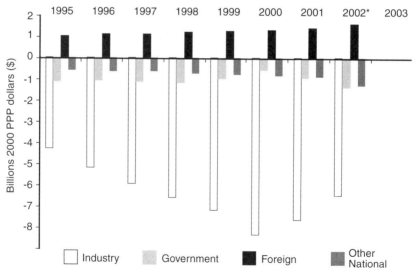

Source: OECD-MSTI. 2002* MERIT estimate. 2003 not available.

At the other end of the spectrum, over the 1980s and 1990s in most European countries public knowledge investments in universities and other public research institutes became subject to increased national public scrutiny, systematic performance assessment and academic peer review. As a result academic performance became even more explicitly the dominant incentive in public research institutes: applied, more immediate relevant research became second rated. Effectively it could be said that applied research became "crowded out" of the university environment. Today, the actual national performance of scientific research, measured, for example, in terms of the number of publications per researcher, or per million of euros spent on public R&D is actually not inferior in Europe to that of the United States. Throughout the years, with the increasing dominance of English as the language of scientific communication, the growth in the total "production" of internationally read and reviewed scientific articles in Europe has been much higher than in the United States.

One characteristic of public research is, to some extent, its national embeddedness.[8] From this perspective, the policy towards increasing "competition" between national universities and public research centers, led undoubtedly to important quality impulses to public research in many European countries, but did ultimately *not* lead to specialization of research in Europe[9] but rather, one might argue, to further research duplication. Practically every national university jumped on the same, new, promising research areas (life sciences, nanotechnology, information technology, new materials, etc.), competing nationally, Europe-wide and world-wide to recruit leading researchers. This resulted in a multitude of different, relatively small research groups, each of them seeking additional funding and networks through European funding programs.

The opposing "crowding out" trends in the nature of private research dominated by internationalization and specialization on the one hand and public research dominated by nationalization and duplication on the other hand, warrant a policy of activating public, fundamental research institutions in playing their role in a much more

---

[8] As a parenthesis, it can be noted that, based on this perspective, the concept of "*national* systems of innovation" developed by (primarily European) authors in the innovation literature such as Christopher Freeman, Charles Edquist, Bengt-Ake Lundvall and Richard Nelson: differences between countries in the set-up and nature of *national* institutions, in particular university education and the public research infrastructure, seems to be able to explain to a large extent differences between countries in innovation strength.

[9] With only a couple of exceptions in areas of so-called "big science" where the use of large instruments and other expensive infrastructures warrants ultimately close cooperation between different countries scientific communities.

dynamic fashion as local attractors of private R&D activities and generators of private firms' research renewal. In short, the activating knowledge policies falling under this heading have to deal with (re-) activating the formal and informal connections between the public and private knowledge investment of the various European "national" systems of innovation. The building of such new formal bridges could take various forms, exploiting to the maximum the institutional variety in Europe. One may think of the technology platforms currently proposed by the EC. Topics should obviously not only include private sector research interests but also public research interests (security, mobility, etc.). Alongside such re-activating linkage policies, one should also focus on activating all other forms of joint knowledge production policies: e.g. policies providing stronger and more effective incentives for scientific entrepreneurs, policies aimed at increasing mobility between public and private research labs, policies opening up private research labs to public (and other private) research interests, etc.

4. Activating Human Knowledge

In the end, private or public research investments depend to a large extent on the availability of highly qualified research personnel. The greatest part of research expenditures, about 70% of total R&D resources on average, goes to the salaries of research personnel. The available data on scientific personnel, formalized under the term "scientists & engineers" (S&E) presented in Figure 4.3, point again to an increasing gap between the U.S. and Europe in privately oriented research. Not only is the percentage of S&E in total employment in the private sector 2 to 3 times higher in the U.S. and Japan than in Europe, but its growth is also significantly lower in Europe than in those countries.

The availability of sufficiently qualified personnel is central in the development of any "sustainable" knowledge economy, also within the context of the Barcelona objective. Without the availability of highly qualified research personnel, the aim to increase substantially knowledge investments in less than a decade, will merely lead to a tighter labor market for S&E and the "poaching" of personnel by the private sector from universities and other public research centres or between European countries. Looking at the current labor costs for R&D personnel, realization of the Barcelona objective implies a need for an additional supply of researchers between now and 2010 of between 500,000 and 800,000 full-time equivalents[10] (EU Gago Report, 2004). This should be added to the specific European problem of an aging population, which also affects the knowledge sector: from the growing shortage of teachers in a large number of European countries to the rapid increase in the greying of academic staff in practically all European countries.

Figure 4.3   S&E as % of labour force (growth rates 1995-2000)

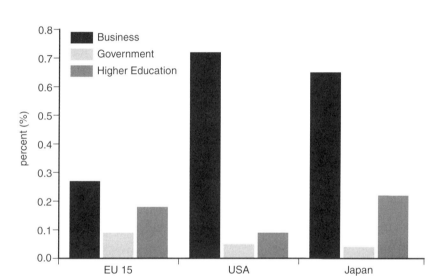

Two factors appear to be of primordial importance in this discussion. On the one hand, the capacity of a country's own educational system to deliver, year upon year, new cohorts of highly-qualified, scientists and engineers; and on the other hand, the attractiveness and dynamism of the profession of researcher and the attractiveness of the surrounding environment—the quality of the local physical environment, facilities available, presence of other research labs, etc.

---

[10] Based on the broad estimations made in the so-called Gago High Level Expert Group, *Europe needs more scientists*, DG Research, April 2004.

1. When referring to the supply of S&E within a country, use is sometimes made of the 'pipeline' analogy, which illustrates how, from secondary education onwards, the flow of scientifically trained S&E finally seeps through to the various components of the R&D world. A number of factors will be important in the flow of sufficient S&E supply to, for example, the private R&D sector, despite a decreasing inflow following e.g. demographic factors at the beginning of the pipeline. Thus, there are countless obstacles preventing pupils, students, graduates, and PhD students, throughout each of the different education and training stages from continuing a research career trajectory. The Appendix to the *Benchmark report on Human Resources in RTD*[11] lists these different obstacles, the different possible policy leverages and objectives. At first sight, these seem to be equally applicable to the U.S. or the EU.

So far, mainly the southern European countries have witnessed a large increase in the numbers of students as part of a European catching-up growth process and the relatively high unemployment rate among youngsters, which resulted in, among other things, a considerable expansion of the number of universities and polytechnics. Yet this is a temporary process, which, incidentally, has not led so far to a proportional increase in the demand from the private sector for highly qualified personnel in these countries. The new accession East European countries represent a very different story. Here the higher education systems have a long tradition in delivering highly qualified S&E particularly in the hard sciences. The lack of knowledge relates primarily to commercial and financial access to worldwide market opportunities. Foreign direct investment exploiting the unused technical human capital potential has been quick in picking up this unused human capital knowledge potential. But here too, the long-term demographic trends are negative; raising questions as to the long-term sustainability of the supply of highly qualified human capital.

2. The importance of the dynamics of the local environment is increasingly recognised as being a crucial factor for innovation and the development of knowledge. Many economic geographers emphasized

---

[11] See *Benchmark report on Human Resources in RTD*, DG Research, European Commission, Brussels, 2002.

the importance of the regional clustering of knowledge activities. Despite the fact that the local supply of S&E remains a crucial determinant for the localisation of private research activities as is clear from the location of many private R&D labs near universities, the demand for knowledge is increasingly also influenced by physical, social and local, cultural factors that will in fact operate as pools of attraction in exerting a pull on highly educated people, in Richard Florida's words: "the creative class." In this sense, the tendency to regionally cluster knowledge centres observed both inside the U.S. and individual European countries is again a logical consequence of the agglomeration and joint production effects of knowledge and its appeal to researchers and entrepreneurs.

Up to now, the various policy proposals aimed at the development of a European Research Area have not really led to a significant rise within Europe of the labour mobility of S&E and European wide knowledge clustering. The barriers to such labor mobility—differences in pension systems, in rules and regulations governing university appointments, in use of foreign languages in higher education teaching—appear all much more significant across European member countries than with respect to the emigration of European S&E towards the U.S. Increased mobility and migration of highly qualified personnel is of course likely to put strongly under question the European ideals of "social cohesion."[12] It is actually surprising that so little thought has been given up to now, to the internal inconsistencies of European ambitions in this area.

To summarize: investments in human capital provide the mirror picture of the knowledge investments described under the previous heading. The crucial distinction here is the one between knowledge, which is codified and can be traded; is embodied in new products or machines. In other words knowledge, which can be "commodified" is ready for use. And on the other hand knowledge, which is tacit, embodied in the brains of individuals, in their competences, in their schooling and training, in their years of life-long experience. Tradable

---

[12] See for example David, P. "ERA visions and Economic realities: A cautionary approach to the restructuring of Europe's research system," EC STRATA Workshop "New challenges and new responses for S&T policies in Europe," Brussels, 22-23 April 2002, mimeo, for a detailed analysis of the possible, undesirable, regional effects of the ERA as a result of mobility effects.

knowledge looses, depending on the effectiveness of intellectual property protection, rapidly, sometimes the day it is brought on to the market, much of its commercial value. It becomes routine, more or less public knowledge. Tacit knowledge by contrast is difficult to transfer and disappears in the extreme case with the death or the retirement of the scientist or researcher.

Recognition of this distinction is essential for policy making. Indeed, it brings to the forefront the local growth dynamics aspects of joint knowledge production based on so-called "co-location" advantages of the physical agglomeration of human knowledge capital. It illustrates why even in our current Internet world with easy access to codified knowledge, scientists, researchers and highly skilled employees still like to cluster together in similar locations. Activating knowledge will hence imply strengthening the local/regional agglomeration aspects of joint knowledge production. In the case of Europe, it means a more fundamental recognition of regional knowledge strengths, of the particular role of regional authorities in helping their regions to become attractor poles for knowledge workers, in having to make regional choices.

Ultimately it is the success of regional knowledge attractor poles, which will determine whether Europe has any chance of achieving its Lisbon ambitions. A knowledge policy that only focuses on international, tradable knowledge, ignores the essential complementarities between codified and tacit knowledge; by contrast a national knowledge policy aimed at belonging to the technological "lead" reflects often an outdated degree of techno-nationalism. Within the current European context of a union of member states, it could be argued that knowledge policies have been too heavily dominated by national aims and have insufficiently recognized the regional dimension of knowledge production and diffusion. This has been exacerbated in many member countries[13] by the national institutional focus of public research funding organisations.

---

[13] The exception being member countries such as Belgium or Spain, where the regional decentralization structures has given way to quite explicit regional research and innovation policies.

5. *Activating Innovation*

So far, the analysis presented has focused mainly on the technological aspects of knowledge creation and development, specifically the link between private and public research expenditure and the demand for highly educated researchers. Outside of this sphere, however, there are other factors that also play an essential role in the innovation process: the introduction of new products onto the market, the implementation of new production techniques, the right organisational set up, the setting up new, innovative companies, the local innovative and entrepreneurial culture, etc.

This raises the question of the possible existence of intrinsic, institutional, social and cultural barriers in Europe that may have a negative impact on knowledge development and innovation. Besides the well-known institutional barriers to innovation in Europe (the lack of harmonization in the area of the European patent, the difficulties in creating an effective European venture capital market, etc.), the question can be raised to what extent certain aspects of the European continental social welfare model might contain intrinsic obstacles to "entrepreneurship and innovation culture," especially in light of Europe's increasing structural disadvantages in the areas of innovation and high-tech entrepreneurship. The Lisbon declaration was not only an expression of the political desire to strive for a Europe belonging by 2010 to the world's most knowledge-intensive regions, but also that this was to happen within the context of a strengthened, 'activated' social Europe that would have an eye for past social achievements. The question that has in fact *not* been addressed in Lisbon is how activating labour markets and what we have termed here "activating knowledge" can go together and when one is confronted with economic trade-offs.

Based on the so-called regulatory barriers index estimated by the OECD, Figure 4.4, represents e.g. for the U.S. and a number of European countries the various, most common barriers to innovation associated with product market regulations, specific burdens on start ups, administrative burdens and last but not least employment protection costs associated with hiring and firing. This last one appears significantly higher in all European countries than in the U.S., with the UK not surprisingly with the lowest index level.

Economists such as Giles Saint-Paul[14] have analyzed the relationship between labor market institutions, and in particular the costs of dismissing employees, and the development of innovations from a purely theoretical perspective. Hiring and firing costs are in many ways the most explicit manifestation of the social welfare state in most continental European countries. They have led to stability in labor relations and represent an incentive for employers and employees alike to invest in human capital. However, in terms of innovation, and in particular the Schumpeterian process of creative destruction, the cost of developing new activities—whether concerned with new product, process or organizational innovations—will crucially depend on the ease with which "destruction" can be realized. Thus, as shown in Saint-Paul's model, the U.S., with lower firing costs, will eventually gain a competitive advantage in the introduction of new, innovative products and process developments onto the market, while Europe will become specialized in technology-following activities, based on secondary, less radical improvement innovations.

Figure 4.4   Regulatory barriers index (OECD)

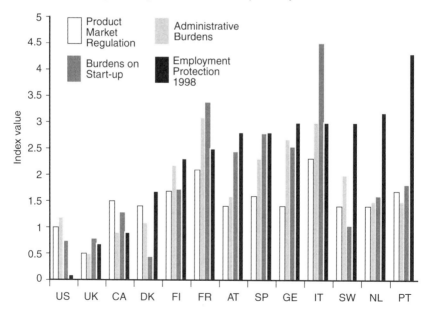

[14] Saint-Paul, G., 2002, "Employment protection, international specialisation and innovation," *European Economic Review*, vol. 46, pp. 375-95.

In other words, the dynamics of innovation, of entrepreneurship, of creative destruction thrives better, practically by definition, in an environment providing higher rewards for creativity and curiosity than in an environment putting a higher premium on the security and protection of employment. Viewed from this perspective, the gap between Europe, and in particular continental Europe, and the United States in terms of innovative capacity, efficiency, and wealth creation may also, at first sight look like the price Europe has to pay for not wanting to give up its social model and in particular social securities and achievements.

To summarize: it might be argued that the Lisbon declaration was not really clearly formulated. A better way would have been: how much of the social achievements of the European model is Europe prepared to give up to keep up with the United States, let alone develop Europe into one of the most prosperous and dynamic regions in the world? Or alternatively: which elements of the European social model are sacred and which elements are worth paying a dynamic growth price for?[15]

Many of the proposals on "activating the labor market" with by now popular concepts like "empowerment" and "employability" appear to go hand in hand with innovation and growth dynamics, others though do not. Some European countries such as the UK and Denmark appear to have been much more successful in reducing dismissing costs than others, and appear to have benefited from it much more in terms of growth dynamics. The central question which must be raised within this context is whether the social security model developed at the time of the industrial society is not increasingly inappropriate for the large majority of what could be best described as "knowledge workers" who are likely to be less physically (and by contrast possibly more mentally) worn out by work than the old type of blue collar, industrial workers. The short working hours, or early retirement schemes might well appear to knowledge workers less of a social achievement, work not really representing a "disutility" but more an essential motivating activity, providing even a meaning to life.

---

[15] As Wim Duisenberg, the previous chairman of the European Central Bank, once stated: maybe we should accept that Europe will always face a growth and productivity gap with the U.S. simply because of existing differences in Europe in language, culture, and customs. As long as we value maintaining those, we will get joy out of our lagging behind the U.S.

There is in other words an urgent need for a complete rethought of the universality of the social security systems in Europe, recognizing explicitly that depending on the kind of work citizens get involved in, social achievements including employment security, a relatively short working life and short weekly working hours are important social achievements and elements of the quality of life, which should not be given up, and the case, probably exemplified by the highly qualified researcher, where exactly the opposite holds. It is in other words urgent time to broaden the discussions in science, technology and innovation policy circles to include social innovation.

Part III
Organizational Reform and Technological Modernization in the Public Sector

Chapter 5

Central Issues in the Political Development of the Virtual State

Jane E. Fountain

Introduction

The term "virtual state" is a metaphor meant to draw attention to the structures and processes of the state that are becoming more and more deeply designed with digital information and communication systems. Digitalization of information and communication allows the institutions of the state to rethink the location of data, decision making, services and processes to include not only government organizations but also nonprofits and private firms. I have called states that make extensive use of information technologies *virtual states* to highlight what may be fundamental changes in the nature and structure of the state in the information age.

This chapter discusses the technology enactment framework, an analytical framework to guide exploration and examination of information-based change in governments.[1] The original technology enactment framework is extended in this chapter to delineate the distinctive roles played by key actors in technology enactment. I then examine institutional change in government by drawing from current initiatives in the U.S. federal government to build cross-agency relationships and systems. The U.S. government is one of the first central states to undertake not only back office integration within the government but also integration of systems and processes across agencies. For this reason its experience during the past ten years may be of

---

[1] The technology enactment model and detailed case studies illustrating the challenges of institutional change may be found in J.E. Fountain, *Building the Virtual State: Information Technology and Institutional Change* (Brookings Institution Press, 2001). The present paper draws from the explanation of the technology enactment model in *Building the Virtual State* and presents new empirical research on current, major e-government initiatives in the U.S. central government.

interest to e-government researchers and decision makers in other countries, particularly those in countries whose governments are likely to pursue similar experiments in networked governance. The summary of cross-agency projects presented here introduces an extensive empirical study, currently in progress, of these projects and their implications for governance.

A structural and institutional approach that begins with processes of organizational and cultural change, as decisionmakers experience them, offers a fruitful avenue to understanding and influencing the beneficial use of technology for governance. Focusing on technological capacity and information systems alone neglects the interdependencies between organizations and technological systems. Information and communication technologies are embedded and work within and across organizations. For this reason, it is imperative to understand organizational structures, processes, cultures and organizational change in order to understand, and possibly influence, the path of technology use in governance. Accounts of bureaucratic resistance, user resistance and the reluctance of civil servants to engage in innovation oversimplify the complexities of institutional change.

One of the most important observers of the rise of the modern state, Max Weber, developed the concept of bureaucracy that guided the growth of enterprise and governance during the past approximately one hundred years. The Weberian democracy is characterized by hierarchy, clear jurisdiction, meritocracy and administrative neutrality, and decisionmaking guided by rules which are documented and elaborated through legal and administrative precedent. His concept of bureaucracy remains the foundation for the bureaucratic state, the form that every major state—democratic or authoritarian—has adopted and used throughout the Twentieth Century. New forms of organization that will be used in the state require a similar working out of the principals of governance that should inhere in structure, design and process. This challenge is fundamental to understanding e-government in depth.

Throughout the past century, well-known principles of public administration have stated that administrative behavior in the state must satisfy the dual requirements of capacity and control. Capacity indicates the ability of an administrative unit to achieve its objectives efficiently. Control refers to the accountability that civil servants and the bureaucracy more generally owe to higher authorities in the legislature, notably to elected representatives of the people. Democratic accountability, at least since the Progressives, has relied upon hierarchical control—control by superiors of subordinates along a chain of command that stretches from the apex of the organization, the politically appointed agency head (and beyond to the members of Congress) down to operational level employees.

The significance and depth of effects of the Internet in governance stem from the fact that information and communication technologies have the potential to affect *production* (or *capacity*) as well as *coordination*, *communication*, and *control*. Their effects interact fundamentally with the circulatory, nervous, and skeletal system of institutions. Information technologies affect not simply production processes in and across organizations and supply chains. They also deeply affect coordination, communication and control—in short, the fundamental nature of organizations. I have argued that the information revolution is a revolution in terms of the significance of its effects rather than its speed. This is because the effects of IT on governance are playing out slowly, perhaps on the order of a generation (or approximately 25 years). Rather than changes occurring at "Internet speed," to use a popular phrase of the 1990s, governments change much more slowly. This is not only due to lack of market mechanisms that would weed out less competitive forms. It is significantly attributable to the complexities of government bureaucracies and their tasks as well as to the importance of related governance questions—such as accountability, jurisdiction, distributions of power, and equity—that must be debated, contested and resolved.

In states that have developed a professional, reasonably able civil service, public servants (working with appointed and elected government officials and experts from private firms and the academy) craft the details and carry out most of the work of organizational and institutional transformation. What is the transformation process by which new information and communication technologies become embedded in complex institutions? Who carries out these processes? What roles do they play? Answers to such questions are of critical importance if we are to understand, and to influence, technology-based transformations in governance. Government decisionmakers acting in various decisionmaking processes produce decisions and actions that result in the building of the virtual state.

Career civil servants redesign structures, processes, practices, norms, communication patterns and the other elements of knowledge management in government. Career civil servants are not impediments to change, as some critics have argued. They are key players in government reform. An extended example may be drawn from the experiences of civil servants in the U.S. federal government beginning in approximately 1993. Working with political appointees and outside experts, career civil servants worked out the details critical to the success of several innovations that otherwise would not have been translated from their private sector beginnings to the organizations of the state.[2] Over time, as their mentality and culture has begun to change, a cadre of superior civil servants have become the chief innovators in the government combining deep knowledge of policy and administrative processes with deep understanding of public service and the constraints it imposes on potential design choices. Their involvement is critical not simply as the "users" of technology but as the architects of implementation, operationally feasible processes and politically sustainable designs.

Technology Enactment

Many social and information scientists have examined the effects of the Internet and related ICTs on organizations and on government. Yet the results of such research often have been mixed, contradictory and inconclusive. Researchers have observed that the same information system in different organizational contexts leads to different results. Indeed, the same system might produce beneficial effects in one setting and negative effects in a different setting. This stream of research, focused on effects and outcomes, neglects the processes of transformation by which such systems come to be embedded in organizations. Because these processes may develop over several years, they cannot be considered transitional or temporary. Transformation becomes the more or less constant state of administrative and governmental life.

---

[2] Many of these innovative developments are presented in the cases included in *Building the Virtual State*. See, for example, the cases concerning the development of the International Trade Data System, the U.S. Business Advisor, and battlefield management systems in the U.S. Army.

The technology enactment framework emphasizes the influences of organizational structures (including "soft" structures such as behavioral patterns and norms) on the design, development, implementation and use of technology. In many cases, organizations enact technologies to reinforce the political status quo. Technology enactment often (but not always) refers to the tendency of actors to implement new ICTs in ways that reproduce, indeed strengthen, institutionalized socio-structural mechanisms even when such enactments lead to seemingly irrational and sub-optimal use of technology. One example include websites for which navigation is a mystery because the organization of the website mirrors the (dis)organization of the actual agency. Another example are online transactions that are designed to be nearly as complex as their paper-based analogues. A third example is the cacophony of websites that proliferate when every program, every project and every amateur HTML enthusiast in an organization develops a web presence. These early stage design choices tend to pave paths whose effects may influence the development of a central government over long periods of time because of the economic and political costs of redesign.

The underlying assumptions of designers play a key role in the type of systems developed and the way in which systems are enacted in government. The Japanese government, known for planning and coherence of response, is currently engaged in development of a national strategy for e-government. This response is distinctly different from a bottom-up approach in which innovation from the grass-roots of the bureaucracy is encouraged. The U.S. Army's design of the maneuver control system, a relatively early form of automated battlefield management, developed in the 1980s and 1990s, was developed with the assumption on the part of system designers that soldiers are "dumb" operators, button pushers with little understanding of their operations. When much of the detailed information soldiers used by soldiers for decisionmaking was embedded in code and made inaccessible to them, there were substantial negative effects on the operational capacity of the division.[3]

---

[3] This case is reported in detail in *Building the Virtual State*, chapter 10.

Figure 5.1   The Technology Enactment Framework

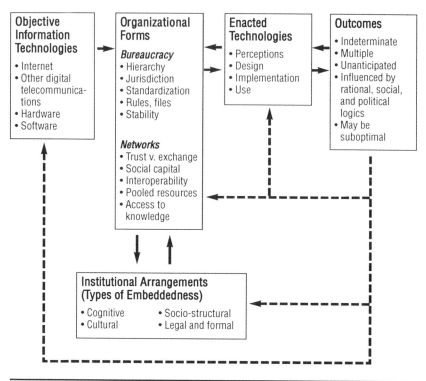

Source: J. E. Fountain, *Building the Virtual State: Information Technology and Institutional Change* (Washington, D.C.: Brookings Institution Press, 2001), p. 91.

I developed the technology enactment framework (presented in the figure above) as a result of extensive empirical research on the behavior of career civil servants and political appointees as they made decisions regarding the design and use of ICTs in government. If information technology is better theorized and incorporated into the central social science theories that guide thinking about how government works, researchers will possess more powerful tools for explanation and prediction. In other words, theory should guide understanding of the deep effects of ICTs on organizational, institutional and social rule systems in government which is not ordered by the invisible hand of the market.

The most important conceptual distinction regarding ICTs is the distinction between "objective" and "enacted" technology depicted in the figure using two separate boxes separated by a group of mediating variables.[4] By objective technology, I mean hardware, software, tele-communication and other material systems as they exist apart from the ways in which people use them. For example, one can discuss the memory of a computer, the number of lines of code in a software pro-gram, or the functionality of an application. By "enacted technology," I refer to the way that a system is actually used by actors in an organi-zation. For example, in some organizations email systems are designed to break down barriers between functions and hierarchical levels. Other organizations may use the same system of email to reinforce command and control channels. In some cases firms use information systems to substitute expert labor for much cheaper labor by embed-ding as much knowledge as possible in systems and by routinizing tasks to drive out variance. In other cases firms use information sys-tems to extend their human capital and to add to the creativity and problem solving ability of their employees. Many organizations have taken a plethora of complex and contradictory forms, put them into pdf format and uploaded them to the web, where they can be down-loaded, filled out by hand and FAXed or mailed for further processing. Yet other organizations have redesigned their business processes to streamline such forms, to develop greater web-based interactivity, particularly for straightforward, simple transactions and processes. These organizations have use ICTs as a catalyst to transform the organization. Thus, there is a great distinction between the objective properties of ICTs and their embeddedness in ongoing, complex organizations.

Two of the most important influences on technology enactment are organizations and networks. These appear as mediating variables in the framework depicted in the figure above. These two organizational forms are located together in the framework because public servants currently are moving between these two types of organization. On the one hand, they work primarily in bureaucracies (ministries or agen-cies) in order to carry out policymaking and service delivery activities.

---

[4] In this conceptualization I draw from and extend a long line of theory and research in the sociology of technology, history of science, and social constructivist accounts of technolog-ical development. What is new in my approach is the synthesis of organizational and insti-tutional influences, a focus on power and its distribution, and a focus on the dialectical tensions of operating between two dominant forms: bureaucracy and network.

On the other hand, public managers are increasingly invited to work across agencies and across public, private and nonprofit sectors—in networks—to carry out the work of government. Thus, these two major organizational forms, and their respective logics, heavily influence the ways in which technologies in the state will be designed, implemented and used.

As shown in the figure, four types of institutional influences undergird the process of enactment and strongly influence thinking and action.[5] *Cognitive institutions* refer to mental habits and cognitive models that influence behavior and decisionmaking. *Cultural institutions* refer to the shared symbols, narratives, meanings and other signs that constitute culture. *Socio-structural institutions* refer to the social and professional networked relationships among professionals that constrain behavior through obligations, history, commitments, and shared tasks. *Governmental institutions*, in this framework, denote laws and governmental rules that constrain problem solving and decisionmaking. These institutions play a significant role in technology enactment even as they themselves are influenced, over the long run, by technological choices.

Note that causal arrows in the technology enactment framework flow in both directions to indicate that recursive relationships dominate among technology, organizational forms, institutions, and enactment outcomes. The term "recursive" as it is used by organization theorists means that influence or causal connections flow in all directions among the variables. This term is meant to differentiate recursive relationships from uni-directional relationships in which, for example, variable A leads to variable B. For example, smoking leads to cancer. But cancer does not lead to smoking. In a recursive relationship, variable A and variable B influence one another. For example, use of ICTs influences governance. And governance structures, processes, politics and history influence the use of ICTs. Recursive relationships specified in the technology enactment framework do not predict outcomes. Rather, they "predict" uncertainty, unanticipated results and iteration back through design, implementation and use as organizations and networks learn from experience how to use new

---

[5] I am indebted to Professors Paul DiMaggio and Sharon Zukin for this typology of institutional arrangements.

technologies even as they incur sunk costs and develop paths that may be difficult to change. The analytical framework presents a dynamic process rather than a predictive theory.

An extension of the model, presented in the figure below, highlights the distinctive roles played by three groups: IT specialists in the career civil service, program and policy specialists and other government officials at all levels from executive to operational, and vendors and consultants.

Figure 5.2   Key Actors in Technology Enactment

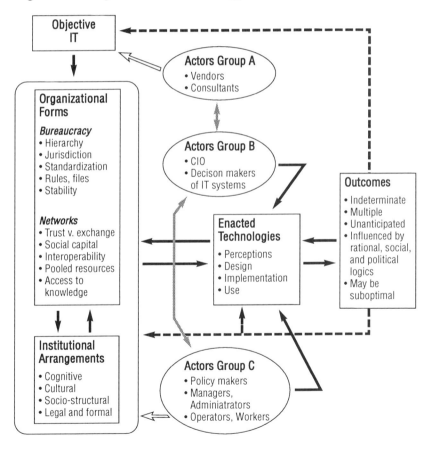

The three groups of actors play distinctive but inter-related roles in technology enactment. Actors in group A, comprised of vendors and consultants, are largely responsible for objective technology. Their expertise often lies in identification of the appropriate functionality and system architecture for a given organizational mission and set of business processes. What is critical for government is that vendors and consultants fully understand the political and governance obligations as well as the mission and tasks of a government agency before making procurement and design decisions. It is essential to understand the context and "industry" of government, just as one would have to learn the intricacies of any complex industry sector. Just as the information technology sector differs from the retail, manufacturing, and the service sectors, so the government sector exists in a unique environment. Within government as well are varying policy domains and branches whose history, political constraints, and environments are important to understand.

Actors in group B, according to this model, include chief information officers of agencies and key IT decisionmakers. These government actors bear primary responsible for detailed decisions of system design. Actors in group C—policymakers, managers, administrators, operators, and workers—have a strong, often unappreciated and overlooked, influence on adjustments to organizational and network structures and processes. It is imperative that some members of this group develop expertise in the strategic uses of ICTs in order to bridge technological, political and programmatic logics. These depictions simplify the complexities of actual governments and the policymaking process. They are meant to draw attention to the multiple roles involved in enactment and the primary points of influence exerted through each role. In particular, the relationships between groups B and C are often neglected when, in fact, they are crucial for success of projects.

Propositions

Six propositions may be derived logically from the technology enactment framework and the political environment that exists in most industrialized democracies.

Proposition 1: Perverse incentives

Public servants face a set of perverse incentives as they make decisions regarding the possible uses of technology in their programs and agencies. Public executives in most states try to accumulate larger budgets and more staff in order to increase the power and autonomy of their department. They learn to negotiate successfully for appropriations for their program and agency. In the theory of adversarial democracy, such conflicts among programs and agencies are assumed to force public servants to sharpen their arguments and rationales for programs. This competition of ideas and programs is meant to simulate a market from which elected officials can choose thereby producing the best results for citizens. The adversarial model of democracy makes the development of networked approaches to government difficult. The impasse can be broken only by significant restructuring of incentives to dampen unwieldy tendencies toward agency autonomy and growth.

For this reason, public executives face perverse incentives. If they implement new information systems that are more efficient, they will not gain greater resources; they will probably enact a situation in which their budget is decreased. If they implement information systems that reduce redundancies across agencies and programs, once again, they are likely to lose resources rather than to gain them. If they develop inter-agency and enterprise-wide systems with their colleagues in the bureaucracy, they will lose autonomy rather than gaining it. So the traditional incentives by which public executives have worked are "perverse" incentives for networked governance.

Proposition 2: Vertical Structures

The bureaucratic state, following from the Weberian bureaucracy, is organized vertically. By that I mean that the government is organized in terms of superior-subordinate relations, a chain of command that extends from the chief executive to the lowest level employees of the government. Similarly, oversight bodies for budgeting, accountability and even for legislation exercise oversight through the chain of command structure. These vertical structures are the chief structural elements of government institutions. Incentives for performance are derived from this structure. This verticality, central to accountability and transparency, also makes it difficult and to use technology to build networked government. The more complex difficulties are not technical. In fact, it is rather easy to imagine how a federal enterprise architecture should be designed. What is difficult is reconceptualizing accountability, oversight, and other basic elements of governance in networked relationships.

Proposition 3: Misuse of capital/labor substitution

In the U.S. federal government, agencies were not allocated significant new resources to develop IT. Congress has assumed that the use of ICTs to substitute for labor would generate resources for technological innovation. Although labor costs can be reduced by using IT, there are a few complexities that should be enumerated here.

First, organizations must learn to use IT. This requires human labor and experienced human labor is critical. It is difficult to downsize and to learn at the same time regardless of popular management imperatives to force employees to innovate through large-scale cutbacks.

Second, although some jobs can be eliminated through the use of ICTs, e-government necessitates many new and expensive jobs. Specifically, IT positions must be created for intelligent operation of systems, for monitoring and protecting data and processes, and for redesigning processes as legislation and programs change. Outsourcing is an option, but is nonetheless expensive and cannot completely replace an internal IT staff. Large organizations have found that IT staffs are expensive. In particular, website content requires labor-intensive attention; protection of privacy and data security in government exceeds industry standards and practices; and some degree of institutional memory and knowledge for networked governance must reside within the permanent civil service rather than in a plethora of contracts. By placing critical strategic knowledge in the hands of contractors, governments put themselves in the position of having to pay for this knowledge multiple times and lose the possibility to leverage this knowledge internally for innovation. Asset specific technological knowledge should reside within governments and must be viewed as a necessary cost of e-government.

Third, the U.S. government has made a commitment to provide public services through multiple channels: face-to-face, telephone, mail, and Internet. Thus, they are faced with the strategic and operational complexities of designing, developing, implementing and managing across multiple channels. For these reasons, and others, the simple idea of substituting technology for labor is misleading and erroneous. In Portugal, it seems necessary to continue to employ multiple channels for services given the demographic differences in Internet use. Here the social decision to respect the elderly population should dominate over technological possibilities for e-government. Other Iberian states have simply eliminated paper-based channels in order to move the population to e-government.

Proposition 4: Outsourcing may appear to be easier than integration

It may appear to political decisionmakers that it is easier to outsource operations than it is for government managers to negotiate the politics of integration, that is, information sharing and working across agencies. In other words, there is a danger that some services and systems will be outsourced in order to avoid the political difficulties of internal governmental integration of back office functions or cross agency functions. But in some cases, outsourcing would be a mistake because the negotiations within the government necessary for integration to move forward form a necessary process of learning and cultural change, through enacting technology. The arduous process of making new systems fit the political, policy and operational needs of the government is, itself, the transformation of the state toward a new form coherent with the information society. Outsourcing may appear to be the easier course of action. But ultimately states must make difficult decisions regarding asset specificity, that is, the knowledge and skills that should reside within the government.

Proposition 5: Customer service strategies in government

Governments have an obligation to provide services to the public. But this is one element of the relationship between state and society. First, customers are in a different relationship with firms than citizens are with government.[6] Customers have several options in the market;

---

[6] See J. E. Fountain, "The Paradoxes of Customer Service in the Public Sector," *Governance*, 2001, for an extended analysis of differences between customer service strategies in economic firms and their use in government. In this working paper I simply mention a few of the more important arguments published previously.

citizens have but one option for government services and obligations. Customers pay for services; but citizens have a deeper relationship and great responsibility toward their government than a fee for service relationship. They do not pay taxes in exchange for services. Tax systems in most states are a form of redistribution, a material system that reflects a social and political contract. In a democratic system of government "of the people, by the people, and for the people," citizens have deep obligations to government and governments have deep obligations to the polity. So the customer service metaphor, particularly in its most marketized forms, is a degradation, minimization, and perversion of the state-citizen relationship in democracies.

Second, in the private sector, larger and wealthier customers are typically given better treatment than those customers who have little purchasing power or who have not done business with a firm in the past. Market segmentation is critical to service strategies in firms but is not morally or ethically appropriate for governments. Moreover, customer service strategies in U.S. firms tend to reward those customers who complain with better service in order to "satisfy" the customer. Those customers who do not complain do not receive better service. This, again, is not morally or ethically appropriate for government. Some citizens cannot exercise voice, or articulate their needs, as well as others. Public servants have an obligation to provide services equitably regardless of the education, wealth, or language skills of the citizen.

As the U.S. government tried to adopt some of the customer service ideas that were popular in economic firms, they did increase responsiveness to citizens. Moreover, public servants experienced a deep change in their attitudes and behavior. In many cases, the culture of agencies and programs changed to become oriented toward citizens rather than toward the internal bureaucratic needs of agencies. These were positive benefits from the customer service metaphor.

But some corporate citizens exploited the notion of customer service to extract benefits from the state. Powerful corporate citizens used "customer service" as a way to pressure agencies to provide benefits and to develop policies and rules that were inequitable and that would advantage some firms or industries over others. Ford Motors, Motorola, and Cisco are indeed large "customers" of the U.S. government. But the regulatory regimes developed for industries cannot serve some "customers" better than others. At the corporate level, the customer service metaphor breaks down as a normative force. For these reasons, the Bush Administration discontinued the use of "customer service" as a government strategy. They use the term "citizen-centric" instead.

Proposition 6: Embeddedness and cultures

One of the chief learnings from the experiences of the U.S. government in the development of e-government has been the strong role of embeddedness and culture. Embeddedness refers to the fact that information systems are situated in the context of complex histories, social and political relationships, regulations and rules, and operational procedures. It is not a simple matter to change an information system, therefore, when it is embedded in a complex organizational and institutional system.

Integration across Agencies: An Example

A marked rise in the use of the Internet, at the beginning of the 1990s, coincided with the beginning of the Clinton administration and the initiation of a major federal government reform effort, the Reinventing Government movement, led by Vice President Al Gore. In addition to the development of regulatory and legal regimes to promote e-commerce, the administration sought to build internal capacity for e-government. A key strategy of the Clinton administration included the development of virtual agencies. The virtual agency, in imitation of web portals used in the private sector, is organized by client—say, senior citizens, students, or small business owners—and is designed to encompass within one web interface access to all relevant information and services in the government as well as from relevant organizations outside the government. If developed sufficiently, virtual agencies have the potential to influence the relationship between state and citizen as well as relationships within government among agencies and between agencies and overseers.

During the Clinton administration, development of cross-agency websites floundered due to intransigent institutional barriers. Oversight processes for cross-agency initiatives did not exist. Budget processes focus on single agencies and the programs within them. There were no legislative committees or sub-committees nor were there budget processes that were designed to support cross-agency, or networked, initiatives. The government lacked a chief information officer, or any strong locus of executive authority or expertise, to direct and manage initiatives lying across agencies and across jurisdictions. These institutional barriers, as well as others, posed deeper challenges to networked government than the usual and oft-cited complaints about resistance to change on the part of bureaucrats. Bureaucrats were simply responding to incentives, norms, and the dominant culture.

In August 2001, in a continuation of the path toward building inter-agency capacity (or networked approaches within the state) the Bush administration released the Presidential Management Agenda. The complete agenda includes five strategic, government-wide initiatives; this paper summarizes one of the five initiatives: e-government.[7] The e-government plan, initially called "Quicksilver" after a set of cross-agency projects developed during the Clinton administration, evolved to focus on the infrastructure and management of 25, cross-agency e-government initiatives. The projects are listed in the table below. (I describe each project briefly in Appendix One.) The overall project objectives are to simplify individuals' access to government information; to reduce costs to businesses of providing government with redundant information; to better share information with state, local and tribal governments; and to improve internal efficiency in the federal government.[8]

The 25 projects are grouped into four categories: Government to Business, Government to Government, Government to Citizen and Internal Efficiency and Effectiveness and a project which affects all others, E-Authentication. Government-to-business projects include: electronic rulemaking, tax products for businesses, streamlining international trade processes, a business gateway, and consolidated health informatics. Government-to-government projects include: interoperability and standardization of geospatial information, interoperability for disaster management, wireless communication standards between emergency managers, standardized and shared vital records informa-

---

[8] For further details see "The President's Management Agenda," p.24 http://www.white-house.gov/omb/budget/fy2002/mgmt.pdf.

[9] Jane E. Fountain, "Prospects for the Virtual State," working paper, COE Program on Invention of Policy Systems in Advanced Countries, Graduate School of Law and Politics, University of Tokyo, September 2004. English language version available at http://www.ksg.harvard.edu/janefountain/publications.htm

tion, and consolidated access to federal grants. Government-to-citizen projects include: standardized access to information concerning government benefits, standardized and shared recreation information, electronic tax filing, standardized access and processes for administration of federal loans, and citizen customer service. Projects focused on internal efficiency and effectiveness within the central government encompass: training, recruitment, human resources integration, security clearance, payroll, travel, acquisitions and records management. Also included is a project on consolidated authentication. (For further information concerning each project see www.e-gov.gov). For a detailed description of the implementation and management of one of the initiatives, Grants.gov, an effort to standardize the grants management process across several agencies, see Fountain (2004).[9]

Table 5.1   Cross-Agency, E-Government Initiatives

Government to Citizen	Government to Government
Recreation One Stop	Geospatial One Stop
GovBenefits.gov	Grants.gov
E-Loans	Disaster Management
IRS Free File (IRS only)	SAFECOM
USA Services	E-Vital
Government to Business	**Internal Efficiency and Effectiveness**
E-Rulemaking	E-Training
Expanding Electronic Tax	Recruitment One-Stop
Products for Business	Enterprise HR Integration
Federal Asset Sales	E-Records Management
International Trade Process	E-Clearance
Streamlining	E-Payroll
Business Gateway	E-Travel
Consolidated Health Informatics	Integrated Acquisition Environment
	E-Authentication

Source: http://www.egov.gov

The 25 projects were selected by the U.S. Office of Management and Budget from more than three hundred initial possibilities. The plethora of possibilities were in nearly all cases developed during the Clinton administration and continue outside the rubric of the Presidential Management Initiative. In al cases, such projects focus attention on the development of horizontal relationships across government agencies. In this sense, the projects move beyond the first stage of e-government which typically entails providing information online to citizens. They also progress further in the use of ICTs than Stage Two E-government, which has tended to focus on putting transactions such as payments to government online.

Their specific objective of a focus on cross-agency consolidation is to reduce redundancies and complexity through standardization of generic business operations in government. A cross-agency approach also limits operational and information processing autonomy—the "stovepipes"—of government agencies and departments (http://www.whitehouse.gov/omb/egov/about_backgrnd.htm).

The projects are overseen and supported by the Office of E-government and Information Technology, a statutory office within the U.S. Office of Management and Budget established by law in 2002. An organization chart detailing the new structures within OMB is presented below. The Administrator for E-government and IT, shown at the apex of the organization chart, is the Chief Information Officer of the federal government and an associate director of OMB reporting to the Director. The position initially was held by Mark Forman, a political appointee, and is currently held by Karen Evans, a career civil servant. The Associate Administrator for E-Government and Information Technology, reporting to the Administrator, is responsible for the 25 cross-agency projects. The five portfolio managers represented in the organization chart—some of whom are career civil servants and others of whom are political appointees—have specific responsibility to oversee the 25 cross-agency initiatives. A management consulting group (not shown), whose members are not government employees but private contractors detailed to OMB have been responsible for most of the day-to-day communications and reporting with the programs. In effect, they serve as staff and liaisons between OMB and the cross-agency projects which are based in and across government agencies.

The new organization within OMB signals a major institutional development in the U.S. federal government. Before passage of the E-Government Act of 2002 (Public Law 107-347), which established the federal CIO and OMB structure, there was no formal structural capacity within OMB to oversee and guide cross-agency initiatives. The structural gap formed a major impediment to the development of networked governance during the Clinton administration. In terms of political development and fundamental changes in the nature of the bureaucratic state, we see in these organizational changes the emergent institutionalization of a governance structure for the direction and oversight of cross-agency, or networked, governance.

The organization chart depicts the 25 cross-agency initiatives reporting directly to portfolio managers within OMB. This representation is meant only to indicate that oversight and guidance of the projects is exercised by portfolio managers. The managing agency for each project is a federal agency rather than OMB. The projects are not part of the OMB hierarchy. The formal authority for each project belongs to the federal agency designated by OMB as the "managing partner," or lead agency.

The matrix presented below arrays federal agencies along the top of the grid and projects along the left side. Agency partners for each project are marked with an x. The managing partner is denoted by an X in bold-face type. For example, the column and row colored blue indicate that the U.S. Department of Health and Human Services is a partner agency in eight initiatives and the managing partner of two projects, health informatics and federal grants.

Each managing partner agency appointed a program manager to lead its project. The program managers are typically senior, experienced career federal civil servants. They have been responsible for developing a consultative process among agencies involved in each project and, in consultation with OMB, they are responsible for developing project goals and objectives. In most cases, program managers were also required to devise a funding plan to support the project in addition to a staffing plan. Neither funds nor staff were allocated as part of the president's plan.

The E-Government Act, the legislation that codified the new organizational structure within OMB, provided for federal funding for the projects of approximately $345 million over four years. But an average of only $4 to 5 million per annum has actually been appropriated by Congress. Strategies developed by each project for funding, staffing and internal governance vary widely and have been largely contingent on the skills and experience of the program manager. So far, the legislature has not adapted organizationally to networked government. This lag in institutional development makes it difficult to build networked systems because appropriations of funds continue to flow to individual agencies and programs within them.

Table 5.2   Presidential Management Initiative E-Government Projects: Partner Agencies and Managing Partners

Projects/Departments	DoC	DoD	DoE	DoEd	DoI	DoJ	DoL	DoT	EP	FDIC	FEMA	GSA	HHS	HUD	NARA	NASA	NRC	NSF	OP	SBA	Smithsonian	SSA	State	Treasury	USAID	USDA	VA
Consolidated Health Informatics	X	X											X									X					
Disaster Management	X	X				X		X			X	X	X	X						X		X					X
E-Authentication	X	X	X	X	X	X		X	X			X	X				X			X		X		X		X	X
Grants.gov	X	X	X	X	X	X		X	X		X	X	X	X				X		X					X	X	X
E-Payroll	X	X	X				X	X								X						X		X			
E-Training		X	X					X				X				X			X			X					
E-Travel		X				X	X					X	X						X								
E-Vital	X	X	X	X			X											X				X		X		X	X
E-Records Management	X	X			X	X									X				X					X		X	X
GovBenefits.gov		X	X	X	X		X	X	X		X		X	X								X	X	X		X	X
Expanding Electr. Tax Products																											
IRS Free File																						X		X			
Federal Asset Sales	X	X		X						X		X		X		X	X			X				X			
Geospatial One-Stop	X	X			X			X	X		X		X	X					X								X
Integrated Acquisition Env.					X			X				X				X				X						X	X
Enterprise HR Integration	X	X	X																X				X			X	
E-Clearance	X	X	X			X											X		X				X				

Table 5.2 Presidential Management Initiative E-Government Projects: Partner Agencies and Managing Partners (continued)

Projects/Departments	DoC	DoD	DoE	DoEd	DoI	DoJ	DoL	DoT	EP	FDIC	FEMA	GSA	HHS	HUD	NARA	NASA	NRC	NSF	OP	SBA	Smithsonian	SSA	State	Treasury	USAID	USDA	VA
Int'l Trade Proc. Streamlining	X					X														X			X	X	X	X	
Business Gateway	X						X	X	X											X				X	X		
E-Loans				X							X		X	X						X			X			X	X
E-Rulemaking						X	X	X	X														X			X	
Recreation One-Stop	X	X			X		X	X													X	X			X	X	
Recruitment One-Stop	X	X			X		X	X						X		X			X			X		X	X	X	
USA Services	X	X									X	X	X							X		X		X		X	X
SAFECOM	X	X			X			X			X	X	X													X	

Source: OMB Project Management Office: E-Gov Partner Agencies Public.xls, unpublished document, no date, Revised, July 1, 2004.

U.S. Federal IT Budget

U.S. federal investments in government IT spending increased steadily from approximately $36.4 billion dollars in 2001 to 59.3 billion in 2004. According to OMB estimates, eighty percent of this spending is for external consultants indicating a high level of contracting out of ICT services. Technical expertise and human capital in the federal government is being greatly weakened as a result under the "competitive outsourcing" policy and lack of human capital with IT expertise in the federal government. But this increase in investment also suggests a commitment to building a virtual state.

Figure 5.3   OMB Office of E-Government and Information Technology Organization Chart

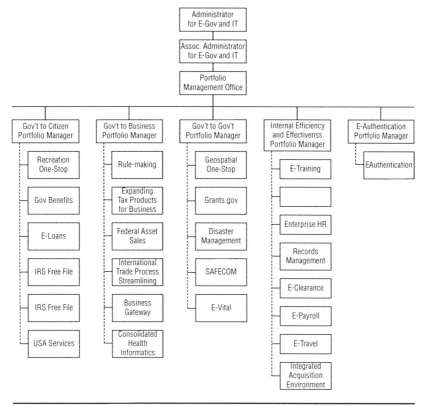

Source: Office of Management and Budget "Implementation of the President's Management Agenda for E-Government: E-Government Strategy" p 19, 2/27/2002, http://www.whitehouse.gov/omb/inforeg/egovstrategy.pdf, and www.egov.gov, accessed 7/1/2004.

Figure 5.4   U.S. Federal Government IT Spending

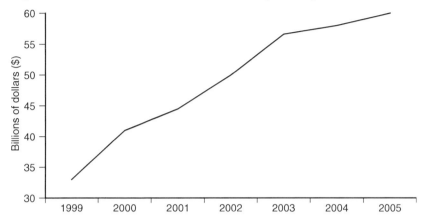

Source: OMB: "Report on Information Technology (IT) Spending for the Federal Government, Fiscal Years 2000, 2001, 2002" , OMB: "Report on Information Technology (IT) Spending for the Federal Government, Fiscal Years 2002, 2003, 2004" Excel spreadsheet: http://www.whitehouse.gov/omb/budget/fy2004/, accessed 7/2/04, OMB:"Report on Information Technology (IT) Spending for the Federal Government for Fiscal Years 2003, 2004, and 2005": http://www.whitehouse.gov/omb/budget/fy2005/, accessed 7-2-04

The E-Government Act tied appropriations to strategic, business and IT plans of agencies and created a fund of $345 million to support cross-agency initiatives and monitoring of their development for fiscal years 2002 to 2004. In contrast to the bottom-up approach of the Clinton administration, the Bush administration approach is top-down, engineering in its approach to systems development, and emphasizes strict and rigorous project management. Yet there have been enormous disparities between the funds actually allocated to the e-government projects and and the congressional appropriation. As John Spotila, former director of Information and Regulatory Affairs in OMB, remarked: "… Even without homeland security absorbing most of the IT dollars, cross-agency projects have never been a favorite of Congress, where appropriations are awarded through a 'stovepipe system' of committees that makes a multi-agency approach difficult."[10] Appropriations for the cross-agency initiatives were $5 million in FY 2002 and 2003 and only $3 million in FY2004. A congressional source

---

[10] Quotation from *Federal Computer Week*, February 18, 2002: http://www.fcw.com/fcw/articles/2002/0218/cov-budget1-02-18-02.asp

recently noted: "We have never been convinced that the fund [requested to support cross-agency initiatives] doesn't duplicate what already exists in other agencies or performs unique functions ... It has never been well-justified, and we don't have a lot of spare cash lying around."[11]

Conclusions

The bureaucratic state is not outmoded, but the nature and structure of the state is changing fundamentally as information and communication technologies are being absorbed into governments. It is not vanishing but remains critical to standard setting, rule by fiat softened by consultation, integrity of processes, and accountability. It is the locus of the "national interest" in an increasingly globalized network of nations. The virtual state is intersectoral, interagency, and intergovernmental yet achieves connection through standardization, rationalization, and systems interdependence.

Although communications researchers have used the concept "co-evolution" to refer to reciprocal relationships between technology and organizations and their co-development, the reference to co-evolution connotes that enactment simply happens. By contrast, I have developed the technology enactment framework to examine how the actions of public officials and other government decisionmakers interact to enact technology. So the technology enactment framework builds specificity and explanatory power into models of co-evolution of technology and government organizations

This chapter has focused on structural and institutional changes to the state in the elaboration of the technology enactment framework and the illustration of recent efforts by the U.S. government to create inter-agency structures and processes. Technology plays a key role in changing the capacity of public servants to engage in knowledge creation and exchange. These informal exchanges among professionals within and outside government through the Internet comprise a powerful change in the public policymaking process. Information

---

[11] John Scofield, spokesman for the House Appropriations Committee, quoted in *Government Computer News*, February 9, 2004. See http://gcn.com/23_3/news/24892-1.html, accessed July 2, 2004.

technology has afforded the capacity for different and greater communication, for different and great information and knowledge sharing, and for greater transparency and display of complex information. All of these change the types of conversations and dialogue for government officials. The daily, informal exchanges are among the most important and potentially far-reaching changes in policymaking and governance.

The virtual state is intersectoral, interagency, and intergovernmental. But it achieves this fluidity and cross-boundary character through standardization, rationalization, and the management of interdependence.

Is the virtual state a non-place?

The idea of a "non-place," drawn from contemporary theory in anthropology, refers to the increasing use of generic systems, applications, interfaces, terminologies, and more to replace unique, particular place-based images, systems, terms and other markers.[12] Generic, corporate systems tend to ignore the particularities of countries, regions, cities, and other local geographic and historic "places." In fact, the desire of corporations to communicate their "brand," intensifies the diminishing of place. For example, the external face of the McDonalds Corporation looks the same in every country regardless of "place." Airports tend to look the same so that a person in an airport may have few markers that provide information about the particular culture of a place.

I have not yet drawn out the implications for government and governance of this increasing homogenization of approaches. But I would say that there might be a loss of attention to the particular problems and political issues that belong to particular places given their unique history and geographic features. This is the general idea of a "non-place."

I do not think that the virtual state in any country will become a "non-place" for many years. But I want to issue a warning about the increasing use of pre-packaged, generic applications, interfaces, and

---

[12] See Marc Augé, *non-places: introduction to an anthropology of supermodernity* (London: Verso, 1995). Translated by John Howe.

systems in governments around the world. These homogenized, stan-dardized products are those of major multi-national firms. They pro-vide organizations and inter-organizational networks with the ability to inter-operate, which is a great benefit to governments and societies. But they diminish local particularities that provide a sense of place and serve to maintain distinctive cultures.

The challenges that lie ahead are not simply technical. Indeed, the technical challenges are relatively simple. The more complex and dif-ficult challenges related to the virtual state are intellectual, govern-mental and practical. As the use of ICTs in government moves forward there is much more at stake than simply increasing efficiency and service levels. Bureaucracies and the bureaucratic model have been the source of government accountability, fairness, and integrity of processes. If the bureaucratic form is changing, what forms, struc-tures, and processes will replace it? Given these governance chal-lenges, business models and business language can be limiting and misleading as a source of wisdom and advice for building the virtual state. Business experience can inform operations and systems develop-ment. But public servants and the polity will have to engage in delib-eration to bring clarity to governance questions.

The role of the public servant is changing but remains critical in democracies. Civil servants play a vital role in domestic—and increas-ingly in transnational and global—policy regimes. Professional, expe-rienced public servants are essential to the virtual state. I suppose that it is obvious to say that professional, experienced public servants are critical. But in the United States, many conservatives would like to eliminate the public service and to use contract workers instead. So, my comment is made in the context of a debate about the privatization of the public service. The argument is that e-government and net-worked government make professionalism and experience even more important within the entire public service. IT is not a substitute for experience and professionalism. It is not a strategy for deskilling the public service although it may be possible to eliminate some jobs made redundant by IT. It is critical also for IT professionals to have better interaction with other professionals.

All public servants need to be knowledgeable about IT, if not in a technical sense then in terms of understanding its strategic and politi-cal importance. Governments must be careful customers of private consultants and vendors. I do not think that most private firms really understand the differences between government and private sector organizations. And most do not care about these differences or view them as their responsibility to understand. Hence, public servants must understand the differences between systems built for the private sector and the requirements necessary for government systems. Vendors generally do not understand the higher standards of account-ability that are the obligation of the state, fair and equal treatment of citizens, access, transparency and, in particular, security and privacy necessary for government systems.

These are not obvious statements in the present business environ-ment. In the U.S. some public servants have been intimidated by Congress and private consultants to believe that they are inferior deci-sion makers, that they are out of date in their thinking and that, in nearly all cases, that the private sector "can do it better than gov-ernment." Public servants, in many cases, insufficiently value their knowledge and experience to negotiate in a strong way with private firms. It is necessary for contractors to build the large systems for government. But it is also necessary for public servants to play a strong role in the design, development and implementation of those systems. They are the decision makers with the experience and depth of knowledge of government operations and politics. Thus public ser-vants are the decision makers who know when to import a system from the private sector and when a system needs to be modified for public use.

Researchers and practitioners are just beginning to explore the potential for cross-agency capacity and policymaking. Extending the ideas presented in this paper beyond inter-agency relationships within the federal state, one can readily imagine that we may have to redefine and modify ideas about federalism due to networked governance. Moreover, the increasing use of inter-sectoral relationships—that is, relationships among the public, private and nonprofit sectors—marks the virtual state. There is strong evidence to support the claim that virtual integration, that is, the location of information and services from different agencies and programs on one website, does in some cases lead to pressure or the desire of decision makers for actual orga-nizational level integration.

Appendix One

25 E-Government Initiatives: Brief Descriptions

Program	Description
Government to Citizen	
Recreation One-Stop www.recreation.gov	"Provides a single point of access, user-friendly, web-based resource to citizens, offering information and access to government recreational sites" http://www.whitehouse.gov/omb/egov/gtoc/recreation.htm
GovBenefits.gov www.govbenefits.gov	"Provides a single point of access for citizens to locate and determine potential eligibility for government benefits and services" http://www.whitehouse.gov/omb/egov/gtoc/govbenefits.htm
E-Loans www.govloans.com	"Creates a single point of access for citizens to locate information on federal loan programs, and improves back-office loan functions" http://www.whitehouse.gov/omb/egov/gtoc/online_loan.htm
USA Services	"Develop and deploy government-wide citizen customer service using industry best practices [to] provide citizens with timely, consistent responses about government information and services via e-mail, telephone, Internet, and publications" http://www.whitehouse.gov/omb/egov/gtoc/usa_services.htm
IRS Free File http://www.irs.gov/app/freeFile/welcome.jsp	"Creates a single point of access to free on-line preparation and electronic tax filing services provided by Industry Partners to reduce burden and costs to taxpayers" http://www.whitehouse.gov/omb/egov/gtoc/irs_free.htm

Government to Business

E-Rulemaking
http://www.regulations.gov/

"Allows citizens to easily access and participate in the rulemaking process. Improves the access to, and quality of, the rulemaking process for individuals, businesses, and other government entities while streamlining and increasing the efficiency of internal agency processes"
http://www.whitehouse.gov/omb/egov/gtob/rulemaking.htm

Expanding Electronic Tax Products for Business

"Reduces the number of tax-related forms that businesses must file, provides timely and accurate tax information to businesses, increases the availability of electronic tax filing, and models simplified federal and state tax employment laws"
http://www.whitehouse.gov/omb/egov/gtob/tax_filing.htm

International Trade Process Streaming
http://www.export.gov/

"Makes it easy for Small and Medium Enterprises (SMEs) to obtain the information and documents needed to conduct business abroad"
http://www.whitehouse.gov/omb/egov/gtob/trade.htm

Federal Asset Sales
http://www.firstgov.gov/shopping/shopping.shtml

"Identify, recommend, and implement improvements for asset recovery and disposition, making it easier for agencies, businesses, and citizens to find and acquire/buy federal assets."
http://www.whitehouse.gov/omb/egov/gtob/asset.htm

Business Gateway
http://www.business.gov/

"Reduces the burden on businesses by making it easy to find, understand, and comply (including submitting forms) with relevant laws and regulations at all levels of government"
http://www.whitehouse.gov/omb/egov/gtob/compliance.htm

Consolidated Health Informatics

"Adopts a portfolio of existing health information interoperability standards (health vocabulary and messaging) enabling all agencies in the federal health enterprise to "speak the same language" based on common enterprise-wide business and information technology architectures"
http://www.whitehouse.gov/omb/egov/gtob/health_informatics.htm

Government to Government
Geospatial One-Stop
http://www.geo-one-stop.gov/; http://www.geodata.gov/

"Provides federal and state agencies with single point of access to map-related data enabling the sharing of existing data, and to identify potential partners for sharing the cost for future data purchases"
http://www.whitehouse.gov/omb/egov/gtog/geospatial.htm

Disaster Management
http://www.disasterhelp.gov/

"Provide citizens and members of the emergency management community with a unified point of access to disaster preparedness, mitigation, response, and recovery information from across federal, state, and local government .... Improve preparation, mitigation, response and recovery for all hazards through the development of interoperability standards that enable information sharing across the nation's emergency management community ...."
http://www.whitehouse.gov/omb/egov/gtog/disaster.htm

SAFECOM`
www.safecomprogram.gov

"Serves as the umbrella program within the Federal government to help local, tribal, State and Federal public safety agencies improve public safety response through more effective and efficient interoperable wireless communications."
http://www.whitehouse.gov/omb/egov/gtog/safecom.htm

E-Vital

"Establishes common electronic processes for Federal and State agencies to collect, process, analyze, verify and share vital statistics record information. Also promotes automating how deaths are registered with the states (Electronic Death Registration (EDR))."

http://www.whitehouse.gov/omb/egov/gtog/evital.htm

Grants.gov
http://www.grants.gov

"Creates a single portal for all federal grant customers to find, apply and ultimately manage grants on-line."

http://www.whitehouse.gov/omb/egov/gtog/egrants.htm

Internal Efficiency and Effectiveness

E-Training

"Create a premier e-training environment that supports development of the Federal workforce through simplified and one-stop access to high quality e-training products and services ..."

http://www.whitehouse.gov/omb/egov/internal/training.htm

Recruitment One-Stop

"Outsources delivery of USAJOBS Federal Employment Information System to provide state-of-the-art on-line recruitment services to job seekers including intuitive job searching, on-line resume submission, applicant data mining, and on-line feedback on status and eligibility."

http://www.whitehouse.gov/omb/egov/internal/recruit.htm

Enterprise HR Integration

"Streamlines and automates the electronic exchange of standardized HR data needed for creation of an official employee record across the Executive Branch. Provides comprehensive knowledge management workforce analysis, forecasting, and reporting across the Executive Branch for the strategic management of human capital."

http://www.whitehouse.gov/omb/egov/internal/enterprise.htm

E-Clearance

"Streamlines and improves the quality of the current security clearance process"
http://www.whitehouse.gov/omb/egov/internal/eclearance.htm

E-Payroll

"Consolidates 22 federal payroll systems to simplify and standardize federal human resources/payroll policies and procedures to better integrate payroll, human resources, and finance functions."
http://www.whitehouse.gov/omb/egov/internal/epayroll.htm

E-Travel

"Provides a government-wide web-based service that applies world-class travel management practices to consolidate federal travel, minimize cost and produce superior customer satisfaction. The E-Travel Service will be commercially hosted ..."
http://www.whitehouse.gov/omb/egov/internal/etravel.htm

Integrated Acquisition Environment
www.BPN.gov
www.ContractDirectory.gov
www.EPLS.gov
www.FedBizOpps.gov
www.FedTeDS.gov
www.FPDS-NG.com
www.PPIRS.gov
www.WDOL.gov

"Creates a secure business environment that will facilitate and support cost-effective acquisition of goods and services by agencies, while eliminating inefficiencies in the current acquisition environment."
http://www.whitehouse.gov/omb/egov/internal/acquisition.htm

E-Records Management

"Provides policy guidance to help agencies better manage their electronic records ... Four major issue areas: Correspondence management, Enterprise-wide electronic records management, Electronic Information Management Standards, Transferring permanent records to NARA."
http://www.whitehouse.gov/omb/egov/internal/records.htm

E-Authentication
E-Authentication

"Minimizes the burden on businesses, public and government when obtaining services on-line by providing a secure infrastructure for on-line transactions, eliminating the need for separate processes for the verification of identity and electronic signatures"
http://www.whitehouse.gov/omb/egov/ea/eauthentication.htm

Chapter 6

Uses of Internet and Mobile Technology in Health Systems: Organizational and Social Issues in a Comparative Context

James Katz, Ronald E. Rice and Sophia Acord

Introduction

The Internet provides an opportunity to the public and healthcare professionals to access medical and health information, improve the efficiency and effective, timely healthcare. The rise of mobile systems and the widespread adoption of the cell phone mean that mobile applications are an exciting and rapidly expanding domain for such applications. Many new offerings are being developed through digital appliances, computer terminals and mobile devices. Yet important empirical questions remain to be answered at every level about how effective these systems are, how people in various socio-demographic sectors actually use these systems, what their different effects are on those sectors, and whether their expense justifies the efforts involved. Important too are issues of how quickly and in what format they should be created, who should bear the costs of development and dissemination, how to ensure their dependability and sustainability, and what their immediate and longer term social implications might be.

In earlier work, we have highlighted structural problems with Internet healthcare applications (Katz & Rice, 2001). More recently, we have observed that (1) there has been substantial resource commitment, resulting in the creation of many useful centralized services (some commercial, some governmental); (2) however, despite their utility, perceived and actual inadequacies of these services have stimulated disparate groups to organize their own compensatory, decentralized and local networks of health information resources. These include Internet listservs, "blogs" (that is, online interactive diaries or

"Weblogs") and local telephone circles. Often these para-institutional sources are designed to respond to patient needs as perceived by patients and care-givers, and response to the way they formulate and articulate their health concerns. But just as questions must be raised about the bias, flexibility and ease-of-use of the centralized systems, questions must also be raised about the bias, accuracy and accountability of the new flexible ones. (4) As new communication technologies are developed, they are also explored for novel e-health uses. Here a recent example is radio-frequency identification (RFID) tags that allow medical paraphernalia, prescription drugs to be traced, monitored and controlled. Indeed, RFID tags are already being used to track and treat patients in hospital settings. These technologies can not only deliver services cost-effectively but will inevitably save lives. They may even prevent the outbreak of epidemics. However, some of these new technologies raise not only serious questions for students of privacy and ethics, but fear of them may lead to avoidance behavior on the part of sick people. This in turn could lead to potentially catastrophic consequences for both the individual and the general population.

Clearly for both centralized and decentralized Internet health resources, there are still many issues to be resolved at the cultural, user interface, institutional and system levels. Of particular concern for those seeking to develop practices at the community level, attention needs to be given to issues of (4) how new systems reconfigure physician/patient relationships and how they re-distribute the respective benefits and drawbacks to both sides of the relationship (Rice & Katz, 2006), (5) to what degree they open channels of communication to help patients and physicians come to terms with new technologies in mutually-beneficial ways and help them communicate about how to best use new technologies for medical ends, and (6) how to create socially sensitive e-health services that are also socially equitable in terms of accessibility (Katz, Rice & Acord, 2004). And of course we are concerned about (7) what role cultural and social aspects impede the deployment of new, cost-effective healthcare and medical services.

In our analysis, we perceived a dialectical process: each of the above analytical themes stems from an original problem perceived by one or more stakeholders, which in turn gives rise to specific forms of Internet use. From these there arise new contradictions, which suggest potential, often novel, solutions. So advancement in effective Internet and mobile healthcare systems require not only empirical data on the specific reception of each system by its users, but also a larger framework that understands the logic of self-interest and cultural moorings that affect each system in a larger setting. For instance, analysts need to consider ways in which people try to use the Internet and mobile to serve their own needs, and how, when doing so, they become enmeshed in, or seek to subvert, the inherent logic and vested interests of health institutions and information systems.

Assessment of these problems involves issues that go beyond good intentions and laudable aims (or other motives) of providers. They should include consideration of the inherent bureaucratic logic of one-way information flow. This logic governs traditional relations of healthcare organizations with their clients, even as these operations are extended into digital domains and widespread access. Further, as this process unfolds, it often includes within it a market logic of packaging information for return on investment, and at the very least some concern about program efficiency. These inherent logics sometimes lead to confusion on the user's part since the user may not understand the deeper motivations and rationales. Yet organizations, if they are to have a continued existence and reap the rewards of sunk costs and prior efforts, must also attend to their vested interests.

Moreover, the specific area of health is further complicated by considerations of (and conflicts among stakeholders over) value orientations toward the rules governing individual and group privacy, commercial free speech, access to markets, legal and medical regulations, and effectively informing, protecting, and enabling patients as well as physicians and other healthcare workers. Increasingly, too, there are concerns of legal accountability and human rights. Thus, responses to identified problems that do not address these limitations are unlikely to be viable over a longer term. This is in contrast to the ways some new technologies are deployed, which might be described as "create a new technology, deploy it in a few sites, and then ask people how much they like it." Ultimately, then, it seems reasonable that further research on e-health applications needs to take into account (and be predicated upon) the *needs* of all stakeholders involved in the medical sphere (e.g., patients, physicians, hospitals, policy makers, regulators, and payers).

Before delving into the themes, we should mention our perspective, which we dub "Syntopian" (Katz & Rice, 2002). The Syntopian perspective rejects both dystopian and utopian perspectives on the social uses and consequences of information and communication technology. Rather, it emphasizes how people, groups, organizations and societies adopt, use and reinvent (Johnson & Rice, 1987; Rice & Gattiker, 2000) technologies to make meaning for themselves relative to others. Hence, while possibilities are limited by the nature of the given technological tools, systems and their uses are (potentially) surprisingly flexible. Thus technology becomes shaped by individual needs and social contexts. The perspective also highlights that the internal logic of both formal organizational systems and personal social systems are fully applicable to the Internet (Castells, 2000).

In this chapter, we focus on delineating some recent developments in the use of the Internet and related technologies for healthcare. The emphasis is on the situation in the US, though we draw on other countries as well for comparative and descriptive purposes. We try to highlight the macro social issues that could be of interest to policymakers and suggest possibilities that could merit consideration by system designers or healthcare service professionals.

Internet Technology and E-health Resources

E-health resources have wide appeal in the US; quality, utility sometimes problematic

Clearly e-health is something that has great appeal to Internet users throughout the world, especially in North America. Numerous surveys have shown that in the US in particular there is heavy use among consumers and especially physicians (Katz, Rice & Acord, 2004). Many institutions have devoted vast resources to putting medical information online (Boston Consulting Group, 2003). In the US, this includes PubMed and Medline via the National Library of Medicine, which are generally accessible online from Internet-connected computers, regardless, generally speaking, of where around the globe they might be located. These resources are often free, which, though partly understandable, is also in many ways astonishing. (Portugal, incidentally, has committed to putting large amounts of information in

Portuguese on line and making it readily accessible to its citizens. As a case in point, to provide better access to governmental data, Portugal reportedly offers free public access in some parish churches—"eGovernment in Europe," 2004).

However, websites such as the NHS library or MDConsult.com, which aim to provide accurate and secure information to health-seekers, suffer from readability problems (Ebenezer, 2003) and are rarely designed for patients (Tench et al., 1998). Moreover, at least in the US and Canadian contexts, patients are generally unaware of these high-quality data sources (Sigouin & Jadad, 2002), so they are often not places to which consumers are likely to turn, at least in the first part of their attempts to seek information. Hence, health seekers tend to use general search engines, such as Google (Boston Consulting Group, 2001, 2003). However, the more centralized and commercial websites found in this manner generally lack customer interaction features. Instead they provide only unidirectional information (Cudmore & Bobrowski, 2003). For example, fewer than one out of three pharmaceutical company websites offer a way to respond online to consumer requests. Fewer than half of health-supply websites respond to online requests or questions (Pharmaceutical, 2003). Yet government health sites are even less interactive (Rice, Peterson & Christine, 2002). Further, these more general health sites may not provide the specific, contextual information appropriate to the user's needs, and may have both identifiable and hidden commercial and other biases.

Personal websites have role

Personal, rather than commercial, educational or government, health websites play a significant role in the construction of medical knowledge online, and represent the growth of interest in 'local' knowledge. In a search for rheumatoid arthritis, 34% of relevant sites were posted by an individual, more than those posted by a non-profit organization, and over 6 times more than those posted by an educational institution (Suarez-Almazor et al., 2001). Yet, very little research has been done on the ways in which health-seekers use this information source, as its existence is often overshadowed by online support groups. It is likely that "blogs," or web logs (which are essentially on-line diaries with an interactive component that encourages others to leave comments), will be playing a growing and complementary role in these processes.

Physician websites becoming an important resource

In the US, it appears that about one-third of physicians have a Web site, of whose development obstetrics/gynaecology and internal medicine specialists have been the most prevalent (AMA, 2002). Howitt et al. (2002) studied UK websites and found that, apart from e-mail sent to the practice, possibilities for electronic communication were low, as was the general quality of information. Sanchez (2002) notes that the vast majority of physician websites focus on practice enhancement tactics, rather than specific patient service. In contrast to the supply side of the healthcare equation, Norum et al. (2003) report that cancer patients want to see more information on hospital websites that is directly related to the delivery of healthcare. For example, these include waiting time before a physician is available, treatment services, and office location information (Pastore, 2001). Services like WebMD are providing physicians with an array of electronic support, including websites and secure email. Patients have reported that these sites are cumbersome, in part due to the concerns about liability and the assumption of responsibility.

Desire for useful online information from physicians is also typical of Spain, apparently, even though there is overall less Internet health-seeking and more traditional ties to local providers. This desire is reflected in a study of Catalonian patients. Panés et al. (2002) found that 84% of Internet health-seeking patients (which represented 44% of all patients) suffering from irritable bowel syndrome wanted a local website from their own clinic; 65% were willing to pay for this service. It seems that patient demand continues to exceed physician supply of useful information both in the US and Spain.

Health kiosks: Crossing a digital divide?

Health kiosks are uncommon in the US and tend to be situated in clinic waiting rooms (indeed the proportion seems to be declining for reasons of inutility and cost). For example, Sciamanna et al. (2004) experimented with a kiosk giving tailored advice on fitness and smoking. Although fewer than one/third of the participants had ever used the Internet to seek health information, over 80% found the kiosk easy to use. However, less than half of the doctors looked at the report provided by the kiosk or discussed it with the patient. Goldschmidt and

Goodrich (2004) placed bilingual kiosks in clinic waiting rooms and noted that 68% of people said they found all the information they were looking for, and that flu shots increased by 24% following the installation. In contrast to the US (which seems to use kiosks to reduce information demand on the physician), other countries are experimenting with health kiosks containing pre-sorted information, to reach communities which may not have Internet access or know-how. Jones et al. (2001) found that among an elderly Spanish population without Internet access, 25% were interested in the kiosk idea. While in terms of professional opinions about their utility, kiosks do not rate high, they may yet be a significant way to disseminate medical information to socially remote communities or in specific delivery locales.

Physician education resources

There is great potential for the Internet to help educate and update physicians. For instance, Casebeer et al. (2003) details the positive impact that a Web-based physician tutorial on preventative care (in these specific case, sexually transmitted diseases) had on the knowledge of the experiment group versus the control group.

Policy Concerns of Centralized Applications

Due to the decentralized, unregulated nature of the web, and even the contested nature of what constitutes valid and quality medical information, the accuracy and usability of online information are extremely pressing policy problems (Berland et al., 2001; Kunst et al., 2002; Rice, 2001; Zeng et al., 2004). As just one example, websites that offer so-called alternative medical treatments have been described as containing dangerously inadequate or misleading information (Ernst & Schmidt, 2002; Hainer et al., 2000; Molassiotis & Xu, 2004). Organizations such as HON (Health on the Net) have devised guidelines to rate the quality of e-health information, and some current websites carry the HON seal of approval (Wilson, 2002). However, it is not clear really to what degree health-seekers use general search engines because they are not familiar with approved medical resources, or because they are specifically looking for alternative treatment ideas. As there is no way to prevent the dissemination of hazardous information, the best use of resources seems to be to develop sanctioned general web health portals and raise public awareness about ways to look for reliable health information, especially by the patients' physicians. The recent success of WebMD Health (after staggering losses in 2001) demonstrates the fruits of such policies.

In addition, it does seem as if health-seekers realize the dangers of bad health information online and want the development of local-medical sources such as physician websites. In responding to this need, the biggest factors are ensuring readability, privacy, and publicity in accurate medical sources, as well as informing patients of clinical studies for new treatments. As Seidman, Steinwachs and Rubin (2003) point out, there still needs to be developed a robust tool, accessible to health-seekers, to identify quality information on the Internet.

Yet these concerns should not blind us to the enormously important role online health information is already playing. For instance, Wagner et al. (2004) report that patients who suffer chronic diseases (in this case diabetes) find that the information gained through online channels help them manage their situation. Moreover, there is another way in which quality interacts with the Internet, and this is in terms of rating the quality of physicians and healthcare providers (especially hospitals and insurers). Indeed, this is one area in which we could predict a revolution that will benefit the public even at the cost of some individual or institutional reputations.

Apart from the quality or design of Internet health applications, there are still major differences in exposure and access. It is not always clear whether the fault or limitation inheres in the application or in the target population. But in the USA, at least, there are consistent "digital divides" in access to healthcare information. These include socioeconomic status, gender, race (Houston & Allison, 2002), health status, language (Berland et al., 2001, found Spanish-language sites suffered from even worse quality issues), age (Meischke et al., 2005)[1] and physical disabilities such as elderly immobility (Katz & Aspden, 2001) or visual impairment (Davis, 2002). Most importantly, much data support claims that higher education levels corresponds with Internet use (Giménéz-Perez et al., 2002; Licciardone et al., 2001;

---

[1] In fact, in a recent study in Washington State, only 7% of seniors who suffered heart attacks *and* had Internet access ever looked for information on their conditions online (Meischke et al., 2005).

Pandey et al., 2003). Kakai et al. (2003) found that people of higher education levels prefer to get their health information through seemingly objective, scientific, and updated forms, such as the Internet, while those of lower educational levels prefer to have their information come from mass media and other people because they say they like the human approach. Perhaps one way to increase delivery to the "have-nots" may be to develop health kiosks in ways that appeal to the elderly and non-native language speakers; of course attention to location and usability would be paramount, as well as situated teaching campaigns to train local populations in their use.

Cultural factors are also important in understanding the policy implications of various e-health applications (Yom, 1996). Kakai et al. (2003) found differences in preferred information sources along ethnic lines, as Caucasian patients preferred objective, scientific, and updated information obtained through medical journals, research institutions, and telephone and Internet sources, while Japanese patients preferred media and commercial sources such as TV, magazines, books, and other written sources. Non-Japanese Asians and Pacific Islanders tended to favor information sources marked by person-to-person communication, such as physicians, social groups, and other cancer patients. In the US, black women had a 60% lower likelihood of using computer-based resources than did white women (Nicholson et al., 2003), and non-white people are less likely to use the Internet to look up health information for breast cancer (Fogel et al., 2002). Social and cultural factors of populations and communities hence appear to be important considerations when developing targeted e-health applications (Morahan-Martin, 2004).

Thus, despite the widespread development of Internet e-health applications, these resources do not seem to be accessible to, or at least accessed by, large portions of US society. Nor do they often seem recognized as a source for medical knowledge in communities and cultures that are already much more familiar with face-to-face physician interaction. The challenge remains then to create health information systems accessible in ways that fit lifestyles and choices of underserved groups, motivate healthcare providers to provide personal encouragement for and information about using online resources, and encourage these groups to develop knowledge and routes of accessibility to e-health websites.

Internet Technology—Multidirectional

E-health applications also should not stop at merely providing uni-directional information, although this is important. Keeping in mind the way most non-students learn, it is important to develop on-line possibilities for multi-directional interaction between health-seekers and appropriately tailored information.

Physician webcams

Bamford et al. (2003) implemented a country-wide network of physician webcams in the UK through the implementation of double-headed microscopes in 35 histopathology departments across the UK. A year after installation, they found that 71% of the physicians had not even used the networking software. All of those physicians who had used it found it effective for diagnosis and exchanging opinions. Bamford et al. conclude that the project did not achieve its aims to due excessive workloads preventing physician training, IT staff reluctance to render assistance, but above all, user attitudes.

Email

Many physicians do not use email because they are not compensated for the time involved to check, assess, and respond (Anderson et al., 2003; Harris Interactive, 2001; Rice & Katz, 2006); and there are liability and confidentiality issues that preclude using email. In contrast, American healthcare consumers overwhelmingly say they would often like to be able to contact their physicians by email rather than through office visits (CyberAtlas, 2002; Norum et al., 2003). Patients would like to email for prescription refills, non-urgent consultations, and to receive test results (Couchman, Forjuoh & Rascoe, 2001). However, it is noteworthy that 75% of patient emails to physicians included requests for medication/treatment information or actions, or specific diseases/symptoms (Sittig, 2003). Hassol et al. (2004) found that most patients preferred email communication and face-to-face communication with their physicians (depending on the matter), while US physicians preferred telephone to email communication. Of those 20-30% of physicians who do use email or electronic communication, many see improved patient satisfaction and some note improved efficiency and care (Harris Interactive, 2001).

In this context, it is unsurprising that researchers have attempted to develop software that would identify terms in patients' emails that could be then linked to medical information to be emailed back to the patients without the need for a physician response (Brennan & Aronson, 2003). This system may be efficient, but it is also likely to raise some serious concerns in the minds of the patients; it may be that patients want email because they seek a *human* response, which may be paradoxically more difficult through traditional physician-patient channels.

Sometimes it is suggested that "out-sourcing" of medical information provisioning could help the developed countries as well as developing ones. This idea is already widespread in many technical and consumer support fields, most notably in computer user problem resolution. However, there appears to be scant interest on the part of healthcare consumers for such services at this point. For instance, Hassol et al. (2004) evaluated interest in various ways in which offshore physicians could be contacted by patients. They found mild interest in telephone contact methods among Americans, but no interest whatsoever in an email service.

Health information management systems

Mendelson and Salinsky (1997) note that the early failure of many Community Health Management Information Systems (CHMIS) (similar to CHINS, or community health information networks) was due to the lack of private sector support for integrated, state-wide systems. In addition, the general public distrust of state-sponsored health care systems combined with the proprietary interests of the players involved served to eliminate them in the majority of states (Eder & Wise, 2001; Katz & Aspden, 2001). However, in states where health databases exist, such as Wisconsin Health Information Networks, the direct access to clinical and administrative data saved up to $68,000 a year for private practices and up to $1 million for hospitals (Mendelson & Salinsky, 1997).

Using electronic medical records in hospital databases was demonstrated to help ensure consistent and correct coding by physicians, as well as context-sensitive treatment in Germany, by Muller et al. (2003). Patient-accessible health records have been found to be a valuable step forward, with satisfaction, rates in the 65-85% range (Hassol et al., 2004; Joustra-Enquist & Eklund, 2004; Wang et al., 2004).[2] Yet there is both resistance to them by staff due to local cultural practices and larger concerns about privacy and security. Radio-frequency identification (RFID) systems are expected to blend database management and mobile tracking together in extremely fruitful ways, although problems of cost and integration remain to be solved before they can see widespread deployment.

Outside of the US, the EU has implemented a general e-health strategy for the years to come,[3] and Tachinardi (1998) describes an ongoing project in Brazil to build a network of e-health applications including a unified health record for the exchange of patient data, and a virtual hospital of health information and medical journals for physicians and lay patients..

Discussion groups

Online discussion groups respond to many of the needs unfulfilled by the centralized information providers. In some cases, these groups extract information from professional journals (Wikgren, 2001) and recreate it in a way to make it more applicable and understandable among the users. Many discussion groups include physicians (Katz & Aspden, 2001). Practically all conditions and situations have groups,

---

[2] Wang et al. (2004) developed a web-based personal health record for patients to collect and manage their health information (medical history, past surgeries, medications, and allergies), to request self-referrals, and to store a record of their consultations. The PHR also includes a messaging system that can be structured into the workflow of referral management as well as allowing more general communications. A preliminary study was conducted with 61 patients. Thirty-two patients completed a survey in which 85% of respondents were satisfied with the usability and 94% were satisfied with the overall online referral process. Joustra-Enquist and Eklund (2004) report on SUSTAINS, a web-based health care account in which the patient can login (with a login sent to their mobile phone) and review medical results and prescriptions and information, and exchange written information with physicians; participants reported that it is beneficial for both parties. According to Hassol et al. (2004), 65-85% of Americans in an experiment with electronic health records reported them easy to use, and that they understood all the information; a small minority reported confidentiality concerns.

[3] By the end of 2005, each member state should have a national roadmap for e-health, focusing on e-health symptoms and electronic records, and there will be an EU public health portal. By the end of 2006, member states should have a common approach to patient identifiers and identity-management, as well as interoperability standards for health data message and electronic health records. By 2008, health information networks should be commonplace (European Commission, 2004).

including those that deal with chronic conditions or embarrassing conditions (Millard & Fintak, 2002) and rare diseases (Patsos, 2001). Participants also report across-the-board benefits for themselves (Pew, 2000; Pew 2002) and for their loved ones (Till, 2003). They especially seem to like the fact that use offers empathy (Preece & Ghozati, 2001), personal empowerment (Sharf, 1997), and emotional support (Winzelberg et al., 2003). In fact, many report that symptoms seem reduced or alleviated by membership (Lorig et al., 2002; McKay et al., 2001; Winzelberg et al., 2003). This is not surprising in part because if people did not perceive benefits, they would not be using the systems. The social-psychological and emotional benefits are the qualities that are often lacking in treatments provided by physicians and institutions. Beyond the perception of psychological and emotional benefits, however, perceptions of actual health changes and improvements may be highly inaccurate and may even lead users to engage in treatment practices that are harmful.

E-commerce and online bidding

MedicineOnline.com offers an auction service in which patients can elicit physician bids for surgeries (Baur et al., 2001). It is unclear who uses this service, however, and what impact it has. At the same time, online "retail" e-commerce is likely to grow quickly, in part because of the desire to reduce costs and, in many societies including the US, to open channels of competition. This is likely to affect the cost of, and hence demand for, many elective procedures. Cosmetic surgery and whole-body magnetic resonance imaging (MRIs) are likely to be among those that are going to be competitively marketed online. Certainly there is already much promotion among dentists for both routine and cosmetic procedures through traditional distribution channels, and it is likely that the Internet will also become an important method of advertising for many common procedures and for attracting patients to under-utilized hospitals and treatment centers.

Web-Based interventions

The US has experimented with web-based health interventions, while other countries tend to focus on mobile phone text-based interventions (Curioso, 2006). For the US, one web-based diabetes care management system saw an improvement in testing and check-up regularity among its users (Meigs et al., 2003). Overall, Wantland et al. (2004) found that web-based interventions were much more likely to achieve noticeable results than non web-based interventions in behavioral studies. These included areas of increased exercise time, knowledge of nutritional status and knowledge of treatments. However, in the UK, Eminovic et al. (2004) tested a web-based triage service with a nurse and found on average that it took twice as long to diagnose and treat complaints as with the NHS direct hotline. This study suggests the importance of interpersonal and cultural aspect in developing e-health applications.

Mobile Communication Technology: Bi-directional and Multidirectional

Telephone

The telephone can function as the basis for local support networks, often designed to harmonize with local culture. (Indeed it has been an important component in healthcare for more than a century!) In the US, this may be seen in the case of the Native American Cancer Survivors' Support Network (Burhansstipanov et al., 2001). This example is actually a cultural adaptation, based on dissatisfaction with tribal clinics. There was no use of local tribal authorities, in order to prevent the loss of confidentiality characteristic of small communities. Instead, survivors from other communities provided support via telephone. A similar project, the Aldre Vast Information Centre, took place in western Sweden (Hanson et al., 2002). In response to the requests of older people and their families, the project established telephone, videophone, and Internet support to older citizens and their families. The project had positive results in empowering these people to make better health care choices. As an alternative to face-to-face clinic-based behavioural counselling, Glasgow et al. (2004) describe how interactive voice-response telephone calls can generate comparable results.

The telephone is relied upon in Iberian countries in some ways like the Internet is in the US. A Spanish study of a call centre for oncology patients reports a decline in emergency hospital visits (42% to 24%), and an overall short call length (3-5 minutes) (Ferrer-Roca et al.,

2002). This study demonstrates that telephone networks can be valuable for local patient support networks, as well as acting as effective paths to medical care. And, the short overall call time may indicate that such multidirectional networks will not take the toll on a physician's time that they fear. Likewise, a study of one Spanish telephone-intervention (Marquez Contreras et al., 2004a), found that telephone interventions increase treatment compliance as well as overall health.

Mobile phone

While Americans are relatively heavy seekers of Internet health information, there are relatively few mobile phone health applications in the US. The reverse is the situation in many other developed and developing countries (Curioso, 2006). Studies from Spain provide an illuminating contrast in usage patterns. Giménez-Pérez (2002) found that although only 36.5% of patients were regular Internet users, 76.6% of the patients owned a mobile phone, and 96% of those used it more than once a week. As a result, health applications involving mobile phones in Spain are more effective. Marquez Contreras et al. (2004b) conducted a controlled group study with hypertension patients; members of the intervention group were sent reminder text messages to their mobiles 2 days a week. Hypertension was significantly lower (51.5%) in the control group compared to the intervention group (64.7%). In another Spanish study, Vilella et al. (2004) found that text messages were an effective way to remind patients of immunization schedules prior to travelling abroad. Likewise, Bielli et al. (2004) report on an Italian study which analyzed the use of mobile phones for patients' health reporting. It was successful for 58% of patients; those who did not use it were older, less educated, and less familiar with new communications technology (mobile phone calls, mobile phone SMS, Internet, and email).

Similarly, trials in Asia report significant success with mobile phone health applications. Kubota et al. (2004) discuss a mobile application in which text messaging was used to send information about body weight reduction to study participants. Their study claims successful weight loss in 32% of the cases. Tang et al. (2004) report on a Hong Kong study that created a system for medical digital picture/scan information distribution and archiving using the physician's mobile phone as the base. A central server handled the pre-sorting and pro-cessing of images. A Philippine study by Tolentino et al. (2004) describes a mobile phone based system for event reporting to develop an anaesthesia surveillance system.

Zhang et al. (2004) attribute much credit to mobile phone networks in the widespread success of public education during the SARS epidemic in China. Press reports at the time of the SARS epidemic described how public health workers in Hong Kong who were combating SARS would receive training and operational orders via SMS (short message service). The general public used SMS to alert others about which apartment buildings had infected residents (and hence should be avoided). At the same time, in the People's Republic of China, some people who were alerting others via SMS about SARS risks in their area were arrested by police and charged with spreading socially destructive rumors. The SARS example shows how mobile applications can be important in major health emergencies, but also shows how mobile communication can be a source of concern for officials seeking to control public behavior and movement of information.

Quite tellingly, research in Asia suggests strongly that there are substantial benefits available via mobile health applications for the elderly (once they have undergone the necessary training, of course). Ogawa et al. (2003) report on the success of using mobile phones with a pen-type entry sensor to provide and assess home care needs for elderly patients. Miyauchi et al. (2003) used mobile phones attached to sensors in order to inform medical services if elderly patients fall and are immobile, or are otherwise immobile, for set periods of time. Yoshiyama et al. (2004) also used mobile phones with digital photograph technology to effectively allow elder home care patients to communicate with their physicians.

Certainly there are some US applications employing mobile phone interventions. Several studies have been devoted to health improvement and self-management strategies as opposed to the management of specific chronic illness. For instance a study by Obermayer et al. (2004) used mobile phone text messages to deliver smoking-cessation intervention to college students, with a positive result. A similar study by Lazev et al. (2004) reports on the success in using mobile phone text to reach a low-income HIV-positive population in a smoking cessation program. The participants would not otherwise have land phones or transportation to a clinic, so the mobile allowed them to get real-time counselling in life situations. Durso et al. (2004) also assessed how mobile phones could be used to communicate with older patients diagnosed with diabetes.

Morrissey (2004) blames concerns of electromagnetic interference with medical equipment for the poor availability of mobile phone networks in hospitals, claiming that alleviation of these concerns can lead the development of helpful physician and staff mobile communication. Klein and Djaiani (2003) note that this interference occurs only in close proximity to hospital equipment, and should not prevent the use of mobile phones in patient care areas and away from sensitive equipment, where access to and use of mobiles would encourage compliance with hospital policies.

Mobiles to fight AIDS and malaria in developing countries

It is worth including in our analysis a brief mention of the way mobile technology is being used to control malaria and AIDS. In the case of AIDS, free text messaging services are available in Kenya, where users can send text questions and receive free answers. As well, the free service sends out daily tips on how to prevent infection and deal with the disease's consequences. This service is provided by NGO One World (BBC, 2004). In Mali, local mobile company Ikatel sends free text messages with PSI-created health slogans twice a month to each of the company's 350,000 clients, and also prints AIDS and malaria prevention slogans on at least one million of the pre-paid phone cards most used by low-income customers. Sample messages include: "Protect your family against malaria—use an insecticide-treated mosquito net" (Plus News, 2004).

Certainly, given the mobile's success in social and business settings, there can be great expectations for the usefulness of the technology in fighting disease, especially in poor countries. These mobile health applications are interesting examples of how health information can be inserted directly into the daily lives of targeted populations, which contrasts with more traditional systems that are physically and psychologically remote from the active health-seeking population.

Mobiles healthcare databases highly useful in developing countries

In Rwanda, mobiles are used for connecting remote hospitals with centralized laboratories and supply houses. This saves enormous amounts of time and greatly increases efficiency. This initiative is based at the Earth Institute of Columbia University in New York City. Another mobile database operation may be seen in India. There, a rural healthcare project utilizing mobile phones won the UN's 2003 World Summit Award for e-Health. It triangulates mobile phones carried by field representatives to interconnect patient data, computers used by doctors in clinics, and a central database. Thus, distance-diagnosis is possible, saving on transportation costs, and other obstacles to health care (Simha, 2003).

Advanced mobile videophone and multi-media messaging

Chu and Ganz (2004) describe an ingenuous mobile medical application which uses commercial 3G wireless cellular data service to transmit a trauma patient's video, images, and electrocardiogram signals to a trauma specialist when the patient is in a remote location. Similarly, Weiner et al. (2003) used videoconferencing in nursing homes for unscheduled, night-time consultations. This study found that mobile multimedia applications were especially effective in dealing with mental health patients.

Mobile telemedicine

Telemedicine often is the use of satellite mobile communications technology to transfer information from patient to physician without the need for face-to-face interaction (Feliciani, 2003). Mobile telemedicine systems are used to convey images and information from location to location, such as from a remote clinic or an ambulance to a trauma centre (Heaton, 2006; Tahoka et al., 2003). Studies of systems include a German remote heart monitoring system, in which cardiac patients have their heart signal monitored and transferred to their mobile phone, and from there transmitted to their physician. Another one was a system in Brazil that allows remote physicians to confer via desktop computers with metropolitan cardiologists, and TelCardio Mobile, which allows important data and test results to be transferred to physicians via mobile phones and PDAs. As a result, consultation and diagnosis can occur independently of a local infrastructure. There are many other telemedicine developments in India, the UK, and the EU, which allow the remote monitoring of patients by physicians in a hospital, via information transmitted over a mobile phone (Tahoka et al., 2003).

Important rationales for telemedicine are efficiency and effectiveness: physicians can do more with their time, and specialists can be remotely accessed by general clinics in low-income and sparsely-populated locations. Exemplifying the former, Holleran et al. (2003) describe the benefits of providing physicians with a wireless handheld device that is Web-enabled. The device can receive patient information anywhere, thus allowing physicians to respond in both a timely and an informed manner. A comparable approach has been developed by Chen et al. (2003). Although based in New York, their HealthNet system is used to provide better health care to Brazil's low-income northeast population. Examples of applications include fetal care and cardiology using telediagnosis and rendering second opinions about needed medical procedures (Barbosa et al., 2003).

Policy Implications of Internet and Mobile Health Technology

Ultimately, under most conditions it seems that healthcare applications have to resonate with a culture/society's dominant form of technology use. If either the provider or the patient side of the equation is resistant, difficulties will ensue. While the Internet has been characterized as an ideal way to disseminate information both locally and globally, for a variety of reasons discussed above, it has not succeeded in connecting up large portions of the population. Rather, telephone and mobile telephone health applications are relatively more popular in European and Asian countries; this is also reflected in the extraordinarily rapid spread of the mobile phone, which makes the heretofore seemingly rapid spread of the Internet seem slow by comparison.

Fahey (2003) warns that relying on cell phones to send text messages will lead to further inequality in health care along socioeconomic divides. However, other studies, such as Lavez et al. (2004), demonstrate the opposite. In fact, the very portability of mobile phones and PDAs, enhanced by further device-to-device wireless technologies, actually make them versatile candidates to provide health care to remote areas, elderly individuals, transient workers, and individuals with disabilities (Curioso, 2006). (Sorri et al., 2003 developed a digital induction loop to improve the use of cell phones by the hearing impaired by means of reducing incompatibility with hearing aids.)

Concerning cross-cultural comparisons, it seems that most US telemedical developments are aimed at supporting physicians (such as mobile PDA-devices), while most non-US applications seem to be aimed at supporting patients (e.g., two-way health reporting through mobile phones).

To sum up, it seems that the original predictions about the problems of centralized systems continue to be borne out. Certainly unidirectional health applications continue to be developed, and succeed to some extent. But in trials and experiments, patients continue to ask for two-way communication and localized sensitivity. The abundance of mobile phone health applications in non-US countries, although their development came later than the original US health websites, seems to demonstrate the important role that the cultural-historical use of technology has on the acceptance of e-health devices. Above all, patients in remote areas or lower-income communities, as well as the elderly, generally find *interactional* e-health applications far more desirable than centralized sources. This differential is likely due to the cultural emphasis in these groups on non-mechanistic, face-to-face interaction. On the other hand, the active, independent, and non-confrontational health-seeking culture in the US lends itself well towards Web-based applications. In this regard, it will be interesting to track e-health developments as US mobile phone usage and EU Internet usage continue their respective rise. Yet, no matter the technology (Web or mobile phone), decentralized and interactional e-health applications seem to be taking an ever more prominent role in healthcare. Many programs that use them as their base also seem to be enjoying relative success. Presumably further development of these resources will add value to, and stand alongside of, the still-developing older formats of centralized, unidirectional healthcare information resources.

Bibliography

American Medical Association (AMA). (2002, July 17). "Physicians' use of Internet steadily rising." Retrieved July 16, 2003, from http://www.amaassn.org/ama/pub/print/article/1616-6473.html.

Anderson, J. G., Rainey, M. R., & Eysenbach, G. (2003). "The impact of cyberhealthcare on the physician-patient relationship." *Journal of Medical Systems, 27*(1): 67-84.

Bamford, W. M., Rogers, N., Kasssam, M., Rashbass, J., & Furness, P. N. (2003). "The development and evaluation of the UK national telepathology network." *Histopathology, 42*(2): 110.

Barbosa, A. K., de A Novaes, M. & de Vasconcelos, A. M. (2003). "A web application to support telemedicine services in Brazil." *AMIA Annual Symposium Proceedings 2003*: 56-60.

Baur, C., Deering, M. J., & Hsu, L. (2001). "Ehealth: Issues and approaches." In R. E. Rice & J. E. Katz (Eds.), *The Internet and Health Communication.* Thousand Oaks, CA: Sage. Pp. 355-383.

BBC. (2004). "Texts aim to fight Aids in Kenya." December 1, 2004 at 9:56 AM. Retrieved February 5, 2004 from http://news.bbc.co.uk/2/hi/technology/4054475.stm.

Berland, G. K., Elliott, M. N., Morales, L. S., Algazy, J. I., Kravitz, R. L., Broder, M. S., Kanouse, D. E., Munoz, J. A., Puyol, J. A., Lara, M., Watkins, K. E., Yang, H. & McGlynn, E. A. (2001). "Health information on the Internet: Accessibility, quality, and readability in English and Spanish." *Journal of the American Medical Association, 285*: 2612-2621.

Bielli, E., Carminati, F., La Capra, S., Lina, M., Brunelli, C. & Tamburini, M. (2004). "A wireless health outcomes monitoring system (WHOMS): Development and field testing with cancer patients using mobile phones." *BMC Medical Informatics and Decision Making, 4*(1): 7.

Boston Consulting Group (BCG). (2001, April). "Vital signs update: The e-health patient paradox." Retrieved July 30, 2003, from http://www.bcg.com/publications/publications_splash.jsp.

Boston Consulting Group (BCG). (2003). "Vital signs: E-health in the United States." Retrieved July 30, 2003, from http://www.bcg.com/publications/publications_splash.jsp.

Brennan, P. F. & Aronson, A. R. (2003). "Towards linking patients and clinical information: Detecting UMLS concepts in e-mail." *Journal of Biomedical Informatics, 36*(4-5): 334-341.

Burhansstipanov, L., Gilbert, A., Lamarca, K. & Krebs, L. U. (2001). "An innovative path to improving cancer care in Indian country." *Public Health Reports, 116*: 424-433.

Casebeer, L. L., Strasser, S. M., Spettell, C. M., Wall, T. C., Weissman, N., Ray, M. N. & Allison, J. J. (2003). "Designing tailored Web-based instruction to improve practicing physicians' preventive practices." *Journal of Medical Internet Research, 5*(3): e20.

Castells, M. (2000). *End of Millennium*, 2nd ed. Oxford: Blackwell.

Chen, E. S., Hripcsak, G., Patel, V. L., Sengupta, S., Gallagher, R. J. & Cimino, J. J. (2003). "Automated identification of shortcuts to patient data for a wireless handheld clinical information system." *AMIA Annual Proceedings 2003*: 809.

Chu, Y. & Ganz, A. (2004). "A mobile teletrauma system using 3G networks." *IEEE Transactions on Information Technology in Biomedicine, 8*(4): 456.

"City selects Doc@Home for remote monitoring trial." (2003, June 9). [Online]. Retrieved January 24, 2005, from http://www.e-health-insider.com/news/item.cfm?ID=444.

Couchman, G., Forjuoh, S. & Rascoe, T. (2001). "E-mail communications in family practice: What do patients expect?" *Journal of Family Practice, 59*(5): 414-418.

Cudmore, B. A., & Bobrowski, P. E. (2003). "Working the Web." *Marketing Health Services, 23*(3): 37.

Curioso, W. (2006). "New technologies and public health in developing countries: The cell PREVEN project." In M. Murero & R. E. Rice (Eds.), *The Internet and Health Care: Theory, Research and Practice*. Mahwah, NJ: LEA, in press.

CyberAtlas. (2002, April 12). "Americans want online access to doctors: A report from Harris Interactive." *NUA Internet* Surveys. Retrieved July 15, 2003, from http://cyberatlas.Internet.com/markets/healthcare/article/0,,10101_1008331,00.html.

Davis, J. J. (2002). "Disenfranchising the disabled: The inaccessibility of Internet-based health information." *Journal of Health Communication*, 7(4): 355-367.

Durso, S. C., Wendel, I., Letzt, A. M., Lefkowitz, J., Kaseman, D. F. & Seifert, R. F. (2004). "Older adults using cellular telephones for diabetes management: A pilot study." *Medsurg Nursing*, 12(5): 313

Ebenezer, C. (2003). "Usability evaluation of an NHS library website." *Health Libraries Review*, 20(3): 134.

Eder, L. B. & Wise, D. E. (2001). "Web-enabled hospitals in the United States: Influences on adoption processes." In R. E. Rice & J. E. Katz (Eds.), *The Internet and Health Communication*. Thousand Oaks, CA: Sage. Pp. 309-328.

"eGovernment in Europe: The State of Affairs." (2004). *International Journal of Communications Law and Policy*. Issue 8, winter. Retrieved February 7, 2005 from http://www.ijclp.org/8_2004/pdf/leitner-paper-ijclp-page.pdf.

eESC/TB11 Health. (2005). "Open smart card infrastructure for Europe." (vol. 2). Retrieved January 25, 2005, from http://www.eeurope-smartcards.org/Download/01-4.pdf.

Eminovic, N., Wyatt, J. C., Tarpey, A. M., Murray, G. & Ingrams, G. J. (2004). "First evaluation of the NHS direct online clinical enquiry service: A nurse-led web chat triage service for the public." *Journal of Medical Internet Research*, 6(2): e17.

Ernst, E. & Schmidt, K. (2002). "'Alternative' cancer cures via the Internet?" *British Journal of Cancer*, 87(5): 479-480.

"European Commission presents e-health action plan." (2004, May 5). Retrieved January 26, 2005, from http://europa.eu.int/idabc/en/document/2524.

Fahey, D. (2003). "Reminding patients by text message: Text reminders could lead to increased health inequalities." *British Medical Journal*, *327*(7414): 564.

Feliciani F. (2003). "Medical care from space: Telemedicine." *European Space Agency (ESA) Bulletin*, *114*: 54-9.

Ferrer-Roca, O. & Subirana, R. (2002). "A four-year study of telephone support for oncology patients using a non-supervised call centre." *Journal of Telemedicine and Telecare*, *8*(6): 331.

Fogel, J., Albert, S. M., Schnabel, F., Ditkoff, B. A., & Neugut, A. I. (2002). "Use of the Internet by women with breast cancer." *Journal of Medical Internet Research*, *4*(2): e9.

Giménéz-Perez, G., Gallach, M., Acera, E., Prieto, A., Carro, O., Ortega, E., Gonzalez-Clemente, J. M., & Mauricio, D. (2002). "Evaluation of accessibility and use of new communication technologies in patients with type 1 diabetes mellitus." *Journal of Medical Internet Research*, *4*(3): e16.

Glasgow, R. E., Bull, S. S., Piette, J. D. & Steiner, J. F. (2004). "Interactive behavior change technology: A partial solution to the competing demands of primary care." *American Journal of Preventative Medicine*, *27*(2 Suppl): 80-87.

Goldschmidt, L. & Goodrich, G. L. (2004). "Development and evaluation of a point-of-care interactive patient education kiosk." *Journal of Telemedicine and Telecare*, *10*(Suppl 1): 30-32.

Hainer, M. I., Tsai, N., Komura, S. T., & Chiu, C. L. (2000). "Fatal hepatorenal failure associated with hydrazine sulfate." *Annals of Internal Medicine*, *133*(11): 877-880.

Hanson, E., Andersson, B. A., Magnusson, L., Lidskog, R., & Holm, K. (2002). "Information centre: Responding to needs of older people and carers." *British Journal of Nursing*, *11*(14): 935.

Harris Interactive. (2001). "The increasing impact of ehealth on physician behaviour." Report by the Boston Consulting Group. *Health Care News*, *1*(31): 1-14.

Hassol, A., Walker, J. M., Kidder, D., Rokita, K., Young, D., Pierdon, S., Deitz, D., Kuck, S. & Ortiz, E. (2004). "Patient experiences and attitudes about access to a patient electronic health care record and linked web messaging." *Journal of the American Medical Informatics Association, 11*(6): 505-513.

Heaton, L. (2006). "Telehealth in indigenous communities in the Far North: Challenges for continued development." In M. Murero & R. E. Rice (Eds.), *The Internet and Health Care: Theory, Research and Practice*. Mahwah, NJ: LEA, in press.

Holleran, K., Pappas, J., Lou, H., Rubalcaba, P., Lee, R., Clay, S., Cutone, J., Flammini, S., Kuperman, G. & Middleton, B. (2003). "Mobile technology in a clinical setting." *AMIA Annual Symposium Proceedings 2003*: 863.

Houston, T. K. & Allison, J. J. (2002). "Users of Internet health information: Differences by health status." *Journal of Medical Internet Research, 4*(2): e7.

Howitt, A., Clement, S., de Lusignan, S., Thiru, K., Goodwin, D., & Wells, S. (2002). "An evaluation of general practice websites in the UK." *Family Practice, 19*(5): 547-556.

Information Society, Portugal. (2004). "E-Health." Retrieved January 26, 2005, from http://www.infosociety.gov.pt/egov/ehealth.aspx.

Johnson, B. and Rice, R. E. (1987) *Managing Organizational Innovation: The Evolution from Word Processing to Office Information Systems*. New York: Columbia University Press.

Jones, R. B., Balfour, F., Gillies, M., Stobo, D., Cawsey, A. J. & Donaldson, K. (2001). "The accessibility of computer-based health information for patients: Kiosks and the web." *Medinfo, 10*(2): 1469-1473.

Joustra-Enquist, I. & Eklund, B. (2004). "SUSTAINS—direct access for the patient to the medical record over the Internet." *MEDINFO 2004*(CD): 1673.

Kakai, H., Maskarinec, G., Shumay, D. M., Tatsumura, Y., & Tasaki, K. (2003). "Ethnic differences in choices of health information by cancer patients using complementary and alternative medicine: An exploratory study with correspondence analysis." *Social Science &*

Medicine, 56(4): 851-862.

Katz, D. G., Dutcher, G. A., Toigo, T. A., Bates, R., Temple, F., & Cadden, C. G. (2002, March-April). "The AIDS clinical trials information service (ACTIS): A decade of providing clinical trials information." *Public Health Reports, 117*(2): 123-130.

Katz, J. E. & Aspden, P. (2001). "Networked communication practices and the security and privacy of electronic health care records." In R. E. Rice & J. E. Katz (Eds.), *The Internet and Health Communication.* Thousand Oaks, CA: Sage. Pp. 393-416.

Katz, J. E. & Rice, R. E. (2001). "Concluding thoughts." In R. E. Rice & J. E. Katz (Eds.), *The Internet and Health Communication* (pp. 417-430). Thousand Oaks, CA: Sage.

Katz, J. E., Rice, R. E. & Acord, S. (2004). "E-health networks and social transformations: Expectations of centralization, experiences of decentralization." In M. Castells, *The Network Society: A Cross-cultural Perspective.* Cheltenham, UK: Edward Elgar. Pp. 293-318.

Klein, A. A. & Djaiani, G. N. (2003). "Mobile phones in the hospital—past, present and future." *Anaesthesia, 58*(4): 353-357.

Kubota, A., Fujita, M. & Hatano, Y. (2004). "[Development and effects of a health promotion program utilizing the mail function of mobile phones]." [Japanese] *Nippon Koshu Eisei Zasshi Japanese Journal of Public Health, 51*(10): 862.

Kunst, H., Groot, D., Latthe, P., Latthe, M. & Khan, K. (2002). "Accuracy of information on apparently credible websites: Survey of five common health topics." *BMJ, 324*(9), 581-582.

Lazev A, Vidrine D, Arduino R, Gritz E. (2004). "Increasing access to smoking cessation treatment in a low-income, HIV-positive population: The feasibility of using cellular telephones." *Nicotine and Tobacco Research, 6*(2): 281.

Licciardone, J. C., Smith-Barbaro, P., & Coleridge, S. T. (2001). "Use of the Internet as a resource for consumer health information: Results of the second osteopathic survey of health care in America." *Journal of Medical Internet Research, 3*(4): e31.

Lorig, K. R., Laurent, D. D., Deyo, R. A., Marnell, M. E., Minor, M. A., & Ritter, P. L. (2002). "Can a back pain e-mail discussion group improve health status and lower health care costs?: A randomized study." *Archives of Internal Medicine, 162*(7): 792-796.

Marquez Contreras, E., Casado Martinez, J. J., Corchado Albalat, Y., Chaves Gonzalez, R., Grandio, A., Losada Velasco, C., Obando, J., de Eugenio, J. M., & Barrera, J. M. (2004a). "Efficacy of an intervention to improve treatment compliance in hyperlipidemias." [Spanish] *Atencion Primaria, 33*(8): 443.

Marquez Contreras, E., de la Figuera von Wichmann, M., Gil Guillen, V., Ylla-Catala, A., Figueras, M., Balana, M. & Naval, J. (2004b). "Effectiveness of an intervention to provide information to patients with hypertension as short text messages and reminders sent to their mobile phone (HTA-Alert)." [Spanish] *Atencion Primaria, 34*(8): 399.

McKay, H. G., King, D., Eakin, E. G., Seeley, J. R., & Glasgow, R. E. (2001). "The diabetes network Internet-based physical activity intervention: A randomized pilot study." *Diabetes Care, 24*(8): 1328-1334.

Meigs, J. B., Cagliero, E., Dubey, A., Murphy-Sheehy, P., Gildesgame, C., Chueh, H., Barry, M. J., Singer, D. E., Nathan, D. M. (2003). "A controlled trial of web-based diabetes disease management: The MGH diabetes primary care improvement project." *Diabetes Care, 26*(3): 750-757.

Meischke, H., Eisenberg, M., Rowe, S. & Cagle, A. (2005). "Do older adults use the Internet for information on heart attacks? Results from a survey of seniors in King County, Washington." *Heart & Lung, 34*(1): 3-12.

Mendelson, D. N. & Salinsky, E. M. (1997). "Health information systems and the role of state government." *Health Affairs, 16*(3): 106-120.

Millard, R. W. & Fintak, P. A. (2002). "Use of the Internet by patients with chronic illness." *Disease Management & Health Outcomes, 10*(3): 187-194.

Miyauchi, K., Yonezawa, Y., Maki, H., Ogawa, H., Hahn, A. W. & Caldwell, W. M. (2003). "A new microcomputer-based safety and life support system for solitary-living elderly people." *Biomedical Sciences Instrumentation, 39*:179-82.

Molassiotis, A. & Xu, M. (2004). "Quality and safety issues of web-based information about herbal medicines in the treatment of cancer." *Complementary Therapies in Medicine, 12*(4): 217-227.

Morahan-Martin, J. (2004). "How Internet users find, evaluate, and use online health information: A cross-cultural review." *CyberPsychology & Behavior, 7*(5): 497-510.

Morrissey, J. J. (2004). "Mobile phones in the hospital: Improved mobile communication and mitigation of EMI concerns can lead to an overall benefit to healthcare." *Health Physics, 87*(1): 82.

Muller, M. L, Burkle, T., Irps, S., Roeder, N. & Prokosch, H. U. (2003). "The diagnosis related groups enhanced electronic medical record." *International Journal of Medical Informatics, 70*(2-3): 221-228.

Nicholson, W. K., Grason, H. A., & Powe, N. R. (2003). "The relationship of race to women's use of health information resources." *American Journal of Obstetrics and Gynecology, 188*(2): 580-585.

Norum, J., Grev, A., Moen, M. A., Balteskard, L. & Holthe, K. (2003). "Information and communication technology (ICT) in oncology: Patients' and relatives' experiences and suggestions." *Supportive Care in Cancer, 11*(5): 286-293.

Obermayer, J. L, Riley, W. T, Asif, O. & Jean-Mary, J. (2004). "College smoking-cessation using cell phone text messaging." *Journal of American College Health, 53*(2): 71.

Ogawa, H., Yonezawa, Y., Maki, H., Sato, H., Hahn, A. W. & Caldwell, W. M. (2003). "A Web-based home welfare and care services support system using a pen type image sensor." *Biomedical Sciences Instrumentation, 39*: 199.

Pandey, S. K., Hart, J. J. & Tiwary, S. (2003). "Women's health and the Internet: Understanding emerging trends and implications." *Social Science and Medicine, 56*(1): 179-191.

Panés, J., de Lacy, A. M., Sans, M., Soriano, A. & Pique, J. M. (2002). "Frequent Internet use among Catalan patients with inflammatory bowel disease." [Spanish] *Gastroenterología y hepatología, 25*(5): 306.

Pastore, M. (2001, Feb.). Physicians' web sites, ehealth plans mark future of healthcare. Retrieved July 03, 2003 from http://cyberatlas.Internet.com/markets/healthcare/article/0,,10101_594991,00.html.

Patsos, M. (2001). "The Internet and medicine: Building a community for patients with rare diseases." *Journal of the American Medical Association, 285*(6): 805.

Pew Internet and American Life Project. (2000, Nov.). *The online health care revolution: How the Web helps Americans take better care of themselves.* Retrieved July 16, 2003, from http://www.pewInternet.org/reports/toc.asp?Report=26.

Pew Internet and American Life Project. (2002, May). *Vital decisions: How Internet users decide what information to trust when they or their loved ones are sick.* Retrieved July 17, 2003, from http://www.pewInternet.org/reports/toc.asp?Report=59.

"Pharmaceutical, health care products and service industries must remedy the online customer experience they provide, according to the customer respect group's spring 2003 sector study." (2003, May 5). *Business Wire*. Retrieved July 13, 2003, from http://home.business-wire.com/portal/site/home/index.jsp?front_door=true&headlineSearchConfigBO=v2*G0.

Plus news (2004). Mali: Using telephones to fight HIV/AIDS. UN-OCHA Integrated Regional Information Networks. Retrieved February 2, 2005 from http://www.plusnews.org/AIDSReport.ASP?ReportID=4233&SelectRegion=West_Africa&SelectCountry=MALI.

Preece, J. J. & Ghozati, K. (2001). "Experiencing empathy online." In R. E. Rice & J. E. Katz (Eds.), *The Internet and Health Communication.* Thousand Oaks, CA: Sage. Pp. 237-260.

Simha, Rakesh. (2003). Indian e-Health Project Wins Top UN Award. OneWorld South Asia. 23 November. Retrieved February 5, 2005 from http://southasia.oneworld.net/article/view/73925/1/.

Rice, R. E. (2001). "The Internet and health communication: A framework of experiences." In R. E. Rice & J. E. Katz (Eds.), *The Internet and Health Communication: Expectations and Experiences.* Thousand Oaks, CA: Sage. Pp. 5-46.

Rice, R. E. & J. E. Katz (2006). "Internet use in physician practice and patient interaction." In M. Murero & R. E. Rice (Eds.), *The Internet and Health Care: Theory, Research and Practice*. Mahwah, NJ: LEA, in press.

Rice, R. E. & Gattiker, U. (2000) "New media and organizational structuring." In F. Jablin and L. Putnam (Eds.), *New Handbook of Organizational Communication*. Newbury Park, CA: Sage. Pp. 544-581.

Rice, R. E., Peterson, M., & Christine, R. (2002). A comparative features analysis of publicly accessible commercial and government health database web sites. In R. E. Rice & J.E. Katz (Eds.), *The Internet and health communication: Expectations and experiences*. Thousand Oaks, CA: Sage. Pp. 213-231.

Ruiz, J. C., Escallada, R., Cotorruelo, J. G., Zubimendi, J. A., Heras, M. & Arias, M. (1999). "Model of a telematic network for communication between centers in a kidney transplant area." *Transplantation Proceedings, 31*(6): 2358.

Sanchez, P. M. (2002). "Refocusing website marketing: Physician-patient relationships." *Health Marketing Quarterly, 20*(1): 37.

Sciamanna, C. N., Novak, S. P., Houston, T. K., Gramling, R. & Marcus, B. H. (2004). "Visit satisfaction and tailored health behavior communications in primary care." *American Journal of Preventative Medicine, 26*(5): 426-430.

Seidman, J. J., Steinwachs, D. & Rubin, H R. (2003). "Conceptual framework for a new tool for evaluating the quality of diabetes consumer-information Web sites." *Journal of Medical Internet Research, 5*(4): e29.

Sharf, B. F. (1997). "Communicating breast cancer on-line: Support and empowerment on the Internet." *Women and Health, 26*(1): 65-84.

Sigouin, C. & Jadad, A. R. (2002). "Awareness of sources of peer-reviewed research evidence on the Internet." *Journal of the American Medical Association, 287*(21): 2867-2869.

Sittig, D. (2003). "Results of a content analysis of electronic messages (e-mail) sent between patients and their physicians." *BMC Medical Informatics Decision Making, 3*(1): 11.

Sorri, M., Piiparinen, P., Huttunen, K., Haho, M., Tobey, E., Thibodeau, L. & Buckley, K. (2003). "Hearing aid users benefit from induction loop when using digital cellular phones." *Ear and Hearing*, *24*(2): 119-132.

Suarez-Almazor, M. E., Kendall, C. J. & Dorgan, M. (2001). "Surfing the Net—information on the World Wide Web for persons with arthritis: Patient empowerment or patient deceit?" *Journal of Rheumatology*, *28*(1): 1-2.

Tachinardi, Umberto. (1998). "Internet and healthcare in Brazil: the role of the Working Group for Healthcare (GT Saúde)." *Computers in Biology and Medicine*, *28*(5): 519-529.

Tang, F. H., Law, M.Y., Lee, A. C. & Chan, L.W. (2004). "A mobile phone integrated health care delivery system of medical images." *Journal of Digital Imaging*, *17*(3): 217.

Tench, C. M., Clunie, G. P. R., Dacre, J., & Peacock, A. (1998). "An insight into rheumatology resources available on the World Wide Web." *British Journal of Rheumatology*, *37*(11): 1233-1235.

Till, J. E. (2003). "Evaluation of support groups for women with breast cancer: Importance of the navigator role." *Health and Quality of Life Outcomes*, *1*(1): 16.

Tolentino, H. D., Dela Cruz-Odi, M., Lazatin, P. F., Egay, L., Arenas-Corleto, T., Marcelo, A., Maramba, I. & Bandola, E. (2004). "Design and implementation of an open source prototype telephony and Web-based critical event reporting system for continuous quality improvement program in anesthesiology. *MEDINFO 2004*(CD): 1883.

Vilella, A., Bayas, J. M., Diaz, M. T., Guinovart, C., Diez, C., Simo, D., Munoz, A. & Cerezo, J. (2004). "The role of mobile phones in improving vaccination rates in travelers." *Preventive Medicine*, *38*(4): 503.

Wagner, T. H., Baker, L. C., Bundorf, M. K. & Singer, S. (2004). "Use of the Internet for health information by the chronically ill." *Preventing Chronic Disease*, *1*(4): A13.

Wang, M., Lau, C., Matsen, F. A. 3rd & Kim, Y. (2004). "Personal health information management system and its application in referral management." *IEEE Transactions on Information Technology in Biomedicine*, *8*(3): 287.

Wantland, D. J., Portillo, C. J., Holzemer, W. L., Slaughter, R. & McGhee, E. M. (2004). "The effectiveness of Web-based vs. non-Web-based interventions: A meta-analysis of behavioral change outcomes." *Journal of Medical Internet Research*, *6*(4): e40.

Weiner, M., Schadow, G., Lindbergh, D., Warvel, J., Abernathy, G., Perkins, S. M., Fyffe, J., Dexter, P. R. & McDonald, C. J. (2003). "Clinicians' and patients' experiences and satisfaction with unscheduled, night time, Internet-based video conferencing for assessing acute medical problems in a nursing facility." *AMIA Annual Symposium Proceedings 2003*: 709-713.

Wikgren, M. (2001). "Health discussions on the Internet: A study of knowledge communication through citations." *Library and Information Research*, *23*: 305-317.

Wilson, P. (2002). "How to find the good and avoid the bad or ugly: A short guide to tools for rating quality of health information on the internet." *British Medical Journal*, *324*(7337), 598-602.

Winzelberg, A. J., Classen, C., Alpers, G. W., Roberts, H., Koopman, C., Adams, R. E., Ernst, H., Dev, P. & Taylor, C. B. (2003). "Evaluation of an Internet support group for women with primary breast cancer." *Cancer*, *97*(5): 1164-1173.

Work Research Centre, Dublin. (2004). "Social cohesion/inclusion in the information society—the regional dimension." BISER Domain Report No. 9. Retrieved January 25, 2005, from http://www.biser-eu.com/10%20Domains%20Report/BISER_Cohesion_fnl_r.pdf

Yom, S. S. (1996). "The Internet and the future of minority health." *Journal of the American Medical Association*, *275*: 735.Yoshiyama, N., Hashimoto, A., Nakijima, K., Hattori, S. & Sugita, F. (2004) "[An applied research on effective health care planning using cellular phone with the digital still camera function]." [Japanese]. *Gan To Kagaku Ryoho 31*(2): 208.

Zeng, Q., Kogan, S., Plovnick, R., Crowell, J., Lacroix, E-M., & Greenes, R. (2004). "Positive attitudes and failed queries: An exploration of the conundrums of consumer health information retrieval." *International Journal of Medical Informatics*, *73*, 45-55.

Zhang, S. X., Jiang, L. J., Zhang, Q. W., Pan, J. J. & Wang, W. Y. (2004). [Role of mass media during the severe acute respiratory syndrome epidemic] [Chinese] *Zhonghua liu xing bing xue za zhi, 25*(5): 403.

Chapter 7

E-Learning and the Transformation of Education for a Knowledge Economy

Betty Collis

Introduction

Major changes are occurring in society in the ways in which we work and interact with each other. Collectively we are experiencing a change to a *knowledge economy*. I will focus on several of the main characteristics of functioning productively in a knowledge economy and give some examples of how these characteristics can relate to transformations in educational processes in the corporate setting, for ongoing professional education, and in higher education. However, for a transformation to take place many changes must occur in the institutions, regulating bodies, and world views of those involved.

Functioning Productively in a Knowledge Economy

The term "knowledge economy" is an evolving phrase without a precise definition. A search of the Internet on 5 February 2005 identified nearly a million hits, many of which are portals with multiple links. The knowledge economy is related to changes in society worldwide, particularly globalization, information/knowledge intensity, and networking and connectivity.[1]

Characteristics of a knowledge economy include: the increased mobility of services, information, and workforce; the need to derive local value from information often in creative ways that go beyond expected performance; the need to work in multidisciplinary and distributed teams; the need to use information technology (IT) for knowledge management, sharing, and creation; the need to update and change ones skills throughout one's lifetime; and the need to "act autonomously and reflectively, joining and functioning in socially heterogeneous groups" (The World Bank Group, 2003, p. 17). "These attributes produce a new type of marketplace and society, one that is rooted in ubiquitous elec-

---

[1] As an example see http://www.skyrme.com/insights/21gke.htm

tronic networks" (Kelly, 1998, p. 2). A concise summary of the skills needed to function productively in a knowledge economy is given by the Ministry of Economic Development in New Zealand:

"Know-why and know-who matters more than know-what

There are different kinds of knowledge that can usefully be distinguished. *Know-what*, or knowledge about facts, is nowadays diminishing in relevance. Know-why is knowledge about the natural world, society, and the human mind. *Know-who* refers to the world of social relations and is knowledge of who knows what and who can do what. Knowing key people is sometimes more important to innovation than knowing scientific principles. *Know-where* and *know-when* are becoming increasingly important in a flexible and dynamic economy."[2]

Personal knowledge management skills as well as a knowledge management infrastructure for the organization or professional body supporting knowledge workers are critical to the learning needed for a knowledge economy.[3] The National Health Service in the UK for example identifies personal knowledge management skills for those in the healthcare professions as including: skills in asking the right questions; searching skills including in defining and identifying the sources of evidence it is appropriate to search for when faced with a particular decision; storing information for effective reuse; and being able to critically appraise the evidence that is obtained.[4]

All of these relate to new approaches to learning in which technology is a constant tool, and from these to a transformed model of education.

Given this societal context, the need for schools, higher education, professional development, and corporate learning to change is obvious. The World Bank (2003) contrasts traditional learning with learning for a knowledge economy as moving away from the teacher and textbook as sources of knowledge towards the teacher as a guide for finding and interpreting real-world information; away from learning being delivered to learners who receive it toward learning by doing and participating as close to the real world as possible; from assessment being based on responding to questions with pre-determined right and wrong answers

---

[2] http://www.med.govt.nz/pbt/infotech/knowledge_economy/knowledge_economy-04.html

[3] See for example, the portal of resources at http://www.sveiby.com/library.html

[4] See http://www.nelh.nhs.uk/ebdm/knowledge_individuals.asp

to assessment being based on competence development as documented by a variety of forms of performance including those that require integrating one's work with the work of others. Developments in higher and professional education as well as corporate learning are gradually occurring that reflect these shifts. Information and communication technologies are necessary tools, but only when used in ways appropriate to the ways people will work and learn in a knowledge economy.

Much of what is currently called e-learning, where a computer system selects learning objects for knowledge transfer, is in fact counterproductive to the development of competencies for a knowledge economy. The following examples show interpretations of e-learning that, in contrast, relate to the competencies needed for functioning productively in a knowledge economy.

Examples from Professional and Higher Education

Corporate: In corporate settings, the benefits of informal learning including with knowledge management tools and resources are well known, but corporate training still tends to operate via traditional models reflecting a knowledge transfer orientation. Much of what is called e-learning in the corporate sector involves providing knowledge transfer through the computer so that the employee does not have to "attend" a classroom session itself oriented around knowledge transfer from the expert to the learners. Such an approach to learning, while speeding up and personalizing the knowledge transfer process, will not lead to the sort of transformation that is called for in a knowledge economy. Instead at Shell International Exploration and Production (Shell EP) an approach to e-learning in which participants in courses make use of the skills and tools of knowledge management and learn from each other related to their actual workplace problems and experiences has emerged in over 70 courses since 2002 (Margaryan, Collis, & Cooke, 2004). Because participants in the courses represent many different backgrounds and experiences, these differences are built upon to improve the process of learning from each other. For example, one course brings together experienced well engineers and geologists who must work on multidisciplinary teams in the workplace in order to identify new sources of oil. While each of the participants needs to update himself in his own discipline, he also needs to work productively with his non-discipline colleagues. Thus the course is organized around a model of participants contributing resources and sharing experiences via company knowledge management systems and a common course Web environment during the first portion of the course while still remaining in their workplaces, and then when coming together for a one-week face to face session still using the Web environment to support their working in multidisciplinary teams. While in the classroom component they deepen their own discipline knowledge by learning from the contributions made by the others in their discipline to the Web environment. But they also take responsibility for helping their non-discipline teammates to be able to adequately understand and explain different perspectives to the workplace problems. Assessment is based on how efficiently and effectively this knowledge sharing, building and coaching takes place.

The sorts of e-learning involved in Shell EP do not emphasize the use of e-modules oriented around knowledge transfer, although these are available to support the knowledge-building processes. Instead Web technology is used to support the knowledge sharing, knowledge building, and coaching activities of the participants, as well as to integrate the organization and assessment of these activities in an efficient and manageable way accessible to everyone in the course from their own workplaces.

Professional development: The ongoing professional development of practitioners outside of a particular corporate setting is predominately a matter of life-long learning where there may or may not be professional accrediting bodies or societies to steer the learning process. Here the role of *communities of practice* for learning becomes essential. Etienne Wenger describes a community of practice as being "formed by people who engage in a process of collective learning in a shared domain of human endeavour…" where "members engage in joint activities and discussions, help each other, and share information. They build relationships that enable them to learn from each other" (http://www.ewenger.com/theory/index.htm). Thus communities of practice are important to ongoing professional development.

In a review of best practices in 2000 for professional development (Bowskill, Forster, Lally, &McConnell, 2000), the importance of the use of electronic networks for on-going professional development was highlighted. Key strategies include:

- The use of guests or experts from within the communities, for example as guest lecturers interacting with others via the use of online tools. The interactions may be in preparation for a face-to-face event or may be in response to specific requests for help or support;

- The use of shared archives, such as those from online discussions, from workshops, from knowledge management systems, or from other forms of contributions from the members of the community of practice;

- Mentoring and coaching, supported by online resources and tools.

Figure7.1   E-learning in terms of content and communication with communities of practice representing the intersection of the richest forms of each

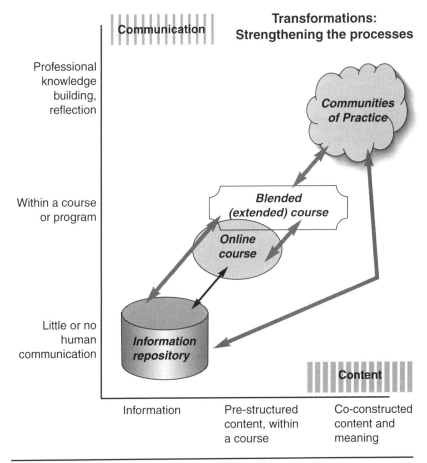

Source: Collis & Moonen, 2005.

For all of these, network tools provide access to the community over time, distance, and depth. Such communities can also contribute to the learning of others not (yet) active in the community, for example through making their archives available via the Web or an intranet, or by engaging young professionals still in training into some of the dialogues and dynamics of the community. Figure 1 shows how such interlinkages can involve communities of practitioners with practitioners in training and their instructors.

E-learning is here seen in terms of two dimensions: Content and communication. Communities of practice use communication for knowledge sharing and co-construction as the richest form of e-learning.

Higher education: Electronic portfolios are increasingly being used as reflection and assessment tools in higher education5. There are many definitions for a portfolio from before the time of electronic portfolios, such as "a purposeful collection of student work that exhibits the students' efforts, progress and achievement in one or more areas. The collection must include student participation in selecting contents, the criteria for selection, the criteria for judging merit, and evidence of student self-reflection" (Paulson, Paulson, & Meyer, 1991, p.60). An electronic portfolio uses electronic technologies, allowing the portfolio developer to collect and organise portfolio artifacts in many types (audio, video, graphics, text) in a way that is scalable and accessible over time, distance, and modality. An electronic portfolio provides a comprehensive storage medium for the results of individual assessments, accommodating a potential variety in the instruments themselves as well as providing assessment opportunities at different time frames and for different performance indicators, in particular indicators dealing with less-tangible results. There can be a number of different levels of use of electronic portfolios, such: (a) a collection of artifacts, (b) collection of artifacts with reflective statements, (c) the previous with self-assessment, (d) a course-centered portfolio, (e) a program-centered portfolio, (f) a standards-centered portfolio, and (g) a learner-centered portfolio. At the University of Twente in the Master of Science program for Technology in Education and Training, the use of electronic portfolios goes beyond the benefits for the individual student. Students set up their portfolios not only to provide evidence of their own individual growth relating to the competencies of the program, but also develop a portion of the portfolio as a learning resource for students who will enter the program in subsequent years, helping them to understand what the competencies mean in practice.

For uses of the electronic portfolio that involve accessing the resources in a scalable and convenient way, network tools are needed, thus electronic portfolio use becomes a form of e-learning.

Affordances and Barriers

These examples illustrate how the social and technical developments of the knowledge economy can be applied to different learning settings, within formal courses and programs and for informal professional development. Network technology, particularly including groupware tools and tools for self-expression, provide key affordances. However, there are many potential barriers. For example, for the use of electronic portfolios to make an impact in education, standards and procedures for integrating these as assessed processes and products within courses and accreditation procedures are needed and must be applied in a consistent way for marking and grading. These processes will be new for both instructors and students alike, and can lead to uncertainty, excessive time demands, and disputes relating to grading decisions. From the institutional perspective issues relating to the cost of the electronic tools, the management and monitoring of the network systems involved, and security are issues that must be handled.

More generally, for the instructor or trainer and the learners, new roles and processes must be accepted and managed and for universities, training centres, and accreditation bodies new flexibilities must be introduced. The skills and insights for participating in a variety of knowledge communities over time and distance need to be stressed and assessed as much as (if not more) than the acquisition of knowledge. Fundamentally this may lead to a clash among cultures in an organization. The organisational cultures of the e-learning contexts can be seen as worlds where different values and attitudes can be applied (Boltanski & Thevénot, 1991). The organisation culture is a key variable in the motivation for why a transformation might take place. Boltanski and Thevénot (1991) describe six different cultures within organisational contexts. Table 7.1 shows the characteristics of these different worlds in terms of features which are relevant for the transformation of an educational organization from traditional to knowledge economy orientations.

Table 7.1   Relevant characteristics of the worlds (Strijker, 2004, adapted from Boltanski & Thevénot, 1991)

	Verbs	Value Features
The Industrial World	To organise, to control, to formalise, to standardise	Efficiency, performance
The Domestic World	To behave; to respect traditional roles	Responsibility, convention, hierarchy; rules
The Civic World	To debate, to gather, to inform	The group, collective action, collective entities
The World of Opinion	To convince, to persuade	Reputation, credibility
The Merchant World	To buy, to sell, to negotiate, to deal, to rival, to accumulate	Business; competition, rivalry
The World of Inspiration	To create, to discover, to research	Singularity, innovation, originality

An organization that reflects the Domestic World, as is the case with many higher education institutions, will not be transformed with a model of e-learning that also reflects this world. Instead, the examples relating to the knowledge economy that have been mentioned here are closer to the World of Inspiration. A mismatch of cultures can prevent the realization of e-learning initiatives (Strijker, 2004).

The knowledge sharing communities in large organizations, supported by knowledge management tools and processes and effective coaching and mentoring in the workplace, are the closest current match to the requirements for productive participation in the knowledge economy. In such corporate settings, the need to adapt to the changing business environment is a strong motivator for change and for new models of organizational learning. However, such models of learning oriented around knowledge sharing, management, and co-creation are infrequently seen in higher education. For a transformation of education to occur national policy and accreditation processes and institutional assessment and degree requirements will need to better reflect the societal transformation that is already emerging. And network technologies must be used for "know why," "know who," "know when," and "know where" much more than "know what" in the primary processes of education.

References

Boltanski, L., & Thevénot, L. (1991). *De La justification, Les economies de la grandeur*. NRF Essais, Gallimard.

Bowskill, N., Foster, J., Lally, V., & McConnell, D. (2000). Networked professional development: issues for recipients and providers. In Asensio, M., Foster, J., Hodgson, V. & McConnell, D. (Eds.)

Networked Learning 2000: Innovative approaches to lifelong learning and higher education through the internet (pp. 49-56). University of Lancaster, UK. Available via the Internet at

http://www.shef.ac.uk/education/research/RTPLandMc.shtml

Collis, B., & Moonen, J. (2001). *Flexible learning in a digital world: Experiences and expectations*. London: Kogan Page.

Collis, B., & Moonen, J. (2005). Standards and assessment of e-learning. In P. Resta (Ed.). *Teacher development and e-learning* (in press). Paris: UNESCO

Kelly, K. (1998). *New rules for the new economy: 10 radical strategies for a connected world*. New York: Penguin.

Margaryan, A., Collis, B., & Cooke, A. (2004). Activity-based blended learning. *Human Resource Development International*, 7(2), 265-274.

Ministry of Economic Development of New Zealand (2005). *What is the knowledge economy?* Available via the Internet at http://www.med.govt.nz/pbt/infotech/knowledge_economy/knowledge_economy-04.html

Paulson, L., Paulson, P., & Meyer, C. (1991). What makes a portfolio a portfolio?. *Educational Leadership*, 48(5), 60-63.

Strijker, A. (2004). *Reuse of learning objects in context: Human and technical perspectives*. PhD dissertation, Faculty of Behavioural Sciences, University of Twente, The Netherlands. Available via

the Internet at http://130.89.154.170/proefschrift/

The World Bank Group, (2003). *Lifelong learning in the global knowledge economy*. Available via the Internet at http://www1.worldbank.org/education/lifelong_learning/lifelong_learning_GKE.asp

Chapter 8

Reshaping the State and its Relationship with Citizens: the Short, Medium and Long-term Potential of ICT's

Geoff Mulgan

Introduction

Government has always been concerned with information and communication as much as control and coercion: writing was born out of tax collection, bureaucracy was pioneered as a means of managing territories and people with the use of records, commands and intelligence (the very word statistics comes from the German 'Staat'), and all states have paid close attention to rituals and propaganda.

Each wave of technology has changed the options available for the organisation of government, shaping how much can be managed, delegated, commanded or coordinated, and there has been a coevolution of techniques of governance—the new knowledge of professionals, methods of raising taxes, measuring and monitoring—and of communications technology, such as scripts, roads, telegraphs, satellites and more recently the web and the grid.

This evolution has not always been fast. It took over a century from the invention of the telephone to its widespread application to government services—for example placing nurses backed by diagnostic software in call centres. But the last 10-15 years have brought a dramatic acceleration (albeit one that has probably slowed in the last 2-3 years) in the application of new technologies making use of the web in and around government, an acceleration accompanied by a probably unprecedented, real time, running commentary from academics and consultancies.[1]

---

[1] For example Accenture, *E-government leadership: High performance, maximum value* (London: Accenture, 2004).

In terms of the maturity of applications the front runners remain Canada, the US and Singapore; but there are probably some 8-10 countries at roughly similar stages of development, often making parallel mistakes, but steadily transforming the day to day business of government. E government is a perfect example of the rapid trend towards continuous benchmarking by governments and the acceleration of cross-border learning, albeit much less tempered by hard evidence than fields like macroeconomics and labour market policy (and more vulnerable to hype from vendor companies).

This paper draws both on international and on UK experience and aims to show that the question of e government is inseparable from broader questions of government: how it is evolving, in response to what forces, with what tools, and taking what shapes. I suggest a framework for assessing impacts in terms of public value. And I suggest that some of the most promising developments involve a shift from government providing structures, to government providing infrastructures on which more diverse forms of social organisation can be based.

Public value and e.government

Grandiose claims have been made for e.government, including that it would deliver:

- Major efficiencies

- Increases in overall societal productivity and competitiveness

- Transformations in the relationship between citizen and state

The now familiar distortions of rhetoric that have accompanied ICTs for several decades have been present again during the phase of major investment in e applications. Behind these claims the central issue for any state is whether e applications contribute to legitimation—the trust that is essential to collecting taxes, electoral success and the day to day functioning of government. This legitimation can be understood more precisely as an activity of value creation by the state. Broadly speaking states that create public value will tend to be legitimate, able to act, to recruit, to persuade citizens to share information and so on. The fundamental issue of e.government is how much it creates—or destroys—public value.

This question of public value has been the focus of a good deal of recent work. The core arguments of public value theory[2] are:

- that in democracies states exist to create and add public value—meeting the needs and wants of citizens

- that value is generally provided through a combination of: outcomes, services and trust (or the quality of the relationship between states and citizens).

- that public value has to be constantly discovered through politicians and officials interrogating public demands, discovering relative priorities

- that this value is different in nature from private value, and from the conventional accounts of welfare economics, in part because it is shaped out of dialogue and politics rather than existing as an objective reality

- that a clear understanding of value has to come prior to any meaningful discussion of efficiency or productivity (otherwise reforms which appear to increase efficiency risk destroying value).

E government has evolved as a means of contributing to value in all three areas—outcomes, services and trust—and this provides a useful rubric for understanding its evolution, assessing its current and future performance, and avoiding the pitfalls of technological determinism and hype. It also provides a helpful counterweight to overdetermined accounts of ICTs in government which postulate very general new principles linked to the broader evolution of a knowledge society or economy: instead, as I will show, some of the directions of change are contradictory.

---

[2] Summarised in Creating Public Value by Mulgan, Kelly and Muers (Strategy Unit, Cabinet Office, 2003); other relevant literature includes Mark Moore's book 'Creating Public Value' published in 1995, and a special issue of the Australian Journal of Public Administration

Outcomes

First, outcomes. The following are some of the varied ways in which the broad family of e.government applications can assist governments in the achievement of outcomes for which they are held accountable (such as lower crime, unemployment, better health &c):

- The simplest applications are models of information provision that help to deliver superior outcomes—for example online systems that provide comprehensive jobs databases have helped employment services to improve their outcomes in Sweden, the US and other countries. Often these have required new kinds of public private partnership.

- Somewhat more sophisticated are online curricula that assist home based working. These are beginning to have an impact, building on the various public and private on-line learning services now available (ranging from the UK's National Grid for Learning and Open University to the University of Phoenix and the plethora of private distance providers). They can provide a base of common knowledge, along with diagnostic tools as well as learning.

- Within public services a growing impact is being achieved by much more transparent performance data: a well known example is the use made of crime statistics for regular peer review sessions and performance management in the New York COMSTAT system. In the UK there is now web access to near real time performance data on schools, police forces, hospitals and welfare providers. This sort of transparency is still resisted by many professions.

- A panoply of policy measures have been tried out to enhance knowledge intensive economic activity. Despite many false starts (for example in the promotion of clusters and technopolises) these have become increasingly sophisticated: the ICS Polynet project led by Sir Peter Hall and conducted for the European Commission will show the rapidly evolving synergies between different advanced business services and the interplay of communications bandwidth, regulatory environments, transport (air and high speed rail), key institutions (big firms, markets and universities) and labour markets.

- Within fields of public policy we are beginning to see the use of more sophisticated knowledge management systems to spread best practice, research findings and organise communities to share tacit knowledge: the Cochrane collaboration provides one end of this, the UK NHS health collaboratives are another example. Private sector experience with knowledge management has been decidedly mixed; these public examples too involve major issues around culture, incentives and day to day practice. The networks of mutual learning established in the UK around programmes like Surestart (for under 5s) and the New Deal for Communities (regenerating poor areas) are good models for the future.

- Some governments are using more sophisticated tracking of data to improve outcomes. In the UK the move to tracking of all children at risk is an important—and controversial—example. One of its potential virtues is that it enables much more holistic organisation of government across organisational boundaries.

- Looking further ahead there are major potential gains to be achieved from the application of grid computing to efficient outcomes—mapping patterns in real-time using data collected from medical trials or public services in order to accelerate learning.

- Finally, a longer term implication of some current applications is to make knowledge more widely available not just to professional practitioners but also to the public in order to improve outcomes. In the UK NHS strategy is based in part on an assumption that the public will over time take greater responsibility for their own health, supported by online diagnosis and information systems; easily organised forums to bring together people with similar conditions; and wider understanding of the links between personal behaviour and health outcomes.

In all of these areas egovernment is bound up with the broader trends towards making government more consciously knowledge based, shaped by evidence, and also providing much greater quantities and quality of knowledge for society and the economy to organise themselves.

Services

The second area of public value, services, has been the main focus of rhetoric about e.government in recent years. Much of this has primarily drawn on consumer models of service delivery, themselves often drawn from manufacturing.

Uses of e applications in services have tended to follow a fairly common pattern of evolution running from:

- Information—provision of websites containing existing information, some of which is banal but where in some cases even quite modest measures like making all health inspections of restaurants available online can have a big impact in terms of public value

- Communication—for example NHS Direct providing online diagnosis, or the moves to brigade different services together in more interactive ways; providing frontline staff (eg police officers, housing repair teams) with PDAs and other mobile devices to speed up response to public issues.

- Transactions—for example putting all financial transactions online as in Singapore (where most transactions can be performed online, including payment of fines and taxes); Australian visa services which are fully electronic from end to end; or the UK's Courts OnLine service which allows citizens to launch minor cases in a purely electronic way.

- Open access—moving beyond functional transactions to enrich service delivery cultures through allowing many more comments and informal knowledge to be combined on the web.

- In the longer term offering users the means to pull together a mix of elements to customise services to their own needs. The UK's Direct Payments model for the disabled is one variant of this: providing a choice over mixes of money, service provision all backed up by both face to face and online information and help. These models come closer to the service approaches favoured in premium areas of the market—highly personal, responsive—and move further way from the mass models still predominant in most private sector service.

Canada has probably gone furthest in the deliberate targeting of user satisfaction with services, addressing the 5 main drivers of satisfaction (timeliness, knowledge, extra mile/smile, fairness, and outcomes) and showing a steady improvement between 1998 and 2002 at every level.

These evolutions of service delivery models raise some difficult issues. One is that each further state of evolution requires some shared data systems across organisational boundaries, and some common protocols. Some countries have felt able to adopt unique identifiers as in Finland; but in many others there is insufficient trust in the state to allow this. Another is that integration of services across boundaries may be easier for non-state organisations given the nature of bureaucratic and professional interests: those states most willing to allow porousness across boundaries may reap gains fastest. A third is that these all enable more networked organisational structures with greater decentralisation of operational decision making in ways that are likely to threaten the power of middle tiers.

All are in part about altering the mix of channels to maximise public value—which implies automating some services and intensifying the personal nature of others.

Trust

The most difficult area of public value has always been the third—trust. Here, the development of e government is bound up with the broader opening up of the state to scrutiny, and the changing nature of the conversation held between states and the public. The picture is complex. Most citizens relationships with states are abrupt, unsatisfying and disjointed—voting in an election, serving on a jury, receiving schooling, being paid pensions and so on.[3]

There have been some common moves to reframe the environment for trust, including:

- Greater use of pre-legislative scrutiny, with legislation online prior to its agreement

---

[3] See Touching the State, Design Council, London, 2004

- The move towards permanent consultation and conversation[4], bound up with the spread of Freedom of Information legislation. Governments are to some extent being turned inside out as previously secret performance information becomes public.

- Methods of policy making with wider communities involved—for example the relatively open methods used by bodies like the UK Strategy Unit, including publication of project plans and working papers; likewise at local level the normalisation of online committee timetables, minutes, webcasts &c

- Changing practices in politics and parliaments, as politicians open themselves up to email, dialogue (and learn to cope with new ways of orchestrating campaigns). The British Labour Party's Big Conversation designed to help frame its forthcoming manifesto is an interesting example of a new approach both to face to face meetings and to use of the web

- New vehicles for citizen involvement—such as the BBC's very successful iCan project; mysociety.org which is producing social software such as theyworkforyou.org which provides easy access to all elected representatives; and upmystreet.com's geographically tagged message boards

- Social programmes addressing digital divides (cheap or free computers; access to institutions; training programmes);[5] the UK now has near universal access to free internet (via some 6000 government supported sites in the UK)

- Wired neighbourhoods—encouraging greater mutual support and social capital (building on findings such as Keith Hampton's study of Toronto in the late 1990s which showed that residents who were connected online had far more day to day interaction with other residents than those who were not connected).

---

[4] For example the UK's rule of 12 weeks consultation on policy proposals

[5] Engaging the community in e-government: a briefing paper from the Strategic Support Unit (Improvement and Development Agency, 2005)

All of these are in part about changing the nature of the conversation between state and citizen—making it more reciprocal, open and nuanced. However, these trends are complex.

i) Greater transparency combined with aggressive news media can reduce trust (as some countries have learned with FOI).

ii) there are complex dynamics in public engagement—sometimes as in Porto Allegre public expectations can rise so fast that even successful programmes of involvement can lead to disappointment

iii) Analysis of trust in public institutions shows that the key determinants are how institutions behave—competence, integrity, speed of admitting mistakes—rather than any more structural trends.

Tensions around outcomes, services and trust

Outcomes, services and trust can be closely linked. In several countries the major barriers are now perceived to be public take-up rather than government provision. This of course raises the question of whether they are right to be sceptical of the offers being made. A related issue is whether the key barriers are questions of trust, in particular confidence in government's commitment to confidentiality. In some countries this may require stronger principles to underpin use of personal data—for example that identifiable personal data should remain under the control of the individual; guarantees of maximal anonymity to organisations providing data to governments; and strong sanctions for misuse of data.

This is just one of many complex ways in which trust, outcomes and services interrelate. In some countries the paramount issue is security against threats; where government is seen to respond inadequately one result may be greater mutual public distrust. Legitimacy therefore depends on often quite coercive enhancements to surveillance, with crime, DNA and other databases, linked together in ways that often conflict with privacy and civil liberties concerns.

Some of the key improvements in services and outcomes depend on there being sufficient legitimacy to impose strict common standards. There is a long history in communications of new categories liberating everyday relationships and strengthening community: the Penny

Post invented by Rowland Hill in 1840 required consistent addressing systems for every building in Britain; half a century later the telephone required consistent numbers for every building too, yet amidst this radical standardisation new scope was given for an infinite diversity of conversation, care and love. Similarly imposition of some common protocols in IT, and maximising interoperability, is coming to be the most important priority for innovation in technology. This implies a partial swing to greater centralisation.

Another link is that legitimacy and trust depends on value for money in delivering outcomes and services, yet IT programmes have been notorious for overrunning on costs. The UK NHS modernisation programme for example, the largest single IT project globally, has recently been estimated to cost £30bn, twice the earlier estimate. Part of the problem in securing reliable estimates is that many of the potential benefits flow from radical, and unproven, changes to organisational structures—allowing much greater decentralisation within tighter frameworks for accountability, performance and financial control. Different models for organising purchasing also appear to have achieved very different levels of value for money. [6]

The many measures to address inequality and exclusion also bring their own contradictions. Many past ICT programmes subsidised or provided hardware without any evidence of demand and this error has been often repeated under the rubric of tackling the digital divide. Few if any of the programmes offering technological solutions to what are essentially social problems have worked: informal social connections continue to be much more important than physical access in terms of opportunities; and many expensively provided networks have remained underused or used for very different purposes from those intended. [7]

---

[6] Dunleavy P., Margetts H., Bastow S. and Tinkler J., 'Government IT performance and the power of the IT industry: A cross-national analysis' (Paper to APSA 2004 Conference).

[7] I have written many pieces on this topic, including 'Communication and Control: networks and the new economies of communication (Polity, 1991). A good recent overview is William Davies, 'Don't assume that improving IT alone will breach the digital divide' (*The Times*, 25 January 2005, available at www.ippr.org.uk)

Radical, systemic and incremental innovation in egovernment

This leads to the fundamental issue of the nature of innovation. Much of the daily reality of e.government has been distinctly incremental and cautious, despite ambitious rhetoric, and the impact on underlying state structures have been extremely limited.

This has also been true in the past of uses of communications technology in and around the state. A good example is the use of television in tertiary education: proposed by Michael Young in the UK in the late 1950s, introduced a decade later in the form of the Open University, and subsequently used by very large numbers of students. However, the practices of existing universities continue to be almost untouched, and not a single UK university uses OU course material (other European universities have been equally conservative in their methods).

In the same way most of the new models for using ICT in public services have been introduced alongside older models rather than displacing them—in the UK for example, Learndirect sits alongside traditional further education colleges. The reasons have to do with funding structures (which do not fund outcomes); power; and professional cultures.

For many years observers have commented on the scope for radically different organisational models of service delivery, combining transparency, accountability, decentralisation, and shared platforms. These promise a future of much greater citizen control over processes and services, supported by a mix of online, telephone based and face to face support, as well as greater front-line autonomy.

However it remains the case that there is not a single example of an entire public services that has been radically reengineered to make the full use of new technology. There are some good reasons for caution—risk, uncertainty and the likelihood that significant customer groups would not be able to use new technologies. But vested interests are also a large part of the explanation, as a result of which the new is added as a layer on top of the old, thus making it impossible to realise efficiency gains. This is part of a general feature of governments—that they find it easier to start programmes than to stop them—and a general feature of reform that it has to involve some contestability, and some creation of new structures of power to challenge the old.

Future issues

Looking to the future three areas of possibility stand out, all of which raise important questions about the radicalism of innovation and the potential of European governments to take advantage of future opportunities:

- One is the likely growth in the role of third parties acting as validators of information; as holders and managers of personal data; and as designers and managers of public data and online services. A good example of the latter is the role of upmystreet,com in providing superior local public information to anything provided by the UK public sector. The growing power of third parties may be extremely challenging to some governments and even further erodes government's monopoly even over its own information.

- A second is the potential for open source methods. The term 'open source' has been much misused, and much of the potential of open methods in the public sector is rather different from the specific characteristics of open source in fields like software, encyclopedias and news. However, there is great potential for governments to open themselves out; to make previously internal management information external; to extend the open principles of coordination that have been used in the EU to every aspect of public organisation; and in some cases to extend open methods to fields like legal services. Again the implications may be threatening to existing interests.[8]

- A third is the further evolution of government towards matrix models of organisation, with as much structured horizontally as vertically to meet the needs of population groups or to solve problems. This has long been the promise of ubiquitous communications. The UK has made extensive use of horizontal budgets, ministerial roles, task forces and targets (under the label 'joined up government) on the premise that unless the main drivers of governmental behaviour—budgets, political

---

[8] The forthcoming paper 'Wide Open' by Geoff Mulgan and Tom Steinberg (Demos 2005) explores the potential for open source methods and proposes a new terminology for differentiating its various meanings.

rewards, targets—are aligned to horizontally change is unlikely to happen. Finland has attempted to integrate horizontal goals much more deeply into government strategy. The US attempts to integrate intelligence and security operations are another current effort.[9] Stronger internal IT and knowledge management systems make it possible for government to become much more flexible, more task and project oriented, breaking away from classic administrative structures. However, most European governments remain traditionally organised into functional silos and change requires strong political will.

Conclusions: public value and the state as infrastructure

The broad future technological trends around e.government are reasonably predictable—more abundant bandwidth, capacity and speed; further digitisation; further miniaturisation; blurring of boundaries between hardware and bodies and biology; personalisation; more intensive conflicts over property rights and privacy; widening use of grid technologies. The precise forms that will be taken by technologies and their uses are far harder to predict—as recent experience over texting, blogs and mobile devices has shown.

But the bigger idea that lies behind many of the trends in e.government is not so much a technological idea. It is rather that states are reshaping themselves to be less structures that directly provide services or achieve outcomes; instead they are becoming more like infrastructures, orchestrating complex systems with greater capacities for self-organisation, and engaged in co-creation of outcomes with citizens and civil society. This requires strong provision of common protocols; easily useable public systems; and legible underlying rules. Some of the effects will be to make government less visible—with more complex underlying processes but simpler interfaces. Some of the effects will be to make government more modular (for example in the design of funding, support systems and care), as part of the broader personalisation of the welfare state—maintaining principles of equity and universality but allowing much more variation and personalisation within the system.

---

[9] Partly prefigured in Fountain Jane E. *Building the Virtual State: Information Technology and Institutional Change* (Washington DC: Brookings Institutions, 2001

This is the radical potential of e.government. It promises both greater differentiation and greater integration: differentiation of services and public relationships, alongside greater integration in achievement of outcomes, service design and social inclusion. To the extent that it does this it contributes to public value, and more broadly to the productive contribution of the public sector to the wider economy.

Part IV:
Media, Communication, Wireless
and Policies in the Network Society

Chapter 9
The IP TV Revolution

Jonathan Taplin

Introduction

This chapter outlines the critical transition from a media world of analog scarcity (a limited number of broadcast channels) to the coming world of digital abundance where any maker of content (films, music, video games) could have access to the world's audience through a server based on demand media environment. Today, all of the technical innovations needed to rollout this IPTV (Internet Protocol TV) system are in place. What is missing is the information policy initiatives which are being held up by entrenched powers frightened of change. This paper seeks to clarify what the new environment would look like and how the transition to IPTV could aid all of the existing media stakeholders. We believe that the new environment would also enable an explosion of creativity as the distribution bottleneck that has existed for one hundred years of media history could be unlocked.

The Analog to Digital Transition

The realization of a transition from the world of bandwidth scarcity to a new world of media abundance could not have happened without the seminal transition from analog to digital. The import of this can be seen in the chart below.

As we move from the analog age of videotape and broadcast TV, the ability of content owners and independent filmmakers and musicians to reach their audiences without needing the distribution power of multi-national media companies has important meaning for the future of an independent media system. To understand the transition to a Media On Demand age enabled by Internet Protocol, it is first necessary to understand the role of the traditional media powers.

Figure 9.1   Analog to Digital Transition

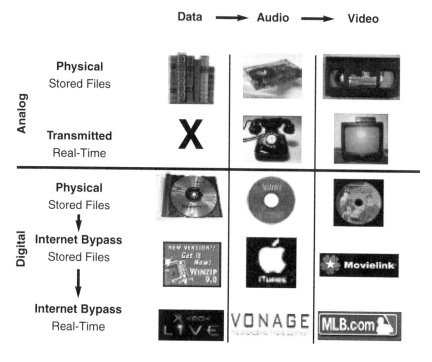

Source Sanford Bernstein & Co.

Background

Since the invention of radio at the beginning of the 20th century, our mass media has functioned in one way. Programmers looked to advertisers to pay for the cost of the media in return for access to the audience for their marketing campaigns. The rise of great multinational consumer product companies (Procter & Gamble, Unilever, Coca Cola, Ford, Daimler Chrysler, Nestle, Phillip Morris) coincided with the rise of radio and then television. This relationship was based on the law of scarcity. In order for Proctor and Gamble to grow it had to turn out an increasing number of basic commodity products (soap powder, toothpaste) whose only differentiation was in their marketing. And they quickly found that the only way to differentiate Tide from any other *identical product* was through TV or Radio advertising. In a world of a few commercial broadcast networks that existed on both Radio and TV in every major country, the *scarcity* of prime time advertising slots led to what William Paley (Founder of CBS) characterized as "a license to print money." For the audience the bargain was simple. You didn't have to pay for programming as long as you were willing to put up with the commercials. The other part of the bargain was that you paid $3.00 for a box of Tide, the ingredients of which cost about twenty-three cents, the remainder being marketing, packaging and profit.

This somewhat Faustian bargain worked well for all parties until about ten years ago. It was at this point that the growth of cable and satellite networks and the intrusion of new privatized broadcast networks began to make it very hard for a single television program to aggregate the mass audience needed for a basic commodity consumer product. Whereas in 1980 an average hit show on France's TF1 could draw 1/3 of the TV audience, today the highest rated program might draw 1/8 of the TV audience. So as the audience got disaggregated, so did the advertising business. A classic example would be MTV. By putting on very cheap programming (they got the videos for free from the record companies), MTV was able to undersell advertising to companies interested in reaching teenagers. This in turn allowed them to create outsized cash flows based on an average audience of about 500,000 viewers for any one program. The risk reward ratio was so great that between 1990 and 2000 over 220 new niche cable & satellite networks were created.

In the late 1990s a second disruptive factor to the classic TV advertising model entered the picture. This was the construction of the worldwide optical fiber backbone. The enthusiasm of the capital markets to supply funding to any entity willing to secure right of way led to a classic oversupply condition the pain of which was shared by both firms and governments. As any shareholder of Cisco, Nortel or Lucent will tell you, there was more than enough pain to be shared. Strategic planners at those three companies as well as many of their competitors and suppliers made one major miscalculation. They looked at the amount of fiber optic cable being delivered in 1999 and 2000 and projected the number of routers, switches, lasers and other gear that would be needed to enable that fiber. They then geared up their production capacity to be able to provide this. And then a curious thing happened. The orders never came. Partially because wave division multiplexing allowed carriers to get as much as 100 x throughput for each strand of fiber and partially because local Broadband connectivity did not continue to grow exponentially, the backbone providers simply left the "dark fiber" in the ground. So the telecom crash hit both the suppliers (Cisco, Nortel, Lucent) and the carriers (Global Crossing, AT&T, British Telecom, France Telecom, etc).

But what was a problem in 2001 becomes an opportunity today. The conversion to an IP-TV platform is possible because although we have already constructed a completely new way for Media to function in the society, we have chosen not to enable it. It is as if we had constructed the Autobahn in the 50's but neglected to build out the on and off ramps. In the last 6 years we have built an Internet Protocol (IP) based broadband network of such immense capacity that it is safe to say that we will not have to lay another mile of backbone fiber for the next ten years. Qwest, one of the companies that built out the backbone, ran an ad last year where a tired salesman pulls into a motel and asks the clerk if they have movies in the rooms, to which the clerk replies "every movie ever made." This is not an idle boast. Qwest's 34 strands of fiber could technically serve up every movie ever made on demand to every hotel room in the U.S. The only problem is that they have only "lit" four strands.[1] In order to realize such a dream we have only to imagine for a second, the notion of Universal Broadband. Today most western countries have what is called Universal Telephone service, meaning that every household has the availability of a minimum level of subsidized service. The notion would be to extend this provision to data and video. Although the existing build out of Broadband to the home has been progressing well, with Merrill Lynch estimating 110 million worldwide home broadband subscribers by 2007[2], a transition to a new system of IP-TV could only be enhanced by more Universal Broadband service.

Assume that by 2008 every home had Universal Broadband with an Ethernet jack in the wall to which you could plug any browser based IP media terminal (Figure 9.2) connected to a TV monitor with 2 MBPS connectivity capable of receiving streaming DVD quality video on demand.

---

[1] Author Interview with Joe Nacchio, CEO of Qwest, November 2000
[2] Merrill Lynch, *Broadband Report Card*, Oct. 19, 2004

Figure 9.2   Nevius Media Center Server

This system would use the one international set of standards (IP, HTML, MPEG) and would not in anyway be "choosing a winner" from the existing competitive technology and media companies. In addition the ability to use the tradition remote control and a Browser ensure a classic TV 'Lean-back" experience (Figure 9.3).

In this world anyone who wanted to "Publish" media would have no more trouble than putting up a web site today. They could sell their programming by subscription, "Pay per view" or give it away for free with targeted advertising. They would not have any "gatekeeper" determining who could reach their audience. Many of the worries about Media Concentration would be seen as the old paradigm of "Scarcity" as opposed to the IP world of total abundance. As the web has shown, no classic media company from the 70's and early 80's is a dominant force on the Internet. Yahoo, Google, AOL and Tiscali are all from a new era and make a lie to the notion that the old-line players always win in an open playing field. While it is clear that the marketing power of major media conglomerates like AOL Time Warner or Viacom/CBS would have huge power in the marketplace, it would be the power to persuade, not the power to control. Needless to say such an open system would depend on maintaining a regulatory stance of Network Neutrality as defined by U.S. FCC Chairman Powell's "Four Freedoms of Broadband"[3]. The EU telecom regulatory bodies have begun to weigh in on this matter and it is perhaps the most critical regulatory issue of our time.

---

[3] Freedom to Access Content. Freedom to Use Applications. Freedom to Attach Personal Devices. Freedom to Obtain Service Plan Information

Figure 9.3   Media Center Control System

But beyond the entertainment uses of such a network lies the world of education. Both the current Real Networks and Microsoft IP Video Codecs make it possible to publish video at VHS quality at 500 KBPS and DVD quality at 1.5 MBPS. These tools could enable the most important Distance Learning initiative in history. When MIT announced that it was going to allow people to audit it's courses on the internet, it was but one more sign that the extraordinary institutions of learning in our country are ready to embrace IP based distance learning. Not only can kids catch up on their courses on line, but also the whole world of continuing education for adults would be transformed. The fact that the technology companies of every EU country are always trying to raise the number of foreign technology workers they can employ is symbolic of the inability to retrain our workers for the high paying jobs of today. Universal broadband to the home would enable a platform for Universities and private Training Companies to sell their services to the country as a whole.

Now the obvious question that arises is: Why would the current Media Powers whose enormous market capitalizations have been built on a world of scarcity ever allow such a world of abundance to come into being? The answer quite simply is that they would make more money. To understand this we must look at the five constituents that control the current media universe: Producers, Advertisers, Distributors, Telecom Suppliers and Talent.

Producers

Producers develop, create, and finance programming. Though many Producers are also distributors (AOL-Time Warner, Viacom, Disney, Bertelsmann) it is important to separate the two roles in order to understand the IP-TV Challenge. As an example, let's take Discovery Networks. Originally begun as the Discovery Channel, their task was to buy existing nature programming from around the world as cheaply as possible and package it for distribution under the Discovery Channel brand. This proved to be quite lucrative as the demographic of educated affluent customers attracted to this programming was being sought by higher end advertisers (Mercedes, Merrill Lynch, etc) who were just beginning to move their ads from high end print publications (Wall Street Journal, New Yorker, Vanity Fair, etc) into television. Needless to say for Mercedes to advertise on a Network sit-com was a total waste of money and so the cheap pricing of Discovery Channel was a relatively efficient buy. However, two things happened from the point of view of Discovery as a Producer that has changed the economics. First they began to run out of programming they could acquire cheaply and therefore had to begin producing their own shows at a much higher cost per hour. Second, as the number of cable distribution channels began to grow (and then explode with satellite and digital cable) Discovery believed it had to defend it's brand against imitators and so grew niche networks (Animal Planet, Discovery Health), each of which had to be programmed 24 hours a day, seven days a week, 365 days per year.

Today the programming budget for the twelve Discovery Networks is probably in excess of $1.5 billion per year[4]. Now the audience for this type of programming has not grown by a factor of 24x, so they are basically cannibalizing their own and their advertisers audience. If you extrapolate this out to the universe of almost 300 "Programming Services" on cable or satellite, you can see that the economics of a 500-channel universe will become increasingly tenuous. Discovery

---

[4] Legg Mason Estimate, July 2004

alone is responsible for programming 105,000 hours of television per year. Even assuming that half the hours are re-runs, the programming will have to get cheaper each year in order for them to reach break-even on the new networks as there is no way the advertiser will continue to pay higher rates for an increasingly fractured audience (the average Discovery digital channel is reaching less than 80,000 viewers per program).

Contrasting this with our Universal Broadband Network, one could easily see how Discovery could cut by half its programming budget and produce twenty great hours of new "on demand" programming a week with extraordinary production values. The most fanatic viewer of Discovery type programming probably does not have more than ten hours per week to spend watching this type of programming. But if they did, Discovery could cheaply archive every single episode of programming it owns and make those accessible on a pay per view or subscription basis. For the viewer, the programming could be watched when they wanted to watch it, with full VCR-like controls and Discovery could offer a "My Discovery" option that would push pet shows to the pet lover and alligator wrestling to the fans of that genre. Since the object of Discovery's business is to sell advertising, it could offer the pet food advertiser very targeted opportunities to not only advertise to the specific audience they wanted, but to also sell their product through interactive ads with e-commerce capability. All of the technology to enable this vision currently is in place. More importantly, the costs of streaming the programming are going through a dramatic downswing (Table 9.1).

Advertisers

The movement of Euros away from the broadcast networks to cable and Satellite networks continues, but this year even cable networks have had to lower their rates. The famous maxim by U.S. department store mogul John Wanamaker that "50% of my advertising expenditures are wasted. I just don't know which 50%" is truer than ever. This problem has been exacerbated by the introduction of the Personal Video Recorder (PVR), originally under the brand name TiVo and now introduced as an add-on to the standard cable set top box. The potential effect of widespread diffusion of PVR's is quite dramatic (Table 9.1) and could lead to a quicker adoption of the IP-TV paradigm.

Table 9.1   Downward Internet Streaming Costs

	Today	End-1 Yr	End-2 Yr	End-5 Yr
Stream: Megabits/Second	0.300	0.300	0.300	0.300
Cost per Gigabyte	$1.150	$0.690	$0.414	$0.069
Annual Improvement		(40)%	(40)%	(40)%
Usage Megabits per Hour	1,080	1,080	1,080	1,080
Gigabytes per Hour	0.14	0.14	0.14	0.14
Cost per Hour	$0.1553	$0.0932	$0.0559	$0.0121
Cost per Streamed Units ($)/Min.	0.0026	0.0016	0.0009	0.0002
Hours of Usage per Day	8	8	8	8
Hours of Usage per Year	2,920	2,920	2,920	2,920
Streaming Cost per Year @ 8-Hr Day	$453.33	$272.00	$163.20	$35.25
Streaming Cost per Month	37.78	22.67	13.60	2.94
Sub. Fees for 40 Basic Cable Nets	7.98	8.38	8.80	10.18
Annual Increase in Subscriber Fees		5%	5%	5%
Total Content and Web Transport Costs	$45.76	$31.05	$22.40	$13.12
Add Cable Op. EBITDA Margin	35%	35%	35%	35%
Total Charged Consumer	$61.77	$41.91	$30.24	$17.72

Source: Sanford Bernstein & Co.

The ability of the Internet to target an audience was seen as a way out of the misplaced advertising trap, but it quickly became clear that the ubiquitous banner ad lacked the basic power of the ad industry: emotion. As banners proliferated, the web surfer simply didn't even see them, much less click through (click-throughs were lower than 1%). A video quality broadband network affords advertisers the Holy Grail; the ability to target like the web combined with the ability to run full screen 30-second commercials that allow interested users to click-through to the e-commerce page of the advertiser. If you are moved by the Gap ad, you can immediately buy the clothes. Furthermore, the ad buyer can specify a demographic target (females, 14-18, in specific zip codes) and only pay for that target. In recent tests with this broadband technology, click through rates on interactive video ads were more than 30%.

Table 9.2   PVR Penetration and Commercial Skipping Estimates

PVR Negative Impacts	2004E	2005E	2006E	2007E	2008E	2009E	2014E	2016E
PVR Assumptions								
22 PVR Penetration	6%	11%	16%	20%	22%	25%	25%	35%
23 PVRS @ Year-End	7	12	18	22	25	28	42	46
24 Growth of PVRs	103%	85%	50%	22%	14%	12%	6%	4%
PVR Impact Calculations								
25 Pct of Recorded Commercials Skipped	70%	70%	70%	70%	70%	70%	70%	70%
26 Pct of Total Commercials Skipped in PVR Households	14.81%	15.96%	17.16%	18.40%	19.69%	21.02%	27.43%	29.99%
27 Effective Average Homes Reduced by PVRs	(0.96)	(1.92)	(3.09)	(4.05)	(4.92)	(5.88)	(11.46)	(13.68)
28 Advertising "At Risk" in All PVR HHLDs ($mil)	$(560)	$(1,172)	$(2,015)	$(2,782)	$(3,587)	$(4,522)	$(10,834)	$(13,980)
29 Pct of TV Advertising "At Risk"	(1)%	(2)%	(3)%	(4)%	(4)%	(5)%	(10)%	(11)%
30 Adding Demographic Premium	125%	125%	125%	125%	125%	125%	110%	110%
31 Adjusted "At Risk" in All PVR HHLDs ($ mil)	$(700)	$(1,465)	$(2,519)	$(3,478)	$(4,484)	$(5,653)	$(11,917)	$(15,378)
32 Adjusted Pct of TV Advertising "At Risk"	(1)%	(2)%	(4)%	(5)%	(5)%	(6)%	(11)%	(12)%

Source: Sanford Bernstein & CO

Distributors

In a new world media order, the role of distributor would change. Today, the six basic conduits for video media are theaters, broadcast TV, cable TV, satellite TV, video rental stores, and broadband IP networks. The classic producer/distributor like AOL Time Warner seeks to market its product through every one of these channels. And in each of these channels there is a third party who can demand a share of the revenue from the transaction.

To begin to understand this new world of IP-TV it will be important to differentiate between Broadband Carriers and Broadcasters. Broadband carriers would be comprised of all DSL providers (FT, BT, Telecom Italia, Deutsche Telekom, etc) all cable providers with upgraded Hybrid Fiber/Coax plants, all ISP's offering Broadband service (AOL, Tiscali, MSN) and all fixed wireless providers. Broadcasters would consist of all over the air TV networks and all Satellite networks. In an IP-TV world the Broadband Carriers would make their money by providing metered service much like your cellular or utility service. Heavy users of streaming media would pay more than light users. Distributors of content could then sell to the Carrier's customer base on an Open Access basis and use the three basic models for payment: monthly subscription, pay per view or ad supported content. Clearly the Broadcasting model would not be able to compete because of lack of a two-way network. However, this transition to IP-TV would be gradual and still the "Event" type of programming like sports or award shows which demands a specific mass audience to be present at a specific time would be a staple of the broadcasting universe for a long time.

Telecom Suppliers

The last few years has seen a steep downturn in the Telecom economy. The obvious reason was that without reasonably priced broadband connectivity in the last mile, no one needed to enable the immense backbone networks that had been built. Companies like Cisco, Nortel, and Lucent saw their market caps fall by 50%. Because much of the last mile Broadband connectivity is controlled by the national telecoms, there was a clear bottleneck in the system. Recent attempts at regulatory relief have proved only partially successful. It is here that the European market must make aggressive moves to keep up in the Broadband economy. Although the necessary fiber backbone for a Trans-European IP TV system is in place, the local build out of robust broadband capacity to the home is lagging both Asian and the U.S. In the U.S. the huge capital investment by cable companies in hybrid fiber coax has led to their ability to offer 6 MBPS downstream to the home. (Figure 9.4)

Figure 9.4   U.S. Cable Capital Expenditures

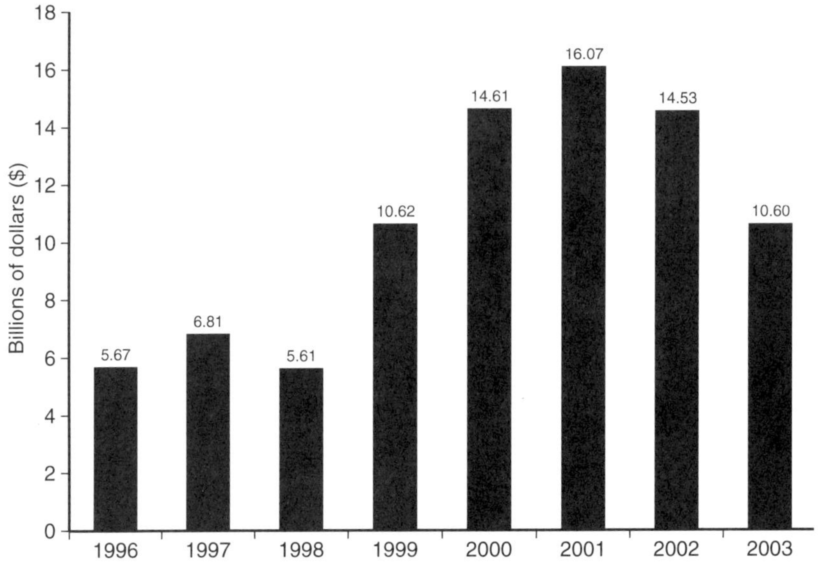

Source: Kagan World Media, *Broadband Cable Financial Databook*

The recent announcements by both by U.S. carriers SBC and Verizon to build out their fiber to the home networks also presage a real boost to the IP-TV vision. By unlocking the bottleneck, thereby creating a need to enable the immense dark fiber backbone, the European Telecom Economy could be put back on solid footing and a potentially fatal blow to the regions economic health could be avoided.

Talent

It is one of the great ironies of the age of media consolidation that giants like Fox, Time Warner and Canal + promote themselves as "Brands." In the world of entertainment, the artist is the brand. The navigation metaphor of Apple's I-Tunes, a digital music service that has sold 54 million downloads in one year acknowledged this reality. All you needed to do was type in the name of the artist. It is actually impossible to search by record company "brand." Further empowering the notion of the artist's primacy is the arrival of powerful new inexpensive digital tools for both music and video production. This production doesn't have to be as expensive as it is and the true artist will work for much less if he or she has a real stake in the gross earning power of their work.

So how would the arrival of Universal Broadband help foster a new artistic renaissance in the culture? If the world of distribution scarcity has built a wasteful media economy, it would stand to reason that a world of abundant, cheap digital technology and distribution might help the true artist escape the current media "Hit" economics. If the only things being financed are aimed at the mass audience that appeal to the raunchiest lowest common denominator, then the artist with a different perspective has a hard time getting financed. This realization is leading some in the entertainment business to realize that the tyranny of the 80-20 rule could be broken. Chris Anderson of Wired Magazine has described a new selling model called "The Long Tail," in which on-line retailers are finding that even the most obscure content sells at an acceptable level on line. Although the average large record store might have a total of 40,000 individual songs in it's racks, the digital music service Rhapsody currently has over 500,000 (Figure 9.5) and song number 499,999 sells well enough to pay for itself.

Is IP-TV a pipe dream? Some Mobius-shaped fantasy? By year-end 2005 there will be 40 million homes in the EU with Broadband. An additional 5 million college students have access to broadband at their University. Moving the signal from the PC to the TV will evolve over the next 12 months as new set top boxes, game consoles and wireless home networks proliferate. What is needed is the combination of political will and the vision to realize that the educational and cultural needs of the country will be enhanced by the widespread deployment of IP-TV.

Figure 9.5   Monthly Download Performance of Rhapsody-Source-Wired Magazine

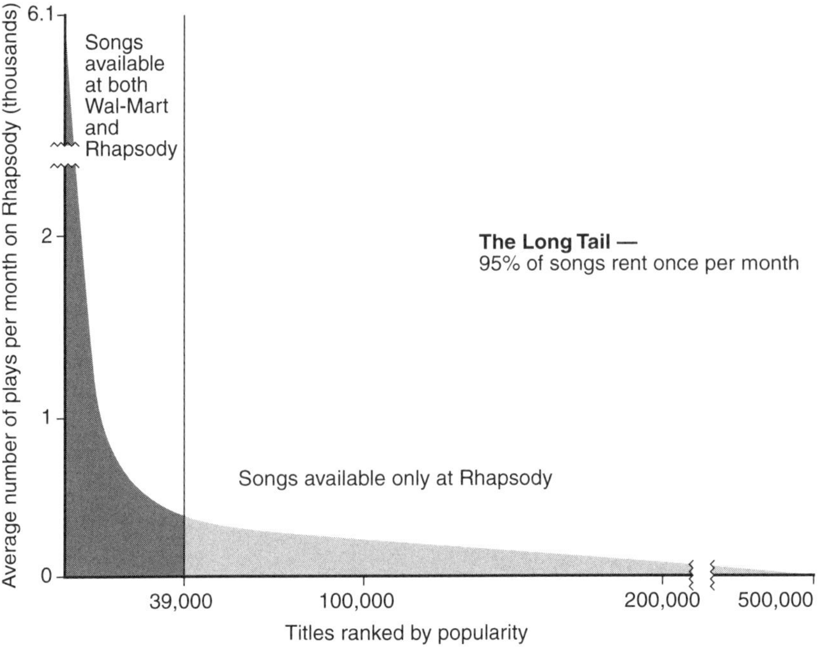

Source: Wired magazine

We are in the Media Interregnum. In the past lies the failed orthodoxy of the domination of all media by a few major corporations, subjecting artists, citizens, politicians, marketers and the technology economy to their will. In the future lies a Renaissance of media, entertainment and learning fueling a new technology growth economy that will lift our minds and our spirits and keep our economic growth on track in the process. This radical change in the media landscape will not arrive without some serious turf battles between owners of content and owners of "pipe." Cable and Telephone companies will naturally migrate towards a "walled garden" approach to Broadband, hoping to preserve their "gatekeeper" status between content owners and their customers. Already in the U.S. the cable companies have gotten the FCC to reclassify broadband to an Information service from its previous classification as a Telecommunications service. This is not a trivial difference. Telecommunications services have a "common carrier" component, preventing the owner of the network from discriminating in any way. As the Center for Digital Democracy states, "The principle of nondiscriminatory communication has long governed our telephone system and the Internet itself, allowing any party to transmit any message to any other party without interference by the network operator. This principle of free expression should be maintained for broadband as well. High-speed Internet users should be allowed unimpeded communications with any network device, use of any lawful service, and transmission of any data." In order to move into a new world of IP-TV that will be the preferred platform for all of the constituencies of the digital age, the EU can take the lead to preserve the open nature of Broadband Internet and usher in a new age of IP TV.

Chapter 10

Television and Internet in the Construction of identity

Imma Tubella

Introduction

The world of communications has changed radically due to the development of digital technologies. The multiplicity of Television channels and Internet and the access to information in all its formats from around the world has had a strong impact on traditional media and, at the same time, as Thompson (1997) points out, digital technologies have transformed the spatial and temporal organization of social life, creating new forms of action and interaction, new kinds of social relationship and new ways of relating to others and to oneself.

The new forms of social interaction allowed by Internet oblige us to reconsider the meaning of concepts as community or identity. The big impact of Internet on the expression and perception of social identities is relatively clear: it spans cultural spheres and geographical boundaries and allows communication from many to many. The real difference between the Internet and all preceding media forms is the role it gives to people: millions connected in many to many relationships and interactions. In Internet, common space is a direct result of synergy and connectivity.

One of the most important factors for the development of collective identity is and has been communication. If we understand the concept identity not as a given reality but as a work in progress, we will appreciate the important role of communication as the cement of its building process.

There are two types of identity building which are relevant here: individual identity understood as the sense of oneself as an individual endowed with certain characteristics and potentialities, and collective identity, understood as a sense of oneself as a member of a social group. It is a sense of belonging, a sense of being part of a collectivity.

Both the sense of oneself and the sense of belonging are shaped by the values beliefs and forms of behaving transmitted from the past, but also highly influenced by symbolic materials transmitted by media. In this sense, some authors refer to media as substitutes of tradition.

Giddens (1991) tries to understand the persistence of national identities and propose to be considered by analyzing how citizenship is created and recreated in local situations in the context of the everyday uses and production of culture. During many years, Television has taken the place of vernacular literatures in the construction of a common imaginary and complicity.

My principal concern in this chapter is that while traditional media, in special television, play an enormous role in the construction of collective identity, Internet influences the construction of individual identity, as individuals increasingly rely on their own resources to construct a coherent identity for themselves in an open process of self formation as a symbolic project through the utilization of symbolic materials available to them. This is an open process that will change overtime as people adapt new symbolic materials. This is a relatively easy process for individuals but much more difficult for collectivities who have tendencies to remain fixed in their traditional values.

The difference resides in the fact that the use of television in the construction identity is vertical, from one to many and opposite, the use of Internet in this process of self formation depends of the will of each individual. It is a horizontal use, from many to many.

The narrative of self identity, individual or collective, is continually modified in the process of retelling. The main issue here is to know who the teller is, especially in the case of collectivities. If we think that media in part are the teller, we will understand the importance they have in the process of self formation.

Individuals have gradually more access to what Thompson (1997) describes as non-local knowledge. It is interesting to point out the process of appropriation, because non-local knowledge is always appropriated by individuals in specific locations. The case of *Dallas* is a very interesting one. In Catalonia, *Dallas* has been a powerful tool for the normalization of Catalan language. I will return to this issue when analyzing the Catalan situation in terms of the role of media in the construction of Catalan identity. Now, children in Catalonia play in Catalan because they watch *Chin Chan* in Catalan. In my childhood, I used to play in Spanish when I was acting as a teacher, as a shopper or as a seller. I only used to speak in Catalan when I acted as a mother. Then, Catalan was forbidden, even for Hollywood actors.

My point of view is that the process of self formation as individuals and as collectivities becomes increasingly dependent on access to mediated forms of communication. How do Information Technologies, and specifically Internet, affect individuals and communities? What constitutes a community in the world of electronic mediation? What are the essential ingredients? Who are the new mediating forces?

As professor Cole writes in the introduction of his last version of the World Internet Project[1], a lot of academic studies have examined the impact of television on viewers' lives, but researchers now realize that we missed a golden opportunity by not looking at individuals and their behavior prior to their acquisition of television sets and going back to the same people year after year to see how exposure to the medium changed them and at the same time, I would add, society. In Catalonia we don't have a panel, we just have an important research program about the transformation of individuals and society due to the impact of Internet[2], but we have some empirical data that can help our attempt to answer these questions.

In our research in Catalonia we assume that network society is not just the result of the impact of information technologies on social structures, but a new social form using communication as one of the central factors defining it, and becoming the emblematic figure of our current society. It is because of this that the study of the use of the communications media is essential to understand the transformation of social life and the creation of new forms of exercising power disassociated from the fact of sharing a common space. However, study of the practices that include Internet use and how this use has modified them, if it has, gives us elements of empirical analysis that help us to situate the levels of interaction and connectivity of Catalan society. On the other hand, questions such as communication practices in relation to the use of language, or to construction of meaning and, therefore, of identity, are also important parts of our analysis.

---

[1] http:// www.digitalfuture.org

[2] Projecte Internet Catalunya: http://www.uoc.edu/in3/pic/eng/pic1.html

The Catalan case

In Catalonia, collective identity is central to the political debate. On the other hand, radio and television have been key institutions through which listeners and viewers have come to imagine themselves as members of the national community. It is not strange that the very first law approved by the Parliament of Catalonia in 1982 just as democracy was being recovered was the Law for the Creation of the Catalan Broadcasting Corporation with the purpose of linguistic, cultural and national normalization.

Catalan Television (TVC) began broadcasting on September 11, 1983, some months before Basque Television did as well, breaking the monopoly of television in Spain and, therefore, the centralist Spanish discourse. By 1990, eleven autonomous broadcasting organizations had been approved, seven of which had already begun broadcasting on a daily basis, in an outlaw situation due to problems with the Spanish State.

What did cultural normalization mean at this moment and in this context? In 1975, data from the official census say that only 60% of people living in Catalonia could speak Catalan. In 1986, two years after the creation of Catalan Television, the census says that 64,2% could speak it; and in 1995, this percentage was 79,8%. In our research we observe that Catalan knowledge is currently almost universal, reaching a 97,7%. If we look at Catalan Television audiences in programs like *Dallas* or football in 1984 and 1985 we observe that a big amount of people watching these programs in Catalan were Spanish speakers who couldn't speak Catalan language. The growth in this knowledge is impressive in relation with the delay to reach it. In this way some linguists[3] speak of it as a cultural revolution.

Catalonia is a nation that has always cultivated a strong desire to express and strengthen its identity on both cultural and national levels. From a Catalan point of view, cultural identity is not just a different language but a set of habits, traditions, values, beliefs, and ways of living, thinking and behaving, in other words, a certain style of life. In this sense, media play a very important role as an operational instrument.

---

[3] Francesc Vallverdú, El català estàndard als mitjans audiovisuals, CCRTV, April 1996

In the field of communication practices in Catalan society, our Project Internet Catalunya of 2002 ratifies a well-known fact: the most frequent daily practice is watching television (90.8%). What is perhaps not so commonly known, and which we have considered to be a communication practice, is that the second most common use of daily time is speaking with people at home, playing with children or similar activities (80.8%). Listening to the radio occupies the third place (64.3%), followed by listening to music (57.6%). Press and magazines occupy the sixth place (45.7%). In 2002, Internet was used in Catalonia by 34,6% of the population. Currently, this percentage has grown to 39,7%.[4]

The communication practice most affected by Internet use in 2002 and certainly now is television. A 16.6% of people watched less television since they were connected to the Internet. Of this 16.6%, 61.7% were under 30 years old.

In a research done a year later in Portugal by the Centro de Investigaçao e Estudos de Sociologia in which our questionnaire[5] was partly used, we can see that the situation was quite different. There was almost no difference between users and non users in their daily use of TV (98,9% and 99,4%, respectively)[6]. At this time, we were thinking about the possibility of networking Portugal and Catalonia to evaluate, in a comparative level, transformation in media use. Unfortunately, we didn't have the opportunity to pursue this in depth. Maybe some day we will be able to do it.

In the United States, the same year, users began to report spending less time with TV, newspapers and magazines (about 45 to 60' a week less than nonusers. Some users reported spending more time with online newspapers[7]. In 2005, the biggest gap in media use between users and non-users continues to be the amount of time they watch television. In 2004, internet users watched about 4,6 hours of television less per week than non-users.[8] The majority of those who watch television

---

[4] IDESCAT 2004

[5] da Costa, A.F.; Cardoso, G.; Gomes, MdoC; Conceiçao, CP (2003), A Sociedade em Rede em Portugal, Lisboa, ISCTE

[6] Although in terms of time spent on each activity we find considerable differences of up to more than 40 minutes less television viewing among internet users in Portugal.

[7] The digital future report, www.digitalcenter.org

[8] op. cit

every day are Internet non-users while, in contrast, the majority of those who watch it weekly are users and 40% of those who never watch it are also users.

Nevertheless in Catalonia, television is still the reference media for information (74.6%). This percentage in Portugal is 97,8%. For local events the second most frequent method is personal communication. In Portugal, we observe the same situation but, even if personal communication occupies the second place, the distance between Television (99,3%) and "speaking with family, friends and other people" (84,0%) is higher than in Catalonia.

In contrast, in 2002, Internet was used as an information source by just 1% of the Catalan population and only to find out about international events. General population mainly trusted radio, while Internet users trusted printed media.

As far as language related to communication practices is concerned, Spanish dominates the printed media, far ahead of Catalan. On television, in contrast, both languages are almost even, with 47,6% of the population watching television in Catalan.

In Internet the dominant language is Spanish. On one hand, this is due to a question of the amount of contents in this language, yet on the other hand, to a question of choice.

In general, among Internet users, 89% do not habitually use English, 53,7% do not habitually use Catalan and 20,5% do not habitually use Spanish.

The next practice that has very slightly diminished is watching videos or DVDs, followed by reading books and listening to the radio. It is always the youngest group that has the highest tendency to migrate towards the Internet. In contrast, the communication practice that has increased most is listening to music (5%), possibly due to the Napster phenomenon, followed by playing computer or console games.

In short, Catalan population had and still has two main communication practices: watching television and talking to people in their immediate environment, specifically within the family environment, corresponding, as we shall see, with the dominant, overall major feeling of identification, the family.

In the 20th century, "home" has been a breathing space from work and public life, a place where one can pull back from the world, enjoy one's personal privacy, build familial relations and individual objectives. Increasingly, however, people are able to work, learn, shop, participate in civic events and campaigns and even vote from home. The separation of work and leisure evaporates and the meaning of privacy, home and community is changing significantly.

Therefore, television is still the reference communication medium, yet in contrast, people trust radio more. From the point of view of consumer confidence, radio occupies the first place as 29.6% trust it more, compared to 25.8% who have more confidence in the printed press and 20.8% who trust television. If we analyze consumer confidence levels in the Internet, we see that those who trust it a lot are mainly users (89.3%), although 67% of those who say they trust it very little are also users.

Identity and communication are language, but so are emotion, sentiment and individual and collective representation. In this sense, Catalonia, in spite of the great leap forward that Catalan Television represents, has a serious control deficit in its own representation. In the process of construction of meaning, or of a certain creation of collective consensus, we should ask what the role of communications media should be and, specifically, that of Internet as a tool for social and collective cohesion, because identity is a source of meaning and sensibility, but it is also shared sensibility, and the communications media are the creators of sensibility.

As important as History itself is the history that the community is able to explain to its fellow members, the history of myths and beliefs created as an element of cohesion. If this statement is correct, we should agree with the importance and the influence of the communications media in the construction of a common discourse and collective representation.

Finally, a key question for our research is, what role does Internet use or non-use play in building Catalan identity? Because if identity is a network of interactions where the true importance lays not in simple existence but in transformation, in representation and construction of meaning, in difference and not in negation, and if collective identity is furthermore the capacity to communicate, what role does Internet play in the transformation of this identity? Is it simply a transmission tool in which the only significant factor is the level of use, or does it in some way conform to a differential model? What relationship is there, if any, between population profiles, identity practices and Internet uses? What shared values are there between elements of dominant identification, identity characteristics and the values of the new social structure based around the web, such as individual freedom or open communication?

Building Catalan identity in the network society

In our research in 2002 we arrived to an initial conclusion: the perspective of identification, the traditional referents for identity construction such as language, culture or one's country change and we find new dominant identification referents such as the family or the individual, which are also basic elements of collective identity construction and key aspects for cohesion in a network society.

A key differential factor in Catalonia as a network society could be the search for a collective, complex strategy of adaptation to the change produced by the characteristic phenomena of economic, cultural, social, demographic, political and, in general, structural globalization. If this has a social visibility, it could constitute a powerful construction element for meaning and representation of collective will. That is, to go from a differentiated project of unity, natural to a resistance identity needing the element of dominion to construct a meaning and aspects such as language, territory or history on which to support itself, a network node with its own personality and will to exist, a new definition is needed. Our data show us that the period of resistance identity was overcome because there are certain basic aspects of what we could call "being Catalan," the most significant of which is language, which has been normalized. In this scenario, it is normal for resistance to tend to dissipate.

In contrast, elements that generally are not considered in traditional identity constructions like projects for personal autonomy have, in Catalonia, a positive association to construction of identity.

If, as we have seen, one of the clearest differential factors in Catalonia, today, is language, and a second differential factor is level of personal autonomy, the possibility opens before us for construction of a project identity going beyond the traditional elements of identity construction and one that integrates others that are much more in agreement with the economic, social and political structure of the information society.

In summary, then, one of the basic ideas emerging from our research, clearly demonstrable in empirical terms, is that once we have analyzed the different dimensions of the projects for personal autonomy, we have verified that on one hand, the more autonomous people are, the more Catalan identity they have and, on the other hand, the more autonomous people are, the more they use the Internet and with more intensity.

If we demonstrate that the Internet is a clear agent for construction of personal autonomy and that for cultural reasons, the younger the population, the more they use it, we could conclude that, although in Catalan identity practice, age works *in contra*, when a project for personal autonomy exists alongside Internet use, identity practice is strengthened in general, but specifically among the young.

This also confirms our hypotheses about the importance of personal will in identity construction that has materialized in a project, the reflection of a collective strategy we discussed above, and which we have also called project identity. Project identity can be built not on the basis of difference, but on a basis of shared beliefs and values, or on personalized patterns of behavior.

Television is a territorial medium, broadcasting in the same space at the same time. Internet is not. The territory of Internet is the language you know, the language you are able to understand. Let's remind here that in Catalonia 89% of Internet users never use English in the net, 53,7% never use Catalan and 20,5% never use Spanish. That gives us a first picture of the Internet territory for Catalan users. Perhaps the main contribution of Internet in the construction and reconstruction of identity and community is the break down of the old idea of a territorial based community and belonging. Today territory is still relevant but there are other important factors to be considered, for instance, connectiveness and cooperation.

Television, a mass medium, has been a space of influence but by definition, vertical and passive: one to many. Internet, a many to many medium is horizontal, a space of participation, a space of connection. Increasingly we must think in terms of spaces of transmission.

Could we affirm that we are in a transition time from collective identity to cooperative identity, from passive identity depending on third parties to active identity building processes depending just on a one self project? What it seems clear is that identities are constituted within a system of social relations and require the reciprocal recognition of others. If this is true we can say that Internet facilitates the recognition because facilitates a bidirectional communication. Today, identity is not only influenced by what you see but by how you look.

The creation of new social and politico-economical geographies requires new strategies of community self conceptualization and identity. In modern societies, much of this sense of shared identity is communicated through media technologies. These technologies help to transmit shared symbolic forms, a sense of group culture and, at the end, to foster what de Tocqueville called "Fellow feeling, Renan commandership and Anderson deep horizontal commandership. Some authors claim that modern societies are defined by the degree to which the transmission of fellow feeling to symbolic forms is no longer restricted to contexts to face to face interaction. Other authors, such as Robert Putman, think in terms of social capital as features of social life—networks, norms and trust—that enable participants to act together more effectively to pursue shared objectives that permit cooperation among them.

We observe important differences between project identities, with clearly defined shared objectives involved in the horizontally membership building and the legitimating identities using vertical authority. The study of the maintenance of identity in diasporas and the cultivation of a virtual home, using Internet and being connected with the motherland and with fellows on the world, is a good example of horizontal community building.

How does the cultural use of Information Technologies differ from the cultural use of Television? I don't have still empirical evidence of it I hope that my research in progress about the time management of the population concerning the use of media and information technologies in general is going to illuminate my way.

Currently, I can affirm that the use of Information Technologies in Catalonia is transforming the construction of identity from a concept of given destiny where television has played an important role as a tool of cohesion and representation, to a much more dynamic concept involving collective and cooperative action, where the role of Internet, mobile phones, and Information Technologies in general is central.

We are just at the starting point of a two years research program about transformations of media in Catalonia because of the impact of Information Technologies. At the same time, we will analyze the transformation of identity building because of this new influence. We will be able to compare the central role of Television on this construction during the last twenty years and observe what happens now with young people migrating to Internet. We hope to go deep in our data from our first research and to proof the use of Internet as an empowerment tool connected with the birth of a new kind of identity construction based in the individual will and in the capacity to formulate projects, not just to resist but to cooperate.

References

Castells, M. (2001): La Galaxia Internet, Barcelona, Areté

Castells, M.; Tubella, I.; Sancho, T. and others (2003): La societat xarxa a Catalunya, Barcelona, Plaza y Janés

Giddens, A. (1991), Modernity and Self Identity: Self and Society in the late modern age, Standford University Press

Goffman, E. (1969): The presentation of Self in Everyday Life, London, Penguin

Grodin, D. & Lindloft, T. ed. (1996): Constructing the Self in a Mediated World, Thousand Oaks, CA, Sage

Habermas, J. (1992) *"Citizenship and National Identity: Some reflections on the future of Europe,"* Praxis International, 12 (1), 1-19

Morley, D. & Robins, K. (1995): Spaces of Identity: Global media, electronic landscapes and cultural boundaries, new York, Routledge

Schlesinger, Ph. (1997) "From cultural defense to political culture: Media, politics and collective identity in the European Union," *Media, Culture and Society*

Smith, A. (1991): National Identity, London, Penguin

Thompson, J.B. (1995) The Media and Modernity: A Social Theory of the Media, Cambridge, Polity Press

Turkle, S. (1995), Life on the screen: Identity in the Age of the Internet, New York, Simon & Schuster

Wellman, B. (2001) *"Phisical place and cyberspace: The rise of networked individualism."* Internet Journal of Urban and Regional Research

Chapter 11

Geeks, Bureaucrats and Cowboys: Deploying Internet Infrastructure, the Wireless Way

François Bar and Hernan Galperin

Introduction

The deployment of communication infrastructure has traditionally been associated with big investment programs undertaken by large entities such as telecommunications operators and government agencies. The reason is quite simple: only these entities were able to amass the sizeable capital and attain the necessary economies of scale involved in deploying wired networks. However, three parallel trends are converging to permit departure from that tradition: the emergence of more flexible spectrum policies, which has removed regulatory barriers to entry; the advent of new wireless technologies, which has fundamentally changed the cost equation in favour of wireless solutions; and the entrance of many small business and non-profit actors eager to play new roles in the creation and management of wireless communication networks.

While advances in wireless technologies have significantly reduced the deployment costs for communications infrastructure, their transformative impact on the architecture and control of communication networks is often overlooked. Because wireless technologies are not subject to the same economies of scale as traditional wireline technologies, they allow end-users—often acting collectively through cooperatives and other local institutions—to deploy and manage systems themselves in ways not previously possible.

This in turn pushes the boundary that divides control between users and providers much deeper into the network, opening the possibility of a radically decentralized approach to system expansion, based on the integration of local wireless networks built and managed by users. While most of today's networks continue to be built by large organizations, the evidence increasingly points to a potentially disruptive shift in the way wireless communication networks are being deployed and operated (Best, 2003; Bar and Galperin,2004).

The tension between these two alternative logics of network deployment is well illustrated in the case of wireless Internet access services. One the one hand, mobile telephony operators have made considerable investments to deploy third-generation (3G) networks that allow mobile customers to access a variety of IP-based services. On the other, wireless enthusiasts, small entrepreneurs, and local governments are increasingly taking advantage of a new breed of wireless networking technologies to build wireless local area networks (WLANs), particularly in areas neglected by large operators. 3G networks follow the traditional model of large investments in infrastructure equipment for centrally-planned and controlled networks; WLANs on the other hand consist of small investments in terminal equipment by independent actors at the local level without coordination or a pre-conceived plan. While both are evolving in parallel (and some argue, are complementary), the tension is evident in recent policy debates about how to allocate limited resources (notably the radio spectrum) and the role played by local governments and cooperative organizations in the deployment of advanced wireless networks.

The paper is organized as follows: in the first part we review the evolution of the new breed of WLAN technologies, in particular Wi-Fi, and discuss its implications for the architecture and control of emerging wireless broadband networks. We draw on the social constructivist history of large technical systems and the work of economic historians concerned with the evolution of technology to understand the largely unexpected success of Wi-Fi. Next we review the evidence on the bottom-up deployment of wireless networks by local actors, focusing on three types of initiatives driven by different deployment dynamics: end-user cooperatives (affectionately referred to as "geeks" in our title), wireless ISPs ("cowboys"), and municipal government ("bureaucrats"). The conclusion discusses the policy and institutional issues most likely to affect the balance between centralized and decentralized deployment of wireless broadband networks in the near future.

From the cordless Ethernet to the wireless mesh: The unexpected evolution of Wi-Fi

WLAN technologies refer to a broad family of non-cellular wireless communication solutions which in practice includes most of the technologies currently under the purview of the IEEE 802.xx standardization activities. While this encompasses a range of technologies with different attributes and at various stages of development, the focus of this paper will be on the suite of IEEE 802.11 standards also known as Wi-Fi. The reason is simple: this family of WLAN standards has gained broad acceptance, leading to significant cost reductions due to volume production, and the level of penetration in a variety of consumer devices (from PCs to PDAs to mobile phones) is fast reaching infrastructure scale. Wi-Fi has evolved in a somewhat accidental manner, through an evolutionary path not envisioned by its original creators and early backers. This is a rather consistent pattern in the evolution of technological systems (e.g., Nye, 1990; Fischer, 1992). In the case of Wi-Fi, it was initially conceived as a wireless alternative for short-range connections between computers within homes and offices (i.e., a cordless Ethernet). However, it soon became clear that Wi-Fi could also be used to extend the reach of computer networks into public spaces. Moreover, both equipment vendors and wireless enthusiasts also realized that, with the appropriate hardware and clever tinkering, point-to-point connections could be made over several kilometers. The important role played by early adopters in the innovation process and testing of the technology under different conditions is again consistent with previous patterns of technological evolution (the best known case being that of amateur radio operators in the early 20th century).[1]

Wi-Fi has experienced extraordinary growth since 1997, when the IEEE finalized the original 802.11 specifications.[2] It is worth noting that the technology emerged amidst competition from alternative standards for WLANs, notably HomeRF and HiperLAN.

---

[1] See Douglas (1987).

[2] Today, Wi-Fi comes in three basic flavors: 802.11b, which operates in the 2.4GHz frequency range and offers speeds up to 11Mb/s; 802.11a, which operates in the 5GHz frequency range and offers speeds up to 54Mb/s; and the most recent 802.11g, which is backwards compatible with 802.11b but offers speeds up to 54Mb/s. Work continues on new variations that will improve the range, security and functionality of Wi-Fi, such as 802.11e (Quality of Service), 802.11r (roaming), and 802.11s (meshing).

Interestingly, because these standards emerged from within the computer rather than the telecom industry, the standardization process has been largely led by the private sector, organized around industry consortia such as the HomeRF Working Group and semi-public organizations such as the IEEE. Compared to the contentious case of 3G standards (see Cowhey, Aronson, and Richards, 2003), the role of governments and multilateral organizations such as the ITU has been rather minor.[3]

It is estimated that there are currently about 60 million Wi-Fi-enabled devices worldwide.[4] Among the many factors that explain the success of Wi-Fi, three are particularly noteworthy. First, Wi-Fi can deliver high-bandwidth without the wiring costs, which makes it an effective replacement both for last-mile delivery as well as for backhaul traffic where the installation and maintenance cost of wired infrastructure is prohibitive (it is estimated that wiring expenses can comprise up to three-quarters of the upfront costs of building traditional telecom networks). Second, there is widespread industry support for the standard, coordinated through the Wi-Fi Alliance, an industry organization including over 200 equipment makers worldwide.[5] As a result, equipment prices have dropped rapidly, and users can expect compatibility between Wi-Fi client devices and access points (APs) made by different vendors. A third key to the technology's success lies in the lack of regulatory overhead: Wi-Fi networks have blossomed on unlicensed bands, namely, thin slices of radio spectrum reserved for lowpower applications in which radio devices can operate on a license-exempt basis—though this is not always the case in the developing world (see Galperin, forthcoming). This has allowed for a wide variety of actors to build WLANs without any of the delays and expenses traditionally associated with obtaining a radio license from telecommunications authorities.

---

[3] Today the development of HomeRF has been largely abandoned, and while the new generation of the HiperLAN standard (HiperLAN2) gained some momentum in the EU as a result of ETSI (European Telecommunications Standards Institute) rules related to the use of unlicensed spectrum in the 5GHz band that delayed the launch of 802.11a products in the European market, analysts agree that this Wi-Fi competitor will, at best, fill a small niche in the corporate market.

[4] Presentation by Devabhaktuni Srikrishna, CTO, Tropos Networks (December 2004). Available at www.arnic.info.

[5] The Wi-Fi Alliance was formed in 1999 to certify interoperability of various WLAN products based on the IEEE 802.11 specifications. Since the beginning of its certification program in 2000, the group has certified over 1,000 products.

The major drawback of Wi-Fi is the short signal range. Even though point-to-point connections have been made over several kilometers, Wi-Fi networks typically extend for a few hundred meters at most. This makes the technology generally unsuitable for long-haul transmissions. Nonetheless, related technologies are emerging to address this problem, notably 802.16x (also known as WiMax). This new standard is expected to offer point-to-point connectivity at 70mb/s for up to 50 kilometers, making it an ideal alternative for traffic backhaul. Nonetheless, establishing baseline protocols for WiMAx that would allow interoperability between equipment from multiple vendors has proved more complex than in the case of Wi-Fi. Interestingly, the unexpected success of Wi-Fi, coupled with the potential challenge that new WLAN technologies represent to 3G networks being deployed by mobile telephony operators (Lehr and McKnight, 2003), has significantly raised the stakes in the standardization process, bringing many more players to the bargaining table and making agreements more difficult to reach.

The new generation of WLAN technologies challenges many assumptions associated with the deployment of traditional telecom networks at the local level. Laying conventional fiber and copper wires, or even installing expensive cellular telephony base stations, is not unlike paving roads. It requires large upfront investments, economies of scale are pervasive, and the architecture of the network has to be carefully planned in advance because resources are not easily redeployed. As a result, networks are typically built by large organizations in a top-down process that involves making many ex ante assumptions about how the services will be used, by whom, and at what price. However, these assumptions are easier to make in the case of well-understood, single-purpose networks (such as roads and sewage) than in the case of ICT networks, where applications and uses often result from the accumulated experience of users themselves (Bar and Riis, 2000). Moreover, outside wealthy urban areas, demand for advanced ICT services is complex to aggregate and difficult to predict.

New WLAN technologies create an alternative to the top-down network deployment model associated with traditional telecom infrastructure. Because of the relatively low fixed capital expenditures, the use of unlicensed spectrum, the wide acceptance of open transmission standards, the scalability of the technology, and the lack of significant economies of scale in network deployment and management, infrastructure investments in Wi-Fi networks are within the reach of a variety of local actors—from private entrepreneurs to municipal governments to agricultural cooperatives. Moreover, these investments are for the most part in increasingly powerful wireless terminals capable of adapting to their operating environment, which allows for more edge-base control of network uses and innovation. This allows for a flexible infrastructure to expand from the bottom-up, without a preconceived plan, and driven by those who best understand local demand for advanced information services—local users and organizations.

Moreover, it is possible to imagine a future in which ad-hoc networks spontaneously emerge when enough Wi-Fi devices are present within an area (Benkler, 2002; Agarwal, Norman, and Gupta, 2004). Today, most Wi-Fi networks are deployed to replace Ethernet cables within homes and office, with the simple goal of allowing mobility for users within a confined network environment and physical space. This is similar to the way cordless phones allow limited mobility for fixed telephony within a limited range of the base station. Yet because there is no fundamental difference between Wi-Fi access points and clients, all Wi-Fi devices can be programmed to detect other devices within range and create ad-hoc connections. Traffic can then be routed through a series of short hops, bouncing from one device to the next until it reaches a backhaul link, and effectively bypassing much of the existing wired infrastructure at the local level. Of course, this only works if there are enough Wi-Fi devices in an area, but this becomes increasingly possible as Wi-Fi prices come down and as Wi-Fi radios are built into more user devices.

Assuming a dense enough distribution of such radios, network coverage would become nearly ubiquitous. Collectively, the end-devices would control how the network is used.

New communication services could be invented and implemented at the edge of the network, and propagated throughout the network from peer to peer.

Consider the prediction that by 2008, 28 million cars will come equipped with local networking devices.[6] These would not only serve to connect various systems within the vehicle, but to support communications with outside systems, for applications ranging from telephony to safety and cashless payment systems. Ultimately, since cars are typically always within less than a hundred feet from one another (and have a built-in power supply), one could imagine how they would provide the basis for a mobile networks. Of course, many technical issues remain to be solved for such networks to become practical, including the development of adaptive routing software that can keep up with intermittent mobile nodes. But the rapidly growing number of Wi-Fi devices present in the environment creates at least the theoretical potential for such wide-area wireless grids to emerge, with wires progressively receding in the background.[7]

The evolution of WLAN technologies is today at a critical juncture, with many possible trajectories lying between two extremes. One represents the extension of the established deployment model to the world of wireless broadband communications: licensed by the state, wireless service providers deploy centrally controlled, closed-architecture networks, their economic strategies resting on tight control over spectrum and on the ability to raise massive amounts of capital to secure licenses, build out networks, and subsidize terminal equipment. The other represents an alternative approach whereby users and local institutions make small-scale investments in radio equipment to build local networks from the bottom-up, in an unplanned manner, and collectively organize to exchange traffic and share common network resources. While there is much theoretical debate about the feasibility of such alternative network deployment model (e.g., Benkler, 2002; Sawhney, 2003; Benjamin, 2003), we take a different approach by examining the actual evidence of such bottom-up network deployment in the case of Wi-Fi networks.

---

[6] ABI Research, 2003, Automotive Wireless Networks Opportunities for Wi-Fi, Bluetooth, RFID, Satellite and Other Emerging Wireless Technologies (http://www.abiresearch.com/reports/AWN.html).

[7] There is much historical precedent about the displacement of older technologies by new technologies once considered complementary or feeders to the incumbent system. It is worth recalling that railways were once considered appendices to the canal system, that the telephone was once considered a feeder for the telegraph network, and that the direct current (DC) and the alternating current (AC) electricity systems were once considered complementary (Nye, 1990; Fisher, 1992; Sawhney, 2003).

Our focus is on three types of local public Wi-Fi networks, each driven by different sets of actors and based on different logics of deployment: wireless cooperatives, small wireless ISPs, and municipal governments.

Decentralized models of wireless broadband deployment: Reviewing the evidence

Wireless cooperatives

Some of the most publicized grassroots efforts to provide wireless Internet access to the public have been led by so-called wireless cooperatives. Though wireless

cooperatives come in many colors and flavors, these are generally local initiatives led by highly skilled professionals to provide wireless access to the members of the cooperative groups who build them, to their friends, and to the public in general (Sandvig, 2003).

These for the most part comprise little more than a collection of wireless access points intentionally left open by these wireless enthusiasts and made available to anyone within range, although there are more sophisticated architectures generally based on backhaul connections made between these access points. For example, the Bay Area Wireless User Group (BAWUG) operates long-range connections (2 miles and more) linking clusters of access points, while in Champaign-Urbana a wireless community group is building a 32-node mesh network that will function as a testbed for the implementation of new routing protocols.

Wireless cooperatives pursue a wide variety of goals: some simply provide a forum for their members to exchange information about wireless technologies, while others are actively engaged in building wireless networks to experiment with the possibilities of Wi-Fi technologies, such as the Champaign-Urbana group referred to above. While the exact number of community networks is difficult to establish (in large part precisely because these are small community initiatives that do not require licensing by a central authority), there are over 100 documented initiatives in the U.S. alone, each typically ranging from a few nodes to a few dozen nodes.[8] Interestingly, many of these free wireless cooperatives operate in some of the wealthiest U.S. cities such as San Francisco, San Diego, and Boston. There are also many individuals (or organizations) who volunteer to open their access point to the public without necessarily belonging to an organized cooperative, and advertise this fact on directories such as nodeDB.com.

Despite much publicity, the assemblage of these community networks is today of small significance in terms of the access infrastructure it provides. Further, it is unclear how many people are effectively taking advantage of them. In cases where the community organizations track usage of their open networks, there seems to be relatively few takers.[9]

Anecdotal evidence indicates that the main users of these community networks are the wireless community members themselves (Sandvig, 2003). Nevertheless, these networks are playing an important role in the emerging ecology of Wi-Fi. If nothing else, they represent a clear disincentive for investments in commercial hotspots operations.[10]

Moreover, much like in the case of radio amateurs in the 1910s, wireless enthusiasts have made significant improvements to the reach and functionality of Wi-Fi networks, including routing protocols for mesh networks, authentication tools, and the real-life testing of signal propagation and interference problems.[11]

Somewhat surprisingly, coordination among the various community wireless groups has been relatively limited, with different groups often duplicating efforts in terms of basic access provision over the same area or development of competing software protocols.

---

[8] For a seemingly thorough listing see http://wiki.personaltelco.net/index.cgi/WirelessCommunities.

[9] See for example the usage statistics of Seattle-wireless at http://stats.seattlewireless.net.

[10] 10 Verizon cites the availability of free wireless access in several areas of Manhattan as the reason why it decided to offer free Wi-Fi access to its existing DSL customers.

[11] It is interesting to note that the notorious Pringles "cantenna" used by many Wi-Fi enthusiasts has a precedent in the history of radio, for early radio amateurs often used Quaker Oats containers to build radio tuners.

However there are recent signs of increased cooperation to pursue common policy goals (e.g., availability of unlicensed spectrum) as well as technical cooperation. [12] There are also grassroots efforts to connect small local networks to share backhaul capacity and exchange traffic in a mesh-like architecture. For example, the Consume project is a London-based collaborative effort to peer community Wi-Fi networks. The group has developed a model contract for cooperation called the Pico Peering Agreement, which outlines the rights and obligations of peering parties (in essence, it is a simplified version of existing peering agreements between Tier 1 backbone operators).[13]

Much like in the case of open source software, wireless community efforts are based on the voluntary spirit of like-minded (and technically-proficient) individuals who agree to provide free access or transit across their network. While simple contracts such as the Pico Peering Agreement might prove useful for peering among small community networks, more complex financial and legal arrangements are likely to be needed for scaling-up the current patchwork of community access points into a larger grid that provides a true connectivity alternative for those limited technical expertise and for local institutions with more complex service demands. Yet, while the impact of wireless community initiatives has yet to match that of the open-source movement, experimentation with cooperative models for the deployment and management of WLANs has exciting opened new possibilities for network deployment at the local level.

Municipal governments

A second category of non-traditional actors that are increasingly engaged in building and managing wireless broadband networks are municipal governments. This is certainly not the first time in U.S. history that municipalities are engaged in the deployment of telecommunications networks or the provision of services (see Gillett, Lehr, and Osorio, 2003). Yet the advances in wireless technologies discussed above have created a more attractive environment for local government involvement in the provision of wireless broadband services,

---

[12] It is worth noting that the inaugural National Summit for Community Wireless Networks was held in August 2004.

[13] Available at www.picopeer.net.

particularly among those communities neglected or poorly served by traditional broadband operators (notably cable and DSL providers). The impetus is particularly strong among communities where municipally-owned public service operators are already present—for example, among communities with Municipal Electric Utilities—for the existing resources (such as trucks and customer service and billing systems) significantly lower the cost of municipal entry into broadband wireless services. In pursuing these deployments, municipal governments have a considerable advantage over commercial entities or community groups: they control prime antenna locations in the form of light posts and traffic signs, all of which have built-in electrical supply that can serve to power wireless access points.

The number of cities deploying wireless broadband networks has been growing very fast in recent years. According to one estimate, as of June 2004 there were over 80 municipal Wi-Fi networks in the U.S. and the EU, with more in the planning stages in large cities such as Los Angeles and Philadelphia.[14] The scale, architecture, and business models of these municipal networks vary widely. Some municipalities are simply building so-called "hot zones" (essentially a small cluster of public access points) along downtowns, shopping districts, and public parks. By providing free Wi-Fi access, these cities hope to help attract businesses to these areas, boost customer traffic, or lure conference organizers to their convention centers by making it easy for conference-goers to stay connected. This was for example the explicit goal behind the launch of free Wi-Fi access by the city of Long Beach, CA in its downtown, airport and convention center areas.[15]

A more ambitious model involves generally small municipalities that seek to deploy citywide wireless broadband to service government buildings, mobile city workers, security and emergency services. This is for example the case of Cerritos, CA, a small Southern California community without cable broadband and only limited access to DSL services. The city partnered with wireless access provider Aiirmesh to

---

[14] Munirewireless.com First Anniversary Report (June 2004). Available at www.muniwireless.com.

[15] Interviews with Chris Dalton, City of Long Beach Economic Development Office, February 6, 2004 (see also John Markoff, "More Cities Set Up Wireless Networks," New York Times, January 6, 2003). It is also worth noting that during our visit to downtown Long Beach we detected several private access points open for public use.

offer access to local government workers (in particular mobile employees such as city maintenance workers, code enforcement officers and building inspectors), while at the same time allowed the company to sell broadband services to Cerritos' residents and businesses. Similar publicprivate partnerships are mushrooming in a number of small and mid-size U.S. cities, including Lafayette, LA, Grand Haven, MI, Charleston, NC, and others.[16]

A significant number of these municipal networks use a mesh architecture: rather than connecting each Wi-Fi base station to the wired network, as in the case of residential access points or commercial hotspots, devices relay traffic to one-another with only a few of them hard-wired to the Internet. They are programmed to detect nearby devices and spontaneously adjust routing when new devices are added, or to find ways around devices that fail. Municipalities have an inherent advantage in pursuing a mesh architecture since as noted they control a large number of prime locations for antenna locations, such as light posts, traffic signs or urban furniture, dispersed through the city and equipped with power supply. A prominent example is Chaska, MN, a city of less than 20,000 where the municipal government built a 16-square miles mesh network and operates the service on the basis of an existing municipal electric utility.

Municipal wireless networks drew little controversy when confined to small cities or communities underserved by major broadband operators, or when these initiatives primarily addressed the needs of government employees. Yet, as soon as larger municipalities announced plans to build metropolitan area networks (MANs) that would cover large geographical areas, the debate over the proper role of local governments in the provision of wireless broadband erupted, and incumbent operators swiftly sought legislation blocking municipal Wi-Fi projects.

The theoretical case in favor of local government provision of wireless broadband rests on three key assumptions: first, that broadband access is part of the critical infrastructure for communities to prosper in economic and social terms; second, that for a variety of reasons market forces cannot adequately fulfill the demand for broadband

---

[16] For descriptions of these municipal wireless projects in the U.S. and elsewhere see http://www.muniwireless.com.

access within the community (for example, because externalities prevent private operators from fully capturing the benefits of widespread broadband access); and third, that under these circumstances local governments can run wireless networks and deliver these services (either directly or under a franchise agreement) more efficiently than private firms (Lehr, Sirbu, and Gillett, 2004).

While the first assumption seems plausible, the other two depend on a number of specific circumstances that prevent overarching generalizations (such as those typically made on both sides of the debate). In communities underserved by existing broadband operators, there is clearly a role for local governments to play in spurring the availability of broadband at competitive prices. This is particularly the case when other municipal utilities already exist, so that economies of scale and scope can be realized in the provision of a bundle of government services (e.g., electricity, water, broadband). At first glance, the market failure rationale is less convincing for areas where a competitive broadband market exists, although even in these cases it is entirely possible to argue for a limited government role in the provision of wireless broadband (for example, in running the fiber backhaul, in specialized applications for government operations, or in conjunction with economic development projects). Ultimately, a better understanding of the potential costs and benefits of municipal wireless initiatives under different contexts is needed to allow conclusions about the appropriate role of local government in the wireless broadband environment.

Wireless ISPs

A third category of new actors taking advantage of the properties of new WLAN technologies are the Wireless Internet Service Providers (WISPs.) These are new forprofit companies providing internet services to residential and business customer over wireless networks, including internet access, web hosting, and in some cases more diverse services such as virtual private networking and voice over IP. Over the past two years, the FCC has taken a keen interest in WISPs, seeing them in particular as a way to bring broadband internet access to rural areas. This regulatory support is further strengthened by rural development funding programs, such as the USDA's Community Connect Grant Program aimed at providing "essential community facilities in rural towns and communities where no broadband service exists."[17] In November 2003, the FCC held a *Rural Wireless ISP Showcase and Workshop* to "facilitate information dissemination about Rural WISPs as a compelling solution for rural broadband service."[18] In May 2004, FCC Chair Michael Powell announced the creation of the Wireless Broadband Access Task Force, to recommend policies that could encourage the growth of the WISP industry.

In the U.S., WISPs are present in a diversity of communities ranging from large cities (like *Sympel, Inc* in San Francisco or *Brick Network* in St Louis), to rural towns (like *InvisiMax* in Hallock, MN). However, their impact is perhaps most significant in rural and small towns, where they are often the only broadband access solution. While there is much enthusiasm about this new segment of the ISP industry, little information is available.[19] Different sources cite widely divergent numbers of WISP providers. In September 2003, analysts In-Stat/MDR estimated there were "between 1,500 and 1,800 WISPs" in the U.S.[20] During the *Wireless Broadband Forum* held in May 2004 by the FCC, Margaret LaBrecque, Chairperson of the WiMax Forum Regulatory Task Force claimed there were "2500 wireless ISPs in the U.S. serving over 6,000 markets."[21] At the same meeting, Michael Anderson, Chairperson of part-15.org, an industry association for license-free spectrum users, said there were "8,000 license-exempt WISPs in the United States actively providing service"[22], most of them serving rural areas. The FCC's own Wireless Broadband Access Task Force puts that number at "between 4,000 and 8,000."[23]

While these numbers obviously lack precision, they are also strikingly large. Considering there are about 36,000 municipalities and

---

[17] See http://www.usda.gov/rus/telecom/commconnect.htm.

[18] See http://www.fcc.gov/osp/rural-wisp/

[19] The authors gratefully acknowledge research help from Namkee Park, USC, in tracking down some of the available information.

[20] Cited in Bob Brewin, "Feature: Wireless nets go regional," *CIO*, September 14, 2003.

[21] Transcript of the FCC Wireless Broadband Forum (5/19/2004), p. 63. Available at: http://wireless.fcc.gov/outreach/2004broadbandforum/comments/transcript_051904.doc. 22 Ibid. at p. 89.

[22] "Connected on the Go: Broadband Goes Wireless," Wireless Broadband Access Task Force Report, FCC, February 2005, p.5.

[23] *2002 Census of Governments*, at http://www.census.gov/govs/www/cog2002.html

towns in the U.S., of which the large majority are small (29,348, or 82%, have less than 5,000 inhabitants; 25,369, or 71%, have less than 2.500 inhabitants)24[24], and considering that there are several WISPs serving more than one community (Table 11.1), the coverage that this new breed of access providers are providing in rural and small communities is remarkably extensive. The small scale of these operators is illustrated in Table 11.1 While the larger WISPs serve less than 10,000 subscribers, the majority of them are mom-and-pop operations serving only about 100 customers each.25 This indicates an extremely fragmented industry structure, largely resulting from very low entry costs: with an upfront investment as low as U$10,000 in off-the-shelves equipment, a small entrepreneur can build a system able to serve about 100 customers, with a payback ranging from 12 to 24 months.[25] In fact, many WISPs have been started by frustrated customers fed up with the difficulty of getting affordable high-speed connections in their small communities, and who decide to front the cost of a T1 connection and spread that cost by reselling the excess capacity to neighbours over wireless links.[26] However, one common problem is the availability of T1 lines (or comparable) for backhauling traffic. Unlike urban ISPs, many WISPs have to pay additional long-haul charges to interconnect with Internet POPs located in major cities, which raises provision costs significantly.

The WISP sector is an infant industry, with most players entering the market in the last three years. The availability of both private and public financing, coupled with the slow roll-out of broadband by traditional carriers in most rural and small communities, has fueled the remarkable growth of this segment. For the moment, there seems to be significant demand from customers, and ample policy support, to

---

[24] Stephen Lawson, "Wi-Fi brings broadband to rural Washington," NetworkWorldFusion, *08/23/04.*

[25] See for example "How Much Does a WISP Cost?," Broadband Wireless Exchange Magazine at http://www.bbwexchange.com/turnkey/pricing.asp.

[26] As *Part-15.org* Chairman (and CIO of WISP PDQLink) Michael Anderson recalls, "I think most of the WISPS, the licensed exempt guys, the smaller, less than 10 employees, 100 miles from any metropolitan area, those guys, for the most part, started their business because of the frustration of not having the availability of broadband in their areas, which makes them either suburban or rural. I think in '98, '97, when I started wireless from ISP, I had the same frustrations. I was paying U$1700 a month for a T-1 at the office and four blocks away at my home the best I could hope for was a 288kb/s connection." Transcript of the FCC Wireless Broadband Forum (5/19/2004), p. 117.

sustain the current growth rates. Yet, at least two factors call for attention. The first is the entry of traditional wired broadband providers, such as cable operators and telcos, who in several cases have come to rural areas to challenge WISPs with lower priced offerings. The second is the long-term sustainability of these small-scale operations which often depend on a few larger customers. In early days of telephony, grassroots efforts were also critical to extend telecommunications to rural America, yet after a wave of consolidation in the early 20th century only a few remained independent (Fischer, 1992). While new WLAN technologies have similarly spurred a new generation of small telecom entrepreneurs, it remains to be seen how sustainable these networks will be in the long run.

Table 11.1   "Top 10" Wireless Internet Service Providers

Headquarters	Wireless ISP	Subscribers	Communities served
Omaha, NE	SpeedNet Services, Inc.	7,000	235
Prescott Valley, AZ	CommSpeed	4,579	–
W. Des Moines, IA	Prairie iNet	4,001	120
Amarillo, TX	AMA TechTel Communications	4,000	–
Erie, CO	Mesa Networks	3,000	–
Moscow, ID	FirstStep Internet	2,709	16
Lubbock, TX	Blue Moon Solutions	2,000	–
Owensboro, KY	Owensboro Municipal Utilities	1,550	–
Orem, UT	Digis Networks	1,516	–
Evergreen, CO	wisperTEL	1,000	31

Source: Broadband Wireless Magazine (at http://www.bbwexchange.com/top10wisps. asp, as of 2/23/05) and company data.

Conclusion

David (2002) has aptly described the Internet as a fortuitous legacy of a modest R&D program which was later adapted and modified by various economic and political actors to perform functions never intended by its pioneers. Wi-Fi has similarly emerged from a rather modest experiment in spectrum management launched by the FCC in 1985 that has unexpectedly resulted in the proliferation of local wireless networks in homes, offices, and public spaces. Much like the Internet challenged traditional telecom networks, with this new architecture comes a new distribution of control over wireless networks. However fast new wireless technologies evolve, this will be an evolutionary process whereby various stakeholders, not simply equipment manufacturers and incumbent carriers but also local governments, start-up providers and especially endusers, will interact to shape the technology in different ways. While some battles will be market-driven, other will take place in the courtrooms, in regulatory agencies, and within standards-setting organizations. Having outgrown their original purpose as an appendix to the wired infrastructure, Wi-Fi networks now stand at a critical juncture, for they embody technical possibilities of potentially disruptive character, and yet it is in the decisively social realm of economic and political interactions that their future is being cast.

With tens of millions units sold in just a few years, there is now a critical mass of Wi-Fi radios in the environment. All signs point to the continuation of this trend in the coming few years: Wi-Fi devices are becoming very cheap and embedded in a wide array of consumer devices, from cell-phones to televisions, appliances and cars. Once density reaches a certain threshold, the traditional deployment architecture and models of control will need to be revisited, for the system is likely to reach capacity as too many devices compete for scarce resources such as frequencies and backhaul links. This will inevitably lead to regulatory battles about how to reform the existing legal edifice for wireless communications, largely based on the broadcast model of a few high-power transmitters connecting to numerous low-power, limited-intelligence devices. The ongoing debate between unlicensed vs. property rights-based models of spectrum management illustrates this point.

One of the central questions for the evolution of WLANs is whether the large, and fast growing, number of radio devices in the environment could be coordinated differently to create a fundamental challenge to existing networks. We believe we are fast approaching a point where this might happen, because of two related developments. The first is the bottom-up dynamics associated with Wi-Fi deployment discussed in this paper. As households, grassroots community groups, small entrepreneurs and local institutions build their own networks, the incentives will increase to share resources, reach roaming or peering agreements, and devise new cooperative mechanisms to manage this decentralized wireless infrastructure as a public grid. The possibility to do just that is tied to the second development, the recent emergence of open-source mesh protocols that can knit together neighboring Wi-Fi devices into a single network. At this point, mesh technology has been worked out for centrally deployed network devices, and much technical work remains to be done for ad-hoc mesh networks to become a reality. Nonetheless, as with other technologies, experimentation by users and corporate R&D will eventually result in a workable solution. More challenging, however, will be to create new organizational arrangements to manage the wireless grid. As noted, because it was conceived under assumptions drawn from an earlier generation of wireless technologies, the existing regulatory regime limits the growth of and stifles experimentation with bottom-up WLAN deployment. Revisiting these assumptions is a necessary step to allow these exciting new ways of building and running networks to flourish.

References

Agarwal, A., D. Norman, and A. Gupta (2004). *Wireless grids: Approaches, architectures, and technical challenges*. MIT Sloan School of Management Working Paper 4459-04.

Bar, F, and H. Galperin. (2004). Building the wireless Internet infrastructure: From cordless Ethernet archipelagos to wireless grids. *Communications and Strategies 54*(2): 45-68.

Bar, F, and A. Riis. (2000). Tapping user-driven innovation: A new rationale for universal service. *The Information Society* 16:1-10.

Benjamin, S. (2003). Spectrum abundance and the choice between private and public control. New York University Law Review 78: 2007-2102.

Best, M. (2003). The wireless revolution and universal access. In *Trends in Telecommunications Reform*. Geneva: ITU.

Benkler, Y. (2002). Some economics of wireless networks. *Harvard Journal of Law and Technology* 16(1): 25-83.

Cowhey, P., J. Aronson, and J. Richards. (2003). The peculiar evolution of 3G wireless networks: Institutional logic, politics, and property rights. In E. Wilson and W.

Drake (eds.)., *Governing global electronic networks*. Cambridge, MA: MIT Press.

David, P. (2002). The evolving accidental information super-highway. *Oxford Review of Economic Policy* 17(2): 159-187.

Douglas, S. (1987). *Inventing American broadcasting, 1899-1922*. Baltimore: Johns Hopkins Press.

Fischer, C. (1992). *America calling: A social history of the telephone to 1940*. Berkeley: University of California Press.

Galperin, H. (forthcoming). Wireless networks and rural development: Opportunities for Latin America. *Information Technologies and International Development*.

Gillett, S., W. Lehr, and C. Osorio (2003). *Local broadband initiatives*. Presented at the Telecommunications Policy Research Conference, Alexandria, VA.

Lehr, W., and L. McKnight. (2003). Wireless internet access: 3G vs. WiFi? *Telecommunications Policy* 27(5-6): 351-370.

Lehr, W., M. Sirbu, and S. Gillett (2004). *Municipal wireless broadband: Policy and business implications of emerging access technologies*. Available at http://itc.mit.edu/itel/docs/2004/wlehr_munibb_doc.pdf

Nye, D. (1990). *Electrifying America: Social meanings of a new technology*. Cambridge: MIT Press.

Sandvig, C. (2003). *Assessing cooperative action in 802.11 networks*. Presented to the 31st Telecommunication Policy Research Conference, Washington D.C.

Sawhney, H. (2003). Wi-Fi networks and the rerun of the cycle. *Info* 5(6): 25-33.

Chapter 12

Free Software and Social and Economic Development

Marcelo Branco

Introduction

We live in a period that has become known as the "information age," in which we have the possibility of interacting with new technologies that establish new forms of communication between people and between people and things. We are experiencing a revolution, at the center of which are the information and communication technologies.

As a result of this, we are also witnessing profound alterations in our social, political and economic relations, heightened by the permanent expansion of communications hardware, software and applications that promise to improve economic results, provide new cultural impulses and incentivate personal improvement through the use of the technologies for educational practice.

Far from fulfilling that promise, the cyberspace or the Information Society—which is materializing today with the growth of the Internet—has instead increased the inequality between those who have and those who do have access to the benefits of the network.

For those of us who want a better world, understanding and reflecting on this new level of capitalist accumulation and examining the contradictory potentials of this new period in history, are fundamental factors for updating both are theoretical concepts and our practices as public managers.

Our Life in Cyberspace

The thus far dominant technologies for the supply of information, communication, entertainment and ways of doing business are being replaced by a second technological generation using broad instead of narrow band. The objective is to supply a greater volume of multi-modal (sound, image, text) and multiplexed information simultaneously, which can be transmitted at increasingly higher speeds. Digital codification is the process that makes it possible to converge information stored on a computer (data), cultural products (music, films, books), telecommunications and radio and television transmission processes in one and the same format. This converging technology combines technological capacities that were once separate, meaning that the telephone, the computer, the TV and the sound system will be operating as one unit—a unit that is much more powerful and with a much greater presence in our lives than we could imagine. The Internet is the materialization of this new scenario, fuelled by the efforts of manufacturers, investors, academic researchers, hackers and government policies. Before the advent of the network of networks (the Internet), traditional communications were divided into two categories: one to one or one to some (fax and telephone) and one to many (TV, radio, the press and cinema). In the new environment, in addition to these categories, the possibility of communication of the many-to-many type has also emerged. This not only brings access to greater quantities of information, but also transformation of the economic and social relations—which interact in all branches of capitalist production—in an endeavour to adapt to the "more economic" way of doing business and new form of relations with people. New forms of relationships emerged, and also new communities without precise geographic definition—new producers, new distributors and new consumers with a global and no longer merely local or regional positioning. These new economic, political and social relations—we can call them virtual—are faceless and territory-less. They are now part of our daily routine—our life in Cyberspace.

Digital Exclusion

In the new economic order resulting from the decline of the manufacturing industries and the expansion of the services sector, we have witnessed the birth of the information age and its growing importance as a sources of products, growth and the creation of wealth. "Moving bits instead of atoms is a lot cheaper." The value of knowledge as a "universal good" has forfeited space to the marketing of knowledge. Knowledge/information has become just one more product in the globalized market. This new technological level of capitalist accumulation has ramifications in terms of employment patterns, contributing decisively to the high degree of obsoleteness of jobs in the production industries and, more acutely now, in the services sector. New social agents, new forms of work relationships, new professions are emerging. The possibility of locating production closer to cheaper sources of labour gives rise to new international labour divisions, new forms of control and increasing competition. Capital surfs the cyberspace in search of new business opportunities and new markets, with greater productivity. Brazil and some of the peripheral countries are regarded by those who control the international market as being of vast potential for the consumption of proprietary technologies and contents from the countries of the Northern Hemisphere. This phenomenon reduces us to the role of mere consumers of technology and contents and not protagonists in the new global scenario. We enter the digital scenario as subordinates to the interests of the policies of the central countries and global corporations. Our scientific, technological and economic development also plays a subordinate role, and at the social level, digital exclusion is increasing instead of decreasing. Our countries and regions are becoming even poorer in economic terms and a new poverty dimension is emerging—digital information and knowledge poverty. "The exclusion of people from active participation in, the privileges of, and responsibility in, the information society is perhaps greater than exclusion from access to the privileges of the ruling classes they were subject to in the past." The most visible example of this exclusion is that almost one half of the country have never had their own telephone line and only some 5% of Latin Americans have home access to the Internet.

Digital Consumers, Proprietary Software

The trend towards universal access of the population to the world-wide computer network with technologies we do not master and contents we have no influence on guarantees neither digital democratization nor the socialization of the economic and social benefits provided by the technological advances. On the contrary, we are experiencing a heightening of the inequalities and technological dependence on the central countries. "In the concrete field of information technologies, an age-old phenomenon is being repeated since the 1980s: knowledge, transmitted via a written language code, is being zealously guarded by some, who use it to maintain a power structure that has survived over the centuries. In the 1960s and 1970s, the development in information technologies was due, in part, to the specialists sharing their knowledge. Computer programming codes were shared, meaning that the advances achieved by one were used by others to improve the programme in question. Today, a large part of the computer applications we use has a secret code. They belong to their proprietors and we cannot copy them or share their development. Only the proprietors can modify and improve them. If that is in their interest, of course."[1] The high cost of the software used in computers and the barrier to free scientific and technological knowledge imposed by proprietary licences have hindered and even prevented some regions of the world from benefiting from this revolution in order to provide better quality of life for their citizens.

The Free Software Movement and a New Paradigm for Our Development

In this new scenario, in which the Internet and the information and communication technologies assume a vanguard role, new possibilities of social intervention and new economic relations are also emerging. We can create new spaces for the practice of citizenship and democracy, new spaces for educational practices and bring our technological, scientific and economic development up to new heights. To this end, we must put an end to dependence and subordination and actively develop a new model, with the help of public policies and alternative practices. Some important initiatives are being implemented to invert the dominant trend, offering alternatives with a view to ending digital exclusion. One of the most important of these initiatives is the Free Software Movement, which is building a concrete alternative to the hegemonic model and has proved to be more efficient in scientific terms and more generous at the social level. "For a number of years a group of specialists has been working with the aim of sharing their work. They communicate via the Internet and work on joint projects, no matter what part of the world they are in. They have developed a technology that is so solid that institutions and corporations such as the Government of Brazil, the Regional Government of Extremadura, Google, AOL, Time Warner, Amazon and others use it without problems. We are talking about "free software applications," which can be legally copied. Improvements to a programme are made available to all."[1]

Due to the solidarity aspect—i.e. the fact that it helps open up knowledge to all citizens, that we can adapt computer programmes to each individual need without requiring the permission of large corporations, that in the 21st century our regions and countries can take a leap forward towards technological equality, that we can use, develop and investigate state-of-the-art technologies in real time, with the state of development of first world technology—this new paradigm is more in line with our development interests. This movement, supported by thousands of autodidacts working in cyberspace—the hackers (not to be confused with crackers),— is shared by our young graduates and local companies and offers us the possibility of developing our technological autonomy and independence without the risk of isolation from the international community. On the contrary, we will be in perfect synchronization, with a high degree of knowledge sharing. Our concrete experience with the Brazil Free Software Project[2] and the Brazilian government initiatives has shown the social amplitude and the strategic importance of having public government policies in similar projects. Instead of sending billions of dollars for licences for the use of proprietary software and protected technology to the countries of the North, as we do today, we can transfer those resources to the internal market and further the development of the local economy and the modernization of other sectors of our economy. We must develop a public policy of incentives for the creation and strengthening of local and regional companies that operate in this new paradigm of the information technology market. With the information technology products and services—free from the restrictions imposed by the licences of the software giants—we will make our digital inclusion more accessible and more adapted to our reality, we will boost our local and regional economies, we will make use of the local knowledge coming from our universities and schools and we will share our latest-generation technological knowledge in real time with the other countries on the planet.

---

[1] Regional Government of Extremadura—text on the launch of GNU/LinEx

[2] A non-governmental initiative: www.softwarelivre.org

What is Free Software?

Free Software is computer programmes written in cooperation by an international community of independent programmers communicating via the Internet. They are hundreds of thousands of hackers who reject all associations with "security breakers." "That is a confusion on the part of the mass media," says Richard Stallmann, Chairman of the Free Software Foundation.[3] These software developers reject the pejorative meaning of the term hacker and use it as meaning "some who loves programming and who likes to be capable and inventive." In addition to this, the programmes are handed over to the community an open source, accessible code, thus making it possible that the original ideal can be developed and perfected further by the community. In conventional programmes, the programming code is secret and the property of the company that developed it, so that it is almost impossible to decipher the programming language. What is at stake is the control of technological innovation. For Stallmann, "free software is a question of freedom of expression and not just business." Today there are thousands of alternative programmes developed in this way, with a user community of millions around the world.

Software can only be considered free if it guarantees the four fundamental liberties[4]: a) freedom to use the programme for whatever purpose; b) freedom to modify the programme and adapt it to one's needs (to make this liberty possible, one must have access to the source code, for modifying a programme is very difficult without the code); c) freedom to distribute copies, both free and at a fee; d) freedom to distribute modified versions of the programme, so that the whole community can benefit from the improvements. The most high-profile example of software following this concept is the operating system GNU/Linux, an alternative to Windows developed and enhanced by thousands of co-programmers around the globe. For this reason, its quality has been proven to be superior to that of the software industry rival.

---

[3] www.fsf.org

[4] http://www.gnu.org/philosophy/free-sw.html

A New Form of Production

The main leaders and protagonists of the movement are the hackers—very capable programmers who have gained notoriety for having developed an important programme or useful tool for the movement. The most well known are Richard Stallmann, the head of the movement, and Linus Torvalds, who wrote the kernel for the GNU/Linux operating programme. These "cyberproletarians" who make life hell for Bill Gates, work mainly on a voluntary basis and are responsible for more than 80% of the work effort that has gone into the thousands of free programmes used in the world. The reasons why a hacker may develop a programme on a voluntary basis are the most varied possible: the quest for fame and recognition, the desire to create something useful, indignation at Bill Gages, insomnia… or all of these together. Less than 20% of the free programmes are developed by programmers working in companies with conventional structures. Another reason for the optimal quality of the products is their development in cooperation. From the conception of the software project through all production states, a team of programmers, from all around the world, is very actively involved, communicating via the Internet. All documentation and codes are made available without secrecy, guaranteeing development 24 hours a day, 7 days a week. Another important feature is that unfinished and incomplete products are made available to "user groups" and to any interested party for assessment purposes. The user groups are made up of professionals from other areas, as well as programmers, who detect bugs, suggest modifications and request new functionalities. The product is thus constantly improved. They are not like proprietary products, which, once completed, then seek consumers in the market. They are products that seek to be of use to the community, made to order to attend to already existing needs. Another important lesson to be learnt from the movement is the creation of distributors. In order to undermine the blockage of distribution of these programmes, several international distributors were created that are responsible for the "packaging" of the programmes copied onto CDs and the instruction manuals and for providing support services to the users. It is they who place the "packs" in the shops, making life easier for the users and avoiding that we have to spend hours downloading the programmes from the net to able to set up our computers. This is one form of doing business in the world of free software, given that selling the licence is prohibited.

The largest distributors are: SuSE (Germany); Slackware, Red Hat and Caldera (United States), Conectiva (Brazil), TurboLinux (Asia), Mandrake (France) and Caixa Mágica (Portugal). One should point that the largest of these distributors does not even have 300 employees. There is another distributor which is preferred by the hackers and the majority of public administrations, for it is not a company but a non-profit organisation: Debian.[5] Debian has approximately one thousand voluntary programmers selected in a rigorous technical "selection process" who assume a societal commitment through a "social contract," a kind of code of ethics for the cyber community. It is the technically most stable form of free software distribution, used by various companies and in "high availability" government projects.

Threats to Innovation and Freedom of Expression

Some of the initiatives, in the technological and legal spheres, of interest to the large monopolistic corporations in the information technologies industry may restrict innovation and the individual and collective liberties of the citizens.

Under the pretext of "updating" the national and international laws in view of the growth of the Internet and digital works, these initiatives designed to extend the reach of the copyright laws for digital works in reality can amount to centralized and totalitarian control by the large corporations over the rights of the users and producers of digital works and impede innovation.

A Technological Plan against Liberties

A consortium[6] made up of Microsoft, Intel, AMD, IBM, Sony and other giants is developing the TCPA (Trusted Computing Platform Alliance), which is already in an advanced phase. This technological alliance is producing chips that can be monitored and controlled permanently through the Internet, even without the authorisation of the users of the computers and other electronic equipment. Using the argument that they protect "intellectual property," this new genera-

---

[5] www.debian.org

[6] www.againsttcpa.com/tcpa-members.html

tion of chips can restrict the installation of new computer programmes, the playing of a music CD, a DVD, electronic games, digital books and even the exhibition of certain websites.

The "ex-owners" of the equipment will require prior authorization—or have to use commands introduced via the Internet—for the large corporations in the consortium to be able to run whatever what they want on their computers. In this new scenario, for example, it is possible that a person who buys a music CD will be only to play it three times on their computer. If they want to play it any more, they will have to pay. Or a user may purchase a film on DVD that can only be watched at times that do not compete with certain "prime time" television hours, or for which the user's credit card is debited every time it is played. But above all, new works produced independently or free computer programmes and/or those developed by companies outside the consortium will require an approval so that they can be used by the "ex-owner" of the electronic equipment (computer, DVD player, etc.). This development is also a real threat to the development of free software and to technological innovation and freedom of expression.

We work with a new logic that allows the execution, copying, modification and distribution of a new programme derived from an original. Imagine what it would be like if, in each software development process, we were dependant on centralised authorizations and the opinions of lawyers to run a programme, a new modified version or the copies authorized by the free licences. Many users have already tasted the bitter taste of this restriction of individual liberties. Even without the new TCPA generation chips, Windows XP users, for example, have already experienced "Palladium," which is a form of software control developed by the monopolist industry to impede users from running non-authorized copies of music, videos or applications on their new operating system. Even if you want change some of your computer's hardware components—such as the video card or modem—the users of this new operating system require centralized authorization from MS. Otherwise the new component will not work. It so happens that Palladium—like any other software applications—has already been easily decodified by young hackers, who have given back part of the lost freedoms to the users of the new MS operating system. It will, however, be infinitely more difficult to overcome the restrictions imposed by TCPA (at the hardware level) plus Palladium.

A Legal Plan against Liberties

At the legislative level, this same initiative has also been working with the aim of criminalizing developers of technological and scientific applications that endeavour to produce alternatives to the restrictions imposed by the proprietary technology. In the USA the so-called Digital Millennium Copyright Act (DCMA) is already in force. It severely punishes those who dare to ignore the restrictions. The DCMA is one of the United States laws included in the FTAA package, meaning that such laws can be extended to countries that have signed the treaty. The European Union is also under pressure from powerful lobbyists who are trying to impose a clone of this anti-democratic law and the patentability of software upon the Member States and the European Parliament. This is legislation that is outlawing citizens, based on the extension of laws which were born out of industry regulations, i.e. for material products, and which may have made sense at a certain time to immaterial (digital) products with a (re)production cost of practically zero. This criminalization does not make sense in the new information society. With the argument that one is protecting the commercial interests of digital contents, the rights of the citizens to the legitimate use of materials with their copyright guaranteed under the industrial legislation are being taken away. We have the right to lend and borrow printed books. We have the right to tape or copy a music CD or a video tape for non-commercial purposes. We have the right to partially copy a book in a library or borrowed from a friend to increase our knowledge on certain subjects. However, these rights are threatened in the digital sphere. "Cyber rights" must not have totalitarian and fascist preconditions. These laws and initiatives in the technological fields directly affect all individuals, authors and programmers and should not be dealt with only from the perspective of the monopolistic industry giants.

Brazil at the 1st World Summit on the Information Society

The first phase of the World Summit on the Information Society,[7] an official UNO event that took place on 11 to 13 December 2003 in Geneva, Switzerland, was marked by the profound differences between the interests of

---

[7] http://www.itu.int/wsis/

the rich countries and those of the developing and poor countries lead by Brazil, India, South Africa, Egypt and Argentina.

Sharing Knowledge

One of the main controversies at the Geneva Summit revolved around the Free Software alternative and knowledge sharing as instruments of digital inclusion, innovation incentivation and technological development. Brazil and India led the bloc that argued that emphasis on the sharing of technological know-how between peoples was more in line with the development of a democratic and inclusive Information Society and that it was the only way for the developing countries to close the technological gap.

The Brazilian motion was contested by the group led by the United States, which presented as an alternative emphasis on the consolidation of the intellectual property laws on digital works, an increase in the penalties for and criminalization of users that attempt to copy and share freely through the Internet. The majority of the governments of the rich countries, led by the USA, manifested their interest in maintaining absolute and egoistic control over the technology by protecting themselves with the strengthening of the intellectual property laws.

In addition to being a clearly protectionist policy, this position proposes an information society without information and without shared knowledge. Indeed, a disinformation society. For the poor and developing countries all that would remain is the role of consumers of "canned" technological products produced in the Northern Hemisphere, thus depriving our universities, research centres, private companies, governments and populations of having access to and mastering the technology that is being (or should be) disseminated.

Multilateral, Transparent and Democratic Governance of the Internet

At the 1st Summit on the Information Society, Brazil was one of the countries that highlighted the need for a multilateral, transparent and democratic form of governance of the Internet.[8] A more in-depth debate of this question became a key component of the summit.

---

[8] http://www.softwarelivre.org/news/3126

The debate on the "democratization of the Internet governance" is a very relevant one. The group led by Brazil argues that the control of addresses and names and the management of the Internet should be carried out on a tripartite basis (governments, civil society and the private sector).

Currently, the Internet Corporation for Assigned Names and Numbers (ICANN), the body responsible for establishing the rules for the use of the Internet on a worldwide basis, is unilaterally subordinate to the United States government.

Digital Solidarity Fund

The African countries and a resolution from the "World Summit of Cities and Local Authorities on the Information Society,"[8] held in Lyon, France one week before the Geneva summit, came out in favour of the creation of an International Digital Solidarity Fund. The move is being supported by Brazil and the developing countries bloc. The resources for the fund could come from the taxation of a small part of the profits from the international transactions of the information technology companies or from voluntary contributions.

The representatives of the countries led by the United States want nothing to do with the fund. Not even if it were a voluntary, non-governmental fund. They argue that the "market" should regulate digital inclusion. In other words, if you have the money to buy from the monopolistic mega-corporations from the Northern Hemisphere, you will have the chance to participate in the information society. The rest will just have to join the long line of the digitally excluded.

In Tunis, for a More Inclusive Information Society

At the Geneva summit, there was a dubious and contradictory outcome in terms of these issues, the result of the tough diplomatic negotiations. But the results of the Geneva summit are far from reflecting and identifying new concepts for the Information Society or any type of innovative thought. It was a summit dominated by a "conservative reaction" approach to the new possibilities provided by the digital rev-

---

[9] http://www.cities-lyon.org

olution and the Internet—a reaction against innovation. The debate must continue and we must make both civil society and our governments more aware of these issues in the run-up the second round of the summit in Tunis in 2005. There is a lot to be done.

The results and benefits of the digital revolution must be regarded as human rights and no longer as a mere instrument for the accumulation and concentration of wealth. The digital revolution is on our side!

Part V:
The Network Society:
Global and Local

Chapter 13

Internet and Society in a Global Perspective: Lessons from Five Years in the Field

Jeff Cole

Overview

The World Internet Project (WIP), of which "Surveying the Digital Future" is the part conducted in the United States, originated in 1999 at what is now the USC Annenberg School Center for the Digital Future as the study of the Internet "that should have been conducted on television." For over a generation, it has been a truism that since television was the one mass medium expected to be a mass medium, a panel study should have commenced in the late 1940s as the United States and much of Western Europe and Asia acquired television.

A long-term study of individuals as they became television users would have done much to answer some fundamental questions about the rise of television and its effects on the audience. When American households had their televisions turned on three hours a day in 1960 and were asked where that time came from, most users simply did not know and claimed they simply found the time from "somewhere." A long-term tracking study could have shown whether television time came from time spent talking with family members, from time spent reading books or newspapers or listening to the radio, or from somewhere else. Such a study also could have documented television's effects on consumer behavior to determine whether and how it affected consumer purchases, connection to the civic process, desire to travel, career aspirations and much else.

In the U.S. television is used primarily for leisure and entertainment, while the Internet has the potential, like the printing press, to transform work, play and learning. Therefore, a much more compelling case can be made to track the growth of the Internet than could have been made in the 1940s with television. Believing the impact of the Internet would eventually be much more significant than that of television, in 2000 the World Internet Project launched the study of the Internet that should have been conducted on television.

Methods

Using a RDD sample, the Center creates a carefully constructed representative sample of the American population. Non-users as well as users make up the sample, as it is essential to talk to non-users before they go on the Internet and understand as much as possible about their lifestyle. While the project did not begin before a significant portion of the population was online, the project is at the beginning of broadband at home, online media and the wireless Internet in the United States. In the first year, when the household was contacted, the interviewer crafted a roster on all household members over the age of 12. The computer then randomly chose one of those members and the interviewer spoke only to that person. A parent's permission is required for interviews with those between ages 12-17 and the survey is conducted in English and Spanish.

The interviews cover a wide range of topics. For both users and non-users of the Internet, the interview examines all types of media use and users' credibility toward media. Communication patterns, ranging from telephone use to conversation time face-to-face with family, friends and neighbors, are covered, as is a whole range of questions about buying behavior and shopping decisions. Questions also are asked about use of leisure time, trust in institutions, attitudes toward technology and much more.

Non-users are asked about why they are not online, whether they anticipate ever connecting and what it might take to get them to connect. They are also asked their perceptions of what is happening online. Users of the Internet are asked when they first went online, what made them connect and their perceptions of online life. Users also are asked detailed questions about how they connect to the Internet and from where, how often they connect and for how long and what they do online. In the area of consumer behavior they are also asked about whether they buy online and, if not, what is barring them, as well as general attitudes toward online security and privacy.

The World Internet Project is based on the belief that the technology may continue to grow in important ways and the best way to understand the impact is to watch non-users as they become users, telephone modem users as they move to broadband and all users as they gain experience. In addition to watching that change, the project will also determine whether people drop off the Internet (between 2000 and 2004, about 3% of Internet users left each year—some of them later returned) and whether they ever return and, if so, when and what brought them back. The study also believes that some of the most important impacts of the technology may be in unpredictable areas and, therefore, the best way to see that change is to create a baseline profile of people's lifestyles and to go back to the same people year after year in order to watch the impact and change.

International Partnerships

While technology change is occurring in America faster than in most of the world, the United States is not at the forefront of that change. Penetration rates for the Internet have been higher in Scandinavia than in the United States, and America is just beginning to enter the wireless area for anything more sophisticated than voice communication. While high percentages of Europeans and Asians use their mobile phones for SMS and accessing the Internet, this use of mobile is in its infancy in the U.S. Therefore, to gain a worldwide perspective on the rate and nature of technological change and its impact on lifestyle, the project reached out to partners around the world to conduct parallel studies in their own countries. At the moment, close to 20 other countries are part of the World Internet Project.

In year one, in addition to the United States, surveys were conducted in Sweden, Italy, Singapore, Hong Kong, Taiwan and Japan. The second year saw the addition of Germany, Hungary, Spain, Macao, China, South Korea, Canada and Chile. Additional partners are now in India, Argentina, Israel, Australia, Portugal and the Czech Republic. Great effort is now being focused on finding African and more Latin American partners.

In each country the work is carried out by a university or qualified research institution. Membership in the World Internet Project requires the use of common questions in each nation's survey, although each country is free to add additional questions of particular interest to them or their region. In Asia, Chinese-speaking countries (China, Hong Kong, Singapore and Taiwan) are aligning their efforts to look at issues of common concern.

Lessons Learned from Five Years in the Field

Conducting such a widespread international, longitudinal project begins to yield real results and trends after three years in the field. While the project has four years' or more data from the United States, Singapore, Italy and Sweden, enough countries have produced data from two or more years in the field to begin to discern and understand trends. The latest report from the United States (http://digitalcenter .org) identifies ten major trends that have shown themselves after ten years of the public Internet in the U.S. and after five years of data. Most of those trends can also be found in the industrialized nations of Europe and Asia and in many of the developing nations as well. Not surprisingly, each country has also identified unique issues and trends that have more to do with national culture or development and demonstrate the local character of the Internet around the world. This paper focuses on the common issues, problems and developments that have become clear in a longitudinal look at the social, political and economic impact of the Internet.

The Advantages of Experience Have Diminished

Sometime over the past year, a subtle but important development on the Internet began to emerge: for the first time the advantages of having Internet experience began to diminish and even disappear. The rate of this diminution is greatest for those countries that have had the greatest Internet penetration for the longest time: United States, Sweden, Germany, Japan and Canada.

Over the past five years we have been tracking Internet use, following the same non-users as they became dial-up and then broadband users. From the beginning we saw significant and pronounced differences between the newest users (who had just gone online) and the most experienced users (who had been online seven years or more). Those experience differences accounted for enormous differences in how often users went online and with what type of connection, how long they stayed connected, their attitudes towards the Internet and, most importantly, what they did while connected. Indeed, Internet penetration only moved to large numbers in Europe as users could move to broadband (mostly DSL), bypassing the expensive per-minute phone charges associate with dial-up. In the U.S. and Canada, where low-cost unlimited dial was possible, users stayed on modem connections far longer until broadband costs began to decline over the past two-to-three years.

The most experienced users connected over twice as long as the newcomers and were far more likely to be connected through a high-speed connection. Long-time users also connected from more places, both inside and outside the home. The biggest differences, however, over four years was in what the new and experienced users did while connected. New users were much more likely to be looking at chat rooms, playing games and searching for entertainment information and—most interesting to us—searching for medical information. We were intrigued that medical searching seemed to be one of the heaviest uses by new Internet users: they seemed to have an unlimited curiosity about medical issues, issues about which, perhaps, they did not feel comfortable asking friends, parents or even physicians.

Over the years, experienced users were spending much more time than novices buying online, doing work related to their jobs and looking at news online. Fours years ago the average new Internet users did not make an online purchase until they had been online between 18 and 24 months. The most important factor accounting for this lag was fear about privacy and security, although other fears and concerns came into play. Prospective shoppers four years ago also did not buy online because they feared the product would not be delivered or would be delivered damaged. They were also concerned whether they could trust online descriptions of products. Overwhelmingly, they did not like the absence of live human beings in the buying process.

Sometime in late 2003 or early 2004 everything began to change. Now the differences between new and experienced Internet users have almost disappeared. Although long-time users still connect longer, in most other areas the differences have flattened enormously. New users are only slightly more likely to be looking at chat rooms or playing games online, and they are just about as likely to be looking at news, entertainment information or doing work related to their jobs.

Shopping differences have shown immense change. Today, new users buy online almost from the day they get connected. Indeed, the desire to make an online purchase is one of the most compelling factors causing non-users to get an Internet connection in the first place. The 18-to- 24-month lag period is gone. Both Internet users and non-users believe that prices are lower online and that the availability of products is greater. Merchants successfully convinced many non-users to go online and start buying at lower prices. Many merchants (especially airlines) now charge service fees when buying over the phone or in person, but no service charge when buying on the Internet.

While fears about privacy and security have not diminished over the years, they no longer serve as a barrier that prevents buying: people now buy in spite of the fears. Concerns about damaged products or misleading descriptions have also disappeared as actual buying experience has demonstrated there was little basis for the fears. And the most dramatic change: lack of live humans in the buying process has been transformed from a liability to an asset. Now buyers report they don't want to have to deal with a real person and prefer buying through a computer—unless they experience a problem and need customer service.

The most likely cause four years ago for the vast differences in Internet use by experienced and new users was demographic differences. In the United States, the earliest Internet users were much more likely to be white or Asian, highly educated, male and with higher incomes. They were also much more technologically inclined. Over the past four years, more and more of America has gone online, with the fastest growing groups being African-Americans and Latinos, females, lower income and those with less education. In virtually all the other nations of the project, the first and heaviest users were also the most educated with higher incomes and much more likely to be male.

Another important change is that new users go online knowing what to expect from the Internet having, in many cases, been online before with a friend's or relative's connection. The learning curve for online behavior is much shallower. New users know what to expect when they connect and now get down to business much faster than new users of several years ago. Four years ago new users did much more exploring and experimenting before getting down to business on the Internet. For many of the reasons stated above, now they get to business right away.

Internet Users Watch Less Television

In every country for which we have collected data, Internet users watch less television than those who are not online. The amount of television watched lessens, although not significantly, as users gain experience on the net. It is not surprising that Internet users watch less television than non-users since for many people their at-home, awake time has been dominated by television; if they are to carve out time from their lives to go online, it almost must come from television.

Figure 13.1   Number of hours of watched television per user and non user of internet

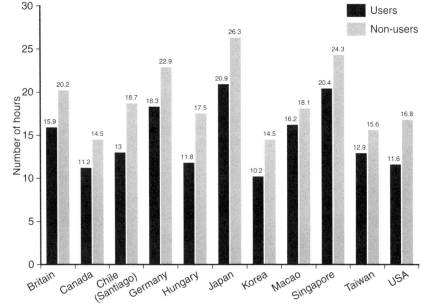

Looking at 2003 data and the 12 countries that collected information on television use, the average across those countries is that non-users of the Internet watched 4.03 hours more television a week than users. The country with the highest television viewing among users and non-users is Japan and the nation with the lowest among the countries measured is South Korea. In Japan non-users watch 26.3 hours of television per week (and users 20.9) while, just a few hundred miles (and a great cultural divide) away, South Korean non-users watch 14.5 hours of television a week and users watch 10.2.

Looking at the gaps between Internet users and non-users and tele-vision use, the greatest gap is found in Chile and Hungary at 5.7 hours a week more television by non-users. It is important to note that in 2003 the Chilean data was urban-based and drawn mostly from Santiago. Had the entire Chilean nation been measured (as it is now), the numbers and the gap might be slightly different. Although the gaps between Hungary and urban Chile are the same, Chileans report watching slightly more television. It is also noteworthy that the biggest gaps between users and non-users occurred in two places that had relatively low television viewing when compared to the nine other countries. The nation surveyed with the smallest gap between Internet users and non-users is Sweden where the difference comes to 1.4 hours a week. Not far behind is the region of Macao (now part of China) where the gap, although very low, is slightly higher than Sweden at 1.7 hours a week.

When Internet users are asked whether they watch more or less tel-evision, it also becomes apparent that the Internet is cutting into tele-vision time. Relatively few Internet users report that they are watching more television. Among those who do, the highest percentage is that in Singapore where 13.4% of users say they are using television more. The country reporting the smallest increase is Sweden where only 0.3% say viewing has increased. Spain also reports tiny increases at 0.9%. Across eight countries, an average of 5.08% report more televi-sion use after discovering the net. Far larger are the percentages reporting watching less television. The average of those saying they are watching less television across the same eight nations is 31.3%, or about six times as many saying they are watching more. The country with the highest percentage of Internet users watching less television is Spain at 41.1%, closely followed by urban China at 39.9% and the United States at 38.3%. The country reporting the smallest number of those saying they are watching less television is Singapore at 19.1%, closely followed by Sweden at 21.2%.

The year-to-year results are able to clearly demonstrate that Internet users watch less television than non-users. Those differences may be due to demographic factors, that in many countries Internet users are somewhat younger or have higher education or incomes. It is compelling to learn that users watch less television, but the more rele-vant research question is whether the Internet is the reason they watch less. Would they watch the same amount of television if there were no Internet? As they access the net does their television use decrease and, if so, in predicable patterns as they gain experience and knowledge of the web? These are the very questions that a panel study can begin to elicit. Great attention is currently being focused in those countries that have been in the field for three or more years to look at changes in lifestyle as people use the Internet. Although it will take another two-to-three years to fully answer these questions, early data show that television use does decline as non-users become Internet users. The scientific answer to this question is of critical importance to the television industry around the world as millions of people move onto the net every year. If these new users begin a process of watching consistently less television, the long-term future of television will be as a vastly smaller and less significant medium than it has been in the past.

Figure 13.2   Changes in time of watched television per user and non user of internet

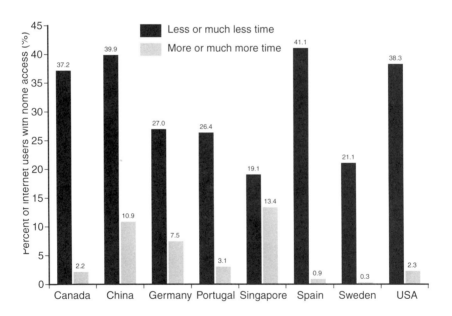

As we measure television watching and its possible displacement by the Internet, two essential observations are coming into focus. First, a majority of Internet users in most countries are multi-tasking and, at least some of the time, are on the Internet at the same time as they are watching television. Television began as a medium that received the audience's full and undivided attention. Only after years of experience did viewers begin to eat or engage in other activities as they watched television. The Internet, on the other hand, because it can be asynchronous, began as one activity among many (talking on the telephone, watching television, sending Instant Messages, listening to the radio) for its users. The American data show that not only do a vast majority of people multi-task while they are online, a small majority are occupied with three or more tasks while on the web. Clearly, the mindset and environment of younger users is not focused on one media activity at a time.

Second, we have also noticed that television displacement begins to change as Internet users move from dial-up use to broadband. Dial-up users at home tend to go into another room away from family members and television and stay online an average of 20-to-30 minutes at a time (with some exceptions). Broadband users are online many more times a day for far shorter periods. Broadband users are more likely to go online with other people around them and, whereas dial-up use tends to displace television program viewing (30-minute blocks), broadband use tends to disrupt television advertising viewing (1-to-2-minute blocks). All of this will ultimately change the nature of television displacement, likely resulting in users not watching significantly less television, but, rather, watching it in a significantly different manner.

Internet as an Important Source of Information

For several generations, survey researchers have been tracking how citizens get their information. In the United States organizations such as Gallup and Roper have tracked where Americans get their information and how that has changed over the years. Internationally, the Internet became a medium for public use in the 1990s, especially after browsers were developed allowing users to access the world wide web (WWW). From the beginning, people turned to the web to get information, whether it was a movie start time, product information or research on a catastrophic illness.

From the beginning, the World Internet Project has been tracking the importance of the Internet as a source of information and entertainment and the ways in which usage changes and may affect other media as well. Clearly, during the first five years of tracking the Internet, it has been perceived much more clearly and strongly as a source of information rather than as a place for entertainment (although it is heavily used to find information about entertainment).

In the United States, the Internet has surpassed television as a source of information and remains heavily used for information in most of the world surveyed in the project. Only in Sweden do the majority of users not consider the Internet to be an important or extremely important source of information. In eight other countries the majority do consider the net to be an important or extremely important source of information. The place with the highest reliance on the web for information is urban Chile where 81.8% say the Internet is at least important in their use of information while only 3% say it is unimportant. Following Chile are Singapore at 77.6% and Spain at 71.8%. Urban China is close to Spain at 69.7%, raising important political questions that the project is striving to study. In the United States and Canada about 60% of Internet users consider the web an important source of information. During the course of the project the trend is toward the perception of the Internet as a place to go to get information and increasingly users are relying on it for that purpose. At the same time, the Internet has made far less significant inroads in the perception that it is a place to go for entertainment.

Reliability and Credibility of Information

As the Internet becomes one of the most important sources of information for people in countries throughout the world, it is essential to track the faith users have in the credibility of that information. The Internet will continue to grow as a source of information in people's lives if those users continue to believe they can trust the information they find there. In most countries television has surpassed newspapers and magazines as the most credible of media. Most of this is attributable to the sense that "seeing is believing." Many critics have argued that, if people had a better understanding of media literacy and the process of editing and special effects that can go into video compilation, they might be more skeptical of the information they receive through television.

Figure 13.3   How important is the Internet for Information purposes

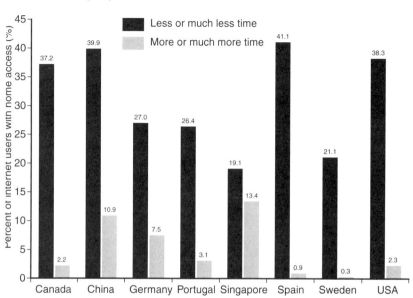

In the United States, faith in the integrity and reliability of traditional print and broadcast media has been high over a period of generations. Because Americans have trusted their media, they largely have not developed the critical media skills necessary to readily distinguish good information from bad or to withhold judgment until after examining the source of the information. The results of the World Internet Project's worldwide data suggest that only people in countries where faith in the reliability of information has not been so traditionally high may have developed more critical media skills.

The American data show that in the first two years of the project, Internet users in the United States had growing faith in the quality of the information they found online. In 2001 55% of American Internet users said they trusted most or all of the information they found on the web (here the term "web " is used so as not to ask about chat rooms or e-mail). In 2002 that 55% grew to 58% and then in 2003 it fell to 53% and then fell again the next year to 50%. Attempting to understand this phenomenon, later questions were asked to distinguish sources of information such as traditional media on the web, government web sites and individual web sites. In 2003 74% of Internet users said they trusted most or all of the information found on the web sites of traditional news organizations, while only 10% said they trusted information on the web sites of individuals. This is a distinction that American Internet users did not make in the first year of our study. The compelling result that has emerged from the course of the work in the United States is that, as people use the web more and more for information, continue to rely on it and develop strong relationships with certain web sites, they have become more skeptical overall about the information on the entire web.

Figure 13.4   How trustful is the information in the Internet

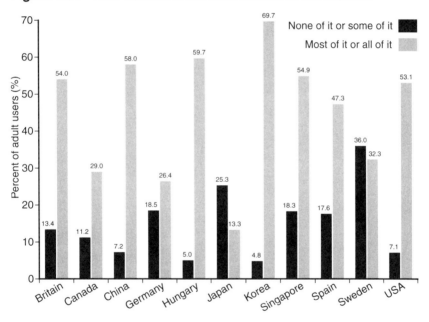

Compared to other countries, the United States is toward the middle with regard to belief in the reliability of online information. Using 2003 data, as mentioned above, 53% of American Internet users said they trusted most or all of the information online. That level of trust is consistent with Britain (54.0%) and Singapore (54.9%). Slightly higher faith in the quality and reliability of online information is found in China (58%) and Hungary (59.7%), while the country in the project that most trusted the quality of online information was South Korea at 69.7%. More skeptical than these countries were Spain at 47% and

Sweden at 32.3%. The countries with the fewest people trusting most or all of the Internet's information were Germany at 26.4% and at the very bottom, far below the others, Japan at 13.3%. As with differences in television viewing, the greatest gulf among the countries with data in the project was between South Korea and Japan.

When looking at the other side of the question and examining the number of cynics who find none or only a small amount of online information credible, it is not Japan but Sweden that tops the list at 36%, while Japan comes in second at 25.3%. The countries with the lowest percentage of users finding little or no information credible is the United States (7.1%), Hungary (5.0%) and South Korea at 4.8%. A great deal of attention is being spent looking at the cultural and technological factors accounting for these differences.

Workers Feel Internet has made them More Productive

One of the most important questions faced by industry is whether the Internet makes workers more productive and efficient with their time or, because of heavy personal use, actually interferes with productivity. Historical studies have looked at the role the telephone played in increased productivity in the workplace. The telephone allowed workers to reach out immediately to other workers in the same location and across their cities, countries and the world. The telephone was far faster than letters and allowed for immediate feedback. Answers to business questions could be found instantly, and the telephone allowed business people to deal with far more people and issues in a single day or hour than was possible with face-to-face visits if such visits were even possible. On this level there is no question that the telephone made workers more productive. But, at the same time, families and friends could reach into the workplace and sap workers' time and energy in a way that also was not possible before. Some employers placed restrictions on employees' use of the telephone for personal matters, frequently to little avail. These histories showed that, while personal use of the telephone could distract workers, overall it significantly improved productivity.

The WIP data has shown that there is significant use of the Internet at work for sending personal e-mail and browsing web sites (the same data also shows an equally or perhaps even more significant use of the net for work-related activities while at home). It falls to other studies to examine actual rates of business productivity over the next generation and to look at the ways the Internet and other technologies may affect this productivity. (A very important effort in this direction is the BIT Study being conducted by Uday Karmarkar at UCLA's Anderson School of Management. The study is currently measuring the ways in which Internet technology is affecting business in close to 10 countries (http://www.anderson.ucla.edu/documents/areas/ctr/bit/Annualreport.pdf).

While the WIP Project cannot measure actual increases or decreases in productivity, it can gauge whether workers believe this technology has affected their productivity. It is clear that across the world workers strongly believe the Internet has affected their business productivity in a positive way. It is important to note that many of these workers add, frequently with some unhappiness, that this increase in productivity means that they take on even more work (not always voluntarily) with the result that they are working more and harder than ever before. The U.S. data also show that a majority of workers believe their use of e-mail and the web is being monitored, sometimes closely, by their employers. A third complaint (to be examined later) is that this technology has tied them to their work and offices whether at home or on vacation.

Figure 13.5   Does the Internet improve your productivity at work?

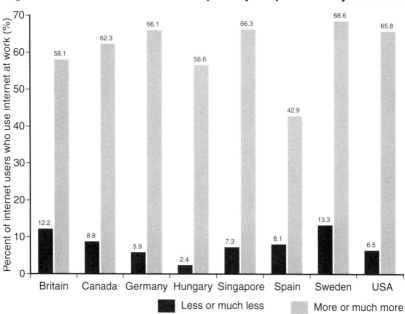

Looking at eight countries in the WIP, first it is striking that only small minorities of workers believe that access to the Internet has negatively affected their work productivity. Across eight countries, an average of 8% of workers feels their productivity has declined because of the Internet. The country most likely to feel this is Sweden at 13.3%, followed closely by Britain at 12.2%. The nation least likely to feel that productivity has declined because of the net is Hungary where only 2.4% see negative effects. In the middle are Canada (8.8%), Spain (8.1%), Singapore (7.3%), the United States (6.5) and Germany at 5.9%. On the other end, an average of 61% of Internet users across these eight countries feel they became more productive at work once they gained Internet access. Here, most of the nations are clustered close together in the 60-percent range. Interestingly, the highest is Sweden, which also had the highest percentage believing the net made them less productive. Fully 68.6% of Swedes see productivity gains because of the Internet. In the same range are Singapore at 66.3%, Germany at 66.1%, the United States at 65.8% and Canada at 62.3%. Slightly lower are Britain at 58.1% and Hungary at 55.6%, while Spain is still lower at 42.9%.

One of the goals of the project in the next cycle is to separate work into discrete tasks to gain a better understanding of whether workers feel that the Internet has improved productivity in all tasks or whether it is concentrated in only certain areas. The addition of data from developing countries will also make this data even more meaningful.

Frequency of Checking E-Mail High, but may be Changing

By any measure, for almost all Internet users, e-mail has become an established part of their lives. In nearly every country, Internet users report that the attraction of e-mail was usually the major reason or one of the top two reasons for seeking access to the Internet. In the American data, the highest level of satisfaction with the Internet over the past four years has been in the ability to communicate with other people. In a mid-year, special survey taken of U.S. Internet users shortly after September 11, 2001, it was found that e-mail use increased significantly in the days after the terrorist attacks. Moreover, many people reported using e-mail to reach out to friends, many of whom they had not communicated with for long periods, to show caring and support and, in many cases, to repair injured relationships. What was most compelling about these "I care messages" is that, in most cases, the senders indicated they would not have sent a letter or made a phone call; the communication only occurred because e-mail perfectly matched their emotional state and desire to communicate. More than a quarter of Americans on the Internet reported receiving messages from outside the United States within a week of September 11.

Clearly, there are very special needs filled by e-mail that are not filled, or at least in the same way, by the use of the telephone or mail. That e-mail has become an important part of many Internet users' daily lives can be shown by looking at the WIP data. In nine countries the project looked at how frequently Internet users check their e-mail. Across those nine countries, an average of 52% checks their e-mail at least once a day. At the very bottom of that list is urban China at 21%. This low number can be easily explained by the small percentage of Chinese who own their own computers. With many Chinese accessing the Internet through cyber cafes, it is not surprising that only a few are able to gain access at least once a day. High percentages in the other countries report checking more than once a day, with many checking once an hour or more.

Figure 13.6 How frequently Internet users check their e-mail

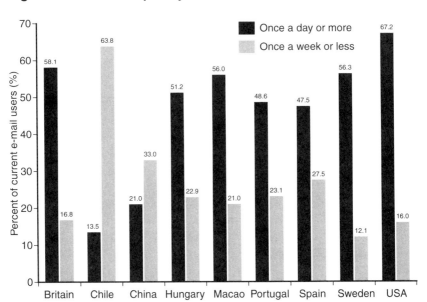

Americans check their e-mail most often, with 67.2% looking at messages at least once a day, followed closely by urban Chile at 63.8%. Other than China, all the countries report a majority or very close to a majority accessing e-mail at least once a day. On the opposite side of the scale, even though Americans are the ones most likely to check e-mail at least once a day, they are not the group with the smallest percentage checking least often (once a week or less). That distinction belongs to Sweden, where 12.1% check only once a week. After Sweden are urban Chile (13.5%) and then the United States. The country most likely to check only once a week is China at 33.1% for reasons stated above.

In the fourth year of the American data a new development was observed that may be the beginning of a trend that will deepen in the United States and perhaps become evident elsewhere in the world as well. Of course, it is also possible that this is a trend that will not truly develop over a period of several years and could prove to be an aberration. Among the most experienced Internet users in the U.S. (those on-line seven years or more), there may be the signs of an "e-mail overload." All of the most experienced users see the great advantages in convenience and productivity that e-mail has added to their business and personal lives, and none of them want to give up either e-mail or the Internet. Although they report high levels of satisfaction with the technology, they also report that they feel this technology is controlling and even, in some cases, defining their lives. Many report that they have become tethered to their e-mail and always feel they have to check and answer messages. This has created in some a constant sense of always having to deal with an issue that did not exist in their lives ten years before. As mentioned, none of them want to abandon e-mail, but report they want to take control of the technology and enjoy the benefits of instant communication without suffering the disadvantages. This phenomenon, referred to in the latest U.S. report as "E-nuff Already," can be evidenced in a number of ways.

Over the first three years of the work, there was always a relationship between Internet experience and frequency of checking e-mail. In the fourth year, there was a change and it was the newest users who were checking more often than the experienced users. When asked how quickly one should reply to a personal e-mail (business e-mail was not looked at here because one may not have a choice of how often to access business e-mail since their job could depend on checking), in the fourth year it was the newest users who believed in the fastest response. Of those online for less than a year, 29.7% felt that a personal e-mail should be answered as soon as possible while less than half as many experienced users (14.7%) felt a reply was called for that quickly. On the slower side, 18.9% of new users felt that a reply in two or three days was acceptable, while 30.8% of the experienced users felt this way.

Figure 13.7   Frequency in replying to their e-mail

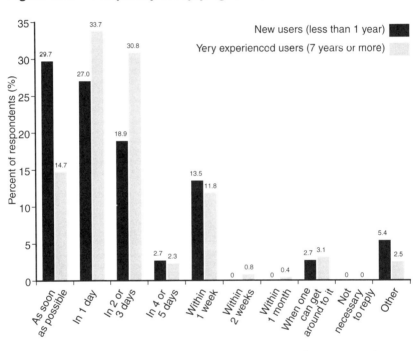

Like television, the Internet has become a significant part of many users' lives. Its importance as a medium of communication and information is already significant and likely will continue to grow and become more pronounced. As it moves from a novelty to an ingrained part of daily (or hourly) life, it will have increasingly unanticipated effects on daily life. Beyond displacing some existing activities, the Internet will change the core of social interaction, politics, learning and entertainment in ways that will be captured internationally as the project grows in size and maturity.

Chapter 14

E-topia: Information and Communication Technologies and the Transformation of Urban Life

William J. Mitchell

What kinds of buildings are required by the network economy and the knowledge society? How should these be distributed spatially within a city? These are the questions that I shall explore in this chapter—first generally, then with specific reference to the context of Portugal.

The technological context

To begin with, we should note that the technological context of the network society is established not just by microprocessors and the Internet, but by an emerging wave of diverse new technologies that find their uses relative to one another. The 2005 Lemelson-MIT list of the top twenty-five technological innovations of the last twenty-five years provides a good sense of this. These innovations proved to be important not just because they provided new capabilities, but because these capabilities met real human needs in a technological context established by earlier innovations and in an evolving social context. The list runs:

1. The Internet
2. The cellphone
3. Personal computers
4. Fiber optics
5. Email
6. Commercialized GPS
7. Portable computers
8. Memory storage discs
9. Consumer level digital cameras

10. RFID (radio frequency identification) tags
11. MEMS
12. DNA fingerprinting
13. Air bags
14. ATM
15. Advanced batteries
16. Hybrid car
17. OLEDs
18. Display panels
19. HD TV
20. Space shuttle
21. Nanotechnology
22. Flash memory
23. Voice mail
24. Modern hearing aids
25. Short range, high frequency radio

Notice that most make practical use, in some particular context, of digital information and inexpensive, miniaturized electronics. Notice, as well, the mutual interdependencies. The Internet needed the personal computer, and the personal computer needed the Internet. Email needed both.

The emergence of fusion space

From an architect's perspective, new technologies often provide new ways of adding value to architectural space. The electric light, for example, made rooms more versatile and valuable at night. The technologies of the network society are no exception. In general, they are producing fusion space—architectural space in which digital electronic technology enables new and socially valuable combinations of people or activities. Here are some examples.

These days, the seminar rooms at MIT fuse the hitherto distinct activities of group discussion and Web surfing. The students bring their wireless laptop computers to class. Whenever I introduce a topic, somebody Googles it—and then interjects any relevant discoveries back into the conversation. This radically changes the social and intellectual dynamic in the space. It produces a very high level of intellectual engagement, it generates a thrilling, high-speed, vividly grounded discourse, and it shifts the role of the teacher. I can no longer rely on my superior command of the subject matter to maintain my classroom authority!

In university dormitories, isolated working under intense academic pressure turns out to be a triggering factor for student depression, binge drinking, and even suicide. Networking dormitory rooms for personal computers can exacerbate this. But creating fusions of study space and social space—lounges with wireless connectivity, and quiet corners to work as well as areas for socializing—reduces isolation and increases opportunities for peer-group support.

In research libraries, the former functions of the carrel and the telephone box are fusing. You can frequently find young researchers with their laptops open, surrounded by books and journals, talking on their mobile phones. If you eavesdrop, you find that they are not just blabbing, but are getting guidance from their supervisors or coordinating with distant collaborators. Then, when they find interesting pages of text or images, they simply snap pictures with their camera phones. Librarians disapproved of all this at first, much as classical chefs looked askance when they first encountered the new wave of fusion cuisine. Then they started to see it as an important new intellectual practice—and to demand space designed to accommodate it.

Walk around a building that accommodates a high tech company, and you will probably find that a surprising number of the private offices are locked and dark. But look, by contrast, at the electronically supported work going on in airplane seats, high-speed train seats, airline lounges, cafés, hotel rooms, and even park benches. Much of the activity has shifted from classically conceived, single-purpose, assigned space to fusion space.

Imagine an apartment that is jammed with sensors everywhere, and that processes the resulting data stream to recognize the current activities of the occupants. (Kent Larson, at the MIT Media Laboratory, has recently constructed just such a dwelling—known as PlaceLab.) It knows when you are making a cup of tea, or folding the laundry. Now imagine that, based on what it observes of your behavior patterns over time, it offers carefully calculated, well grounded advice on diet, exercise, taking the opportunity to go out for a walk, taking your medication, and other things that will keep you healthy. It fuses the private apartment and the elderly-care nursing home. If you are an ageing baby-boomer, it might enable you to live independently in your community for many more years.

Finally, imagine a school bus that uses its GPS location system to retrieve and present information about the areas that it is passing through. It fuses the geography, history, ecology, and civics classrooms with transportation and the public space of the city.

In all of these cases it is the new, connectivity-enabled fusion of previously distinct activities that is the source of new value.

Rethinking adjacency, proximity, and urban spatial patterns

Let us turn, now, to the changing relationships of urban spaces to the other urban spaces that surround it. A simple hut is a single, undifferentiated space that accommodates many activities, but a larger and more complex building is a system of more specialized spaces with circulation networks and exchanges of various kinds linking them. (The distinction between single-celled organisms and larger and more complex biological systems is a similar one.) At larger scales, we can think of cities as systems of specialized buildings linked by transportation networks and exchanges, and of cities embedded in global transportation networks. Digital telecommunication changes spatial patterns of activities within such networks, but not (as many early theorists thought) by simply substituting telecommunication for transportation, producing the "death of distance," and allowing anything to happen anywhere and at any time.

To clarify the mechanisms at work, it will be useful to introduce an elementary cost model. The cost per unit of time to operate a spatially differentiated, geographically extended, networked urban system might be represented as the sum of:

1. The *fixed costs* (think of them as rents) of assigning particular activities to particular urban locations.

2. The *interactive costs* (time and money spent, over time, on transportation) of the flows of people, materials and goods, energy, and information among locations.

The interactive cost per unit of time is the sum of the costs of the exchanges between pairs of activities at their assigned locations. And the cost of exchanges between any pair of activities is given by:

Distance x Volume x Cost coefficient

The *distance* between the activities depends upon the spatial layout of the system. The *volume* of traffic depends upon the nature of the functional connection between the activities—such as the connection between a factory and a warehouse. The *cost coefficient* depends upon the efficiency of the network connection between the locations.

Historically, the fundamental role of new urban networks has been to reduce the cost coefficients in the system. Tracks for people and vehicles reduced the cost of moving people and goods among locations; pipe networks reduced the cost of moving water and sewage; wires enabled efficient distribution of electric power; and wired and wireless channels now allow fast, inexpensive movement of information.

The first-order effect of introducing an efficient new network or network link, with a low cost coefficient, is to reduce the cost of the existing assignment of activities to locations. In other words, the existing spatial pattern can operate more efficiently. The second-order effect is to allow the emergence of *new* spatial patterns when the system is subjected to pressure to grow or to accommodate new needs. Consider, for example, the introduction of a piped water supply network into a village that had hitherto depended upon a central well. The first-order effect is simply to reduce the human time and energy spent on carrying water to existing houses. A second-order effect is to eliminate the need for houses to cluster within water-carrying distance from the well, and to enable them to spread out along the water lines as the village grows. Another second-order effect may be to change bathing, as the village becomes more affluent, from a centralized, public activity at the point of water availability to a decentralized, private activity that takes place in the private bathrooms of houses. Yet another effect is to destroy the efficacy of the old village well as a social magnet and focus of community life, and to create the need for something new—maybe a café.

The first-order effect of new telecommunication networks is, obviously enough, to provide more efficient information distribution and exchange among locations within existing urban patterns. Less obviously, the second-order spatial effects of introducing wired telecommunication networks, with low cost coefficients for movement of information, are:

1. To reduce the need for adjacency and proximity among activities that primarily exchange information.

2. To allow other, latent demands for adjacency and proximity to become effective.

3. To produce, as a result, spatial restructuring through fragmentation and recombination when the system is subjected to pressure to grow, to accommodate new demands, or to become more competitive.

Consider, for example, the traditional urban bookstore and Amazon.com. The urban bookstore clusters, at one location, the functions of book storage, display and browsing, point of sale, back office activity, and advertising. Amazon.com has taken advantage of digital telecommunications to produce an efficient new spatial pattern. By moving the browsing and point of sale functions online it virtualizes and decentralizes them—making them available at any point of Internet access, and efficiently reaching a large number of widely scattered customers. Simultaneously, it centralizes the book storage function in large, highly automated warehouse and distribution centers located at nodes in transportation networks—enabling economies of scale, taking advantage of low-rent space, and keeping many more titles in stock than an urban bookstore can do in its limited, expensive space. And, through use of sophisticated e-commerce technology, the back office functions are freed up to move to wherever the labor market is most attractive.

If you look at many traditional building types and urban patterns today, you can see processes of fragmentation and recombination at work. Most significantly, perhaps, concepts of "home" and "workplace" are changing—together with concepts of the relationship of the home to the workplace. A standard pattern of the twentieth century was for an information worker to have a home in the suburbs, an office in the central business district, and a daily commute between the two. In the network society, though, the home may double as an electronically connected workplace. There is little evidence that this will turn everyone into housebound telecommuters—though it does open up new work opportunities for the disabled, and for the geographically isolated. For many, though, it means that work times and locations are much more flexible, and that the home must now accommodate a home office. And, in some contexts, it allows homes and workplaces to recombine into new urban villages, with twenty-four-hour populations, composed of live/work dwellings. In some cities, the development of electronic live/work villages is becoming an attractive option for the rehabilitation of historic but underutilized building stock.

Another way to say all this is to say that digital technology can add value to a space in two ways. It can do so directly, by increasing the comfort, efficiency, or versatility of the space itself—in other words, by producing fusion space. And it can do so indirectly, by increasing the connectivity and accessibility of the space for various purposes—that is, increasing the value that it has by virtue of its location within the larger, multiply networked urban system.

Wireless connectivity

Wireless networking overlays an additional set of spatial effects on the fragmentation and recombination produced by wired networks. Depending upon the degree of miniaturization of wireless devices, it can:

1. Simply substitute for wired infrastructure over rough terrain, and in other circumstances where wired connections are difficult or expensive.

2. Provide mobile connectivity to vehicles—enabling flexible and efficient dispatch of taxis, direction of emergency service vehicles, and so on.

3. Free sedentary information work and entertainment from fixed locations, and increase the value of places to sit down and work at a laptop computer.

4. Provide mobile connectivity to pedestrians.

A practical architectural effect of this is to reduce the demand for specialized, assigned space—private offices, cubicles, library carrels and the like—and to increase the demand for unassigned public and semi-public fusion space that can be appropriated for different purposes, by electronically equipped and connected inhabitants, as needed at any particular moment. Furthermore, in congenial climates, outdoor and semi-outdoor spaces can have new uses. With your wireless laptop you can work just as easily on a park bench, in the shade of a tree, as you can in a cubicle in an office tower.

Consider, for example, this very paper. I did not write it in my formally designated "workplace"—my office at MIT. I wrote it on my laptop in a series of hotel rooms, airplane seats, and cafés. I presented it in Lisbon. And I emailed the final text to the editor via a wireless connection in Italy.

All of this challenges the assumptions of the cost model that I introduced earlier, and forces us to reframe strategies for designing and managing urban space. It is no longer adequate to think solely in terms of fixed assignments of activities to locations, and specialization of those locations to their assigned activities—as homes, workplaces, places to learn, places of entertainment, and so on. An increasing component of urban space must consist of flexible, electronically serviced fusion space that is nomadically occupied.

The emerging, associated paradox of portable, wireless connectivity is that it does not produce space that looks "high tech." The better the miniaturized, wirelessly connected technology, the less obtrusive it becomes; it disappears into your pocket and into the woodwork. There is less necessity to organize buildings around technological requirements, such as the requirement for sealed, air-conditioned spaces to accommodate old-fashioned computers, or the requirement for teaching space to be darkened to allow the operation of audiovisual equipment—no longer necessary in an era of high-intensity display screens and video projectors. Without sacrificing functionality, architecture can return to an emphasis upon natural light and air, view and connection to nature, and sociability.

Implications for Portugal

Many of the implications of digital technology for Portuguese architecture and cities are those that have now become familiar throughout the world. We will see a growing role for electronically enabled fusion space, and we will see ongoing fragmentation and recombination of established building types and urban patterns as the effects of digital networking become stronger and more prevalent.

There are, in addition, some particular opportunities. Due to its pleasant climate and strong architectural traditions of making use of outdoor and semi-outdoor space, Portugal has a particular opportunity to take advantage of the architectural and urban potentials of wireless connectivity. And there is also an exciting opportunity for preservation and adaptive reuse of historic building stock in Lisbon and other beautiful urban and village settings by unobtrusively introducing digital infrastructure, and thus adapting historic built fabric to new uses without destruction of its character.

As I trust I have demonstrated, digital connectivity does not diminish the importance of place or of local architectural and urban character, but instead provides powerful new ways of adding value to places. A society is fortunate when it has distinctive, humane, pleasant places to add value to. The challenge for Portuguese architects and urbanists is to effectively relate the new technological opportunities of the twenty-first century to the extraordinary Portuguese context of culture, climate, and architectural and urban tradition.

Part VI:
Policies of Transition
to the Network Society

Chapter 15

Challenges of the Global Information Society

Pekka Himanen

Objective

This chapter looks at the serious challenges that are going on in the information society. Some of them will become acute by 2010 but all of them require imminent action if we are to respond to them success-fully. When this review was originally written, particular emphasis was placed on the situation in Finland and Europe. This perspective remains in this revised version of the text to some degree, although most of the challenges are global.

For the purposes of this review, information society is understood in the broad sense of the word (as in Prof. Manuel Castells' and Dr. Pekka Himanen's theoretical studies; see Castells and Himanen 2002; for additional information, see Castells 2000a, 2000b, 2004;).

From a theoretical perspective, the key concepts include *network form of organisation* and *growth that is based on innovations*. Information economy relies on productivity growth based on innovations, unlike the hype of what is called the new economy. Several studies have shown that, during the past few years, growth has increasingly been generated by technological innovations combined with networked forms of organisation (Sichel 1997; Jorgerson and Stiroh 2000; Jorgenson and Yip 2000; Brynjolfsson and Hitt 2000; Castells 2001; Koski et al., 2002).

Networks are becoming increasingly common, and the role of innovations is growing, also in the labour market. Using Robert Reich's vocabulary, routine production jobs are declining, while the importance of symbolic analytical work and personal-service work is increasing (Reich 1991; for the changes in the labour market, see also Carnoy 2000; Benner 2002). In Richard Florida's vocabulary, the concepts of creative and service jobs are close to symbolic-analytical work and personal-service work (Florida 2002). Creative/symbolic analytical jobs are specifically based on creative problem-solving (or the creative generation of new problems). However, the role of the creative component is also emphasised in jobs that are based on interaction. Creativity must be understood broadly: while creativity is an essential part of certain jobs that first come to mind, such as an artist's, researcher's or engineer's, it is also required, for example, in interaction between people and in jobs that involve manual skills.

This review comes to the conclusion that the most critical aspect in the development of the information *society* is the development of the deep-set structures of society, to which we must now pay close attention (cf. Castells and Himanen 2002). The information-society agenda is not the same as an *information network* or *Internet* programme. The development of technology will help only when it is combined with changes in the underlying structures. As the word "information society" usually first brings to mind technical (surface-level) matters, I would like to underline that the approach employed in this review is based on the need to change the deep structures, so topics that are mainly technical in nature, as important as they are, remain outside the scope of this review: Examples include broadband connections (e.g. public libraries as points of access to the network) and information security (e.g. viruses, spam, privacy protection).

This review is not a futurological study. The time perspective of this review covers trends that are already in progress (up to 2010) and to which we must react today if we are to respond to them successfully.

This review describes areas where action must be taken, yet it is not a practical implementation plan. The actions that are proposed in this review form a balanced entity: for example, the suggestions related to a creative economy require the creative welfare society if a balanced outcome is wanted.

Global Trends

In the global development of the information society, we can identify ten major trends that are already in strong progress (building on Castells 2000a, 2000b, 2004; Himanen 2001, 2004b; Castells and Himanen 2002).

1. Increasing international tax competition
2. The new global division of labour
3. Population ageing
4. Increasing pressures on the welfare society
5. The second phase of the information society
6. The rise of cultural industries
7. The rise of bio-industries
8. Regional concentration
9. A deepening global divide
10. The spread of a "culture of emergency"

These trends can be described as follows:

1. Increasing international tax competition

Countries compete for investments and skilled labour by reducing tax rates.

2. The new global division of labour

Routine production moves to cheaper countries (the "China phenomenon"). China and India are particularly on the rise, and other emerging large countries include Indonesia, Pakistan, Russia and Brazil. The most developed countries cannot rely on routine jobs in the future, so they must specialise in creative work that is based on higher expertise and work to improve productivity both through increased added value and the development of production processes. At the same time, large developing countries whose role in the global market is increasing offer extensive markets for the products supplied by developed countries. This marks the next phase of economic growth.

3. Population aging

Population aging is one of the most important trends in Europe and in some other regions. In these countries, population aging means a shift from the "society of the young" via the current "society of the middle-aged" to the "society of pensioners." This shift will already have taken place in many countries by 2010, when the labour force will be declining sharply.

4. Increased pressures on the welfare state

Population aging leads to problems in financing the welfare state, both because of an increase in direct expenses and a rising dependency ratio. At the same time, greater global tax competition and the new global division of labour put increased pressures on the welfare state. The welfare state can be maintained in the future only if its productivity is improved through innovations. The future of the welfare state is a creative welfare state.

5. The second phase of the information society: from technological to social development

The first phase of the information society focused on the development of technology, such as network connections. In the second phase, which has now begun, technological development will continue; however, the focus will shift to larger social matters and the main focus will be on changing the ways in which we work.

6. The rise of cultural industries

The information economy is expanding particularly in the field of culture, including music, TV, film, computer games, literature, design and learning materials. This process is affected by technological convergence, i.e. the digitalisation of content and the coupling of information technology, communication technology and media.

8. The rise of bio-industries

The next phase of the information society will see the rise of bio-industries. Genetic engineering will become another key technology besides IT. Medicine, biotechnology and welfare technology are other examples of emerging fields. The importance of these sectors is increased by population ageing (for example, gerontechnology, i.e. technology that makes life easier for the elderly).

Regional concentration

For the first time in history, the world's urbanisation rate has exceeded 50%. Large concentrations of expertise account for an increasing proportion of innovations and economy, as being at the leading edge of global competition requires larger entities. Regional concentration continues and pressures on further concentration increase.

9. A deepening global divide

If we carry on with "business as usual," inequality and marginalisation will continue to become aggravated both globally and nationally. During the first phase of the information society, i.e. from the 1960s to the turn of the 21st century, the income gap between the poorest 20% and the richest 20% of the world's population doubled and is now approximately 75:1. This development is maintained particularly by the distortions of world trade and the knowledge divide between developing and developed countries, so the situation can be improved considerably only by changing the structures of world trade and by bridging the information divide.

10. The spread of a "culture of emergency"

The pace of development is accelerating, which increases the volatility of economies and creates a "culture of emergency" in workplaces. Deepening social gaps increase tensions, which in turn fuel the emergency culture. This trend is characterised by increasing instability. The challenge of achieving development that is sustainable in both human and environmental terms plays the pivotal role in such a risk society.

This above list of major trends is by no means meant to be an exhaustive description of all societally important developments, but it is one made from the limited aspect of the development of the information society.

Development Scenarios

If we look at this development from the geographical perspective, it can be said that the fiercest competition is carried out by and between three leading regions: the United States, Asia and Europe (see Figure 15.1 below).

Figure 15.1   Global Challenges to the Information Society

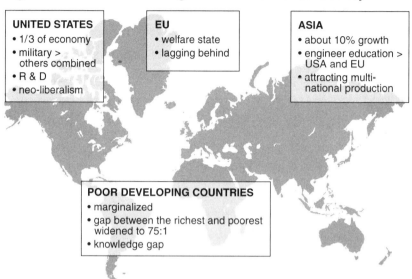

UNITED STATES
• 1/3 of economy
• military >
  others combined
• R & D
• neo-liberalism

EU
• welfare state
• lagging behind

ASIA
• about 10% growth
• engineer education >
  USA and EU
• attracting multi-
  national production

POOR DEVELOPING COUNTRIES
• marginalized
• gap between the richest and poorest
  widened to 75:1
• knowledge gap

On a global scale, Europe is currently at a disadvantage, while the US model clearly has the upper hand.

The United States alone accounts for one-third of the world's economy and half of the R&D work carried out in the world, and its military budget almost equals that of the rest of the world. Many Asian countries develop at an annual rate of almost 10%, and global production and markets are increasingly moving to Asia. In the IT field, for example, by 2010, half of the world's semiconductors are consumed and a third of them are produced in Asia (excluding Japan). For example, China currently produces more experts in science and technology than the EU or the United States (in 2000–2002: in China, 590,000; in the EU, 440,000; in the US, 385,000). A global market for expertise has emerged, where the development of Asia forms a completely new challenge to Europe. The EU clearly lags behind the United States, for example in terms of the region's attractiveness to Asian experts.

Allowing some simplification, there are currently three especially dynamic models in terms of technology and economy, yet they are based on very different social models. These can be called by the following titles (taking the representatives that are most often referred to; for additional information, see Castells and Himanen 2002; Himanen and Castells 2004b; Wong 2004):

1. The "Silicon Valley model," i.e. the American neo-liberalist model —the predominant model (United States)

2. The "Singapore model," i.e. the Asian state-run model in which the objective is to attract multinational companies to the region —an emerging model (also in China and India)

3. The "Finnish model," i.e. a European combination of the information society and the welfare state, which is represented in its most advanced form in the case of Finland.

Outside these regions and models, the status of the poorest developing countries continues to weaken. For example, most of the African countries between the Sahara and South Africa are becoming pauperised. One-fifth of the world's population subsists on less than a dollar a day and has no access to health care or education. A continuously widening knowledge divide underlies the increasing welfare divide.

Each of the above models has currently problems that can be characterized with the following scenarios:

1. The Silicon Valley model refers to the neo-liberalist scenario of *"leaving the weak behind."* Although this scenario is technologically and economically dynamic, it comes with a high social price. For example, the Silicon Valley area itself produced 60 millionaires a day at the end of the 1990s, but they had to move to fenced residential areas, because a society that leaves some of its citizens in the margin is a society of fear. One-fifth of the population lives below the poverty line, has no health insurance and is functionally illiterate. In Silicon Valley, the opportunities to receive education depend on the economic position of your family, so a class of marginalised people has emerged, for which crime is the only means of survival (particularly the sale of narcotics to those who have succeeded). Paradoxically, the world's biggest proportion of the population that is in prison is in California, a leading region in terms of development! In addition, sending someone to prison for a year is more expensive for society than sending them to Harvard to study! The adoption of the Silicon Valley model would mean unfettered neo-liberalism.

2. The Singapore model is based on tax competition, i.e. *"a race to the bottom."* This has also been a dynamic model, although the limitations and problems of competition have recently become evident. As other countries can always reduce their tax rates more in order to attract multinational companies, production keeps moving to cheaper and cheaper countries. In the case of Singapore, companies have moved, for example, to China and India. The outlook is not good in the long run if the region has not developed adequate local expertise and innovativeness, exactly what has happened in the Singapore case. If a region is to succeed in competition in the long run, it must have innovative ability; it is not sufficient that the government takes action to attract multinational companies. (The Singapore model is also patronising, which is another problem: the government attempts to control its citizens' freedom, although the information society cannot be creative if people do not have free access to information and the freedom to think otherwise. This is a great paradox also for China, which idealises the Singapore model.)

3. The third scenario, i.e. the current European combination of the information society and the welfare state, has the danger of *"the dead hand of passivity."* According to this scenario, people keep protecting all the industrial era structures of the welfare state, but they do not recognise that the future of the welfare state is only possible if the welfare state is reformed with the same kind of innovativeness that the information economy has gone through. In practice, passivity leads to a situation where welfare needs to be cut back more and more and the dynamics of the economy fades. People protect their own vested interests and envy other people for the benefits that they get. This can also be called the society of envy.

Fortunately, there is a fourth scenario. It is possible to combine the welfare state and the information society also in the future if only we have courage to revise this model appropriately. Therefore, under the current circumstances, the welfare state is best defended by those who speak for its reform through innovation. The fall of the welfare state can be prevented by moving from a reactive to a proactive policy: we should no longer focus on reacting to something that has already happened; instead we should act beforehand and boldly lead the way.

The values of the reform of the European model

The following list describes the values which could serve as the basis for the continued combination of the welfare state and the information society. They are updated versions of the values underlying the original European welfare state and innovative entrepreneurialism. A successful reform requires from politicians value-based management.

1. Caring
2. Confidence
3. Communality
4. Encouragement
5. Freedom
6. Creativity
7. Courage
8. Visionariness
9. Balance
10. Meaningfulness

The content of the values can be briefly described as follows:

1. Caring

Caring is the old principle of equality (*egalité*, in the traditions of the Enlightenment, and justice, of the classical period). It can also be called fairness or the inclusion of all. Caring means that we work to create equal opportunities for all. This is the key idea of the welfare state. In the global development, it means that we protect the equal opportunities of all the people in the world. The word "caring" is used in this context on purpose, to emphasise everyone's responsibility for caring for other people (in the Christian tradition, this value is referred to as *caritas*). The idea of this value in a nutshell is as follows: "Imagine a situation similar to ours, except that our roles are reversed."

2. Confidence

Confidence is partly based on caring, yet it deserves to be classified as a value in its own right. It is also a basis of the welfare state. Confidence gives safety and makes fruitful communality possible. The lack of caring and confidence creates an atmosphere of fear.

2. Communality

Communality is the old value of fraternity (the *fraternité* of the Enlightenment). It means openness, belongingness, willingness to include other people and to do things together. This value is yet another foundation of the welfare state. Communality is one of the most energising experiences of life—being part of a larger community that shares your interests. It means living together.

4. Encouragement

The realisation of communality is the precondition of encouragement. Encouragement refers to an enriching community whose members feel that they can achieve more than they ever could alone. In an impoverishing community, individuals feel that they are less than they could be. Encouragement means that you choose to enrich, not to impoverish, other people when you interact with them. Encouragement means that you spur people on, including yourself, to be the best they can and that you give them recognition for their achievements. Encouragement is actually a form of generosity. It can be crystallised as follows: "Not wanting to take anything away from other people; instead, working to make it possible for everyone to have more." Other people should not be considered as threats that must be diminished; instead, they are opportunities that can make the world richer for us all. This is not a scarce resource in the world— there is plenty for everyone. The lack of communality and encouragement creates an atmosphere of envy.

5. Freedom

Freedom is also one of our traditional values (the *liberté* of the Enlightenment). It includes the rights of individuality: the freedom of expression, the protection of privacy, tolerance for differences. It means permissiveness. Freedom can be crystallised as follows: "Whatever adults do of their own free will is all right, provided that they do not hurt other people."

6. Creativity

Freedom creates space for creativity, the realisation of your potential. Creative passion is one of the most energising experiences of life. Creativity is related to the human need for self-fulfilment and continuous personal growth. It takes different forms in different people. Restrictions on freedom and creativity create an atmosphere of control.

7. Courage

Courage is a value and characteristic that is required in order to realise the other values. In the European tradition, courage was considered to be one of the cardinal values as early as the classical period.

8. Visionariness

Visionariness requires courage and, in the same way as courage, it is a forward-looking value. In the European tradition, it can be seen as the continuation of hope, a Christian value. Visionariness refers to insightfulness, the courage to dream, the willingness to make this world a better place.

9. Balance

Balance is a type of meta-value: it refers to the balance between the other values. It means the sustainability of what we do. Since the classical period, this value also has been called temperance or moderation.

10. Meaningfulness

Meaningfulness is partly based on balance and the other values that have been described above, yet it is a value in its own right. In the end, we all want our lives to be meaningful. Thus, the meaningfulness of development depends on the extent to which development promotes intrinsic values, such as the classical values of wisdom, goodness and beauty. Meaningfulness can be crystallised in the following question: "Will this make my life more meaningful?"

Values can be considered to give life a meaning and make life worth living. Although the above-mentioned values build on the European tradition, they are found also in other cultures (the European tradition is based on the multi-layered values of the Enlightenment, i.e. freedom, fraternity and equality; the Christian values of faith, hope and love; and the values of the classical period, i.e. justice, courage, temperance and wisdom—all values that can be found universally).

The importance of these ten values can be described with the following pyramid, which is often referred to in the description of man's psychological needs (e.g. Maslow 1954, 1962).

Figure 15.2   The pyramid of values from the psychological perspective

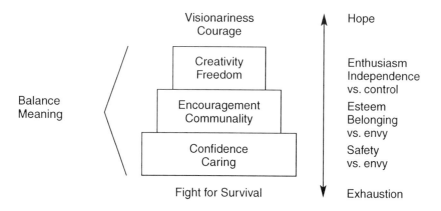

The above description of needs emphasises caring and confidence as the basic human needs, which form the foundation for the social needs for communality and encouragement and the needs for freedom and creativity that are related to self-fulfilment. Courage and visionariness are forward-looking values, while balance and meaningfulness ensure that our actions have a meaning. Psychological experiences, which are listed on the right-hand side of the pyramid, show that you can either move up towards enthusiasm and hope or go down, through control and envy, towards fear and exhaustion. (This pyramid can be used for describing not only society as a whole, but also

its various sectors, such as economy, politics, work, education and individual people. However, the order in which the values are listed and the pyramid form of the figure should not be interpreted as a normative stand on the interrelation between the values.)

Key Concepts of Social Development

In practice, if we are to meet global competition by implementing the above-mentioned development scenario and adopting the values described above, we must take into account the following key concepts related to social development:

1. A creative economy
2. A creative welfare society
3. Humanly meaningful development
4. A global culture

The latter part of this review describes the content of these concepts and the entailing value-based actions that must be taken in order to respond to global trends. The emphasis is largely European, although many of the issues apply much more largely.

1. A Creative Economy

Under the pressures of international tax competition and the new global division of labour, developed countries can only rely on expertise and creativity, as routine jobs and routine production will not help them to compete with the cheap Asian markets. Developed countries must enhance productivity through innovations: creativity will make it possible to increase added value and improve the efficiency of production.

Spearheads of a creative economy: a stronger IT sector, culture and welfare

Developed countries must actively look for new areas of economic activity where creativity can make a difference. Although developed countries should not be fixated on certain fields only, they will find new potential in culture and welfare, the major emerging sectors in the second phase of the information society. Therefore, the creative economy can be strengthened by examining the opportunities of the cultural sector (including music, television, film, computer games, literature, design and learning materials) and the welfare sector (innovations related to the reform of the welfare society, i.e. biotechnology and gerontechnology, which helps elderly people to live independently) so that they become new spearheads for the creative economy in addition to the IT sector. Interaction between IT, culture and welfare will also generate completely new opportunities. The key sectors of the creative economy are shown in Figure 15.3.

The two new spearhead sectors have vast potential. For example, the cultural sector generated a global business of USD 1.1 billion in 1999. This sum was distributed between the following fields (learning materials, which constitute an enormous business as such, are not included):

Table 15.1 Cultural Sector Global Business	USD billion
Publishing	506
TV & radio	195
Design	140
Toys and games	72
Music	70
Film	57
Architecture	40
Performing arts	40
Fashion	12
Art	9

Source: Howkins 2001

The welfare sector, which includes health care, medicine, etc., is an even larger business which continues to grow, for example because of new biotechnological inventions and population ageing. Europe could leverage its expertise in this field, for example in public health care, by exporting it to other regions.

However, success in these areas in the global competition requires increased investment in national R&D activities (financing of creativity). The leading countries are soon investing almost 4.0% of their GNP in these areas, so government decisions along these lines are required if we are to succeed in the global competition in the near future. The most important question is how new public investments are directed: additional financing should be directed to the cultural and welfare sectors.

Financing must also be directed to the development of business models and marketing. Europe, for example, has clear problems at the end of the innovation chain, which is shown below (in practice, innovation does not progress in a linear fashion; the factors described in the figure form an interactive network):

Figure 15.3   Innovation factors

Innovation → Production Process → (Product) → Business Model → Brand

Idea Creativity   Business Creativity

Europe is innovative in terms of products and production processes, i.e. idea creativity, but less creative in terms of business models and brand building, i.e. business creativity that helps to transform ideas into income. Therefore, financing is required in order to promote research and development (including training) related to business creativity.

Richard Florida has combined the creative economy with the concept of the creative class. According to him, this rising class consists of very diverse groups of people, such as researchers, engineers, writers, editors, musicians, film producers, media makers, artists, designers, architects, doctors, teachers, analysts, lawyers and managers. At the turn of the millennium, the creative class accounted for approximately one-third of the work force of advanced economies (Florida 2002).

However, we should not confine the creative economy to a single class of creative professions only, as Florida does. Robert Reich has shown that interaction-based "personal-service" jobs constitute another extensive group of jobs in the information society in addition to the "symbolic analytical" jobs that are similar to those mentioned by Florida. Service professions indeed form an important factor of the economy. The creativity of interaction must, therefore, be seen as another important form of creativity, to which we must pay attention. Work based on interaction also increases productivity, improves the quality of work and provides significant opportunities for employment even for those with a lower education.

In fact, we must understand the creative economy as an idea that permeates all sectors of the economy. Sectors that have traditionally been strong remain significant, and even their productivity can be improved through innovations. Traditional manual skills also require creativity. The above-described spearhead sectors are part of an economy that is based on extensive creativity. The sectors of the creative economy are shown in Figure 15.4.

Encouraging conditions for working

The success of the above-mentioned economy in the global competition depends on the degree to which taxation encourages this kind of activity. If we are to meet these challenges, our taxation system has to promote work that enhances the common good, i.e. taxation must promote job creation, entrepreneurship and creativity and thus make it possible to finance the welfare society.

Figure 15.4   An economy based on extensive creativity and expertise

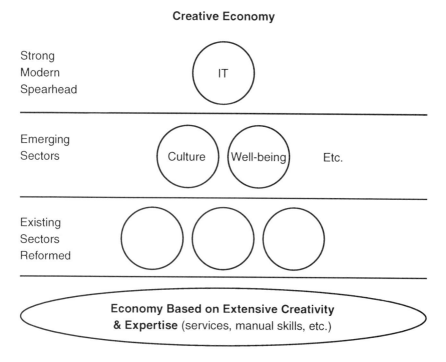

It is essential to note that the welfare society is based on the *tax revenue generated by work*, not by the *tax rate*. Tax revenue can be generated only if the system encourages people to work. Although participation in unhealthy tax competition will not help maintain the welfare state, it must be pointed out that excessive tax rates can also undermine the welfare state.

The welfare society is based on the world's best expertise and work. The financing of the welfare state depends, first and foremost, on the achievement of a high employment rate and on society's ability to associate innovativeness with positive expectations by applying tax rates that encourage work. This will make it possible to finance the welfare society also in the future. A taxation system that encourages work also acts as an incentive for skilled employees to stay in their countries and makes it possible to attract skilled labour from abroad; this will in turn alleviate the problems caused to the welfare state by an ageing population.

Management and work culture in a creative society

The government can, of course, only pave the way for creativity, as government decisions as such do not enhance creativity. However, it is important that the system encourages creativity, instead of restricting it.

The same applies to business. In an information society, companies must provide space for creativity through a management and work culture that promotes creativity (cf. Alahuhta and Himanen 2003, who describe this change, for example, from the perspective of Nokia's experience; Himanen 2001). The work culture and atmosphere are decisive factors in an economy where growth is increasingly based on innovations. The managers' main task is to promote creativity. An increasing number of companies are adopting a new key principle of management by setting ambitious goals that generate enthusiasm. Matters related to work culture will become an important competitive edge.

There is a distinct difference between the industrial society and the information society. In the industrial society, the bulk of the work consisted of routine tasks, and the result of work depended largely on the time that was devoted to it. The old work ethics, according to which work was an obligation that you just had to fulfil and suffering was thought to strengthen the character, made economic sense in the industrial era. In the information society, however, work depends increasingly on creativity. This means that the industrial work culture turns against itself also in economic terms: if people feel that work is nothing but a miserable duty and that the main point is to fulfil orders, they do not feel a creative passion towards their work, and yet this passion would make it possible for the company to continually improve its operations and stay ahead of the competition. The industrial era created a time-oriented management culture that was based on control, whereas the creative economy requires a result-oriented management culture that makes space for individual creativity.

This development is connected with the hierarchy of man's motives, which was presented above. Whatever we do, we are at our best when we are passionate about what we do. And passion evolves when we think that we are able to realise our unique creative talent. People who have such a passionate relationship with their job have access to the source of their inner power and feel that there is more to them than usual. People who feel that their work has a meaning do not become tired of their work; work fills them with energy and gives them joy. We can see this phenomenon not only in business life, but also in any human activity (from learning to science and culture): people can achieve great results because they feel that they are able to fulfil their potential at work, and this meaningfulness makes them even more energetic and boosts their creativity. An encouraging atmosphere enhances well-being at work and job satisfaction.

In our changing economy, people work more and more in co-operation with others, so managers must be able to build enriching communities. Managers must set ambitious goals that generate *joint* enthusiasm, i.e. they must be able to generate interaction that enriches the working community instead of impoverishing it. Interactive skills will bring a key competitive edge.

This development can also be connected to the psychological pyramid of needs. The realisation of creative passion is a powerful experience, yet equally powerful is the feeling of being part of a community that shares your interests and appreciates what you do and who you are. History is full of examples of the power of this phenomenon. For example, in science and art, where money has never been the primary motivator, all great achievements have been made thanks to this power: belonging and being a recognised person. The same power applies to business at its best.

2. A Creative Welfare Society

As global competition becomes tougher and the population ages, the maintenance of the welfare state requires its reform. This reform can be referred to as the building of version 2.0 of the welfare state which guarantees the future of the welfare society.

The philosophy underlying the idea of the welfare state is that people have equal opportunities to realise their potential and are protected against the random misfortunes of life. This includes equal access to education, training and health care, etc. The ethics of this philosophy is that, in principle, everyone could have been born in any position in society and that any misfortune that someone has to suffer could have hit anyone. Ethically, the welfare state is based on the fragility of life and the ability to identify with other people's fates. It is based on the ability to imagine that things could just as well be the other way round: I could be in your position and you could be in mine. This is what caring is all about. A fair society is fair regardless of the cards that fate has dealt you. In a fair society, your fate does not depend on the stars under which you were born, i.e. the economic and social status of your parents. A fair society provides everyone with equal opportunities in life, thus levelling out haphazard circumstances.

In short, the welfare state is based on caring, which is to be understood in the sense of fairness. To put it more precisely, fairness refers to equal opportunities, not a mechanically equal distribution of benefits. If individuals are provided with as equal opportunities as possible, it is only fair that their shares depend on their preparedness to work. Fairness like this encourages everyone to fulfil their potential.

Regarding the concept of the welfare *state*, the government is responsible for providing the equal opportunities and protection. In a welfare state, this duty is allocated to the government, as the government represents the public interests. Although the government is, of course, not able to fulfil this obligation flawlessly, it is the best alternative because it is the only democratically controlled body that protects the interests of all of its citizens. The legitimacy of the government's right to levy taxes is largely based on its obligation to maintain the welfare state: we pay taxes to the government and expect it to provide us with equal opportunities and protect us.

The purchaser–provider split in the organisation of welfare services

However, we must make a specific distinction in relation to the concept of the welfare state. The above definition of the welfare state does not mean that all welfare services should be provided by the public sector. The government is responsible for organising (financing) the welfare services, but they can be provided either by the public sector, companies or non-governmental organisations. In some areas, the government should always also remain the provider. But in many areas, it is useful to separate the purchaser and the provider of the services from each other. In some cases, services can be provided best by parties other than the public sector. A more open competition and co-operation between alternative service providers is in the interests of citizens (as it guarantees that their taxes are used prudently). Therefore, it is better to use the term "welfare *society*" instead of "welfare state." This is the first important step towards the creative welfare society: in many areas, the purchaser and the provider should be systematically split in the provision of welfare services. If the public sector's responsibility always extends from the ordering of services to their provision and evaluation, it will no longer be interested in developing the services. The reformed purchaser–provider model is shown in Figure 15.5:

Figure 15.5   The purchaser–provider model

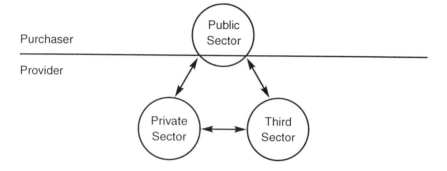

The future of the welfare society is in creativity

The strong global trends, i.e. increasing competition and population ageing, increase welfare expenses, particularly in Europe, and thus increase the pressures for cutting these expenses. In fact, future welfare expenses cannot be covered even with moderate economic growth.

Fortunately, there is another alternative, as we can apply the core principle of the information society to the welfare state: the maintenance of the welfare state by improving its productivity through innovations. This does not mean that productivity would be enhanced by putting more pressure on the employees and by increasing haste at work—in fact, this would even be impossible, as people are already overloaded. Instead, it means that productivity is enhanced through innovativeness, i.e. by combining technological and process innovations (networked organisations). It must be noted that this does not mean the provision of services over the Internet only (although access to services over the Internet is generally a good idea); it means that the processes with which the services are provided are reformed with the help of new technology and new process models.

In practice, the improvement of productivity through innovations requires that the public sector must adopt a similar management and work culture based on creativity to that described above. People should associate creativity with positive expectations. Currently, the system does not encourage improvements, and innovations are curbed. If an individual or a unit does something in an innovative manner and improves productivity, the unit's budget is cut and the individual's work load is further increased. The employees and the employer must agree on a new system, where most of the savings achieved through improved operations will remain in the unit and can be spent for the future development of the unit. In addition, the employer must guarantee that individual employees will personally benefit considerably from the time savings achieved through their innovations. The opportunity to follow a more humane working rhythm and to be able to balance work and family life in a more satisfactory manner is a motivating prize in our increasingly stressful times. The realisation of this kind of work culture requires an agreement between employer and the employee organisations which guarantees the protection of jobs if and when operations become more efficient (if increased productivity jeopardises jobs, any positive expectations related to innovations will fade). Managers must be prepared to act as examples and lead the way. We could introduce a specific training programme for welfare society management and invite the most successful managers of businesses and the managers of best practices in the public sector to share their views and experiences.

As people are prone to consider all changes in the information society to be technical, it must be emphasised once more that, according to research, productivity improves most when technological and process/organisational innovations are combined. This does not mean simply the automation of current operations although, for example, the introduction of electronic prescriptions in health care considerably improves productivity. Instead, entire processes and organisational models must be assessed in order to identify ways of providing the services to patients more efficiently in both economic and qualitative terms. Experiences obtained from business life have shown that the most successful innovations are made when the users of the services or products in question are able to participate in the innovation process. Of course, information networks (such as the Internet) provide efficient new opportunities for participation.

The basis: an inclusive, high-quality education system

The success of the information society and the provision of equal opportunities in the welfare society are, eventually, based on an inclusive and high-quality education and training system. In the information society, where learning continues throughout our lives, schools should not only distribute information but also, and equally importantly, build self-confidence and social skills, as well as help pupils to fulfil themselves by identifying their talents and creative passions. In addition, the challenge of lifelong learning in the information society requires that people must learn to learn—become able to identify problems, generate ideas, apply source criticism, solve problems and work together with other people. Teacher training should pay more attention to these matters.

The success of education in the achievement of these goals is also the foundation of the economy: especially for the small countries, their success depends completely on their ability to leverage the potential of their population to the full. For this to happen, the education and training system must be of a high quality throughout the country, so that the children's opportunities to learn do not depend on the region in which they live or the particular school that they attend.

In the information society, information is used as "raw material," so an open information infrastructure becomes an important factor. Free access to information should be promoted by all possible means: Information generated with public funds should be provided to citizens free of charge whenever possible. This applies to other publicly generated information, such as the historical material of museums. The accessibility of information and knowledge helps people to develop their information-processing skills, while it can also be used as the basis for new information and new innovations.

Innovation is ultimately based on the higher education system. If a country is to succeed in the global competition, it is important that its universities and other higher educational establishments receive adequate financing. It is increasingly important to join forces in the financing of science to be able to rise to the top in international research in the areas specified by the government. The educational units that operate in these areas must be sufficiently large and have adequate international contacts. Small countries, in particularly, must carefully choose the areas in which they want to specialise, because they can carry out leading-edge research and business in a limited number of areas only.

3. Humanly Meaningful Development

The human sustainability of the rapid global development has become an increasingly crucial question in the information society. The development of the information society can currently be characterised by the spread of a "culture of emergency" from the economy to workplaces and from the public sector to people's lives. The information society can also be called the risk society: volatility has increased in the financial market, employment relationships have become increasingly unstable, the public sector does little but reacts to crises, and individual citizens are in a constant hurry. The importance of the protection provided by the welfare society is emphasised in the information society, where all kinds of risk are increasing.

However, if we are to maintain the welfare society, we need new ways of promoting a socially, mentally, physically and culturally balanced development. For example, the current attempts to keep employees at work to an older age are not realistic because few people currently are willing or able to work up to the present official retirement age, let alone longer than that. If a more sustainable development model is not adopted, other actions will prove useless, and vice versa: a more sustainable development model has a significant effect on our ability to finance the welfare society also in the future (morbidity and premature deaths cost enormously through lost work). The best national health programme is the prevention of illnesses and other health problems, i.e. the promotion of health. The following sections focus on the promotion of health in more detail.

Social balance

A new creative work culture was described above. This culture is at best characterised by the energising experiences of self-fulfilment and belonging to an enriching community. Research has shown that good management and a good work culture are important factors that prevent exhaustion. People who are satisfied with their jobs feel well at work, which is positively reflected in their overall lives. Therefore, we can best increase the sustainability of development by paying more attention to employees' job satisfaction and well-being at work.

However, this alone is not sufficient; we also need a better balance between work and leisure, as the creative culture cannot be sustainable in the long term if work and other aspects of life are not balanced. In addition, adequate free time allows people to regenerate their energy and creativity and have a satisfactory social life. However, current trends are going in the opposite direction: an increasing number of people work longer and longer days, work is becoming increasingly stressful and people have less and less time for their family and friends. This is reflected, for example, in children's mental problems that are becoming increasingly common because parents have less time to spend with their family; another consequence is the rising number of broken marriages.

People who work in a continuous state of emergency become exhausted, so they have no energy for active free time. In many countries, one-fifth of workers currently suffer from exhaustion.

A balanced development requires both a reform of the work culture and concrete ways for balancing work and leisure in a more satisfactory manner. We must introduce the principle of reasonableness in our work culture: our era is characterised by increasing requirements, so employees get the impression that their contribution is never quite adequate. Therefore, the principles of management, which were described above, must be complemented with an important addition: managers must set goals that are adequately ambitious so that their achievement generates the feeling of success. However, the goals must be reasonable, so that people are sufficiently often able to succeed and can be satisfied with their achievements. Studies of burnout have shown that people become exhausted if they never feel that they have done well.

As regards concrete action, we need models that balance work and family life better. Of course, the implementation of flexible working-time arrangements depends on the nature of the work in question and must always be planned in co-operation between the employer and the employees. However, employers and employees could conclude an *agreement on more flexible working hours*, which would cover a number of alternatives to meet the needs of individual employees. Examples of such arrangements are:

- Project work, i.e. the specification of work in terms of its results and schedule, so the employee in question is free to decide where and how (in the office, at home, etc.) he/she will work in order to best achieve the agreed results by the agreed time limit.

- A working-time bank, i.e. an opportunity to save worked hours "in a bank" and to use the saved time when necessary by taking days off or by working shorter days (for example, in cases where child care requires). This model can also be developed further, so that employees can cut their working time and have their pay reduced accordingly.

What is important in both these arrangements is that employees can take time off when they need it, not just when it fits their work schedules. Of course, in the name of reciprocity, employees must be prepared to adjust their working hours when the employer requires (this makes it possible to react to fluctuations in demand by cutting working times temporarily and to avoid redundancies). However, not only do these arrangements allow employees to have more free time; they also help to increase job satisfaction, as research has shown that job satisfaction depends largely on the extent to which employees can affect their work. The practical effects of the labour agreement will, of course, depend on the managers' and employees' attitudes towards the new arrangement.

Mental balance

As was noted above, people in many countries retire many years before the official retirement age. Mental health problems have become one of the most important reasons for early retirement. Development has become mentally unbearable for many people.

Continuous stress, which expresses itself as various symptoms such as sleep disorders, is an extremely common mental health problem in the emergency culture. Stress has a relationship with many illnesses, such as heart and stomach diseases. The illnesses and diseases caused by excessive stress incur huge costs to society, to say nothing of the human sufferings that they cause. The above solutions are largely applicable also to this problem.

However, more serious mental health problems, such as the widespread depression and anxiety problems, require that the health care system pays equal attention to psychical and physical health.

Physical balance

In an information society, physical activities are replaced by virtual ones (Internet, TV, computer games etc.). Some people naturally go on with their physical activities, while for other people, physical activity ranks low. We must, of course, respect people's right to choose their lifestyles.

On the international and national levels, however, it seems that in the information society we suffer not so much from information bloat as just physical bloat (this does not mean that information bloat should be underestimated, as it is also a big problem)! Globally, one-fifth of people of working age are overweight. Obesity (and the related eating habits) are known to correlate significantly with cardiovascular diseases.

We also spend an increasing part of our lives in physically bad positions, gorging ourselves on information. Although information work is physically not as strenuous as traditional industrial work, it stresses in another way, through static working positions. (increased teleworking from home has made it necessary to pay attention to work ergonomics also at home, not just in the workplace). The situation is further aggravated by people's increasing habit of spending their free time in the static virtual world (computer, TV, virtual games, etc.).

In the information society, we now need actions that will help improve our physical health and well-being but which are not patronising and respect people's right to choose their lifestyles. Such an approach could be an international exercise campaign, which would inspire people to identify and adopt forms of physical exercise that suit their needs and give them pleasure. The most important point is, of course, that families would help children to identify their favourite forms of exercise and that schools would provide pupils with positive experiences of exercise and thus boost their willingness to pursue physical activities also in their free time. However, the campaign must be extended to workplaces if it is to reach the adult population. The campaign could be implemented in workplaces, for example, so that employees are allowed to exercise during the workday (as part of flexible working-time arrangements).

Other approaches must also be applied. Successful sports heroes could advocate their sports through TV, while less traditional forms of physical exercise should also be highlighted. Here are some examples of sports:

- sports (from running and swimming to tennis and football
- yoga, Method Putkisto, etc.
- gym, aerobics
- lifestyle physical activity (walking to and from work, using the stairs instead of taking the lift, etc.)
- dancing
- going for a walk with friends
- outdoor activities
- cultural tours

Having more exercise would have a considerable positive effect not only on the health of those who exercise, but also on society's welfare expenses as a whole. This development could be promoted by providing people with economic incentives to exercise, for example by giving them the right to use public sports facilities (e.g. swimming halls) free of charge on certain conditions. People could also receive a tax allowance on certain sports expenses. This is the "exercise always pays back" principle, as the investments made in exercise today can save considerable amounts of money in the future. The facilities provided by the information society, for example the Internet, can be used for the preparation of easy-to-use weight-loss and exercise programmes and for the centralised booking of sports services.

In the end, this kind of a balanced culture of creativity would improve the quality of people's lives (through increased job satisfaction and a better balance between work and other aspects of life) and would thus enhance the productivity of work (as companies would be better able to adjust to fluctuations in demand and employees would be more energetic and would achieve better results at work) and guarantee the maintenance of the welfare society.

Cultural balance

Finally, it should be specifically noted that the cultural balance of development also requires self-fulfilment outside work. Underlying this entire review is, indeed, the idea of an active approach to life that is realised not only in the private sector (entrepreneurship) but also in the public sector (innovativeness) and non-governmental organisations (caring, art, hobbies etc.).

Culture and well-being should be understood as intrinsic values, not just as economic tools. This means that we must promote also those forms of culture that are commercially unprofitable. In fact, commerce should be seen as a tool that must only be used to the extent to which it benefits life, i.e. the realisation of intrinsic values.

4. A Global Culture

In global development, we must progress towards joint development that is sustainable on a world scale. This requires greater open-mindedness from all nationalities.

The maintenance of our creative culture also requires such a more open-minded culture. In this way, ethical and economic justifications point in the same direction. We must consider the necessary development to be primarily an opportunity for all.

From a doorman's approach to a welcoming culture

As has been described above, the population of many countries is ageing so rapidly that, already in 2010, their populations start to shrink, unless there is openness to migration.

Immigration is also the only way of improving the dependency ratio, i.e. the ratio of employed people to the dependents (e.g. pensioners). Companies will also need foreign employees when the domestic supply of labour decreases.

In practice, if we are to respond to these challenges, we need political courage to increase the number of immigrants significantly (including high-paid and low-paid employees).

We must become more open-minded if we are to meet the requirements of globalisation. Tolerance must become a value for us Finns and we must show it in our everyday life.

In an ever-globalising world, we cannot keep our borders closed to the rest of the world, neither for ethical nor for practical reasons. We must get away from our previous attitude, the doorman's approach. We cannot act as a stern doorman who divides people into two groups: "You are welcome, you are not."

Figure 15.6 The proportion of the foreign population in different countries in 2000 (%)

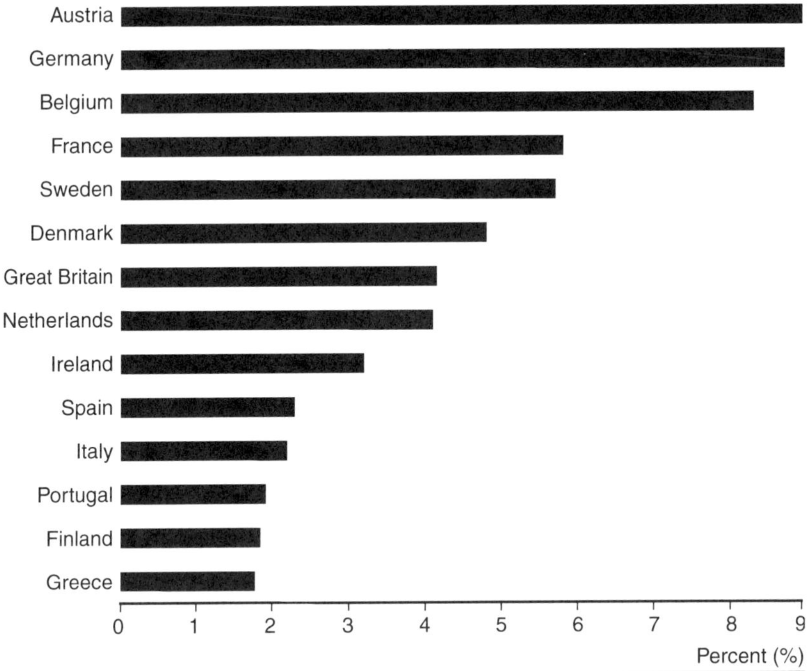

The internationalisation of higher education

One of the best ways for integrating immigrants to society is to be open to foreign students. Students have plenty of opportunities to establish personal contacts during their studies and they often learn the Finnish language easier than other people. Both these matters help to gain a feeling of belonging to the new culture. It would be reasonable to grant foreign students automatically the right to work after graduation. Bureaucracy should be minimised.

However, internationalisation must be seen as a two-way road. We can benefit from global expertise also by encouraging students to include exchange periods in their studies.

The same applies to university researchers. Universities must make serious efforts to recruit researchers globally. Ideally, top international researchers should account for a considerable number of our university professors.

However, just as in the case of students, this is also a two-way process. Science can be globalised also through the international activities of researchers. Therefore, it would be very profitable to grant more financing for research that is carried out overseas, for participation in international conferences, etc., as this is a cost-effective means for obtaining leading-edge international expertise. The international co-operation networks that are established in this way will further help to attract more renowned foreign researchers to the country.

Immigration, studies and research periods carried out abroad and international networks must be considered to be mutually complementing strategies that are all needed.

Attracting skilled labour

Global companies need skilled team leaders and researchers who have international experience. The need for experts exceeds the national supply,<0} so two alternatives remain: companies can either relocate their units overseas or recruit skilled labour from other countries.

Another challenge for these companies is keeping their current experts in their country. Under certain conditions, companies can benefit from the experiences of employees who go abroad to work if and when they return. However, if the number of experts leaving a country exceeds the number of experts coming to the country, the development is unsustainable.

Reasonable income taxation, which was discussed above in the section on the creative economy, is an important key factor that would help to prevent the outflow of experts from the country and attract experts from abroad. Taxation must promote creative work.

However, Richard Florida's research has shown that the attractiveness of a region to experts requires also a more extensive, open-minded culture of creativity. Experts are attracted by multi-cultural environments that are renowned for their openness to diverse ideas and different people, i.e. for their creative drive (Florida 2002). To give an example, one-third of the engineers who work in Silicon Valley, or in the San Francisco Bay Area, are nowadays from India or China, and the total number of engineers who come from overseas is approximately 40% of all the engineers in this area. (Saxenian 1999).

People in the San Francisco Bay Area have adopted an open-minded approach to creativity in terms of both technology and different lifestyles (e.g. this area was the home of the hippie movement, the gay movement and various oriental philosophies in the West). Florida points out that the competition for creative experts is increasingly based on the cultural variety and open-mindedness of the region: this includes vibrant restaurants, a bustling street culture, music clubs, small galleries, new theatre and dance groups and multi-faceted exercise and other leisure opportunities provided by the local authorities. The most important thing is that the region is characterised by the general value of freedom, which extends from the freedom of expression to a vibrant restaurant culture and sexual permissiveness.

Global reciprocity

This review is based on the principle that globalisation must be reciprocal. Therefore, the objective of the proposals made in this review, such as the need to increase immigration, is not just to protect interests of individual countries. Underlying the proposals is a more extensive ideology: caring and sustainable development.

It has been calculated that the opportunity for the citizens of developing countries to obtain work permits, whether for a short or a longer term, and irrespective of the type of work for which they are granted, would be one of the most important ways to improve the situation of developing countries. It would increase their annual income by USD 200 billion, i.e. four times the current development aid. This would be structurally very important, because it would transfer not only money but also expertise and business from developed to developing countries. AnnaLee Saxenian has shown that the brain drain between Silicon Valley and Asia has been replaced by "brain circulation": the Chinese and Indian experts who worked in Silicon Valley are returning to their home countries, where they are setting up businesses and establishing networks between other domestic companies and the best experts of the field (Saxenian 2004). It is unethical to require that capital and goods must be allowed to move freely while employees are denied this freedom. The rights of capital must be complemented with the rights of people. The current situation is awkward, as if we said to goods: "Freedom is your fundamental right. You were born free!" and then told people: "But not you."

In regard to the new global division of labour, we should remember that the partial transfer of routine work to poor countries makes it possible for them to rise from poverty. We must not object to this transfer in principle. We must indeed consider globalisation to be a reciprocal process from which we can benefit but for which we must give something in turn.

Another critical factor that would improve the position of developing countries is free trade, which should be fair in both directions. This could be called a *quid pro quo* agreement: for example, it would benefit the growth of the IT sector both in developed and developing countries, if the developing countries would open up their markets more. However, this requires reciprocity on a *quid pro quo* basis: it is immoral to require that developing countries must deregulate their trade while developed countries protect their markets from the main products supplied by developing countries. This situation can be compared to a relationship where someone suggests a "free sexual relationship" to their partner and adds: "It means that I am allowed to have sex with anyone I want, but you are not!" Developed countries prevent free trade in agricultural and textile products, which account for two-thirds of the exports of the developing countries. It has been calculated that fair trade in agriculture would bring USD 120 billion to the developing countries, i.e. more than twice the entire development aid that they currently receive. This would be an extremely important change for the better, because it would make it possible for the developing countries to improve their situation through their own economic operations. Therefore, it is critical that the government subsidies to agriculture in developed countries are abolished (in a manner that justifies the change also for farmers and other agricultural workers). This would remove a key structural factor that keeps the developing countries in the underdog's position in the global economy. *Quid pro quo.*

The minimum that we should do—albeit it is extremely important in symbolic terms—is to stick to the commitments that the rich countries have made relating to development aid. Rich countries have committed themselves to the United Nations' goal, according to which the development aid provided by developed countries should be at least 0.7% of their GNP. Currently the average figure for all developed countries is only 0.23%. If developed countries stuck to their promises, the developing countries would receive almost twice the current aid, which is USD 50 billion. Our current situation is shameful. The rich countries must stick to their commitment and must use their development aid also to promote a freer transfer of information (including the open source technology). Development aid can be compared with a modest request: "Could you consider using 0.7% of your time caring for other people?

The combination of social justice and the information society has an important role to play in the development of a more sustainable form of globalisation. This review's model of combining a dynamic information society with the creative welfare state is meant to provide some raw material for that critical attempt.

Literature

Alahuhta, Matti ja Himanen, Pekka (2003). *Luovan työn kulttuurin viisi pääperiaatetta* teoksessa Slotte, Sebastian ja Siljo la, Sevi (toim.)

(2003) Cameo. Helsinki: WSOY.

Benner, Chris (2002). *Work in the New Economy: Flexible Labor Markets in Silicon Valley*. Oxford: Blackwell.

Brynjolfsson, Erik ja Hitt, Lorin M. (2000). *Computing Productivity: Firm-level Evidence*. Cambridge, MA: MIT—Sloan School Center for E-business, working paper.

Carnoy, Martin (2000). *Sustaining the New Economy: Work, Family and Community in the Information Age*. Cambridge, MA: Harvard University Press.

Castells, Manuel (2000a). *The Information Age: Economy, Society and Culture, vol. 1: The Rise of the Network Society*. 2nd edn. Oxford: Blackwell.

Castells, Manuel (2000b). *The Information Age: Economy, Society and Culture, vol. 3: End of Millennium*. 2nd ed. Oxford: Blackwell.

Castells, Manuel (2001). *The Internet Galaxy*. Oxford: Oxford University Press.

Castells, Manuel (2004). *The Information Age: Economy, Society and Culture, vol. 2: The Power of Identity*. 2nd edn. Oxford: Blackwell.

Castells, Manuel ja Himanen, Pekka (2002). *The Information Societ y and the Welfare State: The Finnish Model*. Oxford: Oxford University Press.

Florida, Richard (2002). *The Rise of the Creative Class*. New York: Basic Books.

Hallituksen tietoyhteiskuntaohjelma (2004). *Tietoyhteiskuntaohjelma*. Helsinki: Valtioneuvoston kanslia.

Hammer, Michael ja Champy, James (1994). *Reengineering the Corporation*. New York: HarperBusiness.

Himanen, Pekka (2001). *The Hacker Ethic and the Spirit of the Inform ation Age*. New York: Random House

Himanen, Pekka (toim.) (2004a). *Globaali tietoyhteiskunta: Kehityssuuntia Piilaaksosta Singaporeen*. Helsinki: Tekes.

Himanen, Pekka ja Castells, Manuel (2004b). *Piilaakson ja Suomen tietoyhteiskuntamallit* teoksessa Himanen (2004a).

Himanen, Pekka (2004c). *The Hacker Ethic and the Spirit of the Information Age* teoksessa Castells (ed.) (2004), The Network Society. London: Edward Elgar.

Howkins, John (2001). *The Creative Economy: How People Make Money from Ideas*. New York: The Penguin Press.

Jorgenson, Dale ja Stiroh, Kevin (2000). *Raising the Speed Limit: US Economic Growth in the Information Age*. Brookings Papers on Economic Activity, volume 2. Washington, DC: The Brookings Institution.

Jorgenson, Dale ja Yip, Eric (2000). *Whatever Happened to Productivity? Investment and Growth in the G-7* teoksessa E. R. Dean et al.

(2000). New Developments in Productivity Analysis. Chicago, IL: University of Chicago Press.

Kalliokoski, Matti (2004). *Eurooppalaiset tietoyhteiskuntamallit* teoksessa Him anen (2004b).

Kansanterveyslaitos (2002). *Terveys ja toimintakyky Suomessa: Terveys 2000—tutkimuksen perustulokset*. Helsinki: Kansanterveysla itos.

Koski, Heli; Rouvinen, Petri ja Ylä-Anttila, Pekka (2002). *Tieto & Talous: Mitä uudesta taloudesta jäi.* Helsinki: Edita.

Kurjenoja, Jaana (2003). *Kansainvälinen palkkaverovertailu 2003.* Helsinki: Veronmaksajat.

Maslow, Abraham (1954). *Motivation and Personality.* New York: Longman, 3rd edn, 1987.

Maslow, Abraham (1962). *Toward a Psychology of Being.* New York: John Wiley and Sons, 3rd edn, 1999.

Münz, Rainer (2003). *Demographic change, international migration and the recruitment of labour in Europe.* AMPI Background readings.

Parkkinen, Pekka (2002). *Hoivapalvelut ja eläkemenot vuoteen 2050.* Helsinki: VATT.

Saxenian, AnnaLee (2004). *Piilaakso 2000—luvulla* teoksessa Himanen (2004b).

Sichel, Daniel (1997) *The Computer Revolution: An Economic Perspective.* Washington, DC: The Brookings Institution.

Vartiainen, Matti ym. (2004). *Hallitse hajautettu organisaatio.* Helsinki: Talentum.

Wong, Poh Kam (2004). *Singaporen tietoyhteiskuntamalli* teoksessa Himanen (2004b).

Chapter 16

Policies of Transition to the Network Society in Europe

Erkki Liikanen

Introduction

The Lisbon strategy, launched in Portugal in 2000, recognised the importance of ICT for growth in modern economies, and opened the way to the launch of the first eEurope action plan in Feira in June 2000. Since that time parts of the ICT sector have faced a slowdown, but the information society has continued to expand. The creation of a favourable environment for the spread of ICT remains an important responsibility for policy makers.

As information and communication technologies become more pervasive, the future is very much based on the development of new services that run on high-speed networks.

These are the areas where public policy can make a difference, stimulating improvements in productivity growth and in social cohesion.

Broadband is a key enabling technology for the delivery of those services that will help increase the performance of companies and public administrations. In Europe we need competitive companies and better administrations to realise our strategy for economic, social and environmental renewal.

I will focus on three themes:

- First, why it is important to increase productivity and innovation in Europe across all industry and service sectors;

- Second, what is the key role ICTs play in improving Europe's economy and how we in the European Union stimulate this through the eEurope 2005 Action Plan;

- Third, the political approach to sustain the development of the broadband market.

Productivity and innovation

Economic theory shows that welfare, competitiveness and employment can only be sustained in the long run if they are based on productivity growth and innovation.

Over the years, we have favoured in Europe a combination of economic and social progress, with built-in safeguards for equity on the basis of solidarity.

However, economists have recently been warning that Europe's model can only be sustained if we significantly increase productivity and innovation.

GDP can grow by increasing employment or by growing productivity. Productivity growth comes about by investing more in capital or in labour, that is, increasing skills.

The third contribution to productivity growth is called total factor productivity or TFP. This measures growth through better combination of labour and capital, for example through better organisation of business processes enabled by ICT. One might say, TFP is about better recipes for using labour and capital.

Recent studies (such as Van Ark and O'Mahony 2003 and Conference Board 2004) show that the gap in labour productivity growth between the EU and the US has become particularly evident since the mid-nineties. Differences in productivity growth between the two economies are more and more believed to be linked to the production and diffusion of ICTs.

Investment in ICT is clearly a critical enabler of productivity growth, and, for that matter, also of innovation. However, the key question these days is not so much one of technology, but how technology is used and the way it is affecting GDP growth through improved productivity. We should not focus on technology just for the sake of technology.

Investing in computers is not enough. If we want to reap the productivity benefits of ICT, we need to invest, in parallel, in the reorganization of companies and administrations and in skills. This is how ICT will make total factor productivity grow.

European countries embraced ICT later than the US. The diffusion of new technologies is often slow.

Firms can take a long time to adopt them, changing organisational arrangements, implementing effective business processes. Relative to the US, productivity gains in Europe are therefore expected with a lag.

Industry Analysis

The industry-level analysis shows the superior performance of the US in ICT-producing manufacturing (in particular, ICT equipment) and ICT-intensive using industries (in particular, financial services and distributive trades).

Europe in turn has achieved very high productivity growth, outpacing the US, in communication services, and, in particular, in the mobile sector.

This is due to the fact that liberalisation of the telecommunications sector in Europe has taken place within the right legal environment. We could add to this the important role of the single mobile standard, GSM.

These data underline the importance of the growth of the sector of electronic communications for the economy. After the burst of the Internet bubble, telecom operators reduced investments radically as part of their consolidation plans. A return to renewed growth for the whole sector requires a revival in capital spending. Further growth can only be driven by the provision of new services over high-speed fixed and wireless networks such as broadband and 3G. And then the news from 3GSM Cannes event tells that 3G is now becoming a reality. It has taken longer that many expected five years ago.

Policy makers bear the responsibility of setting the right conditions for investment to occur. The implementation of the new EU regulatory framework will provide greater legal certainty for investment. The implementation of national broadband strategies creates additional demand.

Promoting ICT in Europe

The importance of ICT for economic and societal progress is well-recognised in European policies. The European approach is built on 3 pillars:

- First, the *new EU regulatory framework* enhances competition and provides a predictable legal environment.

- Second, *research and development.* More than 4 billion between 2002 and 2006 will be used for ICT related research.

- Third, we are taking action *to promote the use of new services and technology* in areas such as eGovernment, eLearning and eHealth.

The eEurope 2005 Action Plan was based on an interplay between promoting a secure broadband infrastructure and promoting more attractive content, services and applications in eGovernment, eHealth, eLearning as well as eBusiness. This can lead to a virtuous cycle and overcome the chicken-and-egg dilemma, that is, the situation where better content is waiting for faster Internet and vice-versa.

Broadband is one of the most important parts of eEurope. Beyond its impact on the growth of the sector, it ensures the appropriate infrastructure for the delivery of those interactive services necessary for the re-organisation of working and production processes.

The rapid growth of broadband connections over the last two years is encouraging, and ADSL is the fastest growing way of accessing broadband. There are clearly over 30 million connections in the European Union and the growth continues.

Several European countries are now ahead of the US, although well behind Asian tigers such as Korea. To sustain growth, Member States have been putting national broadband strategies in place. These strategies consider action on both sides of the market.

On the *supply side*, two main issues stand out.

- First, competition in the broadband market is still weak. The EU's new regulatory framework is the tool to address this issue.The challenge is to deliver a predictable legal environment that addresses only market imperfections. Those who have succeeded have created certainty to investors, and generated greater competition. Competition is key to stimulate innovation while yielding lower prices and greater choice for consumers. When markets that have been regulated become competitive, regulation will be lifted.

- Second, the limited coverage of remote and rural areas. The rapid growth of broadband is mainly taking place in urban areas. Without public intervention, the digital divide may aggravate. By its own nature, broadband offers opportunities that would otherwise be unattainable in scarcely populated areas. This is a challenge that should be addressed through the national strategies and with the support of the EU's structural funds. On the demand side, investment in e-health, e-government and e-learning applications can play an important role in driving consumers demand for broadband.

But, of course, the main objective is to increase the productivity in the public sector. It means we need more value for money, more quality and quantity for the money spent. This is necessary for many reasons. We are in front of major demographic challenges in Europe. This will increase public expenditure and reduce the share of active population. Higher productivity in the public sector is necessary.

Good governance is vital for boosting economic growth. eGovernment creates here major opportunities by enabling broader transparency and by cutting red-tape. ICT enables also a well-functioning internal market.

But contrary to the private sector, the government needs to push for equity and efficiency at the same time. This makes the work more challenging. But opportunities are also great. Development of e-government services can transform the way the public administration works. eGovernment services enhance the participation of citizens in public life, change the nature of the services offered, and can provide major efficiencies to the public administration. Policies should also encourage *government usage* of broadband applications. *Telemedicine and distance learning* are good examples. Promotion of broadband-enhanced applications has therefore a twofold implication: it encourages the efficient delivery of government services, and it provides incentives for procurement of broadband access, which will help to stimulate supply.

Operators looking for revenues through the provision of new inter-active services will have to find partnerships from outside the telecom-munications sector to create and deliver these innovations. But many challenges need to be overcome. Here I mention just two; security and spam.

Always-on connections make us more vulnerable to cyber-attacks. A new European Network and Information Security Agency, ENISA, is been set up in Greece. And the European Union is seriously addressing the fight against spam. Legislation is in place. It gives legal certainty which is the necessary precondition to combat spam. But legislation alone is not enough. The competent authorities in the EU member states need the necessary resources to effectively trace spam-mers and prosecute them. Industry needs to change marketing prac-tices and continue implementing technical solutions such as filtering and secure servers.

i2010

My successor, Viviane Reding, is about to launch a new initiative i2010. The aim is to make sure that Europe gets the full benefits in terms of prosperity, jobs and growth. This will be done by:

- Promoting a borderless European information space with the aim of establishing an internal market for electronic commu-nications and digital services

- Stimulating innovation through investment in research, the development and deployment in ICT and by encouraging the industrial application of ICT

- Making the European Information Society as inclusive and accessible as possible.

I am very happy to note that the Information Society remains highly on the agenda and that the new Commission is committed. Ms. Reding recently explained the main priorities.

The first 'i' is for information space

The aim is the creation of open and stable markets for electronic communications services and the emerging digital services economy. The next five years will see continuing rollout of broadband. And convergence between the currently separate domains of internet, telephone and television will come to market-place. Broadband coverage in the EU15 is already at 80% of population. But so far we have 8 subscriptions per 100 citizens. It means that perhaps every fourth household is connected.

The recent Commission report shows clearly that those countries in Europe that have the most competition are also the areas that lead in broadband take-up. There are new opportunities from the rollout of third generation mobile phones, which is now finally taking off, other wireless technologies such as RLAN (radio-based local area networks) and satellite.

The use of the Internet to provide voice telephony (VOIP) and television will revolutionise the way in which we communicate, do business and are entertained and there is much to be gained from accelerating this transition.

The Commissioner also has as a target to create an internal market in information goods and services, such as content, games, interactive software and value added services. It is essential to create the conditions to facilitate the production and distribution of online European content, preserving and sharing Europe's different cultural identities, strengthening the single market and the economic strength of this important sector.

The second 'i' is for innovation and investment in ICT

Digital convergence will transform the electronics industry, e-communications and digital content and services over the coming years. The Commissioner has emphasized here three issues: First, the need of private-public partnerships to keep Europe in the vanguard of developments. The aim is to create more certain investment environments and a faster, more efficient rollout of world-leading services for citizens. Second, there is the need to strengthen the position of Europe in research. Europe has *research leadership* in some areas, but it is vulnerable to increased international competition. To take advantage of the next technological wave, Europe has to invest much more than it does today. Of course, more research alone is not enough. Its efficiency and effectiveness must be improved. Third, there is the need to promote *effective adoption* of ICT in firms of all sizes. To achieve the critical mass requires that the Commission works intensively with industrial stakeholders.

The third 'i' is for inclusion and a better quality of life

Commissioner Reding has said that her vision of a European Information Society in 2010 consists of an open, transparent and accessible knowledge society. The information society should be accessible everywhere and to everyone in Europe. I could not agree more.

Europe needs growth to maintain and improve the European social model in the face of demographic ageing and increased international competition. Information Society policies contribute on both sides of this equation. The use of ICT to deliver better and more efficient public services will reduce the costs of delivery and thus make our social systems more sustainable.

To conclude: in the long term, productivity is almost everything, said Paul Krugman, Only through productivity growth can we improve the standard of living. And today we know that here the adoption of ICT, the reorganisation of enterprises and administrations and investment in skills are key factors behind the productivity growth.

Chapter 17

ICT as a Part of the Chilean Strategy for Development: Present and Challenges

Carlos Alvarez

ICT Revolution and its Global Effects

During the second half of the last decade the world witnessed the emergence of a new reality—the Internet—and the great expectations on the effects that this new technology would bring about in many sectors of society. Each month, new publications appeared forecasting the changes that were underway. According to them countless traditional corporations would close down under the attack of new virtual competitors; the processes of vertical and horizontal integration would be reversed and a new batch of entrepreneurs would emerge, generating almost immediate wealth. In the educational field, the availability of computers and Internet in schools would drastically improve student performance while e-learning would quickly spread, guaranteeing education for life. New technologies in democratic processes would permit instant voting on a variety of subjects, ensuring truly popular representation. Governments would benefit from new technologies not only by streamlining their services but also by directing their actions more precisely and by obtaining quick feedback from citizens.

The escalation of expectations, with its correlative financial speculation, came to an end when the bubble burst at the end of 2000. We then entered a phase—in which we are now—where, at the time of being aware of the potential of change that lies within technology we realize that those foreseen changes would come about only as a result of significant efforts in the medium to long term.

The frenzy that took place at the end of the last decade left us with a promising scenario for the future ICT applications. Indeed, important investments in international broadband and wireless telephony infrastructure—whose implementation eventually caused substantial investment losses—provided a solid material base from which to develop multiple applications. Moreover, the maturation of new financial mechanisms such as venture capital completed the scenario to make innovations possible. Markets are now starting to distinguish which business models are generating revenue, providing a key learning experience for entrepreneurs, governments and investors. There are successful businesses—Amazon, e-Bay or Google to mention a few—currently in the consolidation phase, but on a parallel and probably less publicized front, a number of e-government services have emerged around the world, bringing benefits to citizens: transaction times reductions, consolidation of transactions and transparency enhancement in the relationship of government to citizens.

The innovation potential has also expanded. The growing capabilities for information processing, the surge of Internet-based global collaboration networks, plus the development of electronic and biologic sciences have resulted in a wealth of high potential innovations that are starting to bear fruit (interactive television, wireless broadband connectivity and genomics are good examples).

We therefore seem to be facing an auspicious scenario. However, recent examples and the analysis of previous technological revolutions, show that expectations are not always realized. Innovations encounter pre existing cultures, practices and power structures (in business, political and bureaucratic spheres) which sometimes become threatened by the introduction of new technological paradigms. This resistance phenomenon could help explaining high failure rates in the deployment of new administrative information systems in organizations, even when they are expected to increase productivity. Resistance is also evident in the protectionist threats against off-shoring practices, a debated issue in the recent presidential elections in the USA. A similar phenomenon could explain why ICT is still not making a strong difference in students' learning even in places where the incorporation of technology to the classroom has been extensive.

However, there are also cases where results of the incorporation of technologies exceed expectations. This happens when technological revolutions trigger an accumulation of innovations, which attracts talent which in turn produces more innovations through a virtuous circle.

On these grounds, it is key to ask ourselves which are the challenges that governments are currently facing. In the first place, governments should contribute to eliminate, or at least diminish, the obstacles the introduction of the ICT paradigm is facing. However, governments can do more than that to help the change. Governments can become 'early adopters' of technology, showing their commitment to the introduction of technology and innovation. This is specially beneficial to encourage private investment. Government may also act as a facilitator helping to solve conflicts, or compensating those sectors that could be negatively affected by the changes.

In parallel, government has a big role of creating conditions to allow change to happen. Raising awareness and providing education for people are necessary conditions. It is also useful that entrepreneurs are encouraged to grasp new technologies to be able to modify them and produce new ones. Government also has to help creating the necessary flexibility in the public sector to allow change and innovation. An especially critical aspect in the regulation agenda is the telecommunications market.

From a government perspective, the coming years should be faced in a mood of serene optimism. A combination of alertness to be able to generate quick responses to opportunities together with a hard work disposition to be able to take the necessary actions to fully realize projects while overcoming the many obstacles that may appear.

ICT Revolution and its Impact on Chile's Strategic Agenda

Strategic Objectives: Growth, Equality and Democratization

In 1990, Chile recovered its democracy after 17 years of General Pinochet's dictatorship. A new center-left government called *Concertación de Partidos por la Democracia* came into office with a program having economic growth, social equality and the strengthening of democracy, as main priorities.

After three successive democratic governments, there is hardly any doubt regarding the success obtained for the goals set out. The Chilean economy has sustained a 5.5% average growth between 1990 and 2004, more than duplicating its per capita income. The percentage of population living below the poverty line dropped from 40% to 17% during the same period, without observing, however, substantial changes in income distribution (before transference). In the area of democratic consolidation, three presidential and four parliamentary elections have taken place since 1989 under completely normal conditions; several laws have corrected the authoritarian bias in the Constitution and the different powers of state operate without any major obstacles.

Current Situation

After the success of this period, the original strategic goals continue to dominate government's agenda. Nevertheless, and precisely as a result of the achievements and the changing world scenario, these challenges must be approached in a different way.

In the area of economic growth, if Chile wants to increase its current per capita income of close to US$10,000 (in PPP terms), to the levels of south European countries, it should sustain the 7% annual average growth rate witnessed during the 1990's (which decreased to a yearly average of 3,8% in the 2000-2004 period). Although Chile enjoys a high growth potential as reflected by the WEF Report on Global Competitiveness, which positions Chile in 22nd place among 102 countries, there is a growing national consensus that it is imperative to step up efforts in two deficit areas: education and technological innovation.

ICTs and their Impact on the Strategic Agenda

The inception of the Internet and the constellation of innovations that accompanies it have been perceived by the Chilean government as a great opportunity to advance in its strategic agenda. The potential of ICT to contribute to future tasks in Chile is very high. This does not mean that ICTs are granted an almost magical capability to produce development, but rather to be able to both allow technology to find its way in different sectors of society as well as to contribute to public policies that deal with the strategic agenda of the country.

Unlike those voices that emerge from both the ICT industry and non-governmental organizations that tend to either overestimate the technological potential or underestimate the obstacles to transform the benefits of ICT in reality for citizens, the Government of Chile has sought to effectively integrate the contribution of ICT into the different public initiatives of its agenda. Hence we are skeptical of approaches where for example, the development of community info-centers in low income areas is viewed as the way to deal with poverty, or about those that argue that the sole availability of computers in classrooms will produce a leap in education quality. If the argument that explains the persistence of important areas of poverty emphasizes the need to overcome the disconnection of the poor from the economic circuits and public assistance networks, and accordingly a program of individual attention to those families is proposed to reestablish the link,[1] then ICTs are viewed as an element of co-assistance for that effort, in the shape of info-literacy programs or counting as information tools to support professionals working directly with such families. By the same token, it is perceived that the problems of quality of the Chilean education are explained by a combination of aspects, such as lack of infrastructure, curricular inadequacies, and deficiencies in teacher training. In this case Internet would have to be used to improve teacher training and lesson preparation,[2] and also included as part of the training program for students.

The future challenge, then, consists of determining how ICTs introduce threats, but especially how they open up opportunities, to create more growth, greater equality and growing democratization; in other words, how ICTs contribute to carrying out the strategic focal points of the agenda:

- An efficient State oriented to address citizens' needs

At this point, there is no doubt that the services sector is the one that has benefited the most from the advent of the Internet. And the main supplier of services in a country is Government. This has been thoroughly understood by the Chilean government, which has introduced Internet-based applications, especially those that strengthen the link with citizens, in an ample effort to modernize the public sector.

This has come to fruition. Recently, a United Nations report placed Chile as number 22 among 191 countries in the quality of its e-govern-

---

[1] Chilesolidario Program

[2] See educational website www.educarchile.cl

ment, surpassing many countries with a higher per capita income. This is the result of high-impact initiatives, such as on-line tax payments (today, more than 80% of tax returns are done through the Internet), issuance of Civil Registry certificates, and the launching of an online public procurement system called ChileCompra, among others.

Results obtained to date show high economic returns on these initiatives, a substantial improvement of relations between government agencies and the public and important stimulus to the extensive use of the Internet, especially among small and mid-size entrepreneurs. All of this leads to the conclusion that the agenda needs to be reinforced by updating those segments that have fallen behind—such as the health sector—advancing in the integration of front-office systems to back-office, and towards the inter-operability of systems among services.

- An economy integrated into the world

Chile opted, more than 25 years ago, to open up to world trade as a key element of its economic strategy. As a small country, its growth is crucially dependant on maintaining a high exporting dynamic. Although it is true there are no indications of exhausting export potential of the main sectors—mining, forestry, fresh fruit, salmon and wine—there is an emerging perception of more complex scenarios, stemming in part from the increasing international competition in these areas or from the emergence of innovations that reduce the relevance of the country's competitive advantages. From this perspective, it is essential to increase the national effort on Research and Development particularly with regards to the use of ICTs to boost competitiveness of the main national export sectors. ICTs can contribute to optimize the exports logistic chain, promote the integration between export companies and their suppliers, establishing efficient tracking systems and consolidating the prestige of the food exported by Chile in the phyto-sanitary area.

Simultaneously, it is necessary to persevere in the incorporation of Internet in small and mid-size companies, since the country's competitiveness not only depends on the efficiency of direct exports, but also on the whole production systems. Efforts to improve public services to companies (Customs, Internal Revenue Service, etc.) are also going in this same direction.

Finally, the fostering of new undertakings with perspectives of global escalation must not be overlooked. On this level, a potential opportunity lies on using the know-how developed by the export sectors.

- A highly dynamic service sector

It is worth mentioning the development of the export services sector, taking into account the huge transformation being experienced by this sector worldwide. Indeed, if estimations can be trusted regarding the fact that in the off-shoring field, no more than 5% of jobs that are potentially feasible, have been outsourced, the next few years will witness a massive demand for international services, which will overwhelm the capacity offered today by countries such as Ireland, India and the Philippines. In this scenario, Chile constitutes an interesting alternative for companies that are seeking to outsource services, owing to a combination of economic stability, a fluid and transparent business environment, a strong ICT infrastructure and access to qualified human resources. Based on this, several studies have positioned Chile in first place as an attractive country for off-shoring among Spanish-speaking countries. This opens up strong opportunities for the country and requires a precise strategy to focus efforts in terms of assuring substantial and sustainable benefits over time.

- An equitable nation

It is common knowledge that ICTs have brought a promise of prosperity to the world, but it also threatens to deepen inequalities, what some have dubbed as the "digital divide." A country such as Chile, which has quite a regressive income distribution—where 20% of higher incomes have access to 52% of the National Income[3]—is particularly exposed to this risk. Hence, all measures designed to confront the digital divide are essential. Fortunately, this was understood from very early on by the democratic governments after 1990 in their design of educational policies, when the Enlaces Program was incorporated as an essential part of the Improvement of Education Quality Program (MECE) destined to foster the formation of ICTs for all students attending public and subsidized schools in the country.

---

[3] Income distribution measured on Total Incomes, which includes social services and Government transfers.

But the digital divide has not yet been completely closed. It is necessary to continue with the efforts at school level and to extend them to other sectors of the population, an essential task for the upcoming years.

- A nation prepared for the future

Perhaps one of the most distinguishing elements of technological revolutions is the unpredictability of its course once it is triggered. Today, we can hardly predict all the innovations that will take place in the next 20 years in the ICTs field, and much less their social and economic applications and impacts. Facing this scenario, the country must be prepared, generating the conditions to allow to quickly adapt to new conditions. This implies, in a first place, the strengthening of technical competencies—not only in the engineering fields—required to comprehend the phenomena that will come and transform them into answers pertinent to national needs. In second place, it will be necessary to generate a capacity to adapt to the existing legal framework that makes viable the array of new technologies. Finally, it is essential that the government is capable of keeping abreast of new phenomena in addition to fostering regulatory frameworks that promote and not inhibit the innovative responses that the period requires.

The Digital Agenda

This section will outline the steps taken by the Chilean government to establish an agenda that gathered the various agencies involved in different aspects of consolidating an ICT strategy for government.

Pioneering Initiatives

There are three pioneering initiatives that constitute the decisive steps towards the introduction of ICTs in Chile and are milestones on which part of the Digital Agenda was based. These are: the regulation of the telecommunications sector; the ENLACES project in education and the introduction of the REUNA Network access to the Internet. A brief description of each one follows.

Deregulation of Telecommunications

At the end of the 1970's the telecommunications sector in Chile was formed by two state-owned companies: a fixed telephony provider on the national market (CTC) and one international long distance telephone operator (Entel), with both sharing the national long distance market. The State was the owner of two other regional fixed telephony companies (CNT and Telcoy) as well as the Post and Telegraph Company. The deregulation process started at the beginning of the 1980's, when fixed telephony licenses were granted to two new fixed telephony companies (CMET and Manquehue) in areas that were already serviced by the dominating operator. At the same time a mobile telephony license was granted to a company to operate in the capital city (Santiago).

During the 1980's Chile witnessed a wave of privatization of companies, including those in the telecommunications sector. The changes that occurred in this sector began with the passing of the General Law of Telecommunications in 1982. It established objective and non discriminatory technical criteria for granting licenses and assigning the number of operators in each market segment. This law defined standards of continuity and quality of service and the time periods for granting the services to the final users. Free price fixing was instated except for those public services of local and long distance fixed telephony where the antitrust agency determined conditions of insufficient competition.

Since its privatization, the telecommunication sector has experienced rapid growth; the telecommunication companies have increased their coverage of services, as well as their internal efficiency. Between 1987 and 2001, for example, the total number of fixed telephone lines in service multiplied six-fold, increasing the telephone density from 4,7 to 23,1 lines per 100 inhabitants.

Those services where regulatory changes introduced competition experienced a strong drop in their tariffs. Hence, after deregulating services in 1994, prices of long distance calls decreased close to 80%. The introduction of PCS mobile telephony in 1998, which increased the number of operators from two to four, together with the introduction of the "calling party pays" modality, reduced rates for the mobile service by approximately 50%. Fixed telephony rates—a service that faced very little competition until recently—remained relatively stable during the 1990's, except during the last price fixing when rates were lowered substantially, especially in the access charges, which fell abruptly.

Similarly, and as a result of a decree that fixed rates of the incumbent fixed telephony provider, dial up connections to the Internet grew by more than 300% during 1999, and the connection cost was reduced by close to 50%. In terms of Internet connections, as of June 2004 Chile had close to 461,000 of dial up and 424,000 broadband connections to the Internet, showing an increase of more than 50% with respect to the previous year.

Chile has upheld a telecommunication policy that stimulates foreign investment, maintaining technological neutrality and favoring an early introduction of new services that diversify access options to telecommunication services. As a result of these factors, Chile exhibits outstanding access indicators to telecommunications services within Latin America and although the numbers are distant from those in the developed world, they are high in comparison with the country's GDP per capita.

Enlaces Network of Educational Informatics

The pilot program of Educational Informatics of the Improvement of Educational Quality Program (MECE) consisted in establishing an inter-school communications network through computers among students and teachers at elementary schools as well as professionals of other institutions related to education. One university became the central node and tutor of the appropriation process of the new technology (use of hardware and software in the educational context), and of the electronic communication culture in schools (use of electronic mail and forums to develop collaborative intra and inter-school work).

The Enlaces Network started up in 1992 with the goal, considered bold at the time, to have one hundred schools connected by 1997, with computer tools that were user-friendly, easy to use, multimedially and pedagogically stimulating, based on the technological conditions of telephone communication at the time in the country. The quick success of the program and the speed of technological transformations, changed the pilot nature of the program in 1994 when the government decided to extend the equipment, based on the population attending each school and new targets of network coverage. At present, the program covers over 90% of computer laboratories and has 75% Internet access in schools.

Thanks to this project, a network of schools was created which has had vast implications on the quality and equality of education across the country. It has placed at the disposal of the schools and high schools, a network and information technologies that open a window to knowledge and information of the world, drastically redefining the limits of what is possible to do and achieve at each school and making it possible to have access to the same resources of information and cultural interchange, regardless of social or geographical location.

The later incorporation of Internet access in schools, a process which is being completed today with broadband and connectivity for rural schools, has meant giving the educational institutions a central role in improving the digital literacy of the population through the current National Digital Literacy Campaign.

National University Network

In 1986, the national meeting of Academic Computer Centers of Chile, was discussing the architecture to be employed in the implementation of an academic network of electronic mail. This interest was echoed by a donation by IBM that allowed the installation of a transmission network of information that became Chile's first electronic mail network in 1987. This network connected five cities from north to south across the country. As time passed, demand grew for this service, which encouraged the installation of additional national and international connections that extended the scope and robustness of the network.

REUNA, the Spanish acronym for National University Network, was created as a consortium of 19 public and semi-public universities together with the National Science and Technological Council (CONICYT) with the purpose of operating this university network, which for some time was the only IP network with public access with national coverage and connected to Internet.

The increasing traffic needs and the limited access to a budget from the government to finance this growing initiative, quickly encouraged

REUNA to become a commercial operator offering Internet and other services. In retrospect, it can be said that the importance of this project was to be a solution that escalated over time and contributed to creating a demand for a new service such as Internet which today is considered a necessity.

Institutional development: from the Presidential Commission on ICT to the Committee of ICT Ministers

At the end of the 1990's, various actors of the Chilean society decided to tackle the challenges our country faced to make our entrance into the society of information. With this aim, by mid-1998, a commission representing all the relevant sectors of the country: government, parliament, civilians, the academic world and the Armed Forces, was formed to advise the President of the Republic. This commission convoked more than 100 experts to debate for more than seven months after which it generated a report of proposals, presented to and approved by the President of the Republic, Eduardo Frei in January 1999.

Fundamentally, the report defined a general view, diagnosing the readiness of the country to face the challenges, specifying the objectives and proposing a set of relevant initiatives. These initiatives included: to strengthen the Enlaces Program, consolidate REUNA, start up infocenters (community access), legislate on the electronic signature, regulate in order to reduce access costs, start up public procurement, and strengthen the state Intranet, etc.

The year 2000 was the year the digital policy was consolidated and the institutional development began. That year, the newly sworn-in President Ricardo Lagos, gave a huge impulse to digital issues. During his Address to the Nation on May 21, 2000, the President outlined his priorities for his six-year tenure of government and one of the highlights of his program was technological reform. In his speech, the President assumed, among others, the following commitments:

i)   Start up a national network with access for the community (infocenters);

ii) Extend the Enlaces Network to 100% of schools in Chile;

iii) Promulgate a law permitting the accreditation and certification of the electronic signature and to provide a safe framework for electronic commerce to expand expeditiously;

iv) Initiate offers of public procurement on the network;

v) Place on-line most of the services and procedures the public sector provides;

vi) Generate an active risk capital industry.

Towards the end of the year, the President headed a public-private
mission to Silicon Valley where to meet important leaders of the ICT
world, and some cooperation agreements were signed.

In order to conduct the ICT issues, because it is a transversal
nature, the President ordered the creation of the Committee of
Information and Communication Technologies Ministers, which was
instated in June, 2000.

The Committee of Information and Communication Technologies
Ministers was constituted with the goal to facilitate government coordination for the elaboration and carrying out of the follow-up of ICT
policies. This Committee was entrusted with proposing policies and
stimulating initiatives for the development of information development, the stimulation of e-commerce, the promotion of the industry
of contents, the expansion of Internet access, to accelerate the social
learning process associated with the use of the networks, as well as for
the digital diffusion of culture and education. The Committee of
Ministers organized its activity in five areas: Expansion of Access;
Formation of Human Resources; E-Government; Companies; and
Legal Framework, and defined the coordinating leaders for each one
of them. The Committee set out to achieve the following proposals:
constitute the National Network of Infocenters; design and stimulate
the digital literacy campaign; complete the informational phase and
start up the transactional phase of e-government; develop a suitable
Legal Framework, especially the electronic signature law.

Digital Agenda: Objectives and Components

In order to give new stimulus to the digital issues, at the end of
March 2003 the President appointed the under-secretary of Economy
as Government Coordinator of Information and Communication

Technologies (ICTs) with the goal of designing a Digital Agenda, together with the private sector and academia, to be presented to the President for approval.

In April, the Digital Action Group (GAD), the name chosen by this private-public committee, was constituted. Its members represent the business world; foundation directors associated with the issue; members of parliament; academics and experts and public authorities from the ministries of Education, of Transport and Telecommunications, of Finance and of the General Secretary of the Presidency.

From May to June 2003, the GAD identified the areas to be contained in the digital agenda. The six areas to be worked on were defined as: Access and Quality; E-Government; Formation of Human Resources; Companies, ICT Industry; and the Legal Regulations framework.

Subsequently, between the months of July to October, the GAD focused on the elaboration of its proposals. To this end, several work teams were created, both public and private. More than 80 people participated in the private groups while the public groups mobilized more than 85 directors and professionals. At the beginning of November, the private and public groups joined their efforts to prioritize and propose a definite series of activities that constituted the Digital Agenda. This activity culminated successfully at the beginning of January 2004 with a proposal for the agenda that was approved by all the members of the Digital Action Group.

As a result a Digital Agenda was elaborated incorporating the following challenges (quoted from the original text of the Agenda):

Widely Available Access

There is no doubt that the country now faces the difficult phase of expanding connectivity. If current economic trends continue, Internet penetration will continue its expansion rate through 2006. However, considering that income distribution will not likely change in the short term, 70% of this growth will take place among the highest income quintile, and only this quintile will reach the level of developed countries. Among the five lowest income deciles, connectivity at home has not yet surpassed 10%.

Broadband growth has been significant, but without a major reduction in access costs—whose average in 2003 was US$55—the growth rate may drastically slow beginning in 2006, especially in homes and microenterprises.

Given this situation, the challenge is to maintain the rate of progress made in providing widely available and increasingly better access by designing a strategy that overcomes obstacles like unequal income distribution, restrictions facing micro and small businesses, and connectivity problems in rural areas and remote regions like Aysén and Magallanes.

The situation is favorable. Three factors will facilitate Internet expansion over the coming years. First, economic growth will be greater than during the 2000–2003 period, and this will provoke an increase in demand. Second, equipment and access costs will undergo a sustained reduction. Third, community broadband access at schools, Infocenters, and cybercafes will expand. This will be particularly important for the poorer half of Chile's population, who do not yet receive the income needed to have a computer at home, let alone an Internet connection.

But it is possible and necessary to do much more. The private sector should develop commercial packages of computers with Internet connections for lower income homes and microenterprises. The Government will mainly subsidize remote and rural areas, low-income communities, and microenterprises. Finally, the Government should expand and consolidate its broadband digital networks, giving special priority to access to public services in regions and towns, including educational and health care establishments.

Education and Training

Enlaces Program and other technical training networks should implement broadband Internet access. The challenges, however, go deeper than just connectivity. The biggest challenge is to expand and intensify full integration of digital technologies as a learning resource for the curriculum and their use in the classroom. This is where investment in digital content, advanced teacher training, and the spread of better practices all constitute fundamental focal points for development.

Even though Chile's educational system has made significant progress and has developed a reform program that the Organization for Economic Cooperation and Development (OECD) described as one of the most ambitious in Latin America, it is not yet in conditions to guarantee the development and equity that this country needs. Its potential is inhibited by the lack of schools that are effectively able to compensate for the inequalities among its students, which are based on social and family background.

There are also deficits in the quality of training systems—particularly for workers with the highest qualifications. In the area of higher learning, there are very few high-quality graduate and diploma programs

In the end, all of these factors limit the country's competitiveness both in the long term and over the next decade. In fact, 75% of the workforce in 2014 will be made up of people who are working or looking for work today. In a decade of accelerated technical change, investment in education and training of current generations of workers is an extraordinarily important imperative.

Online Government (Deficiencies)

Unequal development of electronic government. The gap between the substantial progress of some Central Government services and the delays observed in Local Government is evident. In fact, 320 municipalities out of a total of 341 are connected to Internet and, of these, only a little more than 40% have dedicated access. There have also been serious problems in implementing advances in digital technology use in the health-related public sector. Furthermore, achievements obtained by Government Administration contrast with those of the Legislative and Judicial powers.

Scant capacity and coverage of the Government digital network. Although it has been possible to develop a Government Intranet that connects a little more than 27,000 work stations in the 27 public agencies, this network unquestionably has neither the capacity nor the coverage to comprehend the growing needs of the public sector as a whole.

Insufficient development in digital technology use for an integrated back office. A good part of the government's digital technology efforts has been concentrated on front office developments to assist users and citizens. Except for some important public entities, most public services are only recently introducing back office changes, that is, in management and organization. This weak point becomes clear when it comes to inter-service coordination. Herein lies the main challenge for public administration and the intelligent application of ICT.

Digital security of the public sector. The public sector rests on a complex network of information infrastructure that, as a result of growing interconnectivity, is vulnerable to threats in growing numbers and varieties. The effective protection of this essential infrastructure in the public sector requires determining a digital infrastructure security strategy, with the purpose of lessening vulnerability, mitigating damages, speeding up recovery times in the event of glitches or malicious activities, and being able to identify the causes and/or sources of these activities for analysis and/or research.

Digital Development for Businesses

In 2003, nearly 100% of large and medium-sized firms, as well as 40% of small businesses, were connected to Internet, with the presence of broadband connectivity on the rise. Nevertheless, significant shortcomings continue with regard to more advanced ICT use. Companies use Internet to stay informed about what the public sector is doing and to check the status of their bank accounts and deposits, but they carry out few transactions aside from some basic services that are widely available on the Internet. Only 15% of businesses communicate with their suppliers and clients over the Internet, and only 25% of that number own a website. These figures are not good if we compare them with developed countries, which conduct three to four times more buying and selling transactions online.

The main hurdles perceived by entrepreneurs and managers against adopting digital technologies are unfamiliarity, unawareness of their relevance, insecurity and distrust, communications problems with the people in charge of information systems, complexity, and cost. Ultimately, many entrepreneurs still see no return on investment in advanced ICT uses. However, those who have implemented these solutions have a favorable view: 66% consider that it increased efficiency, 57% find that it increased productivity, and 49% declare to have obtained cost reductions.

The spread of information and communications technologies in businesses has thus far had two big advocates: the public sector and banking. It is likely that they will continue to be the main vectors of massive expansion in the 2004–2006 period. However, the debut of the private and public marketplace (for example, ChileCompra) should spur the growing use of e-trade in production chains. The widespread company use of electronic invoices will also contribute to this.

Take-off of the ICT Industry

In Chile, the information and communications technologies industry is in its infancy—without the exception of telecommunications—and it is mostly made up of small and medium-sized businesses that are not very consolidated. The digital content business is recently emerging; hardware is small; and software is grappling with major challenges. Furthermore, one of the key factors for the ICT industry's take-off—namely, the virtuous circuit among companies, universities, and research centers—has not been present in the Chilean case.

Equally, there are standards and quality certification for products and services worldwide, geared at guaranteeing homogeneity and satisfaction among global clients. Only a few local ITC firms, however, have incorporated these practices to date.

Legal Framework

The building of the legal-regulatory framework for the information society took its first step with the approval of the Electronic Document and Electronic Signature Law. Unlike other Latin American countries, Chile was able to develop an application with a quick and massive impact: the electronic invoice, and now electronic public purchasing. Moreover, in the 1990s, Chile approved the Computer Crimes Law and the Privacy Protection Law, which are important pieces of legal development that the country requires.

The initiatives that should be promoted in the area will be geared toward removing limitations in the legal system in order to provide the appropriate institutional framework for backing and fostering the development of electronic trade, electronic government, and the use of information and communications technologies. Furthermore, people should be given enough security so as to enhance their trust in the operation of electronic platforms.

These challenges were incorporated into an agenda of 34 initiatives shown in the following table.

Table 17.1   Digital Agenda: 34 Initiatives (2004–2006)

Access

1. Consolidation of the means that will facilitate individual and community broadband access for all Chileans.18) Widespread use of electronic invoices.

2. Promotion of the development of Infocenters as service centers.19) Consolidation and expansion of the use of ChileCompra.

3. 900,000 homes and 150,000 businesses connected to Internet by 2006.20) Simplification and online installation of business transactions.

Education and Training

4. Digital literacy for half a million Chileans.

5. Launching of the certification of ICT skills.

6. Promotion of connected and equipped schools.

7. Integration of ICT into curricula.

8. Fostering of technical/professional ICT training.

9. Promotion of world-class content.

10. Command of basic and instrumental English for all schools.

On-Line Government

11. Integrated Platform of electronic services.

12. Broadband digital network for the public sector (Route 5D).

13. Electronic platform for Chile Solidario and social policies.

14. Development of digital technologies in the health sector.

15) Digital development of regional governments and municipalities.

16. Increment in the metrics and efficiency of government information technology spending.

17. Improvement of the security of essential information structures for the public sector.

Digital Development for Businesses

18. Widespread use of electronic invoices.

19. Consolidation and expansion of the use of ChileCompra.

20. Simplification and online installation of business transaction.

21. Electronic billing for fees and online initiation of activities.

22. Development of means of payment for e-trade and consolidation of Payments Portal of the Government.

23. One Stop Shop and foreign trade marketplace.

24. Increased adaptation of Development Instruments.

Take-Off of the ICT Industry

25. Identification of opportunities and focusing of efforts for the development of the ICT industry.

26. Quality assurance through company certification.

27. Intensification of the High-Tech Foreign Investment Attraction program.

28. Heightened promotion of ICT research and development (R&D).

29. Expediting of the ICT industry export process.

30. Financing for creation and start-up.

Legal Framework

31. Elimination of obstacles and promotion of electronic document and electronic signature use.

32. Right of execution of electronic invoicing.

33. E-trade consumer rights.

34. Updating of legislation for protecting intellectual property.

The Agenda was publicly launched by the President in March 2004. The Digital Action Group was mandated to oversee the development and completion of each initiative.

Current Situation: Main Achievements

By the end of 2004, the balance of the digital policy is relatively positive, as is shown by the following aspects:

- There is a Digital Agenda agreed upon between the private and public sector, which is fostered and monitored by the Digital Action Group. This group includes sectors, both public and private, that are coordinated at the operative level. All of this allows institutional recognition and validation to foster and monitor the Digital Agenda.

- There is an Action Plan 2004-2006 with 34 initiatives and 67 activities, the majority of them funded and having defined leadership. This constitutes a guideline for action, an instrument that gives direction, setting goals and establishing evaluation criteria.

- Main results are the following:

a) **Access.** There is National Network of infocenters in place with more than 800 access points across the country which are being transformed from purely access points into service centers, where people can do useful things that simplify their life, such as transactions with government.

b) **E-Government.** An informational phase of E-Government is nearly finished (300 web sites) and a second, more transactional phase has been initiated. Currently, there are more than 200 transactions on-line, many of them having on-line payment. This year, on-line transactions at the municipal level will be initiated.

c) **Human Resources formation.** Government has focused on a digital literacy campaign to comply with a target of certifying 500,000 adults by end of 2005. To date, over 400,000 have received formation in 18-hour courses.

d) **Companies.** A great effort has been made to simplify over 50 out of 80 transactions, identified by businesspeople, and to move them on-line to facilitate their relation with government. With regard to ICT companies, a certification program has been started, whose first results will be observed during 2005.

e) **Legal and Regulatory Framework.** A law and regulation for electronic signature have been passed, three certification companies have been accredited. Moreover, rules and standards on electronic document and interoperability have been published.

Summary and Future Challenges

Major challenges will be involved in the fulfillment of Chile's Digital Agenda in future years. At present there are a number of public and private organizations contributing their effort and enthusiasm to complete the 34 initiatives contained in that Agenda, a task that of course demands important public funds in a country characterized by its fiscal austerity.

However, as this undertaking unfolds, new challenges arise, derived from the innovative dynamics of the ICT sector as such, but also from the clash between innovation opportunities and the "traditional ways of doing things."

Despite important advances, the most important challenge probably still lies in the Human Capital field. Although Chile has made an important effort to provide Internet access to schools, future tasks should also concentrate on improving education quality, in order for it to really make a difference in students' learning. The global nature of this challenge should be also recognized, at a time when not many substantial international collaboration efforts can be encountered. These are needed for best practice transference but also to increase the availability of research resources. In this same direction, the current production of educational content to be put in the Web is not sufficient, especially in Spanish language. As a contribution in this field, efforts associated to the expansion of the EducarChile network to other Latin American countries could be made.

The internationalization of services, unleashed by the arrival of the Internet, calls for a major change in the training of professionals and technicians, as their job opportunities increasingly involve serving geographically distant customers. Substantive curriculum adaptations are needed for careers typically conceived to deal mainly with local markets. Efforts aimed at increasing the flexibility of education modalities and the dynamism of educational institutions themselves are also needed. So far, traditional educational institutions have been rather slow in embracing these trends.

Enterprises in the field of services in general and ICT companies in particular are also being challenged by internationalization. Although Chile embraced open international trade very early on, enterprises in the field of services were initially not greatly affected by it, since they could still rely on some proximity advantages. At present however, they are feeling the first signs of that economic openness, which will compel them to adopt drastic modifications in their competition strategies. Quality assurance, compliance with widely adopted certification standards and international partnership building, among others, will become key factors for that new survival strategy. On the public side, policies should take bold steps to accompany and strengthen this competition process.

There is still a huge potential for public value generation associated to e-Government in Chile. To date, efforts have concentrated on the front-office field, which has produced important improvements in the relationship of citizens and government. However, there is still a long way to walk in the application of ICT to back-office processes, which despite meaning potentially high productivity gains, face major implementation obstacles. In part, these obstacles arise from the complexity of process re-engineering that is required, but they also stem from rigidities in labor regulations associated to the public sector. Measures also have to be taken so that public organizations can benefit from the opportunities that lie in the use of outsourcing mechanisms.

Another emergent challenge has to do with the governance of the e-Government Agenda. This entails finding an adequate equilibrium among stimulating innovation on public executives that are concerned with maximizing public value for their agencies, together with the search of economies based on demand consolidation, systems integration and standardization. Present practice has favored stimulating innovation at the agency level, a factor that has been key to various success stories within government. However, some important opportunities for consolidation and standardization are still waiting to be exploited. The establishment of the Digital Agenda, the assignment of a Governmental Coordinator for ICT and the constitution of a coordinating instance for e-Government initiatives are measures aimed at a better articulation of public efforts. However, this organization still bears a temporary character that should be consolidated into a more permanent form.

From this discussion it is very clear that the challenges ahead are not of a minor nature. In parallel, it is hoped that the technological revolution maintains its pace, producing more opportunities for citizens' benefit, which in turn faces us with the need of structuring a balanced set of initiatives, under constant revision, that at the same time rates the contribution of ICT in a fair measure. To make this happen, it is essential to bear in mind that ICT is a set of instruments to materialize a national strategy, which for Chile means: growth, equality and the deepening of democracy.

Chapter 18

The European Way To A Knowledge-Intensive Economy— The Lisbon Strategy

Maria João Rodrigues

Europe for what? The traditional discourses focusing on the need to ensure peace within borders are no longer working, namely for the younger generations who take this for granted. We need a more forward-looking approach to European citizens' aspirations by focusing on:

- sustaining their living conditions in a global economy;

- making Europe a stronger player in improving global governance;

- creating a more democratic and effective political system.

If these are the priorities, then we need to combine:

- an agenda of structural reforms with the coordination of the macroeconomic policies in the Euro-zone;

- trade policy with innovation policy and with employment policies to redeploy to new areas of growth and jobs creation;

- focused international initiatives with clear and strong views about multilateralism;

- sound enlargement with sound democratic deepening.

Overview of the Lisbon strategy after its mid-term review

The Lisbon strategy launched by the European Council of March 2000 was precisely the elaboration of a European comprehensive strategy for the economic and social development in face of the new challenges: globalisation, aging, faster technological change. Its central idea is to recognize that, in order to sustain the European social model, we need to renew it as well as to renew its economic basis by focusing on knowledge and innovation. This should be the main purpose of an agenda for structural reforms (Rodrigues, 2002).

Over the last five years, this strategy was translated into an agenda of common objectives and concrete measures, using not only the traditional instruments, such as directives and the community programmes but also a new open of coordination, which had already been tested in the employment policy and which then extended to many other ones: the policies for the information society, research, enterprise, innovation, education, social protection and social inclusion (Rodrigues, 2003).

The general outcome in 2004 was clearly very unequal across policy areas and countries. Progress seems quite evident in the connections to Internet, the networks for excellence in research, the one-stop shops for small business, the integration of financial markets, the modernisation of the employment services or in some social inclusion plans. But some important bottlenecks are evident in fostering innovation, adopting a Community patent, opening the services market, developing lifelong learning or reforming social protection. Besides that, some northern countries display better performances then some southern ones, whereas some smaller countries seem to perform better then most of the big ones. This is, of course, a very rough assessment.

In the meantime, the implementation gap was worsened by a communication gap, due to the absence of a communication policy able to connect some existent progress on the ground with this European agenda. In face of these shortcomings, the mid-term review in 2004-05, under the Luxembourg Presidency, came up with some answers to the main problems which had been identified (Kok, 2004, Sapir 2004):

- blurred strategic objectives;

- inflation of priorities and measures;

- lack of implementation, coordination and participation mechanisms;

- lack of financial incentives.

Clarifying the strategic objectives

The first problem to address was about the very relevance of the strategy. Taking into account the new challenges, is the Lisbon strategy still relevant?

The world landscape is changing. The emergence of new competitive players coupled with more evident ageing trends should fully be taken into account by the Lisbon strategy, but its approach remains valid and becomes even more urgent—this was the position adopted by the Spring European Council under the Luxembourg Presidency. "Europe must renew the basis of its competitiveness, increase its growth potential and its productivity and strengthen social cohesion, placing the main emphasis on knowledge, innovation and the optimisation of the human capital" (Council 7619/05, § 5). Stepping up the transition to a knowledge-intensive society remains the central direction. The need to improve the synergies between the three dimensions of the strategy—economic, social an environmental—is also underlined in the more general context of the sustainable development principles (Council 7619/05).

Still, it was considered that the strategy should be re-focused on growth and employment, with some implications for the definition of the political priorities, as we will see below.

Defining the political priorities

The major political priorities of the Lisbon strategy for growth and jobs, after the mid-term review concluded in July are three:

- Knowledge and innovation—engines of sustainable growth;

- Making Europe a more attractive place to invest and to work;

- More and better jobs.

These three political priorities were specified into a short list of 24 guidelines using the Treaty-based instruments called "broad economic policy guidelines" and the "employment guidelines." Moreover, an additional strand was included dealing with the macro-economic policies, under the label "Macroeconomic policies for growth and jobs" (see next Table and Council 10667/05 and 10205/05).

Table 18.1   Lisbon Strategy

Lisbon Strategy
The Integrated Guidelines for Growth and Jobs

Macroeconomic policies for growth and jobs
1. To secure economic stability for sustainable growth;
2. To safeguard economic and fiscal sustainability as a basis for increased employment;
3. To promote a growth-and employment-orientated and efficient allocation of resources;
4. To ensure that wage developments contribute to macroeconomic stability and growth;
5. To promote greater coherence between macroeconomic, structural and employment policies;
6. To contribute to a dynamic and well-functioning EMU.

Knowledge and innovation—engines of sustainable growth
7. To increase and improve investment in R&D, in particular by private business;
8. To facilitate all forms of innovation;
9. To facilitate the spread and effective use of ICT and build a fully inclusive information society;
10. To strengthen the competitive advantages of its industrial base;
11. To encourage the sustainable use of resources and strengthen the synergies between environmental protection and growth.

Making Europe a more attractive place to invest and work
12. To extend and deepen the Internal Market;
13. To ensure open and competitive markets inside and outside Europe and to reap the benefits of globalisation;
14. To create a more competitive business environment and encourage private initiative through better regulation;
15. To promote a more entrepreneurial culture and create a supportive environment for SMEs;
16. To expand and improve European infrastructure and complete priority cross-border projects;

More and better jobs
17. To implement employment policies aimed at achieving full employment, improving quality and productivity at work, and strengthening social and territorial cohesion;
18. To promote a lifecycle approach to work;
19. To ensure inclusive labour markets, enhance work attractiveness and make work pay for job-seekers, including disadvantaged people, and the inactive;
20. To improve matching of labour market needs;
21. To promote flexibility combined with employment security and reduce labour market segmentation, having due regard to the role of the social partners;
22. To ensure employment-friendly labour cost developments and wage-setting mechanisms
23. To expand and improve investment in human capital;
24. To adapt education and training systems in response to new competence requirements.

Source: Council of the European Union, 10667/05 and 10205/05

Hence, for the first time, the EU is equipped with an integrated package of guidelines for its economic and social policies, using Treaty-based instruments. Behind this major political development a quite long maturing process had taken place and the need to enhance implementation was the final argument to be used.

Fostering the implementation

The aim of defining coordinated guidelines for economic and social policies in the EU comes from the nineties, with the preparation of the Economic and Monetary Union. During the Lisbon European Council in 2000, the political conditions were still not ripe to achieve the adoption of an economic and social strategy using more compulsory instruments such as Treaty-based guidelines. Hence, a new method was defined, called "open method of coordination," based on (Council SN 100/00 and Presidency 9088/00):

- identifying common objectives or guidelines;

- translating them into the national policies, adapting to national specificities;

- organising a monitoring process based on common indicators, identifying best practices and peer review.

The development of this method in eleven policy fields since 2000, in spite of some shortcomings (such as bureaucratisation, simplistic benchmarking, etc.), had been quite instrumental in building the necessary consensus about the strategic challenges and the key reforms to be implemented. In 2005, the arguments regarding the implementation and the coordination gap were already enough to ensure a transformation of some of the most important of these "soft" guidelines into "harder" ones, by building on them in order to formulate Treaty-based guidelines (Council, 10667/05 and 10205/05).

Hence, the open method of coordination did play a role in building a European dimension, organising a learning process and promoting some convergence with respect by the national differences. Does this mean that this method is now over? This is not at all the case (see Council 7619/05 § 39 d/ and Commission, SEC 28.04.2005). It can pursue its role, when this is needed which means that the policy making process can work at two levels, one more formal and precise then the other, ensuring the necessary political re-focusing in the implementation.

A second important development regarding the instruments for implementation concerns the national reform programmes for the next three years, to be prepared by all the Member States in the autumn 2005 (Commission, SEC 28.04.2005). These programmes should be forward-looking political documents setting out a comprehensive strategy to implement the integrated guidelines and adapting them to the national situation. Besides presenting the political priorities and measures, these programmes are also expected to point out the roles of the different stakeholders as well as the budgetary resources to be mobilized, including the structural funds with a link to the stability and convergence programmes. The preparation, implementation and monitoring of the national programmes should involve the main political institutions as well as the civil society and, when appropriate, a national coordinator should be appointed. An annual follow-up report is also supposed to be provided by all Member States, leading to a general report to be presented by the European Commission to each Spring European Council.

A last important piece to foster the implementation is the recently adopted Community Lisbon Programme, putting together, for the first time, all the regulatory actions, financing actions and policy developments to be launched at European level regarding the Lisbon strategy for growth and jobs, and organising them by the three main priorities already mentioned (Commission, COM (2005) 330). Some of its key actions are underlined:

- the support of knowledge and innovation in Europe;

- the reform of the State aid policy;

- the better regulation for business operation;

- the completion of the internal market for services;

- the completion of an ambitious agreement in the Doha Round;

- the removal of obstacles to physical, labour and academic mobility;

- the development of a common approach to economic migration;

- the support to manage the social consequences of economic restructuring.

As well as the national programmes for growth and jobs will require a stronger coordination within the governments, this Community Lisbon Programme will require the same from the European Commission and also from the Council of Ministers in its relevant formations: Ecofin, Employment and Social Affairs, Competitiveness, Education and Environment. Regarding the European Parliament, an internal coordination procedure is already under way between different EP commissions and the same should be considered by the national parliaments, as some of their commissions can be concerned.

Developing financial incentives

Different reforms of financial instruments are underway in order to put them more in line with the political priorities of the Lisbon strategy for growth and jobs:

- the Community framework for the State aids is being reviewed in order to turn them into a more horizontal approach, focusing R&D, innovation and human capital;

- the European Investment Bank and the European Investment Fund are also deploying new instruments in support of the strategy for growth and jobs, and were asked to put a special focus on the needs of the innovative SMEs in Europe;

- the Community Programmes can also play an important role, notably if they are also able to become a catalysts of the national programmes for growth and jobs. Three very relevant cases are the 7th Framework Programme for Research and Technological Development, the Community Programme for Competitiveness and Innovation and the Community Programme for Lifelong Learning;

- the Community Strategic Guidelines for the Cohesion policy, which were recently proposed by the European Commission are now strongly in line with the integrated guidelines for the

Lisbon strategy, covering their three main strands: making Europe and its regions more attractive places to invest and to work; knowledge and innovation for growth; and more and better jobs (Commission, SEC (2005) 0299).

The scope of these two last instruments depends, of course, on the size of the financial resources to be given in the next Financial Perspectives (2007-2013) to two central objectives: investing in the Lisbon priorities and keeping regional cohesion.

Beyond all this, a reform was introduced in the Stability and Growth Pact which can have very relevant implications for the Lisbon strategy (Council 7619/05). According to this reform, macroeconomic stability remains a central concern, the limits for the public deficit and the public debt remain 3% and 60% as ratio of the GDP and pro-cyclical fiscal policies should be avoided. Nevertheless, a new emphasis is put on fostering economic growth and on the sustainability of the public debt in order to cope with the demographic trends. Against this background, the Lisbon goals, such as reforming social protection systems and redirecting public expenditure to key investments for growth potential (in R&D, innovation, human capital) are among the relevant factors to be taken into account when assessing the public deficits (either below or above 3%) or when defining the adjustment trajectories, in case of the excessive deficit procedure.

Against the new background provided by the mid-term review of the Lisbon Strategy, let us now focus on one of the most complex issues of the general debate over Europe.

For a sustainable European social model

The reform of the European social model is one of the most complex issues to be focused on the general debate over Europe. This model is the outcome of a long and complex historical process trying to combine social justice with high economic performance. This means that the social dimension should be shaped with the purpose of social justice, but also with the purpose of contributing to growth and competitiveness. Conversely, growth and competitiveness are crucial to support the social dimension and should also be shaped to support it. This also means that there are different choices in both economic and social policies which evolve over time and must be permanently under discussion, political debate and social dialogue. This is the European tradition, highly valued inside and outside Europe as an important achievement to ensure prosperity and quality of life.

This tradition was translated into quite different national models and the most renowned typologies distinguish the Scandinavian, the Anglo-Saxon, the Continental and the South-European types (Esping-Andersen in Rodrigues, 2002 and Sakellaropoulos and Berghman, 2004). Nevertheless, in spite of these differences, some key components were put together in order to build this European social model:

- increasing general access to education and training;

- regulated labour contracts;

- general access to social protection and health care;

- active policies for social inclusion;

- social dialogue procedures;

- predominance of public funding via taxes or social contributions, with a redistribution effect.

These components have been shaped in each historic period, depending on the existent institutional frameworks and actors and on their replies to the strategic challenges of their time.

Reforming the European social model to face new challenges

Nowadays, it is clear that the European social model is facing new strategic challenges, which seem to be:

- globalisation and the new competitive pressures;

- the transition to a knowledge-intensive economy;

- the ageing trends;

- the new family models;

- the very process of the European integration, in its new stage.

The sustainability of the European social model depends on renewing its economic basis as well as on reforming its main components, in order to cope with these key strategic challenges. Against this background, we will identify some of the main priorities for these structural reforms.

Education and Training

Access to new skills will become crucial to get new and better jobs. The education and training systems should be reformed in order to better cope with the challenges of:

- globalisation and the transition to a knowledge economy, by a more dynamic identification of the skills needs and by the generalisation of the lifelong learning opportunities in schools, training centres, companies, public administrations and households, which should be underpinned by an universal pre-schooling education and the reduction early-school leavers. New and more flexible ways to validate competences (such as the Europass) can also play an important role;

- aging trends, by spreading new methods to assess, enhance and use the elderly workers competences;

- new family models, by providing equal opportunities to career choices and more flexible access to lifelong learning over the life-course;

- European integration, by adopting a common framework for key-competences and facilitating the recognition of qualifications and the labour mobility.

Social Protection

Social protection systems seem to need structural reforms to cope with:

- the transition to a knowledge economy, by a more personalised approach in the active labour market policies, by creating learning accounts with drawing rights and by providing more flexibility of personal choices in using the range of social benefits;

- globalisation and new competitive pressures, by giving stronger priority to more effective active labour market policies; by a careful monitoring of the benefits in order to make work pay and to attract more people into the labour market, reducing unemployment and strengthening the financial basis of the social protection systems. A careful monitoring should also be made about the non-wage labour costs as well as the search of complementary (public and private) financial resources;

- aging trends, by promoting active aging, reducing early retirement, providing incentives to remain active, introducing more flexibility in the retirement age. Balancing the financial effort to be provided by different generations may also require a careful reconsideration of the balance between the three pillars of the social protection system;

- new family models, by spreading family care services and facilitating working time flexibility as important ways to reconcile work and family life;

- European integration, with a common legal framework required by the single market concerning minimum standards and portability, to be complemented with the open coordination of the reforms of the social protection systems.

Social inclusion

Social inclusion policies should also be updated in order to cope with the challenges of:

- the transition to a knowledge economy, by putting more focus on developing new social and professional capabilities, beyond the simple income guarantee;

- globalisation, by better targeting the social inclusion programmes and by strengthening the management of the industrial restructuring;

- aging, by promoting active aging and by designing target measures for elderly poor people;

- new family models, by developing family care services and by designing target measures for single parents;

European integration, by an open coordination of the social inclusion policies complemented with European programmes for social inclusion.

Labour regulations

Labour regulations and human resources management should also evolve to meet the challenges of:

- the knowledge economy, by developing learning organisations in the work place, promoting learning careers and "learning first contracts" for young people, organising learning accounts and improving the working time flexibility for training;

- globalisation, by creating more internal labour flexibility (concerning work organisation, working time and wage setting), by combining new forms of external flexibility with security and by strengthening the management of industrial restructuring. The active promotion of better labour standards at international level can also play a crucial role;

- ageing, by encouraging new forms of work organisation, working time management and better working conditions;

- new family models, by facilitating working time flexibility, parental leave and career breaks;

- European integration, by the regular update of the European directives, by removing the obstacles to the mobility of workers at European level and by defining a European frame for economic migration.

Social dialogue

Finally, social dialogue should itself evolve to cope with the same challenges of:

- the transition to a knowledge economy by negotiating learning agreements at company, sector and national level;

- globalisation, by negotiating innovation agreements and the social management of the industrial restructurings at company, sector and national levels;

- ageing, by negotiating about the conditions for active ageing in the collective agreements;

- new family models, by systematically introducing equal opportunities in the collective agreements;

- the European integration, by upgrading the social dialogue concerning the European strategy for growth and jobs.

The changes mentioned above are the outcome of an intensive experimentation, debate and negotiation which is already underway in Europe. Most of these changes are already pointed out by the integrated guidelines of the Lisbon strategy for growth and jobs after a very rich discussion which took place at European level, involving all the European institutions and committing Prime Ministers and ministers of very different areas. These changes will be subject to a larger discussion in all Member States during the preparation of their national reform programmes for growth and jobs.

A re-interpretation of basic values

This larger discussion in the Member States should take into account this more general background of the European social model and the new strategic challenges it is facing nowadays. Moreover, its underlying basic values seem also to be under re-interpretation, notably when:

- it is said that security should be for change, and not against change;

- providing security, the focus is put not only in income guarantee but also in enabling and building capabilities;

- the concern with social justice is putting more emphasis in equal opportunities, even they should be combined with basic solidarity with the weakest members of society;

- the individual responsibility is also highlighted by this concept of equal opportunities, also leading to more freedom of choice over the life course;

- the principles of sustainable development are taken into consideration in the re-conceptualisation of social justice; hence the contributions and benefits regarding social protection should be balanced across generations.

Let us now focus two concrete areas of reform with many implications for the renewal of the European social model: lifelong learning and innovation.

Sharing responsibilities to develop lifelong learning

The commitment to prepare national strategies for lifelong learning is already made in the framework of the national programmes for growth and jobs. The recent overview at European level led to the identification of some possible common objectives which are summed up in the guideline 23 of the integrated guidelines for growth and jobs. More specifically, this strategy should aim at:

- defining the goals for lifelong learning in terms of not only educational levels but also new jobs profiles and competences;

- developing a new infrastructure for lifelong learning;

- creating a diversified supply of learning opportunities able to provide more customised solutions:

  - to develop the new instruments of e-learning and to explore the potential of the digital TV

  - to turn schools and training centres into open learning centres

  - to encourage companies to adopt learning organisations

  - to shape the appropriate learning modes for each target group

  - to spread new learning solutions for the low skilled workers

- fostering the various demands for learning and to create a demand-led system:

  - to improve the framework conditions for lifelong learning

  - to develop a dynamic guidance system over the life course

- to renew the validation and recognition system

- to create compensations for the investment in learning

- spreading new financial arrangements in order to share the costs of lifelong learning between the various stakeholders and encourage the initiative of companies and individuals;

- improving governance for lifelong learning.

This kind of objectives seems to be consensual, but the implementation gap shows that the real problem lies with sharing responsibilities between the relevant actors. Hence, when it comes:

- the identification of goals for lifelong learning: the public authorities should enhance the forecasting procedures, the companies should improve their human resources management, the social partners negotiate learning agreements and all these actors develop partnerships for growth, jobs creation and competence building;

- the development of a new infrastructure for lifelong learning: the public authorities should create knowledge resource centres and regulate the telecommunications and TV industries for this purpose; companies and households should equip themselves with the necessary hardware and software; the same should happen with the education institutions, which should also become content providers;

- a more diversified supply of learning opportunities: education institutions should be turned into open learning centres and provide more tailor-made solutions for each target-group, companies should develop learning organisations and social partners negotiate a wide range of solutions;

- to improve the framework conditions for lifelong learning: public authorities should foster the provision of child care services and social partners should negotiate the appropriate flexibility in working time management, including time accounts and training leaves;

- to develop a guidance system: the public authorities and education institutions should provide better guidance services and individuals should be encouraged to define their personal development plan;

- to renew the validation and recognition system: the public authorities should create centres of competence validation, companies should present intellectual capital reports and individuals define their personal portfolio;

- to spread new financial arrangements for sharing the costs: the public authorities should cover the costs of basic education for all, improving the education of young people and support targeted adult people with tax reliefs or direct incentives; companies should fund job-related training; social partners should negotiate the sharing of training costs in the labour contracts or the collective agreements; the education institutions should mobilise resources for new investment plans and the individuals could be encouraged to manage their learning accounts or special entitlements (drawing rights) for training.

Sharing responsibilities to foster innovation

For more effective implementation of the national programmes, this kind of sharing of responsibilities should be specified for the other policy fields. Another critical example for the success of the Lisbon strategy, the sustainability of the European social model and the renewal of the European competitiveness is the innovation policy. Here again, it seems there is a quite high level of consensus concerning some possible common objectives which are summarised in the guideline 8 of the integrated guidelines for growth and jobs. Innovation policy should aim at developing:

- The provision of R&D: creating conditions to foster the private investment in R&D, notably tax incentives and researchers mobility; reducing the cost of patenting and improving the management of intellectual property rights; fostering the interfaces between companies and universities;

- Competence building: spreading skills for innovation at all levels of education; training for innovation management; enhancing the skills base in each sector or cluster;

- Financial innovation: improving access to venture capital for innovative SMEs; reorientation of public investment to R&D and innovation; tax incentives with the same purpose; new priorities for structural funds;

- Provision of consultancy services: developing the support services for innovation, transfer and diffusion;

- Improving quality and paving the way to new products and services: competition policy; dissemination of quality standards; improving the criteria of public procurement; targeting sophisticated markets;

- Changing organizations: national programmes for organizational development in companies; reforming universities management; modernizing public services;

- Incubating activities: developing incubators; supporting high-tech start-ups;

- Networking: promoting clusters and partnerships for innovation; extending access to broadband; developing e-business.

Nevertheless, a clearer identification of responsibilities is needed when it comes:

- the provision of R&D, which depends on the research institutions and on companies, but also on the framework conditions to be created by the public authorities concerning the tax incentives, the research careers and the intellectual property rights;

- the competence building, which depends on the education and training institutions, but also on the companies and their collaboration with these institutions;

- the financial innovation, which depends on the financial institutions but also on the companies initiatives and the regulatory conditions of the financial markets to be created by the public authorities;

- the quality of products and services, depends mainly on companies behaviour but also on the competition policy, the dissemination of quality standards and the criteria for public procurement to be developed by the public authorities;

- changing organisations, regarding companies but also education and research institutions as well as public services;

- networking, which depends on all actors which interact in the national or regional systems of innovation.

Furthermore, the reforms of the European social model already mentioned above are also designed to support this renewal of the European competitiveness focusing on innovation.

In conclusion, the sustainability of the European social model depends on the success of the overall strategy for growth and jobs, which are now the two key words; and this success depends on a new approach to renew the European competitiveness, a full use of the potential of the single and external market as well as on more scope for growth in the macroeconomic management. Finally, this success also depends on well designed reforms of the European social model itself.

The concrete solutions to achieve this particular combination in each Member State can only be found by itself. That is why, the preparation and implementation of the national reform programmes for growth and jobs opens an opportunity which should not be missed.

Selected Bibliography on the Lisbon Strategy for Growth and Jobs

After the mid-term review

Report of the High Level Group on the Future of Social Policy in an enlarged European Union, European Commission, Directorate-General for Employment & Social Affairs, Oliver Dutheillet de Lamothe (coord.) with the collaboration of Tony Atkinson, Florian Gerster, Maria João Rodrigues, Ludek Rychly, Dieter Schimanke, May 2004.

SAPIR, André (coord.) with the collaboration of Philippe Aghion, Giuseppe Bertola, Martin Hellwig, Jean Pisani-Ferry, Dariusz Rosati, José Viñals and Helen Wallace, with Marco Buti, Mario Nava, and Peter M. Smith, *An Agenda for a Growing Europe—The Sapir Report* (2004), Oxford: Oxford University Press

SAKELLAROPOULOS, Theodoros; BERGHMAN, Jos (eds.), *Connecting Welfare Diversity within the European Social Model* (2004), Social Europe Series, Volume 9, Schoten: Intersentia

RODRIGUES, Maria João (coord.) (2002) with the collaboration of Robert Boyer, Manuel Castells, Gøsta Esping-Andersen, Robert Lindley, Bengt-Åke Lundvall, Luc Soete and Mario Telò, The New Knowledge Economy in Europe—a strategy for international competitiveness and social cohesion, Cheltenham: Edward Elgar

RODRIGUES, Maria João (2003), *European Policies for a Knowledge Economy*, Cheltenham: Edward Elgar

RODRIGUES, Maria João, *Background paper SSH-ERA—For the mid-term review of the Lisbon strategy*, November 2004

(http://europa.eu.int/comm/research/social-sciences/htm/advisory_group_sshera.htm)

KOK, Wim (coord.), *Facing the Challenge—The Lisbon strategy for Growth and employment*, Report from the High Level Group, November 2004

European Commission (2005), *Communication from the Commission to the Council—Draft Joint Employment Report 2004/2005*, COM (2005) 13 final, 27.01.05

European Commission (2005), *Green Paper "Confronting demographic change: a new solidarity between the generations,"* COM (2005) 94 final, 16.03.2005

Council of the European Union (2005), *Conclusions of the Brussels European Council*, Council of the European Union 7619/05, 22-23 March 2005 (Extract).

European Commission (2005), *Working together for growth and jobs—Next steps in implementing the revised Lisbon Strategy*, SEC (2005), 28.04.2005

Council of the European Union (2005), *Conclusions of the Brussels European Council*, Council of the European Union 10255/05, 16-17 June 2005 (Extract)

Council of the European Union (2005), *Integrated Guidelines: Broad Economic Policy Guidelines*, Council of the European Union 10667/05, 28.06.2005

Council of the European Union (2005), *Guidelines for the employment policies of the Member States*, Council of the European Union 10205/05. 05.07.2005

European Commission (2005), *Cohesion Policy in Support of Growth and Jobs: Community Strategic Guidelines*, 2007-2013, SEC (2005) 0299, 05.07.2005

European Commission (2005), *Communication to the Council and the European Parliament, Common Actions for Growth and Employment: The Community Lisbon Programme*, COM (2005) 330 final, 20.07.2005

European Commission (2005), *Communication from the Commission on the Social Agenda*, COM (2005) 33 final, 09.02.05

Afterword: The Network Society and the Knowledge Economy: Portugal in the Global Perspective

Jorge Sampaio

Throughout my almost ten years in office as President of the Republic, I have gradually become more and more aware of the consequences that the growing interconnection between economies and social relations on an international scale—made possible and, to a large extent, induced, by the expansion of the new information and communications technologies—have on the structuring of societies in general, and the Portuguese society, in particular.

Within the general context of economic/entrepreneurial activities, the onset of the Information Society has immediately brought about significant changes, albeit changes which vary in speed from region to region and from sector to sector. Changes which are apparent in terms of work organization possibilities, from the strategic decision-making level to the scope of merely technical operations.

Furthermore, it is indisputable that the trend towards globalization in the financial markets, which is enabled and permanently supported by the digital revolution, has today a direct effect on the security of employment of a great part of the salaried workers in the world and on the population mobility patterns and geography of hunger and disease.

Moreover, it can easily be demonstrated, that the new international economic order, with its subversion of the traditional criteria for the location of industrial activities, tertiarization and the emergence of trans-national financial and commercial strategies, has led to a profound reconfiguration of our cities and urbanization processes and of the relationship they establish with the national territory as a whole.

With the growth of the Internet and real-time communication resources, it is evident, moreover, that for the younger generations, a certain redefining of routines, group solidarity, cultural activities and aspirations has been taking place. And everything indicates that the Information Society is already having real effects on the value systems, beliefs and representations we use to guide our actions and with which we learn to perceive ourselves and others.

For a more impressive image of the social transformation we are currently experiencing and its future implications, one only has to recognize that both the domains of artistic creation and the most sophisticated scientific debate can no longer do without the storage capacity and transmission speed made possible by the new technologies.

Finally, is it not true that even the mobilization of people around great political causes of global importance, on which the possibility of the alternative regulation of globalization itself depends, seems to be developing in direct relation to the access to the global information networks?

While endeavouring to accompany, with the lucidity and rigour possible, the transformations I have quoted above—which, evidently, requires particular attention to everything, big and small, that politicians come across "in the field,"— I am becoming more and more convinced that, despite the amplitude and originality of the changes currently in progress, there are analytical principles and ideological guidelines I have adhered to early in my now considerably long political life, which, in essence, have lost none of their pertinence.

As far as analytical principles are concerned, I would underline the fact that the national territory still constitutes, in the era of global networks, a fundamental reference and observation dimension, both for understanding the economic, cultural, social and even identity-affecting transformations in progress and for defining balanced and effective policies.

Even more so than in other contexts, in societies such as the Portuguese society, which are classified by some as semi-peripheral and by others as being of intermediate development, it is imperative to see the technical and economic modernization movement in the context of the socio-historic decisions of a predominantly national scope in which it emerges. In many cases, such determinations are, in reality, a source of inertia, paradoxical configurations or truly unprecedented forms that must not be diluted in the overall general trends emerging and which are being defined more clearly in other social formations.

On the other hand, at the level of the ideological orientations of political action which I consider to have remained pertinent in the current social relations context, I would highlight all the central importance, which, in my view, should continue to be given in the new globalization context to the active reconciliation of the goals of development with the perfection of the rule of law and the combat against social inequality—three goals that united successive generations of Portuguese citizens during the dictatorship. I believe that, in the current circumstances, it not only makes total sense not to take a step backward on this course at the national level, but also that it is necessary at the international level to both contribute to and to implement, through all means in our control, the range of intentions included in that ideological triangle.

It was in the context of these ideological coordinates that, some years ago, I decided to promote a cycle of conferences and debates involving a large number of Portuguese and foreign specialists, on the effect of the revolution in information and communications technologies on the quality of democratic systems and, through them, on the regulation of globalization.

At the time, the decision was made to deal with the new and old media together, using the issues of electronic democracy, the use of the Internet and the generalization of access to NICTs to once again consider the problems of the relationship between the fields of politics and the media that democracies always have to face.

In a country which, having achieved political democracy and liberalization of the media at a late stage, is still far from establishing consistent levels of auto-regulation in the institutional spaces in question, it would make no sense to attempt to put into perspective the possibilities of consolidating democracy through electronic/digital means without dealing with and questioning the area of the conventional media.

The same concern with the socio-historic peculiarities of this country has led me to take interest in matters of technological development and entrepreneurial innovation in Portugal, simultaneously paying attention to the specificity of our industrial fabric—particularly the importance the so-called traditional industries, the small and medium-sized enterprises, the informal economy and the pre-Taylorist technical and organizational models have within it—and to the considerable deficits in terms of literacy, experimental culture and innovation rooted in Portuguese society.

In relation to this last point, I should add the following. Although it is true that this contextualized approach to development and innovation has protected me from excessively naive visions as to the possibilities of changing the economy and society using the technological impulses in a very short period of time, it is also true that it has never ceased to provide me with surprising sources of optimism.

By way of example, I can refer the knowledge that, in Portugal, a country frequently considered to be unreceptive to innovation, there have been, in traditional industry sectors with strong exposure to international competition and in territorial areas without an entrepreneurial association tradition, remarkably successful experiences in the organized diffusion of the new technologies, on-going training, the generalized expansion of innovation and the sustained increase of competitiveness levels. The fact that I have been able to draw some public attention to such experiences in the scope of the initiatives I have dedicated to technological modernization and business innovation in Portugal is, indeed, a source for great satisfaction for me.

It is understandable that someone like myself, who has spent more than forty years fighting for the full exercise of fundamental civic liberties and questioning themselves as to the concrete possibilities of democracy democratizing itself, should want, as President of the Portuguese Republic, to debate with a certain degree of depth, at the conference cycle I referred to, the opportunities for perfecting democratic life and improving participation of the citizens provided by the new technologies.

I have, however, not done so with the sole purpose of concentrating on the national concerns in this area. As I have said, I sincerely believe that, with the advent of closely interconnected economies and societies, the triangle of convictions constituted around the objectives of development, democracy and social justice should be transferred, without any concessions in terms of quality, to the plan for the combat for recognition of the dignity of human life on the global scale.

After completing his monumental reference work entitled "The Information Age: Economy, Society and Culture," Professor Castells, together with Professor Pekka Himanen, who likewise has honoured us with his contribution to this volume, conducted a study of the Finnish model for transition to the information society and the network society.

In addition to the rigor that characterizes this project, it also had the merit of revealing, in very expressive terms, that, similar to what happened before with the development of the industrial society, progress towards the information society and towards successful integration into the global economy can be made through different histories and cultures, following distinct institutional combinations and achieving equally varied forms of social organization.

In clear contrast to the paradigmatic information society models associated with Silicon Valley and Singapore, the Finnish case presents, amongst other peculiarities, models that result from the presence of a strong Welfare State in social life and the affirmation, no less pronounced, of an own culture, language and identity. Benefiting from high levels of social cohesion, a fully negotiated labour relations regulation system, strong incentives for training and research in the information technologies field and sustained State intervention in creating the infrastructural conditions for the diversification and expansion of its economy, Finland is a good example of how a country with limited resources can, in the short period of only two decades, overcome difficult economic crises and join the ranks of the most competitive information societies.

In the reflection to be made on the opportunities within Portugal's reach in this field, there are certain traits of Portuguese society that simply cannot be ignored.

The most worrying of all has, in my opinion, to do with the low levels of schooling and literacy of the Portuguese population. In thirty years of democracy, we have made important progress towards establishing basic education for all and the number of young people achieving access to higher education is in no way comparable with what the Portuguese could expect during the dictatorship. However, the failure rates in school and drop-out figures continue at high levels, placing Portugal in a particularly unfavourable position in international comparisons on literacy, access to secondary education and qualification of the working population.

As far as another aspect of the education system is concerned—that of lifelong learning—the diagnosis is just as pessimistic: indeed, given the literal or functional illiteracy of such a large section of our adult population, the demand for vocational training continues to be low. Furthermore, the institutional apparatus that promotes the training offer, in which the country's enterprises should have an active and prominent place, is disconnected and not sufficiently consolidated.

Given this scenario, the questions I honestly feel obliged to ask are the following: with such serious deficits in terms of education and basic schooling capital, does it make sense, and indeed is it effective, to concentrate resources in learning and training programs specifically catering to the needs of the Information Society? Is it possible and politically acceptable to skip phases, with the argument, perhaps, that the younger generations are relatively well equipped for integration in the information networks? Or does, in terms of human resource qualification, investment in excellence necessarily lead today, in a society in transition such as the Portuguese society, to unacceptable situations of exclusion?

Considering that it is true that transition to a network society imposes that the use of the new technologies be seen not as an end, but as a means an instrument of transversal utilization, it is necessary to maintain universal access to quality basic and secondary education as the central objective of public policies. Improvement in said quality today must include renewal of the teaching/learning contents and methodologies in harmony with the digital revolution.

Hence, one must promote and divulge exemplary e-learning and e-teaching experiences, but, obviously, without abandoning the educational heritage built up over the years by the education system.

On the other hand, one must recognize that, as vocational training and life-long education are decisive elements in bringing the populations closer to the competence thresholds demanded by the knowledge economy, in countries such as Portugal a great effort has still to be made in raising, in a general and sustained way, the literacy levels of working adults with little school education. To achieve this, we will have to reject, once and for all, all hesitations and postponements in implementing integrated education programmes, particularly if, as has been the case in Portugal, they have been negotiated and agreed upon by the social partners for a long time.

A second problem that concerns me related with the question at hand has to do with the low levels of cohesion (well below the European averages) that characterize the structure of Portuguese society.

Contrary to that argued by certain critics, in his works, Professor Castells has never neglected the excluding tensions related with economic globalization and the transition to the information economy and society. He dealt with this issue in a particularly expressive way in the analyses he proposed on the distinction between generic labour/self-programmable labour, illustrating to what extent the processes in question contain the seeds of long-term unemployment or irreversible segmentations and polarizations in the labour markets. The exemplariness of the Finnish case is in part due to the particular effectiveness of the Welfare State in containing excluding tensions, at least those I referred to above.

In the Portuguese society, which presents considerably unbalanced income distribution patterns, the institutional social protection structure, essentially built up after the reinstatement of the democratic system, continues to be faulty and lacks the degree of consistency required for the systematic control of the risks of precarization and marginalization that come with technological modernization. Knowing that, in addition to this, the budgetary discipline imposed by the Stability and Growth Pact will not, at least in the short term, allow us any financial slack capable of bringing about significant improvements in our welfare model, are we not faced with problems that will be very difficult to overcome?

Part of the solution will no doubt come through improvement in the efficiency of the public administration in managing its resources and in better addressing the needs and legitimate aspirations of the citizens.

In this perspective, the idea that the model of governance has to adapt to the need to provide responses to social problems, which, being very multifaceted, interdependent and transversal, involve at the same time citizens that are more and more informed, was raised several times throughout this book. It is no wonder, then, that one also recommended, in the name of reinforcing democratic transparency and participation, that forms of interactive online access to legally unprotected administration information be promoted. The adequate use, on the part of the public administrations, of flexible information networks makes it possible to give public services levels of transparency and reliability so that they can guarantee the best exercise of citizenship, more effective and specific combat against exclusion, greater accountability on the part of the administration and the creation of an environment of mutual trust between the people and the institutions which will undoubtedly strengthen the daily exercise of democracy and the social welfare system. Improving the management, gaining time and increasing the quality of the services provided should be, in sectors as crucial as health, justice and the social security, objectives around which all professionals and organizations can rally.

The statistics on access to the new information and communications technologies and opening to the global networks tell us that the Portuguese situation reveals, as in many other fields, considerable deficits and a slowness to develop, although the incidence is less in the younger generations and we do have examples of good practice both in the entrepreneurial fabric and in the civil services. Expansion of the access to digital networks, which is indispensable for not generating new forms of exclusion, can, indeed, include—and this was one of the topics put forward by some contributors—the consideration of opportunities related with open source software. The monitoring of developments such as those going on in Brazil today could be of great interest, particularly, as far as Portugal is concerned, in a perspective of promoting our language in the world. To this end, keeping abreast of community directives on the regulation of access to software is an absolute necessity.

On the basis of all that I have said above on the characteristics of Portugal, I am convinced that our difficulties in the transition to the networked society and the knowledge economy cannot be resolved with a voluntarist approach centred on the restricted aspects directly represented by the conventional figures and indicators. But I also do not share the belief that, as long as all other structural obstacles to development are not eliminated, we are condemned to being able to do nothing in terms of joining the networked society and the knowledge economy.

Throughout this book, it was confirmed that it is not the technological innovations that, by themselves, condition the emerging social—perhaps civilizational—changes. On the contrary, it will always be the organizational changes and the institutional models that will lead to the exploitation of the potentials that the new technologies bring with them.

In this context, the clear formulation of strategic guidelines and, above all, making decisions at the right time and on the basis of knowledge of the current economic and social trends are absolutely crucial for stimulating and monitoring the necessary changes. In other words: full exploitation of the information technologies with a view to modernizing companies, the public administration and the State itself can only be achieved if, before this, in each one of the principal fields of economic and social life, the main barriers associated with the conventional organizational models and modes of operation are examined.

Without organizational innovation, technological innovation will never constitute a development factor and effective source of competitiveness. I recognize that, in a country characterized by high degrees of dualism and asymmetry, the role of the State in creating the infrastructural and support conditions for industrial activity, paying particular attention to the universe of the small and medium-sized enterprises, becomes perhaps even more indispensable than in other contexts.

However, state intervention, though necessary, is far from enough. The role of the business community is indispensable in preparing any national economy for successful entry into the age of the information society and globalization. In the final analysis, it is the enterprises that, depending on a given institutional framework and the stock of skills available in the employment system, will actively contribute to adding vale to the wealth accumulated by an economy.

In this closing comment on the published work drawn from the colloquium *"The Network Society and the Knowledge Economy: Portugal in a Global Perspective"* I have given some thought to the difficulties that a society in transition, such as the Portuguese society, has to face in a phase of change that is as dramatic and influential as that we are dealing with today.

The responsible politicians, the economic agents and the Portuguese citizens will, together, have to be the fundamental protagonists of that change. In my capacity as President of the Republic, however, I understand that the terms of the problems to be faced will be clearer and more consolidated if we all have secure knowledge and information on the alternatives we have. The extremely high quality of the contributions presented and published herein are, for me, an absolute guarantee that the organization of the colloquium, that led to this book, was a very positive step in this direction.

In this sense, I will finish off by greeting the illustrious book contributors and thanking them for having accepted my invitation and, above all, for what we can learn from them.